Open Banking

Open banking ends the proprietary control of customer information by banks and allows customers to share their banking financial data with third parties as a matter of right. It can also permit customers to allow others to remove funds directly from their bank accounts in return for goods and services. All of this is done securely with standardised 'application programming interfaces' (APIs). Open banking has developed in different ways and with different objectives across the globe. *Open Banking: Global Development and Regulation* examines the empowering and enabling regulations that facilitate all of this.

This book compares a number of different open banking national strategies. These range from the focus of the UK and EU on enhanced competition to the more collaborative approaches in many East Asian jurisdictions. It also looks at the use of open banking for socio-economic purposes in Brazil and India. Here, open banking forms part of a wider government programme to increase financial inclusion coupled with encouraging economic growth.

This text will be valuable to fintech companies, policymakers and financial services regulators. Its overarching aim is to demonstrate the possibilities and challenges of open banking and how it is changing lives across the world.

Francesco De Pascalis is a Senior Lecturer (Associate Professor) in Financial Law at Brunel Law School and a qualified lawyer.

Alan Brener is an Associate Professor (Teaching) at University College London's Laws Faculty and Deputy Director of the Faculty's Centre for Ethics and Law.

Routledge International Studies in Money and Banking

Alternative Acquisition Models and Financial Innovation
Special Purpose Acquisition Companies in Europe,
and the Italian Legal Framework
*Edited by Daniele D'Alvia, Ettore Maria Lombardi
and Yochanan Shachmurove*

Financial and Technological Innovation for Sustainability
Environmental, Social and Governance Performance
Edited by Artie Ng and Jatin Nathwani

Digital Transformation and the Economics of Banking
Economic, Institutional, and Social Dimensions
Edited by Piotr Łasak and Jonathan Williams

Behavioral Finance in the Digital Era Saving
and Investment Decisions
*Elżbieta Kubińska, Magdalena Adamczyk-Kowalczuk
and Anna Macko*

International Banking in Global Perspective
Edited by Carmela D'Avino and Mimoza Shabani

Non-Fungible Tokens
Multidisciplinary Perspectives
Edited by Usman W. Chohan

Open Banking
Global Development and Regulation
Francesco De Pascalis and Alan Brener

For more information about this series, please visit: www.routledge.com/Routledge-International-Studies-in-Money-and-Banking/book-series/SE0403

Open Banking
Global Development and Regulation

Francesco De Pascalis and Alan Brener

LONDON AND NEW YORK

First published 2024
by Routledge
4 Park Square, Milton Park, Abingdon, Oxon OX14 4RN

and by Routledge
605 Third Avenue, New York, NY 10158

Routledge is an imprint of the Taylor & Francis Group, an informa business

© 2024 Francesco De Pascalis and Alan Brener

The right of Francesco De Pascalis and Alan Brener to be identified as authors of this work has been asserted in accordance with sections 77 and 78 of the Copyright, Designs and Patents Act 1988.

All rights reserved. No part of this book may be reprinted or reproduced or utilised in any form or by any electronic, mechanical, or other means, now known or hereafter invented, including photocopying and recording, or in any information storage or retrieval system, without permission in writing from the publishers.

Trademark notice: Product or corporate names may be trademarks or registered trademarks, and are used only for identification and explanation without intent to infringe.

British Library Cataloguing-in-Publication Data
A catalogue record for this book is available from the British Library

Library of Congress Cataloging-in-Publication Data
Names: De Pascalis, Francesco, author. | Brener, Alan, 1955- author.
Title: Open banking : global development and regulation / Francesco De Pascalis and Alan Brener.
Description: Abingdon, Oxon ; New York, NY : Routledge, 2024. | Series: Routledge international studies in money and banking | Includes bibliographical references and index.
Identifiers: LCCN 2023052441 (print) | LCCN 2023052442 (ebook) | ISBN 9781032363172 (hardback) | ISBN 9781032363196 (paperback) | ISBN 9781003331339 (ebook)
Subjects: LCSH: Financial institutions--Data processing. | Financial services industry--Security measures.
Classification: LCC HG104 .D47 2024 (print) | LCC HG104 (ebook) | DDC 332.1--dc23/eng/20231205
LC record available at https://lccn.loc.gov/2023052441
LC ebook record available at https://lccn.loc.gov/2023052442

ISBN: 978-1-032-36317-2 (hbk)
ISBN: 978-1-032-36319-6 (pbk)
ISBN: 978-1-003-33133-9 (ebk)

DOI: 10.4324/9781003331339

Typeset in Sabon
by KnowledgeWorks Global Ltd.

This book is dedicated to all our families for their constant love and invaluable support.

Contents

Acknowledgements	*ix*
About the Authors	*x*
List of Abbreviations	*xi*

PART I
Open Banking Ecosystem and Policy — 1

1	Introduction	3
2	The Open Banking World	11
3	Open Banking Policy in the UK and EU	33

PART II
Open Banking Regulation — 53

4	Nordic and European Free Trade Association Countries	55
5	The Americas	63
6	Far East	78
7	Middle East and North Africa Region	103

PART III
Business Models, Emerging Economies and the Way forward — 115

8	Open Banking and FinTech Business Models in the UK	117

9	Open Banking, Financial Inclusion and Economic Growth in Developing Countries	147
10	The Road Ahead	165
11	Conclusion	183
	Bibliography	*193*
	Index	*226*

Acknowledgements

Dr Francesco De Pascalis wishes to especially thank Professor Kern Alexander for always being a great mentor and doctoral researcher Kalliopi Letsiou for research assistance.

Dr Alan Brener particularly wishes to thank Sofia Mingo, a former UCL LLM student, and trainee solicitor, who provided invaluable help with research and text editing.

We are grateful for the help of our respective university libraries (UCL and Brunel) who have provided outstanding support for this work.

About the Authors

Francesco De Pascalis is a Senior Lecturer (Associate Professor) in Financial Law at Brunel Law School and a qualified lawyer. He obtained his PhD at the Institute of Advanced Legal Studies (IALS), University of London, in 2015. Before joining Brunel Law School, he worked as a research fellow at the Rechtswissenschaftliches Institut of the University of Zurich, where he is still a member of the Research Network for Sustainable Finance led by Professor Kern Alexander. At Brunel University London, he is a member of the Research Centre for Law, Economics and Finance and the Centre for AI: Social and Digital Innovation. He is a recognised scholar in banking and finance law and regulation, and author of numerous publications in these fields.

Alan Brener is an Associate Professor (Teaching) at University College London's Laws Faculty and he is also Deputy Director of the Faculty's Centre for Ethics and Law. Besides his LLM from UCL and PhD from Queen Mary University London, he is also a qualified Chartered Accountant and member of the Institute of Chartered Accountants in England and Wales. A Fellow of the Chartered Banker Institute, he is also a member of the Institute's Quality and Standards Committee. Prior to starting his PhD, Dr Brener worked for Santander UK and was responsible, at different times, for the compliance and retail legal departments and regulatory policy. Before joining Santander in 2005, from 1996, he headed the compliance departments for the retail banking divisions of Natwest and RBS banks. From 1989 to 1996 Dr Brener was a Senior Prudential and Conduct of Business Regulator for the insurance and collective investments sectors having previously worked on aspects of public policy at the Department of Trade and Industry.

List of Abbreviations

ABS	Association of Banks in Singapore
ACCC	Australian Competition and Consumer Commission
AI	Artificial Intelligence
AIPSP	Account Information and Payment Initiation Service Providers
AISP	Account Information Service Providers
AML/CFT	Anti-Money Laundering/Combating the Financing of Terrorism
ANPR	Advanced Notice on Proposed Rulemaking
ANZ	Australia and New Zealand Bank
APAC	Asia–Pacific
API	Application Programming Interface
APP	Authorised Push Payment
ASX	Australian Securities Exchange
BaaS	Bank-as-a-Service
BCB	Banco Central do Brasil
BCBS	Basel Committee on Banking and Supervision
BI	Bank of Indonesia
BNPL	Buy Now Pay Later
BOBF	Bahrain Open Banking Framework
BTL	Buy-to-Let
CASS	Current Account Switch Service
CBA	Commonwealth Bank of Australia
CBB	Central Bank of Bahrain
CBDC	Central Bank Digital Currency
CBJ	Central Bank of Jordan
CBK	Central Bank of Kuwait
CBUAE	Central Bank of United Arab Emirates
CDR	Consumer Data Right
CEF	Committee on Financial Education
CFPB	Consumer Financial Protection Bureau
CIPD	Chartered Institute of Personnel and Development
CJEU	Court of Justice of the European Union

xii List of Abbreviations

CMA	Competition Market Authority
CMF	Comision Para el Mercado Financiero
CMN	National Monetary Council
CoDi	Cobro Digital
CONAIF	National Council for Financial Inclusion
CPF	Cadastro de Pessoas Físicas
CRD	Consumer Data Rights
CRM	Contingent Reimbursement Model
DESI	Digital Economy and Society Index
DFSA	Danish Financial Supervisory Authority
DIFC	Dubai International Financial Centre
EBA	European Banking Authority
EBITDA	Earnings Before Interest, Taxes, Depreciation and Amortisation
ECB	European Central Bank
EEA	European Economic Area
EFTA	Electronic Fund Transfer Act
EFTA	European Free Trade Association
EKYC	Electronic Know Your Customer
EMA	Electronic Money Association
EMI	Electronic Money Institution
EU	European Union
FCA	Financial Conduct Authority
FCRA	Fair Credit Reporting Act
FEBRABAN	Federação Brasileira de Bancos
FDIC	Federal Deposit Insurance Corporation
FIP	Financial Information Providers
FISC	Financial Information Service Company
FITP	Financial Infrastructure Transformation Programme
FIU	Financial Information Users
FOS	Financial Ombudsman Service
FSC	Financial Supervisory Commission
FSDP	Financial Sector Development Program
FSMA 2000	Financial Services and Markets Act 2000
GCC	Gulf Council Countries
GeM	Government e-Marketplace
GLBA	Gramm-Leach-Bliley Act
GSTN	Goods and Services Tax Network
HKAB	Hong Kong Association of Banks
HKMA	Hong Kong Monetary Authority
IBA	Indian Banks' Association
IBSP	Information Based Service Providers
IFPE	Institución de Fondos de Pago Electrónico
IMF	International Monetary Fund
IMY	Integritetsskyddsmyndigheten

IoT	Internet of Things
IP	Information Providers
IPO	Initial Public Offering
IPS	Indonesia Payment System
ISA	Individual Savings Account
JFSA	Japan Financial Services Agency
KFSI	Korean Financial Security Institute
KFTC	Korea Financial Telecommunications & Clearings Institute
KSA	Kingdom of Saudi Arabia
KYC	Know Your Customer
MAS	Monetary Authority of Singapore
MENA	Middle East and North Africa Region
NAB	National Australia Bank
NCA	National Crime Agency
NPCI	National Payments Corporation of India
NPPA	New Payments Platform
OBIE	Open Banking Implementation Entity
OCC	Office of the Comptroller of the Currency
OECD	Organisation for Economic Cooperation and Development
OFT	Office of Fair Trading
PBOC	People's Bank of China
PISP	Payment Initiation Service Provider
PMJDY	Pradhan Mantri Jan-Dhan Yojana
PNIF	National Financial Inclusion Strategy
PRA	Prudential Regulation Authority
PSD2	Directive (EU) 2015/2366 of the European Parliament and of the Council of 25 November 2015 on payment services in the internal market, amending Directives 2002/65/EC 2009/110/EC and 2013/36/EU and Regulation (EU) No 1093/2010, and repealing Directive 2007/64/EC
PSR	Payment Systems Regulator
QCB	Qatar Central Bank
QNB	Qatar National Bank
QRIS	Quick Response Code Indonesia Standard
RBA	Reserve Bank of Australia
RBI	Reserve Bank of India
RTGS	Real Time Gross Settlement
RTS	Regulatory Technical Standards
SAMA	Saudi Central Bank
SAR	Suspicious Activity Report
SBA	Swiss Bankers Association
SBI	State Bank of India
SBREFA	Small Business Regulatory Enforcement Fairness Act
SCA	Strong Customer Authentication
SEPA	Single Euro Payments Area

SFSA	Swedish Financial Supervisory Authority
SFTI	Swiss FinTech Innovations
SGF	inDex Singapore Financial Data Exchange
SIF	State Secretariat for International Finance
SIF	Single Invoice Financing
SME	Small and Medium-sized Enterprises
SNAP	Regulation No 23/15/PADG/2021 on the implementation of National Standards of Payments using Open Application Programming Interface
SNSP	Regulation No. 23/11/PBI/2021 concerning the National Payment System Standard
TIPS	Target Instant Payment Settlement
TPP	Third Party Providers
TSP	Third-party Service Providers
UAE	United Arab Emirates
UK	United Kingdom
UKFIU	UK Financial Intelligence Unit
UPI	Unified Payments Interface
USA	United States of America
ZDG	Zahlungsdienstegesetz

Part I
Open Banking Ecosystem and Policy

1 Introduction

What is open banking? An overview

Open banking ends the proprietary control of customer information by banks and it allows customers to share their banking financial data with third parties as a matter of right. It can also permit customers to allow others to remove funds directly from their bank accounts in return for goods and services. All of this is done securely with standardised 'application programming interfaces' (APIs).

Although the APIs are a mechanism for operating open banking, the key motive force is financial services regulation. While most regulations are limiting and restrictive, those powering open banking are empowering and enabling. They exist not, for example, to protect institutions and consumers but rather to direct finance towards specific political and socio-economic purposes. It is also a worldwide enterprise.

Each jurisdiction aims to use open banking for different economic and societal purposes. Consequentially while the mechanisms of open banking are common how it operates and its objectives have been developed in different ways and across the globe. This book examines the empowering and enabling regulations that have facilitated this. While, for example, the UK and EU aim to use the forces of commercial competition to improve financial innovation, increase economic growth assisted by lower transaction costs and remove non-financial barriers, conversely, East Asian jurisdictions have taken a more collaborative approach. This book also looks at the important use of open banking for socio-economic purpose in Brazil and India. Here open banking forms part of wider government programmes to increase financial inclusion coupled with encouraging economic growth. This book aims to demonstrate the possibilities and challenges of open banking and how it is changing lives across the world.

About this book

Since its inception and development worldwide, open banking has aroused interest among financial stakeholders. The literature is quite substantial as the term 'open banking' unlocks a myriad of sources.

DOI: 10.4324/9781003331339-2

Those financial institutions directly participating in the open banking ecosystem, namely banks, and those firms providing account or payment initiation-related services (the so-called 'third parties')—have significantly contributed to the literature. Third parties involved in data sharing have produced significant literature on their roles and activities within open banking. Their informational websites and materials help navigate, from a practical perspective, the complexities of open banking, mainly regarding their interactions with other participants and the implications for the whole financial services sector. Third parties' written work and online updates are also relevant to understanding the new products and services that open banking brings and the extent to which the financial world has changed accordingly.

Studies from consulting, financial advisory firms and organisations representing firms focussed on open banking-enabled services give additional contributions. Their work sheds insight into the potential of open banking to reshape equilibrium across the financial sector by creating a more competitive, innovative and inclusive environment. Within this context, the analysis brings forward valuable recommendations to allow financial stakeholders to be in step with the times. Overall, these studies underline the disruptive impact of open banking in the financial industry. As such, they intertwine with further research conducted by consumer organisations reviewing the opportune strategies for making open banking a concrete force behind everyone's financial well-being. These thoughts are coupled with work assessing the security and privacy rights of all the actors interacting in a data-sharing community.

Nonetheless, the global phenomenon of open banking cannot be overlooked. As mentioned, the concept has spread across nations and become a policy objective in many jurisdictions. Under this dimension, open banking is the basis for wider projects, such as open finance and an open data society. Accordingly, further layers of knowledge are provided by policy and regulatory documents detailing the rationale behind the adoption of domestic open banking regimes, their implementation pathway and future expectations.

Scholarly production is also flourishing as open banking is analysed from business, law and economic perspectives. Academic work critically analyses the effectiveness of open banking in driving innovation and making the financial system more competitive and inclusive. By balancing enthusiasm and scepticism, these studies contribute an objective view of the strengths and weaknesses of open banking. These approaches together demonstrate that open banking trend is commanding attention at industry, regulatory and academic levels.

By relying on the abovementioned body of information and written work, this book intends to capture the global reach of open banking through an incisive analysis of its most relevant features and development worldwide. In doing so, it starts with a narrow approach in which the term 'open banking participants' refers to the main players interacting in a data-sharing ecosystem through specific rules and technological resources. Understanding the role of the main participants is the benchmark for analysing the so-called open banking pioneer jurisdictions. Within this context, the book focuses on the early open banking policies in the EU and UK. This part addresses the role of private sector competition operating within a state-mandated regulatory framework. While regulation is usually restrictive, in the case of open banking, the aim is to use regulation to promote innovation and develop new markets in financial services.

This angle is crucial to understanding the expansion of the open banking concept worldwide. At this stage, the book takes the reader on a fascinating journey through the progress various jurisdictions have made in creating and implementing their own open banking frameworks. The scope of the analysis is wide, as the authors conducted research across continents. This part of the book offers a glimpse of the market-driven and regulatory-driven approaches that have characterised the development of open banking worldwide. Significantly, through a cross-jurisdictional analysis, the book makes the readers aware of the full scale of open banking. It is not a phenomenon confined to one or a few jurisdictions; open banking exists worldwide. For these reasons, the term 'open banking participants' will be used in a broad sense, namely, to denote a global ecosystem made of continental areas.

The book further reviews the rise and growth of open banking business models in emerging economies such as Brazil and India and how central banks have taken on the role of mandating how a new market should operate with the aim of promoting economic growth via greater financial inclusion in selected emerging economies. Against this backdrop, one realises that the global development of open banking does not have a leading jurisdiction. There are open banking pioneers and open banking developers who are running faster than the early adopters. Open banking leaders are probably not needed, but it is worth questioning whether jurisdictions that have adopted (or will adopt) open banking can find common ground for benefiting together as participants in a global phenomenon. These are the last reflections the book offers.

The authors are aware that there are some limitations to this study. Open banking is constantly evolving; some jurisdictions are adopting open banking frameworks, improving existing regimes or simply conducting feasibility studies. As a result, some of the jurisdictional settings the book analyses may soon change. Other countries could have also been analysed. Nonetheless, the paucity of information is another limitation that justifies the focus on the chosen nations. Overall, the book selects those jurisdictions that offer more concrete results regarding their open banking adoption and appear to inspire others. In line with its title, the book achieves the goal of providing a substantial picture of the importance of open banking and its regulatory approaches across jurisdictions.

Open banking is not a fad. There will still be much to consider. The open banking debate is not closed through this book but is further stimulated through the information and reflections the work brings forward. As such, the book is a valid companion for all open banking observers.

Book structure

The book is divided into three parts. Part I is entitled 'Open Banking Ecosystem and Policy' and contains this introduction and two chapters. Chapter 2 examines the concept of open banking to provide an understanding of the main open banking actors and their degree of interaction to make it a collaborative data-sharing ecosystem. The analysis first deconstructs the concept of open banking and then explains the role of each participant. The chapter also discusses API as the widely recognised primary technology for data-sharing among participants. Examining all the open banking features allows us to conclude the chapter by outlining its development worldwide and the various approaches. In Chapter 3, we review open banking regulation in the UK and EU. Broadly, while there are a number of significant exceptions, we believe that while open banking is important, it needs to present a much more compelling benefit to consumers before the adoption becomes significantly wider and deeper.

The aggregation and presentation of data does not appear to provide either sufficient competitive advantage or distinct incentives for many consumers to agree to share their financial data. It is also possible that consumers do not trust how their data will be used since the risk of infringement of personal privacy is a very real issue in, for example, Europe which has had a relatively recent history of personal information being misused for political purposes.

In the UK wealth distribution may be described as deep but narrow. The proportion of households in the UK with any significant savings is very low and the wealth gaps between regions and between generations are vast. Most of the wealthiest individuals will have their own financial advisers who will doubtless do their best to shield their clients from divulging more information than is absolutely required by third parties.

Consequently, the pool of the population who may be attractive to product and service propensity modelling is likely to be small. Of this broad cohort, a number are likely to be unwilling to share their financial information.

The issue for open banking services (and challenger banks) is that operating in the retail market in the UK may be limited to a shallow unprofitable pool. The cost of acquiring new customers and retaining them may be too high in relation to their value. Offering a highly commoditised IT service is probably insufficient. Other services to encourage the use of new payment service providers could be developed. This is currently the case of 'buy now pay later' but all credit-based schemes carry a range of additional risks which may be both financial and reputational.

Part II of the book is entitled 'Open Banking Regulation'. It contains three chapters that explore how various jurisdictions have planned, adopted and implemented their open banking frameworks. Chapter 4 considers open banking development in Europe by focusing on the Nordic region (Denmark, Norway, Sweden, Finland and Iceland) and some countries that are part of the European Free Trade Association (Switzerland and Liechtenstein). This chapter highlights the fast-paced development of open banking in the Nordic region because of the steady implementation plans of the EU Payment Service Directive 2 (PSD2). Rapid legislative implementation of open banking is also explained by the digital tradition of the Nordic region, which finally makes open banking very attractive at regulatory, industry and consumer levels. In contrast, this chapter highlights the scepticism of the Swiss authorities towards open banking through its legislative approaches and the progress achieved so far through market-driven approaches.

Chapter 5 addresses open banking developments in the Americas (Canada, the USA, Mexico and Chile). The Canadian Department of Finance is leading work on developing open banking in Canada. The Department of Finance issued a consultation paper on open banking early in 2019. Its focus, similar to that in Australia, was on data sharing and not on payment initiation. Payments Canada is working on modernising its payment infrastructure which could enable this facility if the government chose to pursue a wider form of open banking. There was little in the consultation on developing FinTech and not much on developing competition in financial services. It is possible that the Canadian government does not really see the benefits of competition in financial services. A number of economists see a correlation between banking competition and bank failures in the global financial crisis of 2007/9 with developed economies, with a less competitive banking sector, avoiding the issues experienced by other jurisdictions with more diversified but fragile banking systems.

Payments Canada operates under the Canadian Payments Act 1985. It is funded by both the Bank of Canada and the authorised domestic and foreign banks operating in the country. It is a non-profit making and owns and operates Canada's payment clearing and settlement infrastructure. There is a very limited amount about open banking in its Corporate Plan and it is vague about the way forward in this area.

There have been some initial steps, in the retail payments area, with the Retail Payment Activities Act 2021 which permits authorisation of firms undertaking electronic payment functions (e.g., 'payment processors, digital wallets, money transfer services and other payment technology companies'). However, as mentioned earlier progress is slow and there is little or no mention of competition as a driving force. The approach appears to be a mixture of government 'top-down' development coupled with incumbent bank direction of the development of the payments systems. This cautious approach may be valid based on what happened in the global financial crisis and being a 'follower' may allow Canada to see what works and to select what may be seen as best for the country.

The USA has been discussing reforms via an open banking rule. In this regard, the chapter reviews the debates and roadmaps for achieving an open banking framework in a country where market-driven initiatives have been the predominant approach to developing open banking.

The chapter ends with an analysis of open banking in Latin American countries, namely Mexico and Chile.

All the signs in 2020 were that Mexico would use FinTech in an innovative way to promote financial inclusion. For example, only around 43% of households have a bank account compare with 70% or more in both Chile and Brazil. In Mexico, this figure falls to only 6% in rural areas. It was also hoped that the development of Cobro Digital (CoDi), Mexico's instant payment system, would widen access to financial services. It is very similar to the much more successful (Brazilian) Pix system. However, it appears to have not had a significant take-up even during the COVID-19 period. The Mexican economy remains very heavily dependent on cash transactions. The lack of an adequate financial services infrastructure, especially in rural regions has had an adverse effect on the economy. Certainly, new firms such as Prometeo and Belvo have entered the open banking market in both Mexico and Brazil. However, while acknowledging the relevance of open banking to aid financial inclusion the focus of, for example, Prometeo is on the growing middle class.

Finally, in Chile the issuance of the so-called 'FinTech Ley' incorporating open banking rules offers important points of reflection regarding its role in driving innovation and growth in emerging markets. Chapter 6 moves to the Far East countries (Australia, New Zealand, Singapore, South Korea, Taiwan, China, Hong Kong and Indonesia). Unlike in, for example, the UK and EU, Australia has not focused on open banking and payment systems. Instead, the regulations have concentrated on the customer's ownership of their own data. The background is the dominance of the four major banks in Australia. There were concerns about the dominant market power of these banks and their poor record in looking after the interests of their customers. The 'Coleman Report', advocated increasing competition in banking and it saw customer 'data sharing' with other financial institutions as one way of achieving this.

As a consequence of a series of reports the government introduced new legislation. This developed consumer data access and sharing. This aspect of open banking was subsumed within the general area of consumer data protection. It fell under the auspices of the Australian Competition and Consumer Commission (ACCC).

However, there was a change in direction in early 2020. The then Treasurer set up an inquiry into 'Future Directions for the Consumer Data Right' (CDR) including considering open banking and payment initiation. The inquiry, chaired by Scott Farrell, an Australian lawyer specialising in fintech, issued its report in October 2020. To some extent, the COVID-19 pandemic accelerated this move as many consumers switched to operating online as the country entered a series of 'lock-downs'.

The Farrell Inquiry reported in October of that year and recommended allowing direct account payment initiation authorised by consumers along the lines operating in the UK at the time. At the end of February 2021, the Treasury took over as the lead agency for CDRs from the ACCC and further reports followed.

It is not clear why full open banking, as opposed to data sharing, is taking so long to develop in Australia. The Treasury seems to be making most of the running to get Australia closer to catching up with developments in this area. This may be the reason for the minister taking greater powers. The Treasury sees the new rules allowing third-party payment initiation directly from customer accounts to be phased in over a period of time. However, since May 2022, Australia has had a new government with a new Treasurer, and it is not clear what the direction of travel will be and at what speed in the area of open banking.

Chapter 6 reviews the open banking policies in China, Hong Kong and Indonesia. It underlines the incorporation of open banking within long-term horizon strategies for boosting economic growth. Through this lens, the chapter underlines how regulators in these countries regard open banking as an enabler of innovation and inclusion.

Chapter 7 concludes Part II of the book by assessing the growth of open banking in the Middle East and North Africa. The chapter focuses on the Gulf Cooperation Council (GCC) countries. It shows how the open banking experience in pioneer countries such as the EU, UK and Australia has been observed across these countries and translated into specific legislation that makes some of them (e.g. Bahrain, Saudi Arabia and Jordan) inspirational in their open banking pathway. Some GCC countries have been planning to transition from open banking to open finance. This chapter demonstrates how some jurisdictions are running faster than the pioneer jurisdictions in implementing open banking.

Part III of the book is entitled 'Business Models, Emerging Economies and the Way Forward'. It contains the last four chapters. In Chapter 8, we consider the future of open banking in the UK. Few of the open banking challenger firms are profitable and the worry is that we have been here before. In the late 1990s, a number of innovative internet banks were established (e.g., Egg bank, Smile bank, Intelligent Finance, Cahoot). They are almost all founded by existing large banks or insurance companies but were generally run independently with their own management and 'style'. They used innovative marketing and product offerings to attract internet customers. They were seen as the future as the stodgy 'bricks and mortar' banks closed branches. However, none of these banks or neo-banks really prospered.

Will it be different this time? The new open banking firms remain dependent on continuing funding from various types of investment businesses. It is unclear how much longer the cash spigots will remain open. Some, such as Adyen in Amsterdam, are already highly successful with a clear and focused business model. However, with the exception of Klarna and a few others, the vast majority have failed to distinguish themselves. They have relatively high-cost bases in relation to their income.

A business model dependent on fees and charges income will expose these firms to conduct business regulation. All this will be in highly competitive markets setting limits on pricing strategies. Finally, UK-based businesses with any pretensions to scale will need to set up EU-authorised firms to allow them to have access to the much larger EU financial services markets and significantly greater numbers of consumers.

Chapter 9 continues to highlight that, broadly, jurisdictions such as the UK and EU have focused on setting up a legal framework to promote open banking. It has then been left to competition to work to deliver innovation and lower prices.

However, the challenges faced by developing countries are immense, including large remote and illiterate populations, very limited access to digital technology or even electricity, and often little to no engagement with either central or regional governments or markets for goods and services. It is almost certainly a correct assessment both for the Brazilian and Indian central governments that, in this circumstance, competition will not aid increased financial inclusion and economic growth.

While both India and Brazil appreciate the importance of financial inclusion and economic growth, the approach taken by India is much more comprehensive and balanced with a strategy aimed at each person having their own digital identity. With this they are able, among other things, to access the open banking elements of the payment systems and engage in the financial economy. This includes the mobilisation of savings put to use for the wider economy.

There are many similarities between the Brazilian and Indian approaches. This includes not placing much, if any, reliance on competition to increase financial inclusion. Both also employ the central government and its agencies, including the central bank, for societal as well as economic and regulatory purposes. Both countries have embraced innovation whereas more traditional financial institutions appeared to have been too complacent and lacking in innovation. As already mentioned, direct intervention by the government was seen as the solution and all the indications demonstrate success. They show how open banking may be used for a variety of purposes including facilitating economic inclusion and growth, engaging all citizens in a productive economy and helping governments to reduce, if not defeat, endemic corruption.

These two case studies are useful in showing what can be done and achieved in societies facing considerable challenges.

Chapter 10 reflects on the future of open banking. Based on the global development of open banking, this chapter refers to 'open banking participants' to identify the jurisdictions that embraced open banking. However, being participants means sharing experiences, coordinating and dialoguing with each other. This dimension must be strengthened to make the extraterritorial expansion of open banking a real global phenomenon. Accordingly, the chapter questions the need to align open banking across jurisdictions. Common open banking issues, such as security, consumer education, financial inclusion and the transition from open banking to open finance, are reviewed from these perspectives.

2 The Open Banking World

Construing open banking

What is open banking? This is the critical question to answer for understanding the open banking world. Various inputs can be given to this end. Open banking can be an application that allows bank customers to see their financial history in one place.[1] Through this lens, open banking is the instrument that improves the customer experience in the financial services industry by enabling them to access more suitable, cutting-edge products and services at lower prices, thus achieving inclusion and stronger financial literacy.[2] However, this is not the only perspective.

The application creators are the so-called 'third parties', primarily FinTech companies. From this angle, open banking drives competition by facilitating the entrance of new players into the financial sector.[3] The third-party viewpoint establishes a connection with traditional financial intermediaries, namely banks, which are also essential open banking participants. Within this context, open banking is regarded as an opportunity for traditional financial intermediaries to modernise their business models, increase their revenues, and incentivise customer loyalty.[4] All these perspectives depict open banking as a win-win situation for all the involved actors.

Nonetheless, the discussion is not over. The interrelationship between the open banking players is possible through specific technology, notably the application programming interfaces (APIs). As shown in the next section, APIs are nothing new. However, their use is so widespread in the digital world that they are no longer considered mere technical tools but a link between the conventional and digital business worlds.[5] The technology stance makes open banking synonymous with innovation and significant transformative changes in the financial services industry.

Finally, open banking means 'regulation'. This word does not simply encompass rules and approaches to make open banking deliver its benefits. The regulation also denotes the borderless growth of open banking. As a cross-jurisdictional phenomenon, open banking caught the interest of regulators worldwide, who have designed appropriate legislation and policies to govern, amongst others, the roles and responsibilities of the participants.[6]

DOI: 10.4324/9781003331339-3

Overall, open banking can be defined and analysed through business, technology, and regulatory dimensions. Each angle constitutes a strand of literature through which open banking is currently discussed. Some scholars argue in favour of a general definition of open banking to bridge the misunderstandings and confusions that the various perspectives through which the open banking phenomenon can be appraised (e.g., business, regulation, technology, economics) generate.[7]

This argument has merit. It must be acknowledged that open banking is a multifaceted concept. Open banking can be introduced and defined in different ways depending on the focal point (e.g., use of technology, bank customer centricity, regulatory strategies).[8] Narrow definitions focus on the consumer authorisation given to third parties to access financial data stored in financial institutions.[9] Broader definitions focus on the types of products and services enabled by open banking, while other definitions are based on differentiating open banking from open finance.[10] Furthermore, a lack of consensus on the definition of open banking also results from different drivers behind adopting and implementing open banking frameworks across countries.[11]

However, all the possible open banking definitions finally converge on one fundamental element: 'Data'. Consumer financial data are at the heart of the open banking idea. In other words, open banking is always presented as a data-sharing process. Consequently, far from mapping and contrasting distinct definitions of open banking, it is essential to build a basic but sound understanding of it by first elaborating on the meaning of data sharing, which is also the subject of scholarly discussion. Some authors bring attention to the blurriness surrounding the concept of data sharing due to its many-sided nature.[12] Again, depending on the aspects, one wishes to emphasise (e.g., business data sharing, government data sharing, personal data sharing, peer-to-peer data sharing, inter-organisational data sharing, cross-domain data sharing) there can be various forms and definitions of data sharing.[13] Consequently, it is necessary to develop a definition of data sharing that synthesises its components, characteristics and implications. Recent studies have brought forward the following paradigmatic definition of data sharing:

> Data sharing is the domain-independent process of giving third parties access to the data sets of others. These third parties may be other companies (usually not direct competitors), individuals, or public institutions. The shared data is often used to develop new applications and services. The expectation is to be compensated financially or through other benefits (e.g., receiving data) for providing the data. What the data may be used for and how it is made available is determined within the framework of the (legal) agreements between the data providers, data consumers, and other roles, depending on the use case.[14]

A general definition of data sharing would help define a specific data-sharing process named open banking. However, as mentioned, the objective of the present discussion is not to come to a general or specific definition of open banking, but rather to clarify the subject of this book as a starting point for wider analysis. The deconstruction of the above definition of data sharing helps to this end. As a financial data-sharing process, open banking involves third parties gaining access to consumer data that financial institutions retain and store the moment a bank-customer relationship is formed, usually with the opening of a bank account. Data access is enabled by proper technology, and the ultimate result is the development of new products and services.

Consequently, the first feature of open banking is the interaction between the involved players. Their interaction is necessary to achieve data sharing through technology. For these reasons, open banking is also defined as a 'collaborative' data-sharing process.[15] The participants' interrelationship has legal implications, and, as discussed in the next chapters, either the industries or the regulators dictate the terms of this interplay to guarantee the sound and secure functioning of open banking. Thus, open banking is an ecosystem, a domain where financial data are shared between diversified players. Such an environment has great potential to bring innovation, enhance competition, transform how financial institutions do business and make the financial services industry more inclusive. The roles and values of its participants need to be dissected to further understand the implications of this ecosystem.

API

Any discussion on open banking pinpoints APIs as cogs in the data-sharing process. To explain APIs in basic terms, one should first consider the ways people interact with each other. Nowadays, communication is primarily face-to-face or remote. In the latter example, communication may happen through various means such as computers, applications and websites. This situation is characterised by the interaction between humans and technologies and requires a 'user interface', that is, all the means facilitating this interconnection (e.g., display screen, keyboard, mouse).[16] The human-tech interaction entails exchanging and transmitting information from one system to another, meaning that there should be something in the middle that allows for processing the data received from one system and transmitting them to another. APIs are therefore brought into this context as the software interface facilitating data transmission amongst computers, applications or machines.[17]

To explain how APIs work in practice, we must first consider the following elements: User, client and server. Assuming, for example, that weather forecasts are needed, there are mobile apps providing weather information daily and hourly for any location. In this case, there is a first layer of interaction between the individual who needs the information (the 'user') and their application. The application will receive the data from the user and, in turn, will have to obtain the weather forecast information from a specific website (the 'server'). To get that information, the application (now called 'the client') will have to establish a second layer of interaction with the server's API. Technically, the client sends a data request to the server's API, which finally forwards the server's response back to the client. In this phase, the API will never interact with the individual seeking a weather forecast but with its application.[18] Clearly, APIs are the go-between the application and the web server.

APIs are a complex world, where various categorisations exist depending on their architecture and purpose. Private APIs are the most common and are defined as 'internal' because they will only be used across departments or units within an organisation.[19] Open APIs, as the name suggests, are open to the public and can be freely used. Public APIs are a subtype of open APIs whose access may require charges and authorisation.[20] Finally, using the so-called partner APIs is only limited to certain parties. For these reasons, they have strict authorisations and security requirements.[21]

APIs form an integral part of the modern technology landscape. Their origins trace back to the 1950s when a book by Maurice Wilkes, David Wheeler and Stanley Gill first described APIs and other key computer programming terms.[22] Wilkes and Wheeler provided a rough definition of APIs as a method for establishing communication between computers. Their introduction and definition set the scene for the current APIs' popularity. In line with the increased use of computers in the 1960s, studies on APIs expanded from the computer-to-computer relationship to the communication between a single app and the rest of a computer system.[23] The advent of the Internet in the 1990s also marked an evolution in the use of APIs as enablers of communication amongst computer applications within the internet arena. In so doing, APIs would have opened the way to the burgeoning of web services. Indeed, in the 2000s cloud providers such as Salesforce, eBay and Amazon began exposing their web APIs to third-party service providers, thus sowing the seeds for data sharing and interconnection.[24]

Since then, public APIs have become increasingly pervasive in a wide range of sectors, such as telecommunications, media and films, travel, real estate, healthcare, insurance, transportation and financial services.[25] Nowadays, APIs are not exclusively regarded as mechanisms allowing software to talk to each other but as crucial tools for economic growth. Opening APIs liberates data and strengthens the connection between companies and organisations. Such interrelation allows businesses to monetise data and bolster innovation by creating new products and services.[26] The benefits of data sharing through APIs are not limited to individual companies but accrue to the global economy. Accordingly, 'API Economy' is the buzzword for designating not only the potential for business growth and transformation but also the economic benefits associated with the proliferation of APIs in various key sectors.[27]

Against this backdrop, using APIs as the underlying technology in open banking to enable bank customer data exposure to third parties is apparent.

The widespread use of APIs in other sectors and their global perception as the building blocks of digital services have made them the glue of open banking. Nonetheless, it is worth mentioning that access to financial data can also be obtained through other methods.

In this respect, the open banking literature compares APIs with 'screen scraping' and 'reverse engineering' practices. Through screen scraping practices, third-party applications retrieve data using bank customers' usernames and passwords.[28] In reverse engineering practices, third parties gain access to bank customers' data by analysing the information exchanged between a customer bank application (e.g., a mobile bank application) and the bank server.[29] Technically, such an analysis is possible by decomposing the application's code. As a result, third parties will build their own ('reverse engineered') API allowing them to interact with the bank server like the bank's application normally does.[30] Like screen scraping, reverse engineering involves the use of customers' credentials. These information-sharing practices are regarded as unstable and prone to fraud risks.[31] Banks would not be keen on being engaged in data-sharing processes through screen scraping and reverse engineering. By not involving the use of bank customer login credentials, APIs are instead considered more secure and robust data-sharing tools.[32] API underpins the global development and regulation of open banking mapped by this book, so there is a strong intersection between them.

As will be shown, banks are either mandated or encouraged to open their APIs. Some jurisdictions like Singapore and Hong Kong named 'API Playbook' and 'Open API Framework' their respective open banking frameworks.[33] Even in the USA, where screen scraping practices have always been the predominant way of sharing data, open APIs are now encouraged at the industry and regulatory levels to govern open banking. In 2017, the National Automated Clearing House Association (NACHA) announced an API standardisation programme centred on key areas such as fraud and risk reduction, data sharing and payment access.[34] API is also fostered within the US Consumer Financial Protection Bureau's consultations for implementing Section 1033 of the Dodd–Frank Wall Street Reform and Consumer Protection Act (the Dodd–Frank Act), which will result in the so-called US Open Banking Rule.[35] While establishing the centrality of APIs within the open banking ecosystem, approaches differ worldwide. For instance, banks cannot charge fees for opening their API, while in other countries fees are either granted *tout court* or allowed when third parties go beyond a set number of bank customer data access.[36]

Furthermore, there are differences in the type of API to be deployed, with some countries prescribing a standard API to be used by all the involved actors, while others give freedom of choice or free rein to financial institutions to launch their own APIs.[37] As the fundamental open banking technology, API requires adequate governance and security measures to make open banking an effective and beneficial data-sharing ecosystem. These aspects can be expanded further by reviewing the open banking participants.

Banks

As pointed out in the first section, open banking is founded on the interaction of three players. Each is pivotal to open banking as a collaborative data-sharing ecosystem. Banks are the first participants to be analysed. They expose their customer data to third parties through open APIs. This relatively straightforward process is quite meaningful. Banks have always had a monopoly over their customer data. Their custodianship can be represented as a vault where customer data are locked. This image conveys that banks have absolute control over their customer data. In other words, it is as if customer data are stored in a crypt that is never opened externally because banks possess the keys. Open banking is founded on the opposite credo, according to which banks must open externally if their customers wish. Consequently, one of the most intriguing and revolutionary aspects of open banking is a break with the paradigm of banks having outright leverage over customer data.[38]

Open banking leads to transformative changes that ultimately affect the bank-customer relationship. As discussed in greater detail in the next section, bank customers are given ownership and control over their data because of open banking.

However, these paradigmatic shifts are a great opportunity for traditional financial institutions. Open banking is thought to modernise banks and permit them to keep up with a constantly evolving financial sector.[39] As open banking players, traditional financial institutions will have deeper insights into their customers' lifestyles, needs and objectives. Through a holistic vision of their customers, they will be able to recommend more personalised financial products and services that they can cross-sell and up-sell.[40] Consequently, embracing open banking would permit banks to strengthen customer loyalty, attract new customers, remain competitive in an ever-data and technology-driven industry, and finally have more options for increasing revenues.[41]

Against these possibilities, it is worth providing a snapshot of banks' involvement in the open banking ecosystem. To briefly anticipate the subject of Part II of the book, it must be acknowledged that banks' participation in open banking is either required under law or encouraged (but not mandatory).[42] As a global phenomenon, open banking has clearly some jurisdictions that are regarded as launchpads. Recent studies on open banking began reviewing the progress of Allied Irish Bank, Danske Bank, Lloyds Banking Group, Nationwide Building Society, Barclays, Bank of Ireland, RBS, HSBC and Santander UK as the nine largest UK retail banks that were mandated to start rolling out open banking through the creation of an open-source Open Banking API by January 2019.[43] Despite some postponements against the initial deadline and the fact that not all the nine banks could finally meet new deadlines, other UK banks and building societies took part voluntarily.[44] Similarly, in Australia, the open banking journey commenced with the four major banks (Commonwealth, NAB, Westpac and ANZ).[45] The pattern of mandating first the country's largest financial institutions and then allowing other smaller credit institutions to join has also been followed in other jurisdictions.[46]

There are differences in the bank services covered by open banking, with some jurisdictions piloting retail banking first and then planning implementation in corporate banking at a later stage[47] or providing for both business areas.[48] In other jurisdictions, bank data sharing is not mandatory but governed by the agreements reached by the involved stakeholders. For example, in countries like China, where the development of open banking is mainly market-driven, digital-only banks have developed custom-made APIs and strengthened their partnerships with other financial services providers to increase their market share.[49] No matter whether they embrace open banking because of legislation or on their own initiative, banks are central players in this new ecosystem, with their core retail and corporate services significantly impacted.

For banks, open banking means not only important changes in how they handle their customer data or the possibility of evolving themselves in step with the digital and technological times but also considerable efforts and costs. There are efforts and costs to implementing a robust and secure open banking architecture. The starting point is an adequate API infrastructure. The global development of open banking evidence regulation, standards and guidelines relating to the setup of a proper API architecture.[50] Some approaches encourage banks to develop their API life-cycle governance by going through the following key steps: Ideation of APIs, prototyping and production, publishing, consumption and retirement.[51] At present, a line can be drawn between banks that develop their own APIs[52] and those that rely on external platforms.[53] Overall, open banking is a reality banks must deal with in the modern digitalised and technology-driven financial services industry. Tapping into the API economy is the first step to being part of a phenomenon that establishes new equilibria in using customer data in the global financial sector.

Third parties

Like banks, third parties are also crucial actors in the open banking world. The word 'third parties' is quite generic. In this book, it will be used as an umbrella term to identify entities that provide the same (open banking-enabled) services, though they have different denominations in the various regulatory frameworks worldwide. For example, 'data recipients' is used to designate third parties under the Australian open banking regime.[54] In Chile, the 'FinTech Ley' refers to third parties as 'Information Based Services Providers',[55] they are identified as 'Third-party Service Providers' in Hong Kong,[56] 'Ancillary Service Providers' in Bahrain[57] and 'data account users' in the United States.[58]

These differences also depend on the scope of the legislation. Indeed, names such as 'Data Recipients' and 'Ancillary Service Providers' are buzzwords to designate wider (and different) categories of players governed by regulations that cover open banking and other sectors. In these cases, the major task is to identify the specific open banking third parties.

With this in mind, there are two key questions to address: Who are third parties and what is their role in the open banking ecosystem? Third parties are those financial players who ask banks to access their customer data. As explained in the next section, access is mediated by customer consent. In any case, third parties need to be licensed or authorised by the competent authorities to be open banking players. Indeed, the worldwide open banking experience highlights the importance of having a robust licensing/authorisation regime to guarantee security and effective control in such a sensitive area as data sharing. In accordance with licence requirements, some jurisdictions hold registers or directories that permit taking stock of the number and identity of these players.[59] Overall, the third-party industry keeps growing in connection with the expansion of open banking worldwide.

However, precise figures are always tricky given the rapid changes due to new entries, withdrawals or licence/authorisation revocation by the competent national supervisory authorities.[60] Traditional banking institutions could act as third parties. In its explanation of open banking, Santander expressly mentions this possibility:

> With Open Banking, you can share your data with authorised third-party providers to link accounts you hold with other financial organisations (so long as you give them your permission). An example of an authorised third-party provider could be another bank, building society, or regulated financial institution, such as Barclays, Lloyds, or HSBC that is registered on the Open Banking Directory. You can link your: current account, savings accounts, and credit cards.[61]

Nonetheless, non-traditional banking institutions such as FinTech start-ups, neo-banks, merchants and payment providers largely populate the third-party market.[62] Santander's definition raises the question of the role of third parties and their relationship with banks.

Preliminarily, it is worth clarifying that the data-sharing process enabled by open banking revolves around payment accounts. Countries can have different definitions of payment accounts. Nonetheless, the definition proposed under the EU Payment Services Directive II (PSD2) as 'an account held in the name of one or more payment service users that is used for the execution of payment transactions'[63] is widely accepted. Consequently, open banking pertains to accounts that can be accessed remotely (online or by mobile phone) and enable the execution and receipt of payment transactions.

Until now, there has been an interesting debate on whether savings accounts qualify as payment accounts for open banking purposes. As is known, savings accounts limit the ability of consumers to make payments or withdrawals vis-à-vis current accounts.[64] In the first place, one could conclude their exclusion from the notion of payment accounts and, therefore, from the open banking process. In the EU, the Court of Justice of the European Union (CJEU) stated that saving accounts coupled with a current account do not qualify as payment accounts as defined in the EU legislation.[65] However, the court also specified that looking at the characteristics and operation of such accounts is important. Consequently, a 'savings account' denomination would not be, on its own, determinant to exclude a payment account categorisation.[66] This would mean that certain types of savings accounts such as flexible savings accounts could be within the open banking realm. Ultimately, it is a matter of interpretation and how the open banking adopters delimit the data-sharing scope.

For instance, the UK regulators mention, generically, personal and business current accounts, credit cards and online e-money accounts as payment accounts to be used for open banking purposes.[67] Then, the Financial Conduct Authority (FCA) clarified that payment accounts could include current accounts, e-money accounts, flexible savings accounts, credit card accounts and current account mortgages but not term deposit accounts, child trust fund deposit accounts and cash individual savings accounts.[68] In the FCA's view, even mortgage or loan accounts would be considered a payment service.[69]

By comparison, the Bahraini framework brings into the open banking scope savings accounts, current accounts, term and call deposits, foreign currency accounts, unrestricted investment accounts, restricted investment accounts, etc.[70] The Australian open banking regime under the Consumer Data Right (CDR) contemplated the following products to start the first phase of a wider open data sharing plan: Savings account, call account, term deposit, current account, cheque account, debit card account, transaction account, personal basic account, GST or tax account, personal credit or charge card account, business credit or charge card account.[71] Payment accounts are therefore the basis for understanding where the interaction between banks and third parties occurs.

What is included and excluded in this area is somewhat blurred across jurisdictions. This premise permits us to discern the role of third parties within the broad payment account area. The nomenclature used by leading European open banking jurisdictions can serve this purpose.

European open banking frameworks designate the financial institutions providing and maintaining payment accounts as 'Account Servicing Payment Service Providers' (ASPSPs). ASPSPs range from credit institutions to building societies and payment institutions.[72] ASPSPs are supposed to open their APIs to third parties denominated as 'Third Party Providers' (TPPs). TPPs are divided into two main categories: 'Account Information Service Providers' (AISPs) and 'Payment Initiation Service Providers' (PISPs).[73] Chapter 8 provides a more specific analysis of the operation of AISPs and PISPs, focusing on the UK open banking market. At this stage, it is convenient to fix their main differences. Payment service users (individuals or businesses) can authorise AISPs to access their payment account information to extract data relating to account balances or transaction histories. The type and amount of information to be retrieved vary across open banking adopters. The payment account information to be shared includes the balance and name of the account holder, payment transaction information (including incoming and outcoming payments), payment details (including payees' names) and payment methods (e.g., direct debits, standing order).[74]

In so doing, a new wave of innovative services stands out. For instance, a money management application that aggregates data (e.g., spending habits, balance) from different bank accounts so that users can see their financial positions in one place.[75] Similarly, in the lending sector, through the AISP services, loan applicants can quickly share their financial history with lenders without needing to provide bank statements. Lenders will then be able to expedite the credit underwriting process.[76]

Unlike AISPs, PISPs connect users to their online or mobile bank application to authorise payments directly from their bank account, without needing to use credit or debit card details.[77] Specifically, if a retailer or business has incorporated payment initiation services, their customers may be presented with a payment option usually called 'Pay by Bank', 'A2A Payment' or 'Instant Bank Transfer'. By choosing this option, the next step is the selection of the bank for the payment. Subsequently, the bank selection and payment review direct the customer to their bank application or online interface to log in. The final step is the payment, which re-directs the customer to the merchant's website for purchase confirmation.[78]

Through open APIs, PISPs establish a direct connection between bank accounts. Their services are advantageous for customers and businesses. PISP services are described as 'zero chargebacks' because they do not entail the fees usually associated with bank transfers or card processing.[79] On the one hand, customers will enjoy a more secure payment experience as they will authenticate their payments directly through their applications without the need to manually enter card details or other sensitive information.[80] On the other hand, businesses will receive their money smoothly and avoid the charges relating to bank transfers or their contracts with card providers.[81] Overall, PISP services save time, effort and money.

Against this backdrop, the difference between AISPs and PISPs is apparent. AISPs manage customer data by accessing and collating them (so-called 'read-only' access).[82] They can aggregate and centralise financial data and give both parties, the financial institutions and their customers, a holistic view of their financial positions in one place. Like AISPs, PISPs are also middlemen but provide users with the possibility of initiating payments from their bank accounts to other accounts (so-called 'read-and-write' access).[83] In essence, AISPs can only view and retrieve customer data, while PISPs view data and initiate payments on behalf of account holders.

As mentioned, the open banking experience worldwide assigns different names to the providers of these services. There can be firms focused on one or both services or provide them as complementary to their core services. Some open banking regulatory frameworks contemplate 'read' and 'write' access, while others only 'read'.[84] For these reasons, the word 'third parties' is more appropriate to identify entities having different denominations across jurisdictions, but finally playing the same role within the open banking ecosystem. There are no boundaries to the products and services that can be created by giving access to bank customer data to third parties.

By mapping the open banking-enabled products, recent studies consider personal financial management applications, account verification applications and peer-to-peer applications only the beginning, and identify emerging use cases (buy-now-pay-later, automated clearing house payment initiation, credit decisioning) with the potential to expand into other more complex areas (digital identity, omnichannel payments, real-time payments, request to pay, crypto payments).[85] Globally, third parties are regarded as new entrants in the financial services industry vis-à-vis traditional financial intermediaries. Their presence strictly relates to one of the main pillars behind implementing open banking across jurisdictions: Enhancing competition and driving innovation in the financial services industry. Third parties are an expression of the significant changes that the financial services industry has undergone because of increased digitalisation and the use of advanced technologies, which allowed new players to flourish and made the industry no longer the exclusive domain of traditional financial intermediaries. Their services bring innovative solutions contributing to business growth and a better customer experience.

Consumer consent

We have emphasised the significance of the inter-relationship between banks and third parties, how traditional financial institutions are affected by the novelty of open banking, and the value of services that third parties provide. Such a process is glued by APIs as the prime technology. However, no operation would be possible without the bank customer's consent. Third parties cannot access payment account data or initiate payment operations without the authorisation of the bank customers. Consumer consent is the most significant feature of the open banking trend. To stress the centrality of consumer consent, the Basel Committee on Banking Supervision (BCBS) labels the data to be shared between financial institutions and third parties as 'customer-permissioned data'.[86]

There are various and important aspects to be analysed. It is to wonder how consumer consent is channelled across financial institutions and third parties. Once again, the European open banking regulation, as the milestone for developing and implementing open banking globally, provides useful insights. At the European level, the consent mechanism is structured through several stages of interactions amongst the banks, their customers and third parties. The first stage involves customers and third parties. Specifically, the third party's interface will indicate to the user the type of information requested and its purpose.[87] The second stage directs the user to their bank's interface for authentication.[88] The completion of authentication allows the financial institution to respond to the third-party request (either access to an account or a payment initiation request) and redirect the user to the third-party interface for giving their final authorisation to the data-sharing operations.[89]

All these steps carried through the interfaces of the involved participants help explain consumer consent in practice, namely as a digital, multi-stage mechanism also applied in other jurisdictions following the European open banking evolution. The interaction between the concerned stakeholders brings forth the legal implications of customer authorisation: The validity and genuineness of the consent for finalising open banking operations. Through this lens, open banking frameworks establish interplays with data protection regulations. Moreover, as open banking is a data-sharing process founded on consumer consent, it is crucial to build this ecosystem by drawing on the rules and safety mechanisms laid down in regulation for privacy and data protection.

Across jurisdictions, the demand, plans or consultations for open banking regulation go in tandem with plans for developing or updating data protection frameworks. For example, in the Middle East, Saudi Arabia has been steadily progressing in implementing open banking regulations. Creating their open banking ecosystem is part of a wider package of national reforms that contemplates the development of a robust data protection law.[90] Likewise, Bahrain has planned the setup of their open banking framework by looking at the EU and UK experiences, including the 2018 EU General Data Protection Regulation (GDPR).[91] Other significant examples can be found in Singapore, where open banking practices need to go along with the Data Protection Act rules for the protection of data subjects,[92] and Hong Kong where banks and third parties are required to comply with guidance on the protection of personal data such as the 'Hong Kong Personal Data Privacy Ordinance' and the codes issued by the 'Privacy Commissioner for Personal Data'.[93]

As the EU PSD2 and GDPR have become models of regulation for developing open banking and data protection regulations outside Europe, they are also influential as to the principles underpinning consumer consent. In this respect, Article 4(11) of the GDPR defines 'consent' as evidence of the data owner's acceptance of the processing of their personal information. Consent should be provided and obtained in a way that does not give rise to ambiguity, no matter whether written or spoken. For these reasons, Article 4(11) pinpoints 'freely given', 'informed', 'specific' and 'unambiguous' as the characteristics for regarding consent as the unequivocal authorisation to process personal data.[94] Under the GDPR, consent is also the condition for processing special categories of personal data specified in Article 9(1).[95] In this case, consent must be 'explicit'. The PSD2 also grounds the exchange of customer information between banks and third parties on the consumer's ('payment service user') 'explicit consent'.[96] There is no definition of 'explicit consent' in the GDPR and PSD2. The European Data Protection Board (EDPB) argues that they should be construed differently. While 'explicit consent' under the GDPR is the legal exception against the prohibition from processing certain personal data, 'explicit consent' under the PSD2 is a requirement within the contractual relationship between the consumer and the third party.[97] Where, for example, consumers enter into a contract with third parties for payment initiation services, they need to be aware of the categories of personal data that will be processed and the purpose (namely, payment initiation service). Explicit consent is therefore permission to access and process data originally stored and processed by another financial institution.[98]

Against this backdrop, the EDPB qualifies 'explicit consent' under the EU open banking framework as an 'additional requirement of a contractual nature'.[99] Despite these differences, the EDPB stresses that the PSD2 consent must be reviewed in connection with data protection frameworks, especially with the (consent) characteristics set out in Article 4(11) of the GDPR (e.g., freely given, unambiguous).[100] However, as the next chapters show, open banking has a global reach. While the influence of the PSD2 (and the GDPR) in shaping an open banking culture worldwide cannot be underestimated, there are different ways of interpreting consent and dealing with its legal implications across jurisdictions.

Accordingly, beyond a thorough exegesis of the meaning and connotation of 'explicit consent', emphasis must be put on the fact that consumer consent is not simply the pillar of the PSD2 framework but the mainstay of open banking as a global movement. Open banking regulations and approaches worldwide are premised on this element no matter the specific drivers behind the implementation of their open banking programmes. Open banking regulatory frameworks put financial institution customers at the centre of this data-driven ecosystem by providing them with the right to give and withdraw their consent.[101] These rights result from another fundamental zeitgeist of open banking, namely, giving customers ownership and control of their data. Such a principle is also the fundamental objective behind the expansion of open banking into open finance.[102]

However, consumer ownership and control of their data are not confined to open banking/open finance; it is the bulwark of a wider global strategy towards a fully open data ecosystem.[103] Under this perspective, open banking and open finance are vital steps to achieving a data-driven economy.[104] In a word, today we have open banking, tomorrow we have open finance, and in the future we will have open data. Seen exclusively through the lens of the open banking context, the consumer right to give and withdraw their consent to any operation involving their own data reinforces the feature of open banking as an innovative data-sharing framework, breaking the traditional canon of banks having the monopoly over their customer data. Customer permission to share their data gives them decisional powers as the sole owners of their data. Their authorisation allows them to be an integral part of the open banking world and benefit from the spectrum of new products and services, thus improving their experience in the financial services industry.

24 *Open Banking Ecosystem and Policy*

Against this backdrop, the present discussion can be closed with the question to be addressed in the concluding chapters of the book that reflect the future of open banking: Are consumers aware of their role as owners and controllers of their financial data under the open banking ethos?

Global development

The explanation of the open banking concept and its participants has been accompanied by some country examples. These references underline the global reach of open banking. It is therefore important to complete the present discussion by moving from the open banking ecosystem (characterised by its major actors) to the 'open banking landscape', which allows for realising the magnitude of a borderless phenomenon. Such an analysis provides the basis for a wider mapping of the development of open banking across jurisdictions, which will be the subject of Part II.

There are other actors when we refer to open banking as a 'landscape' because the main question is about the approaches that can be adopted to allow the flourishing and implementation of open banking, and who promotes the necessary strategies. In this respect, the open banking literature has always drawn a line between prescriptive and market-driven approaches. Clearly, under the former data sharing is required by regulators, while in the latter, the adoption of open banking is left to the negotiations and coordination between banks and third parties.[105] In between, the literature also identifies the so-called 'facilitative' approach where regulators and policymakers foster open banking initiatives without mandating financial institutions.[106] In practice, data sharing is incentivised by issuing guidance, open API standards or by encouraging voluntary data sharing platforms.[107] These distinctions are useful for taking stock of how open banking has been developed and promoted until now. However, they are simply a snapshot to the extent that, as shown in Part II, shifts from market-driven to rule-based approaches can be witnessed in connection with the growth of the open banking experience.[108]

Recent data highlight the adoption of open banking in approximately 80 countries. Among them, government-led approaches through open banking regulatory frameworks are the majority.[109] Indeed, as mentioned above, the European and Australian open banking frameworks have been the springboard for issuing open banking legislation in other countries. However, the open banking landscape is heterogeneous, with some countries having consolidated regimes and others at advanced or early stages of implementation.

Beyond the rule-based versus market-driven approaches dichotomy, there are different drivers behind the adoption of open banking, which ultimately influence its regulation and various initiatives. Promoting innovation, competition and financial inclusion have been the main drivers behind the creation and adoption of open banking worldwide.[110] In some countries, open banking frameworks are created as part of a wider digitalisation plan for the financial services industry and society. Particularly, Middle Eastern countries have 'visions' to be achieved in a time horizon for modernising their financial infrastructures and positioning themselves as internationally recognised financial centres, able to be the catalyst of foreign investments.[111]

Accordingly, open banking is regarded as the essential tool for concretising such a domestic vision so that its framework is either included in specific FinTech legislation[112] or domestic banking legislation.[113] Significantly, the variety of drivers underpinning the regulators' approaches also pinpoints different authorities involved in the promotion and implementation of open banking. In many jurisdictions, central banks are the sole authorities responsible for creating, implementing and monitoring open banking services.[114] Other countries give this responsibility to competition authorities[115] or public bodies overseeing financial and insurance markets,[116] which may be required to consult with other authorities in their rule-making process.[117] The complexity of this landscape is also evidenced by the fact that the authorities in charge of implementing open banking frameworks must cooperate with other authorities responsible for data and consumer protection. Furthermore, there are bodies specifically created for setting API standards and monitoring compliance with them.[118] Consequently, there is no unique open banking system worldwide. The open banking idea of sharing customer-permissioned data with third parties through APIs has spread worldwide, giving open banking the connotation of a global phenomenon. Nonetheless, it is a diversified phenomenon because each jurisdiction has its own open banking philosophy. Borrowing the experience of the open banking pioneering countries does not mean duplicating their frameworks but observing and embracing the changes and reforms the financial services industry has undergone. Then, every country will have its own open banking journey driven by its needs and aims. Against this backdrop, Part II will have a country-by-country focus to show the interest that open banking has raised in regulators and their current efforts and plans for enabling data sharing in their own financial sectors.

Conclusion

This chapter touches upon the features of open banking to provide an understanding of its meaning and practicalities. The analysis of the open banking participants and underlying technology brings to attention not only the collaborative model that open banking establishes to achieve data sharing purposes but also the significant transformation that open banking has determined in the financial services industry: The centre-stage role given to customers through their consent to data sharing, the innovation brought by third parties, and how traditional financial institutions can leverage these changes. Financial data sharing is the open banking way, which spreads around the world in such a way that there is a diversified landscape that witnesses its significance and stimulates us to trace the road ahead.

Notes

1 Competition and Market Authority (CMA), *Update on Open Banking* (5 November 2021) <www.gov.uk/government/publications/update-governance-of-open-banking/update-on-open-banking> accessed 08 July 2023; Chris Hooper, 'Open Banking Apps Explained' (*Gocardless*, May 2022) <https://gocardless.com/guides/posts/open-banking-apps-explained/> accessed 8 July 2023; Axway, 'Open Banking. The Art of the Possible in 10 Use Cases' (*Axway*, 2022) <https://resources.axway.com/financial-services-doc/checklist-open-banking-10-use-cases-en> accessed 8 July 2023.
2 Financial Data and Technology Association (FDTA), 'Opportunities in Open Banking' (FDTA North America, April, 2019) 5 <https://fdata.global/north-america/wp-content/uploads/sites/3/2019/04/FDATA-Open-Banking-in-North-America-US-version.pdf> accessed 8 July 2023; Faith Reynolds, 'Open Banking. A Consumer Perspective' (January 2017) 6 <www.openbanking.org.uk/wp-content/uploads/Open-Banking-A-Consumer-Perspective.pdf> accessed 8 July 2023.
3 CMA (n 1); see also Xavier Vives, 'Digital Disruption in Banking and Its Impact on Competition' (OECD, 2020) 11 <www.oecd.org/competition/digital-disruption-in-banking-and-its-impact-on-competition-2020.pdf> accessed 9 July 2023.
4 The Economist Intelligent Unit, *Whose Customer Are You? The Reality of Digital Banking* (Temenos, 2018) 5 <https://impact.economist.com/perspectives/sites/default/files/Global%20Retail%20Banking%20%282%29.pdf> accessed 9 July 2023; Kanika Hope, *Open Banking and the Rise of Banking-as-a-Service* (Temenos, September 2021) 1 <www.temenos.com/wp-content/uploads/2022/06/Open-Banking-and-the-Rise-of-Banking-as-a-Service-V4.pdf> accessed 9 July 2023.
5 Jean Diederich, 'The API Economy. Why Public APIs Are So Important' (Wavestone, October 2017) 2 <www.wavestone.com/app/uploads/2017/10/Api-Economy-2017.pdf> accessed 9 July 2023; Jean P Simon, 'API, the Glue under the Hood. Looking for the "API Economy"' (2021) 23 Digital Policy Regulation and Governance 5, 498.
6 Francesco De Pascalis, 'The Journey to Open Finance: Learning from the Open Banking Movement' (2022) 33 European Business Law Review 3, 397.
7 Gorka Koldobika Briones de Araluze and Natalia Cassinello Plaza, 'Open Banking: A Bibliometric Analysis-Driven Definition' (2022) 17 PLoS ONE 10, 1 <https://journals.plos.org/plosone/article?id=10.1371/journal.pone.0275496> accessed 10 July 2023; see also Ine van Zeeland and Jo Pierson, 'The Concept of Open Banking: From a Remedy to an Ecosystem' (Study Media Innovation Technology, PB44, 8 March 2021) 1 <https://smit.vub.ac.be/policy-brief-44-the-concept-of-open-banking-from-a-remedy-to-an-ecosystem> accessed 10 July 2023.
8 Ibid.
9 Hunter Dorwart, Daniel Berrick, and Dale Rappaneau, 'Development in Open Banking. Key Issues from a Global Perspective' (Future of Privacy Forum, March 2022) 3 <https://fpf.org/wp-content/uploads/2022/08/FPF-Open-Banking-Report-R2-Singles.pdf> accessed 10 July 2023
10 'Open finance refers to the extension of open banking-like data sharing to a wider range of financial products, such as savings, investments, pensions and insurance', see Financial Conduct Authority (FCA), 'Call for Input: Open finance' (December 2019) 1 <www.fca.org.uk/publication/call-for-input/call-for-input-open-finance.pdf> accessed 10 July 2023.
11 See Part II 'Open Banking Regulation'.
12 Ilka Jussen and others, 'Data Sharing Fundamentals: Characteristics and Definitions' (Proceeding of the 56th Hawaii International Conference on System Sciences, January 2023) 5 <www.researchgate.net/publication/363769417_Data_Sharing_Fundamentals_Characteristics_and_Definition> accessed 10 July 2023.

13 Ibid.
14 Ibid.
15 Laura Brodsky and Liz Oakes, 'Data Sharing and Open Banking' (*McKinsey*, 5 September 2017) <www.mckinsey.com/industries/financial-services/our-insights/data-sharing-and-open-banking#/> accessed 10 July 2023.
16 Mike Sharples, 'An Introduction to Human Computer Interaction' in Margaret Boden (ed) *Artificial Intelligence* (Academic Press 1996) 293.
17 Brian Cooksey, *An Introduction to APIs* (Zapier, Inc 2014) 1.
18 Ibid.
19 Mark Boyd, *Developing the API Mindset. A Guide to Using Private, Partner, & Public APIs* (Nordic APIs 2015) 1 <https://nordicapis.com/ebooks/developing-the-api-mindset/> accessed 10 July 2023.
20 Ibid., 53.
21 Ibid., 31.
22 Maurice Wilkes, David Wheeler, and Stanley Gill, *The Preparation of Programs for an Electronic Digital Computer. with Special Reference to the EDSAC and the Use of a Library of Subroutines* (Cambridge, Massachusetts: Addison-Wesley Press, Inc., 1951) 1.
23 Kate Mikula, 'The History and Evolution of API' (*Traefiklabs*, 7 February 2023) <https://traefik.io/blog/the-history-and-evolution-of-apis/> accessed 10 July 2023.
24 Ibid., see also Matt Hawkins, 'The History and Rise of API' (23 June 2020) *Forbes* <www.forbes.com/sites/forbestechcouncil/2020/06/23/the-history-and-rise-of-apis/> accessed 10 July 2023.
25 George Collins and David Sisk, 'API Economy. From Systems to Business Service' (Deloitte 2015) 23 <www2.deloitte.com/content/dam/Deloitte/uk/Documents/technology/deloitte-uk-api-economy.pdf> accessed 12 July 2023.
26 Bill Doerrfeld and others, *The API Economy. Disruption and the Business of APIs* (Nordic APIs 2016) 1 <https://nordicapis.com/ebooks/the-api-economy/> accessed 12 July 2023.
27 Simon (n 5) 498.
28 Basel Committee on Banking Supervision (BCBS), *Report on Open Banking and Application Programming Interfaces* (BIS, November 2019) 4 <www.bis.org/bcbs/publ/d486.pdf> accessed 12 July 2023.
29 Ibid 6.
30 Ibid.
31 Ibid.
32 Ibid., see also The ODI and Fingleton, *Open Banking, Preparing for Lift Off* (June 2019) 1 <www.openbanking.org.uk/wp-content/uploads/open-banking-report-150719.pdf> accessed 13 July 2023.
33 See Part II 'Open Banking Regulation'.
34 George Throckmorton, 'Afinis: Advancing Financial Services Through API Standardization' (*NACHA*, 30 October 2018) <https://cloud.google.com/blog/products/api-management/afinis-advancing-financial-services-through-api-standardization> accessed 13 July 2023.
35 See Part II 'Open Banking Regulation'.
36 Ibid.
37 See below section 3.
38 Bill Doerrfeld and others (n 26) 25; Rachel J Nam, 'Open Banking and Customer Data Sharing: Implications for FinTech Borrowers' (SAFE WP 364, 2022), 1 <https://papers.ssrn.com/sol3/papers.cfm?abstract_id=4278803#> accessed 16 July 2023; Zhiguo He, Jing Huang, and Jidong Zhou, 'Open Banking: Credit Market Competition When Borrowers Own the Data' (2022) 1 <https://cpb-us-w2.wpmucdn.com/voices.uchicago.edu/dist/6/2325/files/2022/08/Open-Banking_20220726.pdf accessed 16 July 2023>; see also Brodsky and Oakes (n 15).

28   *Open Banking Ecosystem and Policy*

39 Jonathan Turner and others, *The Future of Banking is Open. How to Seize the Open Banking Opportunity* (PWC-ODI 2018) 3 <www.pwc.co.uk/financial-services/assets/open-banking-report-web-interactive.pdf> accessed 17 July 2023; Glory Global, *The Future of Banking-Why Traditional Banks are Embracing Open Banking* (2021) 2 <www.glory-global.com/-/media/GloryGlobal/Downloads/EN_GB/Thought-leadership_EN_GB/Glory-Open-Banking-White-Paper-Thought-Leadership-EN-V1-0.pdf> accessed 17 July 2023; Efma and Wavestone, *Open Banking, an Opportunity for Banks to Rethink Their Business Models* (November 2021) 4 <www.wavestone.com/app/uploads/2021/11/Wavestone-Report-2021_26112021.pdf> accessed 17 July 2023.
40 Ibid.
41 Ibid.
42 See the various jurisdictional approaches mapped in Part II 'Open Banking Regulation'.
43 Gavin Littlejohn, Ghela Boskovich, and Richard Prior, 'United Kingdom: The Butterfly Effect' in Linda Jeng (ed) *Open Banking* (Oxford University Press, New York 2022) 173; see also Finextra and APImetrics, *UK Open Banking APIs Performance Analysis: 2018. An Analysis of the Quality and Cloud Service Performance of the UK's CMA9 Group of Open Banking APIs in 2018*' (APImetrics, May 2019) 5 <https://apimetrics.io/wp-content/uploads/2020/06/finextra_apimetrics_cma9_report_2018.pdf> accessed 18 July 2023.
44 CMA, 'Retail Banking Market Investigation' (2017) Roadmap Completion Decision, 1 <https://assets.publishing.service.gov.uk/media/63bed8958fa8f513b40f866c/BANKING_PROVIDERS_Roadmap_Completion_Decision_.pdf> accessed 18 July 2023; see also <www.openbanking.org.uk/regulated-providers/> accessed 18 July 2023 for a list of current UK open banking regulated providers.
45 Australian Competition and Consumer Commission (ACCC), 'Consumer Data Right – Proposed Timetable for Participation of non-major Authorised Deposit-taking Institutions (ADIs) in the CDR' <www.accc.gov.au/system/files/CDR%20-%20Proposed%20timetable%20for%20participation%20of%20non-major%20ADIs%20in%20the%20CDR_0.pdf> accessed 18 July 2023.
46 See Part II 'Open Banking Regulation' (Indonesia).
47 Ibid., (MENA Region).
48 Chapter 3 Open Banking Policy in the UK and EU.
49 Part II 'Open Banking Regulation' (China).
50 World Bank Group, 'Technical Note on Open Banking. Comparative Studies on Regulatory Approaches' (2022) 8 https://documents1.worldbank.org/curated/en/099345005252239519/pdf/P16477008e2c670fe0835a0e8692b499c2a.pdf accessed 18 July2023.
51 See for instance, The Association of Banks in Singapore (ABS) & Monetary Authority of Singapore (MAS), 'Finance-as-a-Service: API Playbook' (2016) <https://abs.org.sg/docs/library/abs-api-playbook.pdf> accessed 18 July 2023.
52 DBS Bank Limited and Oversea-Chinese Banking Corporation (OCBC Bank) in Singapore, the Spanish financial group Banco Bilbao Vizcaya Argentaria (BBVA) and Citigroup in the US all launched their own API portals, see World Bank Group (n 50) 16. Likewise, some European banks under the PSD2 Directive. a group of major French banks (altogether STET S.A) developed their PSD2 API V1.6, while a consortium of 26 major players in the payment industry called 'the Berlin Group' developed the NextGenPSD2 API; both APIs were then adopted by most European banks, see De Pascalis (n 6) 397.
53 Saltedge, Plaid, MuleSoft, Yodlee, Finicity and Tink, are among examples of platforms partnering with financial institutions for the provision of their own APIs enabling connection with third parties for data sharing purposes. See Julian Alcazar

and Fumiko Hayashi, 'Data Aggregators: The Connective Tissue for Open Banking' (Federal Reserve Bank of Kansas City, PSRB, 24 August 2022),1 <www.kansascityfed.org/Payments%20Systems%20Research%20Briefings/documents/9012/PaymentsSystemResearchBriefing22AlcazarHayashi0824.pdf> accessed 19 July 2023.
54 Australian Competition and Consumer Commission (ACCC), 'Competition and Consumer (Consumer Data Right) Rules 2020' (2020) <www.accc.gov.au/by-industry/banking-and-finance/the-consumer-data-right> 17 July 2023.
55 Part II 'Open Banking Regulation' (Chile).
56 Ibid., (Hong Kong).
57 Ibid., (MENA Region).
58 Ibid., (United States of America). Various names are also given to other open banking actors across jurisdictions. Banks are correlated to 'Data Holders', 'Authorised Deposit Taking Institutions', 'Information Providers', 'Account Data Holders or 'Companies', see Part II 'Open Banking Regulation' (Australia), (Chile), (United States of America) and (Hashemite Kingdom of Jordan).
59 For example, 'Register of Accredited Participants' under the Australian 'Competition and Consumer Data Right' <www.cdr.gov.au/find-a-provider> accessed 17 July 2023; see also the UK Open Banking Directory <www.openbanking.org.uk/regulated-providers/> accessed 17 July 2023.
60 See Konsentus, 'Open Banking in Review: Trends and Progress' (22 December 2021) <www.konsentus.com/insights/articles/open-banking-in-review-trends-and-progress/> accessed 18 July 2023.
61 Santander, 'Using Open Banking to Link Financial Accounts You Hold with Other Providers' <www.santander.co.uk/personal/support/help-with-managing-my-money/open-banking> accessed 18 July 2023; see also John Broxis, 'How Many TPPs in Europe?' (*Open Banking Exchange*, 26 July 2019) <www.openbanking.exchange/europe/resources/insights/how-many-tpps-in-europe/> accessed 18 July 2023.
62 Moira O'Neall, 'An Open Door for Open Banking' (21 April 2023) *Financial Times* <www.ft.com/content/2b227007-3468-4b15-8117-68a30e0023a0> accessed 18 July 2023.
63 PSD2 Directive, art 4 ('Definitions').
64 See for instance Nationwide Building Society', 'Savings Accounts Explained' <www.nationwide.co.uk/savings/help/savings-accounts-explained/> accessed 10 July 2023.
65 Case C-191/17 *Bundeskammer für Arbeiter und Angestellte (Austria) v ING-DiBa Direktbank Austria Niederlassung der ING-DiBa AG* [2018] ECJ 2018:809 para 33: 'It follows from all of the foregoing considerations that the answer to the question referred is that Article 4(14) of the Payment Services Directive must be interpreted as meaning that a savings account which allows for sums deposited without notice and from which payment and withdrawal transactions may be made solely by means of a current account does not come within the concept of 'payment account'.
66 Ibid., para 29: 'Accordingly, while savings accounts do not, in principle, fall within the definition of the concept of 'payment account', such an exclusion is not absolute. It follows, in fact, from recital 12, first, that the mere name of an account as a 'savings account' is not sufficient in itself to exclude the categorisation of 'payment account' and, second, that the determining criterion for the purposes of that categorisation lies in the ability to perform daily payment transactions from such an account'.
67 See <www.openbanking.org.uk/faqs/> accessed 18 July 2023.
68 Financial Conduct Authority (FCA), 'FCA Handbook' (2021) PERG 15.3 <www.handbook.fca.org.uk/handbook/PERG/15/3.html> accessed 18 July 2023; see

also FCA, 'Finalised Guidance 16/6–Payment Accounts Regulations 2015. Definition of a payment account' (August 2016) <https://www.fca.org.uk/publication/finalised-guidance/fg16-6.pdf> accessed 18 July 2023.
69 Ibid.
70 Part II 'Open Banking Regulation' (Bahrain).
71 ACCC, 'Phasing' <www.cdr.gov.au/sites/default/files/2021-01/CDR%20phasing%20table%20-%20January%202021.pdf> accessed 18 July 2023.
72 See, for instance, the UK list of open banking regulated providers (n 44).
73 PSD2 Directive, art 4 ('Definitions').
74 See <www.openbanking.org.uk/faqs/> accessed 18 July 2023.
75 See 'Open Banking Apps in Action' <www.openbanking.org.uk/how-open-banking-can-help-consumers/> accessed 19 July 2023.
76 Ibid.
77 Crown Commercial Court, 'How Payment Initiation Service Providers are Changing the Way Citizens Pay Online' (24 December 2021) <www.crowncommercial.gov.uk/news/how-payment-initiation-service-providers-are-changing-the-way-citizens-pay-online> accessed 18 July 2023.
78 Elliot Green, 'Payment Initiation Services: A Game Changer for UK Businesses' (*Wonderful*, 26 January 2023) <https://blog.wonderful.co.uk/payment-initiation-services-a-game-changer-for-uk-businesses/> accessed 18 July 2023.
79 FirstPartner, 'Why Open Banking Payments Need Chargeback' (5 October 2021) <www.firstpartner.net/blog/why-open-banking-payments-need-chargebacks/> accessed 18 July 2023.
80 Green (n 78).
81 Ibid.
82 Open Banking, 'Open Banking Guidelines for Read/Write Participants' (May 2018) <www.openbanking.org.uk/wp-content/uploads/Guidelines-for-Read-Write-Participants.pdf> accessed 18 July 2023.
83 Ibid.
84 'Read' only access is, for example, contemplated in the Australian CDR.
85 Benjamin Glock, 'Unlocking the Opportunity of Open Banking' (*Visa*, 2022) <https://navigate.visa.com/na/money-movement/unlocking-the-opportunities-of-open-banking/> accessed 18 July 2023; 'Yapily, '20 Open Banking Use Cases to Help you Unlock Business Potential' (2023) <https://i.yapily.com/OB-Use-Cases> accessed 18 July 2023.
86 BCBS (n 28) 4.
87 Open Banking, 'Open Banking Customer Experience Guidelines' (30 November 2018) Version 1.1, 5 <www.openbanking.org.uk/wp-content/uploads/Customer-Experience-Guidelines-V1-1.pdf> accessed 21 July 2023.
88 Ibid.
89 Ibid.
90 Part II 'Open Banking Regulation' (MENA Region).
91 Ibid.,; see also Nameer Khan and Hakan Eroglu, 'Embedded Finance in the MENA Region' (MENA FinTech Association, November 2022) 1 <https://mena-fintech.org/wp-content/uploads/2022/11/MFTA-Embedded-Finance-Report-NOV2022-FINAL.pdf> accessed 21 July 2023.
92 The Association of Banks in Singapore (ABS), 'The personal Data Protection Act (PDPA)' (2021) 1-19 <https://abs.org.sg/docs/library/abs-code-banking-practices-pdpa4be4aa9f299c69658b7dff00006ed795.pdf> accessed 21 July 2023; see also Neha Mehta, *Open Finance Global Progress Ebook: Singapore Special Editorial Focus*' (Open Future, 16 May 2022) <https://openfuture.world/open-finance-global-progress-ebook-singapore-special-editorial-focus/> accessed 21 July 2023.

93 'Personal Data (Privacy) Ordinance' (2022) Cap. 486 last update, 1 <www.elegislation.gov.hk/hk/cap486!en-zh-Hant-HK.pdf?FROMCAPINDEX=Y> accessed 21 July 2023; Privacy Commissioner for Personal Data (PCPD), 'Code of Practice/Guidelines' <www.pcpd.org.hk/english/data_privacy_law/code_of_practices/code.html> accessed 21 July 2023.
94 Regulation (EU) 2016/679 of the European Parliament and of the Council of 27 April 2016 on the protection of natural persons with regard to the processing of personal data and on the free movement of such data, and repealing Directive 95/46/EC (General Data Protection Regulation) (GDPR) (2016) OJEU L 119/1, art 4(11) ('Definitions').
95 GDPR, art 9(1) ('Processing of special categories of personal data'): 'Processing of personal data revealing racial or ethnic origin, political opinions, religious or philosophical beliefs, or trade union membership, and the processing of genetic data, biometric data for the purpose of uniquely identifying a natural person, data concerning health or data concerning a natural person's sex life or sexual orientation shall be prohibited'.
96 PSD2, art 67(2)(a) ('Rules on access to and use of payment account information in the case of account information services'): 'The account information service provider shall: (a) provide services only where based on the payment service user's explicit consent'; Article 94(2) of the PSD2: 'Payment service providers shall only access, process and retain personal data necessary for the provision of their payment services, with the explicit consent of the payment service user'.
97 European Data Protection Board (EDPB), 'Guidelines 06/2020 on the Interplay of the Second Payment Services Directive and the GDPR' (15 December 2020) Version 2.0, 5 <https://edpb.europa.eu/our-work-tools/our-documents/guidelines/guidelines-062020-interplay-second-payment-services_en> accessed 21 July 2023.
98 Ibid., 14.
99 Ibid.
100 Ibid., 15: 'The EDPB highlights that the payment service user must be able to choose whether or not to use the service and cannot be forced to do so. Therefore, the consent under Article 94 (2) of the PSD2 also has to be a freely given consent'. See also, World Bank Group, 'The Role of Consumer Consent in Open Banking. Financial Inclusion Support Framework' (1 December 2021) Technical Note, 13 <https://elibrary.worldbank.org/doi/abs/10.1596/37073> accessed 24 July 2023.
101 See for example PSD2, art 64 ('Consent and withdrawal of consent').
102 FCA (n 10) 10.
103 See Commission, 'Communication from the Commission to the European Parliament, the Council, the European Economic and Social Committee, and the Committee of the Regions on a Digital Finance Strategy for the EU' (2020) COM (2020) 591 final, 13 <https://eur-lex.europa.eu/legal-content/EN/TXT/PDF/?uri=CELEX:52020DC0591&from=EN> accessed 24 July 2023.
104 Ibid.
105 BCBS (n 28) 10; Nam (n 38) 8; World Bank Group (n 50) 4; Dorwart, Berrick, and Rappaneau (n 9) 4; Tania Babina, Greg Buchak, and Will Gornall, 'Customer Data Access and FinTech Entry: Early Evidence from Open Banking' (FDIC, 2022) 1 <www.fdic.gov/analysis/cfr/bank-research-conference/annual-21st/papers/gornall-paper.pdf> accessed 27 July 2023.
106 Ibid.
107 See Part II 'Open Banking Regulation' (Japan), (Singapore), (South Korea).
108 Ibid regarding the implementation of Section 1033 of the Dodd–Frank Act.
109 Babina, Buchak, and Gornall (n 105) 11.

110 Part II 'Open Banking Regulation'.
111 Ibid., (MENA Region), (Indonesia).
112 Ibid., (Chile), (Mexico).
113 Ibid., (Japan), (Bahrain).
114 Ibid., (MENA Region), (Indonesia), (China), (Hong Kong).
115 Ibid., with reference to the CMA in the UK or the ACCC in Australia.
116 Ibid., with reference to the Financial Services Commission (FSC) in South Korea or the Comision Para el Mercado Financiero in Chile.
117 For example, this can be the case of the Consumer Financial Protection Bureau in the US, which is required to consult with other bodies for the implementation of Section 1033 of the Dodd–Frank Act, see Part II 'Open Banking Regulation' (United States of America).
118 BCBS (n 28) 10.

3 Open Banking Policy in the UK and EU

Key concepts behind open banking in the UK and EU

Henry Chesbrough, as adjunct professor and the faculty director of the Garwood Center for Corporate Innovation at the Haas School of Business at the University of California, Berkeley, is credited with devising the 'open innovation' concept and has been highly influential in setting out the vision of an 'open' innovative economy.[1] In 2011, he wrote that technology change would increasingly 'commodify' existing financial products and services and that businesses must develop 'open services' to meet these challenges and remain relevant.[2]

There are a number of fundamental concepts behind open banking in the UK and EU and, to a certain extent, in the US. These include:

1 The developing idea that the customer's financial data belongs to the customer and not just to the bank, insurance company etc. Previously, financial firms treated this customer information as belonging to the business. Open banking ensures that the customer has proprietary rights over this information which they can market for value. The UK's Competition and Markets Authority (CMA) issued a report saying that the CMA 'are requiring banks to allow their customers to share their own bank data securely with third parties using an open banking standard. This change … will help customers to find and access better value services and enable them to take more control of their finances. This will also enable new entrants and smaller providers to compete on a more level playing field and increase the opportunities for new business models to develop'.[3]
2 Taking this further the value of this data, coupled with new technologies, would allow new businesses to develop and segment existing customer services to produce new 'value propositions'. This would benefit customers and attract investors.
3 A view that in the right circumstances competition would solve everything. The incumbent banks and credit card companies (which were largely owned by these banks) were too comfortable in the payment services market and were too slow to innovate and took too much out of the 'value chain'.

DOI: 10.4324/9781003331339-4

4 There are a number of market failures in the use and ownership of customer financial data and the operation of payment services. There is little reason to believe that markets will provide the solution without state intervention. Consequently, there is a belief, certainly in the UK and EU that regulation can, and should, be used to change and develop new business models.

5 Regulation may also be necessary due to 'clash of cultures' and expectations. Financial services, and especially banking, is inherently a fragile industry and the relationship between the customer and the firm is one of trust. The latter can evaporate very quickly if there are doubts about the business' financial stability (cf. the 'run' on Northern Rock) or a major failure of a bank's IT system. The latter was highlighted by the technology problems at TSB in 2018 and the 'run on reputation' as the bank's issues swept through social media in a matter of hours.[4] While some aspects of technology can be a source of experimentation, greater risks are run in financial services as a result of the importance of maintaining the fragile levels of public trust. This has been summarised as a clash of cultures between traditional regulation and fintech innovators who may not have experienced the highly controlled world of financial services and its real but sometimes opaque risks. From my own personal experience, I have often seen the look of incomprehension of fintech entrepreneurs when they 'bump into' data protection and financial services regulation.

6 Regulation is often seen as controlling and limiting. However, the objectives of regulation can be seen as necessary to promote key public policy objectives. For example, regulation is often used to correct market imperfections or failures.[5] However, open banking and the corresponding EU enactments are different. It is much more 'dirigist'—adopting a form of 'high tech colbertism'.[6] The regulations encourage and guide innovation and competition.

Open banking—A UK 'success'

The UK government is keen to champion open banking as a great British success. There has been no officially commissioned independent report on the success of open banking in the UK. However, the UK government has declared that its work on promoting open banking has been a success. 'Open banking has been a major success in improving competition in retail banking and securing positive outcomes for consumers and businesses … this initiative has, in the words of John Glen, Economic Secretary to the Treasury, 'taken the world by storm' with around 30 other jurisdictions now following the UK's lead'.[7] However, it is probably fairer to say that the open banking project is still very much a work in progress and it is too early to trumpet its success.

Open banking in the UK and the Ron Kalifa report

The report by Ron Kalifa in early 2022 has set out the UK's path on open banking. The report was commissioned by HM Treasury in 2021 and supported by a number of consultancy and legal firms and by the City of London

Corporation. The review had a broad remit and was aimed at considering how the UK could continue to foster innovation and maintain and promote new technologies across financial services. This was based on ensuring that UK fintech had adequate resources to maintain and advance the 'UK fintech's global reputation for the innovation and transformation of financial services' and create the conditions for the continuing 'widespread adoption of fintech solutions to benefit businesses and individuals'.[8]

In summary, the report is very 'supply' focused. It considers the main barriers and facilitators to fintech firm success. These include government policy and regulation, and access to skilled individuals and sources of investment. It also considers national competitiveness and fintech research and development. Strangely, the voices of the current and potential users of fintech are missing. There is too much of a sense that if you built it they will come. There is also a danger that the report may be seen as promoting the new fintech incumbents with mention of the 'domestic champions, including Revolut and Monzo', with both firms mentioned several times with quotes from their respective CEOs and a public affairs manager.[9]

Issues relating to policy and regulation are addressed later in the report. The sections in the report relating to skills and training cite Singapore as a role model in this area and the recommendations appear entirely sensible. The report identifies the issue of lack of domestic investment in fintech. It suggests a number of varied recommendations including the establishment of a 'market-led, specialist £1bn Fintech Growth Fund'. The report notes work on reducing capital requirements for insurance companies and allowing higher fees charged to defined contribution pension schemes.[10] How these relate to promoting fintech is not clear. The report also recommends tax subsidies for fintech research and development.[11]

The report also recommends a number of changes largely relating to promoting initial public offerings (IPOs) on the London Stock Exchange which has been in long-term decline. Again, these proposals, covering areas such as relaxing minimum free-floats and supporting dual-class shares, go well beyond fintech and open banking and the scope of this book.

The report barely mentioned several of the key obstacles to fintech succeeding. These include user acceptance of many aspects of fintech. The reader would expect to see how, and why, users perceive fintech services as valuable. Online fraud has developed in parallel with fintech. It is likely that fraudster hold their own conferences and discuss reports on the best ways of using and benefiting from fintech fraud and exploitation plans developed and implemented. The risks of fraud are a major issue for users and this area is considered throughout this book. There is also a possibility that users, or potential users, may not trust fintech or not to the extent necessary for it to flourish. Again, this is not addressed or even considered in the report.

It is critical that users view fintech as worthy of trust. This perception is not helped by the report providing Greensill, described as a 'supply-chain provider' as a good example.[12] Greensill went into administration surrounded by scandal, in March 2021.[13] '[T]here has been skepticism about whether

Greensill was a fintech firm. Lord Myners argued that "We have very few fintech companies. Even though the former Prime Minister has described it as a fintech, Greensill was simply not a fintech. It had 700 employees; it was a paper-based company. It was not in the world of technology at all". Lord Macpherson was also clear: "this simply was not fintechery"'.[14]

The Treasury Select Committee report continues: 'Q604 "I am an enthusiast for fintech. Might our enthusiasm sometimes blind us to conventional financial risks? That seems to have been what brought down Greensill. They were not adequately insured, as they explained to us, and there were possibly some other matters. Could this enthusiasm blind us to routine risks?"'

Rishi Sunak: 'That is the challenge that we have as policymakers. We need regulatory frameworks that are pro-innovation yet can still provide consumer protection or systemic protection to the system. That is always the challenge'.[15]

The Kalifa report contains no significant mention of money laundering and its risks in the UK in relation to fintech or more generally. Financial crime and its risks get one passing mention. Again, this area needs to be appreciated as a significant barrier to the successful development of fintech. These risks tarnish the reputation of fintech and may undermine trust in this sector.

The Treasury Select Committee is currently examining HM Treasury's role in combating fraud.[16] This includes consideration of aspects of fintech and fraud.

The UK government continues to try to ensure that the UK is a leader in open banking. It initiated a review of the payment services 'landscape' in 2019 with a 'Call for evidence' in 2020 to which the government responded in 2021.[17] The main thrust of the government's response is to retain PSD II enacted into UK regulations in 2017 and to continue to work on ensuring that the right regulatory structures in the UK such as the Payment Services Regulator and Pay UK are responsible for running the payment platforms.

Open banking governance in the UK

Open banking in the UK is the result of both EU Directives and the actions of the UK's own CMA. It is a long and complex saga. In summary, the competition investigation by what is now the CMA into UK retail banking resulted in the Retail Banking Market Investigation Order 2017, which required the major UK retail banks to take steps to implement Open Banking.[18] This work was overseen by a 'Trustee' empowered to carry out the 'Implementation Trustee Functions' set out in Schedule 1 of the Order.[19] The Trustee would chair and lead a new 'Implementation Entity'.[20]

The latter function is undertaken by the Open Banking Implementation Entity (OBIE).[21] Its role includes maintaining and developing the existing open banking standards; 'playing a central role' in delivering new proposals ... to further support innovation and competition'.[22] The OBIE is also required to 'fairly and effectively take account of the interests of relevant industry and end-user stakeholders, including consumers and businesses'.[23]

The OBIE's success may have been limited. It has been very active but successful outputs are less evident. This perception is not helped by the lack of any independent report on its activities. Moreover, the view that the OBIE has been less than fully effective is evidenced by the publication of a heavily redacted independent report on its operations and governance which found that the OBIE 'had a toxic workplace culture where bullying was commonplace'.[24]

'Wide-ranging concerns about the culture at [OBIE]. The number of interviewees who described the working environment ... as "toxic" is overwhelming. We were also made aware of a number of incidents of alleged bullying and harassment ...'.[25] There was also evidence that the heavily male-dominated culture was perceived as operating as a 'boys club'. Further, the 'sexist comments and comments that could be perceived as harassment towards women were tolerated' within the organisation and the bullying 'may have been racially motivated'.[26]

There were also allegations that the OBIE was an 'organisation devoid of basic governance', with 'no-one at the helm' and with a 'total lack of accountability'.[27] The OBIE was not properly managed and this included serious issues relating to the management of conflicts of interest.[28]

As a consequence the chair of the OBIE resigned.[29] The OBIE also appointed Henk Van Hulle, from the Post Office, as its first CEO together with new non-executive directors and a new chair.[30]

Under the current structure the OBIE operates under CMA oversight.

The role of the UK treasury

The UK Treasury views the UK's development of Open Banking as being very successful.[31] 'It has been a UK success story, with significant take-up and ever-accelerating growth' and it considers that the UK is a role model in this area.[32] Under the current structure, the OBIE operates under CMA oversight. However, the plan is to develop a successor organisation to the OBIE. The new 'entity will take on responsibility for further developing Open Banking. The implementation phase of the CMA Order will end and the banks which are subject to the CMA Order will have remaining ongoing responsibilities. This interim period will end when the long-term regulatory framework is in place'.[33] Once the later framework is up and running it is intended that the replacement for the OBIE will continue to develop open banking.

The joint statement advocates establishing a new 'joint regulatory oversight committee'. This would be led jointly by the FCA and PSR with HM Treasury and CMA membership. The FCA is the regulator and supervisor of firms working in the open banking industry while the PSR is the 'economic regulator for payment systems'. The Treasury sees a need for a 'permanent future regulatory framework for Open Banking' and this would require new legislation.

The plan is to set up a new Joint Regulatory Oversight Committee which would oversee the work of the OBIE successor organisation and 'further support innovation and competition'.

The proposed Oversight Committee would be responsible for:

- 'Making recommendations for the design of the future entity [and the transition to the new entity] and considering any necessary interim governance and funding arrangements with industry and other stakeholders'.
- Considering the vision and strategic roadmap for further developing open banking beyond the scope of the CMA Order, working with industry and other stakeholders. This will include unlocking the potential of open banking payments, enabling end users to share data, managing access, and developing further data-sharing propositions, including greater consumer protection.
- Providing appropriate input on the permanent future framework for open banking.
- Overseeing and advising the future entity once established on an interim basis until the formal regulatory framework is in place.
- Ultimately guiding the transition from the interim arrangements to the permanent future framework'.[34]

The intention is that the 'new entity to replace the OBIE would be required to:

- Maintaining and developing existing standards.
- Play a central role in the implementation of new proposals which might in turn require new legislation to implement.

The report sees the OBIE successor 'fairly and effectively' to 'take account of the interests of relevant industry and end-user stakeholders, including consumers and businesses'.

Finally, the report sees open banking developing in 'open finance'. While not defined in this document it is likely a reference to extending individual user rights over other aspects of their financial lives including insurance, pensions, investments etc. The FCA started to look at aspects of this area in 2019 and 2021 issued a feedback statement on its initial consultation.[35]

There is lots of merit in the current proposals. They are highly structural in nature and bureaucratic in approach. It sets a 'top down' agenda and while there are passing references to consumers and businesses, their 'voice' is in many ways limited. There is a certain paternalism in all this with very little sense that what may be decided should be demand lead. The 'vision', if there is any, appears to be focused on a mixture of technology ('build it and they will come') and economics. The latter is important since conceptually the arrangements conceive that competition will provide the answer provided it operates in the right regulatory framework. This appears to be at odds with the research findings of, for example, Marina Mazzucato where the state needs to be much more active in generating true innovation.[36]

There needs to be a deeper analysis of why open banking has not been more successful. There are a range of possible reasons, but these may be resolved into two main factors:

- A lack of obvious sufficient need in the market.
- Consumer lack of trust.

These two aspects are considered next.

Possible lack of enough demand

It is possible that the technology of open banking in the UK is running ahead of consumer demand. The success of Klarna and similar firms indicates a need for access to consumer products coupled with easy and free credit. However, more generally consumers do not appear to be demanding new payment systems due to the well-developed consumer payments market in the UK. The latter includes a mixture of debit and credit cards as well as payment systems tied to mobile phones and 'wearables'.[37]

However, the multiplicity of payment and access apps may have led to market fragmentation and confusion. For example, the plethora of cashless parking apps has caused many to avoid on-street parking. One article on this subject found that Financial Times readers had many concerns with mobile parking payment apps. The Financial Times journalist reviewed some two hundred responses to their article. The 'biggest gripe was the sheer number of parking apps one needs to download. The fragmented marketplace means many readers need six apps to cover their regular parking locations. One reader had nine'.[38]

I lecture on payment services regulation. Every year for the last few years I have lectured Masters students on open banking. I have conducted a regular, informal survey of these students. The results are necessarily anecdotal but the demographics are interesting. They are all very bright and almost all under thirty. There is a mix of genders and ethnicities and backgrounds with students from across the globe following international careers. In many ways, they form the target market for open banking. However, prior to attending the course none had heard of it. As part of the course, we examined the websites and customer propositions of a number of high-profile open banking firms. However, not one student over the years has expressed any interest in any of these offerings and they failed to see anything which might benefit themselves. However, a few did have Revolut accounts which they used for foreign currency transactions since these were generally fee-free.

There is a demand from the merchants since open banking can reduce their costs and allow them to be less dependent on the main credit card firms and banks. It is possible that current merchant fees of around 2% could be halved if the open banking operators take payments directly from customer bank accounts.[39] This is particularly valuable to retailers operating on thin margins. Many of these advantages have been highlighted by firms such as McKinsey and other consultancy firms.[40]

The existence of s75 of the Consumer Credit Act 1974 is a peculiarity in the UK which predisposes consumers to use credit cards rather than other means of payment. Under this section, within certain limits, a customer who uses a credit card to purchase goods or services, gains a very valuable piece of consumer protection which does not apply to consumers using other payment methods. The legislation automatically makes the credit card company jointly and severally liable for any breach of contract or misrepresentation by the supplier of the goods or services. Consequently, if, for example, the goods are defective or not supplied, the customer can gain redress directly from the credit card company. There is no need to even complain to the supplier.[41]

McKinsey has highlighted three groups of customers who may find open banking a compelling proposition:

- 'While consumers showed innate conservatism toward data sharing, their willingness to share data doubled when they found a particular feature or service appealing or when they understood the value it might bring to their lives—as compared to a general willingness to share data'.
- Financially stressed consumers' with 'limited resources'.
- 'Affluent senior' who are 'tech savvy'. Apparently, some 15% are 'willing to share data for concepts they like'.[42]

The same research has identified a number of key aspects for open banking customer market development. These are:

- Customers who have 'multiple types of financial accounts with multiple institutions'. Open banking allows them the ability to view all of these in one place.
- Small and medium-sized enterprises (SMEs) 'are equally enthusiastic about solutions that integrate payments and other financial services into their existing systems and processes, for instance bringing together bank accounts, accounting, tax, and reconciliation activities into one place'.
- The ability of customers to do their shopping through one system without the need for a debit or credit card. Klarna and Spotify are examples based on this proposition.
- Apparently, '[c]onsumers are already conditioned to shop around for financial-services products. Some 50 percent consistently use comparison websites, a share that goes up to 70 percent in certain segments, such as tech-savvy professionals. Our research shows that customers crave even more information about whether they are making the best use of their money, and they want tools to be able to act on that information'.[43]

There is no doubt that aspects of this are correct. The questions are to what extent are these true and whether a viable business can be founded on the business generated?

For example, the vast majority of people in the UK have no investments and very limited savings.[44] There is further evidence that a significant proportion of the population would have trouble finding £300 in an emergency.[45] This raises the question of whether there is sufficient demand to sustain more than a couple of stand-alone open banking businesses. This is considered both in the next section and in the next chapter looking at business models.

Open banking and consumer behaviour

Open banking is based on a combination of consumer 'ownership' of their financial data and the freedom to exchange this information for value in the marketplace. There is a similar concept behind the consumer's right to select from a wide range of the methods and processes to pay for goods and services. It is underpinned by a belief in individual empowerment. It rests on the fundamental belief that consumer financial choices will operate through competition to provide the best outcomes for themselves. The role of government and regulators should be to liberate the market so that consumers can freely access and exchange their own financial data for value and make electronic payments as they wish. This needs to be permitted with certain safeguards sufficient to provide consumers with sufficient trust in these freedoms.

However, there is an issue as to the extent of any consumer desire, or even interest, in this level of freedom. All the evidence in the UK indicates that while open banking will grow, the level of consumer engagement will remain limited. Research on behavioural economics demonstrates a range of reasons for this. These may include: A lack of awareness and insufficient clarity about what open banking is; too much complexity and choice; a lack of interest in finance and a general inertia and a combination of a lack of trust in financial markets and providers and their own judgement to make the right choices and too much trust in their own bank and credit card providers.[46]

The Oxera and Nuffield Centre research undertook extensive empirical research on why consumers failed to shop around for the best annuities. The benefits of shopping around online could yield significant financial benefits for consumers. The process of obtaining standardised quotations from a number of providers was straightforward but only some 40% moved providers in 2012.[47] The FCA calculated that as a result of failing to shop around and by not moving provider consumers gave up between £115m and £230m of additional pension benefits.[48] In other words, consumers annually simply throw away a substantial sum of money. This research is backed up by a number of similar surveys in financial services. For example, work reported by Bar-Gill in the US mortgage markets consumer myopia, passivity and lack of basic numeracy undermine concepts of free choice and active competition.[49]

The FCA appears to have given up on trying to make the insurance market more competitive by encouraging consumers to exercise market power and shop around in the home and motor insurance markets. The FCA calculated that in these markets, by failing to shop around and not moving insurer consumers gave up in total between some £300m and £345m in cost savings.[50] As a consequence of these findings, the FCA has gone down a highly paternalistic effectively using price controls to protect consumers.[51]

There is a similar issue with consumers not switching current account providers. As part of an initiative to try to increase competition in the market for personal bank current accounts by encouraging consumers to switch current account providers a not-for-profit organisation (Current Account Switch Service—CASS) was set up in 2013. This made changing current account providers very easy and risk-free. The project to encourage account switching has been supported by a large marketing campaign across all demographics using TV, radio and social media advertising. Many banks provide financial incentives to customers to switch their current accounts.[52] Just over 782,000 accounts were switched in 2021.[53] This is the gross figure since every switch represents a gain for one bank and a loss for another. The level of accounting switching is in broad decline, but it has consistently run at about 2% of current accounts.[54] The challenger banks Starling and Monzo were the main beneficiaries of net switching. In the twelve months to the end of September 2021, they gained 63,000 and 27,000 accounts, respectively. In addition, a number of incumbent banks and a building society also made a net gain of account switchers. Lloyds gained 37,000 new accounts, Nationwide building society gained 48,000 new accounts and Virgin Money (largely based on Clydesdale Bank, Yorkshire Bank and the branch network of what was Northern Rock Bank) acquired 37,000 switchers.[55]

Consumer lack of trust

A survey of some 2,600 customers undertaken for the Dutch central bank ('De Nederlandsche Bank') found that only around a quarter had shared their payment information under the auspices of PSD 2 in the past twelve months. Almost all of this group had only agreed to do this with the bank that held their main bank account. The key issue was that 'techs have not yet succeeded in gaining the confidence of consumers'.[56] Customers were also asked about their future propensity to allow payment information to be shared over the next twelve months. Again this was negligible.[57] Admittedly, these are early days for open banking and new customer propositions still need to be developed. Nevertheless, there is a major hurdle that needs to be overcome since customers view their payment information as one of the most sensitive areas of personal data just behind medical records. It was well ahead of, in terms of sensitivity, personal contacts and their internet search behaviours.

OBIE surveys

The OBIE carries out regular surveys. For example, the OBIE 'approached selected TPPs [third party payment providers] to nominate individual active customers to participate in a survey'.[58] These were subject to additional screening questions so that only 'those who demonstrated an accurate comprehension were permitted to participate in the full survey'.[59]

The survey questionnaire was designed to take no more than ten minutes on average to complete. The survey data is somewhat difficult to follow but both women and those aged over 44 were under-represented in the response data compared to national norms. There is no data provided on other demographics such as ethnicity, socio-economic factors etc.

Based on this survey the OBIE report considered that '[s]ignificant proportions of customers claim that these platforms are helping them keep to budgets, reduce unnecessary expenditure, shop around and minimise fees and charges. On the savings side, we see similarly positive findings, with customers reporting that these services have helped them save more and build a financial cushion. 22% of customers of these savings apps say this was their first adult savings account, suggesting a potential broadening of savings participation'.[60]

Other surveys

There are a number of surveys regarding UK consumer awareness and use of open banking claiming that consumer awareness of open banking remains very low. However, it is difficult to evaluate these due to a lack of methodology data.

One of the most insightful comments has said that 'the more pressing issue is that we're not seeing enough of the innovative products that make the most of open banking and which customers really stand to benefit from.

Unsurprisingly, consumer awareness of open banking in the UK is low; 63% of people say they have not made use of open banking and many are unaware even of its existence as a concept.

This is likely because discussions around open banking are dominated by business-to-business topics, such as integrations and APIs, rather than the benefits which open banking can bring to the consumer. In order to raise awareness levels and increase usage, the industry must put the customer and their needs at the heart of the open banking conversation moving forward'.[61]

The last large-scale consumer review of open banking was undertaken by Yougov in 2018. Clearly, this was not that long after open banking started in the UK. It is possible that a current high-quality survey would find that views were not substantially different.

'Open banking has still to enter the public consciousness, with nearly three-quarters of Brits unaware of the initiative, according to a YouGov survey'. Of 2074 adults surveyed only 28% were aware of open banking.

44 Open Banking Ecosystem and Policy

Thirty-nine per cent of those aged over 55 are aware of open banking, compared to 14% of those aged from 18 to 24. 'Those in the more affluent ABC1 group are more likely than those in the CD2E group to have heard of the term (35% vs. 18%)'.[62]

'YouGov provided those who answered the survey with a clear description of open banking. Despite this, 45% do not understand the ways they could use open banking, against 18% who do.

Nervousness about sharing data is a barrier. Over three quarters (77%) would be concerned about sharing their financial data with companies other than their main bank, whilst just 6% would not be concerned (16% weren't sure). Just 12% state that they would be prepared to share their financial data in order to access new and innovative products or services'.[63]

'Another barrier to take up is the general levels of satisfaction people have with their bank. Approaching two thirds (63%) say that they are satisfied with the service they get from their current bank and are therefore not interested in using banking services from other companies. Those aged 55 and over are most likely to say this (72%).[64]

Similarly, the Financial Times has commented that 'even those behind the new regime acknowledge the predicted deluge has so far been more of a trickle ... Some people in the sector say fintechs have overhyped the speed at which they can achieve this overhaul [of payment services technology] to drum up interest from investors ... '.[65]

Conclusion on this section

Open banking is important, but it needs to present a much more compelling benefit to consumers before the adoption becomes significantly wider and deeper.

The aggregation and presentation of data does not appear to provide either sufficient competitive advantage or distinct incentives for many consumers to agree to share their financial data. It is also possible that consumers do not trust how their data will be used since the risk of infringement of personal privacy is a very real issue in, for example, Europe which has had a relatively recent history of personal information being misused for political purposes.

In the UK wealth distribution may be described as deep but narrow. As mentioned earlier the proportion of households in the UK with any significant savings is very low and the wealth gaps between regions and between generations are vast. This is largely based on accumulated pensions and housing. This has benefited London and the South East.[66] Over 80% of the wealth is concentrated in the top three deciles.[67]

Most of the wealthiest individuals will have their own financial advisers who will doubtless do their best to shield their clients from divulging more information than is absolutely required by third parties.

Consequently, the pool of the population who may be attractive to product and service propensity modelling is likely to be small. Of this broad cohort, a number are likely to be unwilling to share their financial information.

'Six in ten consumers admit that they view their current account in a passive way, as a necessity but not something they give a lot of thought to. While this remains the case, it will be very difficult to strengthen competition in the current account market'.[68] Moreover, only a quarter of consumers reported that they had current accounts with more than one provider.[69] Consumers gave a variety of reasons for having more than one current account. These included: 'to manage finances'; to 'generate returns or get good value'; 'to access services from other banks'; 'left one account open' and to 'pay off an existing debt'.[70] It is likely that many consumers are cherry-picking offers and chasing incentives.[71] The revenue by active personal current account has fallen over this period.

'The Office of Fair Trading (OFT) suggested in 2008 that the average current account brought in revenue of £152 for a bank—equivalent to charging consumers £12.67 a month'.[72] However, the revenue by active personal current account has fallen over this period, from £143.7 per account in 2011 to £125.2 per account in 2013 (−13%)' or a fall of some 18% in 2008 and 2013.[73]

All this suggests that there is a relatively small group of financially 'engaged' individuals who are likely to adopt open banking. Many of these may be attracted by technology and convenience. These and others may be attracted by financial incentives—if these are offered. It is also likely that there is another, probably, separate group of wealthy individuals who work through a network of trusted advisors who are more focused on personal financial services. They are likely to use the various premium banking services of the incumbent banks including those with wealth management arms.

The issue for open banking services (and challenger banks) is that operating in the retail market in the UK may be limited to a shallow unprofitable pool. The cost of acquiring new customers and retaining them may be too high in relation to their value. Offering a highly commoditised IT service is probably insufficient. Financial incentives available to customers may work but that would change the value proposition between merchants and payment services operators and the current regulations would need to change. Other services to encourage the use of new payment service providers could be developed. This is currently the case of 'buy now pay later' but all credit-based schemes carry a range of additional risks which may be both financial and reputational.

Developing the EU's approach to open banking

As in the UK open banking was developed as a 'top-down' regulatory initiative. It originated in 2007 with the publication of the first Payment Services Directive.[74] It is a maximum harmonisation Directive introduced with a number of aims:

- Help to develop the Single Euro Payments Area (SEPA).
- Regulate payment institutions and increase levels of competition by encouraging non-banks to enter the market.

- Set common standards for terms and conditions.
- Provide increased consumer protection and transparency.
- Establish maximum processing times for payments.

Shortly after the Directive was implemented by member states the EU commissioned a report on the Directive's effectiveness. The subsequent report highlighted a number of deficiencies and following a consultation the EU issued PSD II in 2015 and required national implementation by January 2018.[75]

The aims of the new Directive were to:

- Assist in the integration of the EU's payment market.
- Promote competition by encouraging new participants in the market including fintech and the development of mobile and internet payment services across the EU.
- Encourage lower prices for payments.
- Increase customer confidence in making more efficient electronic payments by introducing better customer protection against fraud and other abuses and errors. This would require enhanced security arrangements.[76]

In addition to requiring increased security to improve consumer protection and enhance trust the Directive introduced two new innovative arrangements: 'account information service providers' (AISPs) and 'payment initiation service providers' (PISPs). The former collects, aggregates and analyses information from customer payment transactions. The usual business model involves the AISP anonymising and aggregating the information and then selling it. The PISP is a secure payment messaging which, using an Application Programming Interface (API), allows merchants to be paid directly from the customers' bank accounts. This obviates the need for all card-based intermediaries.

Everything hinges on the customer giving explicit consent. There is no need for a contract between the customer and either the PISP or AISP. Nor is a contract necessary between the PISP and the merchant supplying goods or services to the customer.[77] Customer agreements can be either ad hoc, good for a single transaction or set up under a continuing contract which can be terminated without charge with, at most, a month's notice.[78]

The powerful and profitable US-based credit card companies may have been the primary target for these aspects of the Directive.[79] The European Central Bank (ECB) wanted 'an alternative payment route subject to European governance' and the need to promote 'the creation of a European card scheme, which would offer its services at the pan-European level in competition with international card schemes'.[80] As a result, the EU wanted an 'innovative, safe and easy-to-use digital payments services and to provide consumers and retailers with effective, convenient and secure payments methods in the Union'.[81] However, it is worth pointing out that the Directive prohibits merchants from charging customers an additional fee for the use of credit and debit cards.[82]

EU work on open banking continues with a speech by Benoît Cœuré, a Member of the Executive Board of the ECB in 2019 setting out a strategy for payment services across the EU member states for retail the market.[83] This is in the context of the introduction of the new TARGET Instant Payment Settlement (TIPS) which allows real time fund transfers across the EU by payment service providers direct to customers, at anytime, with settlement via accounts at the ECB.

As mentioned earlier there is a strong element of European protectionism—possible even 'natavism' in the EU's open banking initiatives. In the same speech, Cœuré saw the European retail payments strategy as having 'a pan-European vision' with a 'common brand and logo ... adopted to foster European identity [and a] European governance structure [to] enable European payment stakeholders to have a direct influence on the strategic direction and business models' with solutions 'meets the needs of European customers'.[84]

The EU Commission set out its plans in September 2020.[85] A year later, the EU Commission consulted the European Banking Authority (EBA) in a 'Call for advice'.[86] As required by Art 108 of PSD II, the EU Commission is undertaking a review of the Directive.[87] The review has a particular focus on two key aspects: New firms offering 'new services that did not exist or were just emerging' when PSD2 was adopted; and new types of payment fraud that undermine consumer trust.[88]

The EU Commission has a range of developing concerns in the payment services sphere. These include:

- 'New risks stemming from unregulated services, especially technical services ancillary to the provision of regulated payment or e-money services, and assess whether and how these risks can best be mitigated, including by subjecting the providers of ancillary services or outsourced entities to direct supervision'.[89]
- The lack of a level playing field with card companies who have been using various 'charge-back', loyalty schemes and cash-back arrangements to incentivise customers to use them rather than PISPs.[90]
- The risk of PSD II arrangements for criminal purposes. This aspect requires adequate national supervision. It was an issue highlighted by Bloomberg in January 2022.[91]
- The spread of new types of fraud as mentioned earlier and the scope to develop 'digital identities' to still facilitate fast and safe electronic payments.[92]

Conclusion

The UK is 'an unquestionable leader in terms of PayTech development. By the end of 2019, the financial supervision of this country issued as many as 627 PayTech licences, which constituted 43% of all 1475 analysed licences' in the EU.[93] However, for reasons that are not fully clear Cyprus, Malta and

Lithuania have 'already been successful in seizing the opportunity created by the PSD2 regulation. They made the strategic decision to build innovation hubs for PayTech start-ups with promising early results'.[94]

'It remains to be seen whether the review of the EU's payment services legislation will result in a transition from open banking to open finance'.[95]

While the UK and EU continue to lead the way in open banking it remains unclear whether there is a sufficient market to sustain more than a couple of profitable firms. Aspects of this issue are considered in the next chapter looking at various UK and EU open banking business models.

Notes

1. Henry Chesbrough, 'Open Services Innovation: Rethinking Your Business to Grow and Compete in a New Era', (Jossey-Bass, San Francisco, California: 2011) 1.1.
2. Ibid., (Chesbrough) 1.1.
3. Competition and Markets Authority, 'Making Banks Work Harder for Customers', (August 2016), 1–2, <https://www.gov.uk/government/publications/retail-banking-market-investigation-overview>, accessed 24 July 2022.
4. Slaughter and May, 'Independent Review Following TSB's Migration onto a New IT Platform in April 2018', (October 2019), 206–208, <https://www.tsb.co.uk/news-releases/slaughter-and-may/>, accessed 24 July 2022.
5. Joseph Stiglitz, 'Government Failure vs. Market Failure: Principles of Regulation' in Edward Balleisen and David Moss (eds), *Government and Markets: Toward a New Theory of Regulation*, (Cambridge University Press, Cambridge, 2010), 18 and following.
6. Elie Cohen, 'Industrial Policies in France: The Old and the New', (2007) 7 Journal of Industry, Competition and Trade 213–227, 226.
7. CMA, 'The Future Oversight of the CMA's Open Banking Remedies Response to Consultation', (24 March 2022), 2, <https://assets.publishing.service.gov.uk/government/uploads/system/uploads/attachment_data/file/1063319/Consultation_response.pdf>, accessed 2 May 2022.
8. Kalifa Review of UK Fintech, (2022), 105, <https://assets.publishing.service.gov.uk/government/uploads/system/uploads/attachment_data/file/978396/KalifaReviewofUKFintech01.pdf>, accessed 25 April 2022.
9. Ibid., 52.
10. Ibid., 60.
11. Ibid., 55.
12. Ibid., 77.
13. Treasury Select Committee (TSC), 'Lessons from Greensill Capital: Sixth Report of Session 2021–22 Report', (14 July 2021), 46, <https://committees.parliament.uk/publications/6800/documents/72205/default/>, accessed 26 April 2022.
14. Ibid., TSC Report July 2022, 50.
15. Treasury Committee Oral Evidence: Lessons from Greensill Capital, HC 151 Thursday 27 May 2021, <https://committees.parliament.uk/oralevidence/2293/pdf/>, accessed 26 April 2022.
16. Treasury Select Committee, 'Formal Meeting (Oral Evidence Session): HM Treasury's Role in Combating Fraud, <https://committees.parliament.uk/event/13079/formal-meeting-oral-evidence-session/>, accessed 26 April 2022.
17. HM Treasury, 'Payments Landscape Review: Response to the Call for Evidence', (October 2021), <https://assets.publishing.service.gov.uk/government/uploads/system/uploads/attachment_data/file/1024174/HMT_Payments_Landscape_Review_-_The_Government_s_Response__October_2021_.pdf>, accessed 25 July 2022.

Open Banking Policy in the UK and EU 49

18 CMA, Retail, 'Retail Banking Market Investigation—Provisional Decisions on Remedies', (May 2016), <https://www.openbanking.org.uk/wp-content/uploads/2021/04/retail_banking_market_pdr.pdf>, accessed 27 April 2022.
19 CMA, 'The Retail Banking Market Investigation Order 2017, 64 and following', <https://assets.publishing.service.gov.uk/government/uploads/system/uploads/attachment_data/file/600842/retail-banking-market-investigation-order-2017.pdf>, accessed 27 April 2022.
20 Ibid., (CMA The Retail Banking Market Investigation Order 2017), 13.
21 OBIE website, <https://www.openbanking.org.uk/about-us/>, accessed 2 May 2022.
22 UK HM Treasury 'Joint Statement by HM Treasury, the CMA, the FCA and the PSR on the Future of Open Banking', 25 March 2022, <https://www.gov.uk/government/publications/joint-statement-by-hm-treasury-the-cma-the-fca-and-the-psr-on-the-future-of-open-banking/joint-statement-by-hm-treasury-the-cma-the-fca-and-the-psr-on-the-future-of-open-banking>, accessed 16 July 2022.
23 Ibid., (HMT, 25 March 2022).
24 Investigation of Open Banking Limited, Independent report by Alison White, 28, <https://assets.publishing.service.gov.uk/government/uploads/system/uploads/attachment_data/file/1022451/Independent_report.pdf>, accessed 2 May 2022.
25 Ibid., (Alison White Report), 17.
26 Ibid., (Alison White Report), 1819.
27 Ibid., (Alison White Report), 13.
28 Ibid., (Alison White Report), 10.
29 The Guardian, 'Chair of UK Open Banking Body Resigns over Bullying Report', (1 October 2021).
30 Open Banking Expo, 'OBIE Appoints Henk Van Hulle as Its New CEO to Strengthen Governance', 3 February 2022, <https://www.openbankingexpo.com/news/obie-appoints-henk-van-hulle-as-its-new-ceo-to-strengthen-governance/>, accessed 2 May 2022.
31 Supra n 22 ('Joint statement by HM Treasury, the CMA, the FCA and the PSR on the Future of Open Banking', 25 March 2022).
32 Ibid., ('Joint Statement by HM Treasury, the CMA, the FCA and the PSR on the Future of Open Banking', 25 March 2022).
33 Ibid., ('Joint Statement by HM Treasury', the CMA, the FCA and the PSR on the Future of Open Banking', 25 March 2022).
34 Ibid., ('Joint Statement by HM Treasury', the CMA, the FCA and the PSR on the Future of Open Banking', 25 March 2022).
35 FCA, FS21/7: Open Finance—Feedback Statement', (March 2021), <https://www.fca.org.uk/publications/feedback-statements/fs21-7-open-finance-feedback-statement>, accessed 15 July 2022.
36 Marina Mazzucato, *The Entrepreneurial State*, (Public Affairs, 2015), 207 and following.
37 UK Finance website, The Rise of Mobile Payments in 2020', based on research on the UK payments market in 2021, <https://www.ukfinance.org.uk/news-and-insights/blogs/rise-mobile-payments-2020>, accessed 16 July 2022.
38 FT, Claer Barrett, 'Driven Round the Bend by Cashless Parking' (10 June 2022), <https://www.ft.com/content/0fd91ff5-a7b0-46ad-965c-a88d343cb3e5>, accessed 16 July 2022.
39 FT, 'Trustly: Payment Fintech Bypasses the Card Issuers' (16 March 2021), <https://www.ft.com/content/dd8e60bc-e466-4f44-9ca1-2384afdfcc71>, accessed 16 March 2022.
40 McKinsey website, 'Financial Services Unchained: The Ongoing Rise of Open Financial Data' (11 July 2021), <https://www.mckinsey.com/industries/financial-services/our-insights/financial-services-unchained-the-ongoing-rise-of-open-financial-data>, accessed 16 July 2022.

50 Open Banking Ecosystem and Policy

41 Alan Brener, 'EU Payment Services Regulation and International Developments' in Iris H-Y Chiu and Gudula Deipenbrock (eds), *Routledge Handbook of Financial Technology and Law*, (Routledge, Abingdon, 2021), 167.
42 McKinsey website, 'Financial Services Unchained: The Ongoing Rise of Open Financial Data', (11 July 2021), <https://www.mckinsey.com/industries/financial-services/our-insights/financial-services-unchained-the-ongoing-rise-of-open-financial-data>, accessed 17 July 2022.
43 Ibid., (McKinsey).
44 FCA, 'The financial lives of consumers across the UK, 2017', 68–72, <https://www.fca.org.uk/publication/research/financial-lives-consumers-across-uk.pdf>, accessed 17 July 2022.
45 Nuffield Politics Research Centre, 'Red Wall: Red Herring? Economic Insecurity and Voting Intention in Britain', (May 2022), 35–6, <https://politicscentre.nuffield.ox.ac.uk/media/5142/nprc-econ-insecurity-report_bridges_final.pdf>, accessed 17 July 2022.
46 Oxera and the Nuffield Centre for Experimental Social Sciences, 'Increasing Consumer Engagement in the Annuities Market: Can Prompts Raise Shopping Around?' (June 2016). Research prepared for the Financial Conduct Authority, 17, <https://www.oxera.com/wp-content/uploads/2018/07/consumer-engagement-in-annuities-market-1.pdf-1.pdf>, accessed 19 July 2022.
47 Financial Conduct Authority, 'Thematic Review of Annuities', (2014) TR 14/2, 29, <https://www.fca.org.uk/publication/thematic-reviews/tr14-02.pdf>, accessed 19 July 2022.
48 Ibid., (Thematic review of annuities'), 29.
49 Oren Bar-Gill, *Seduction by Contract, Law, Economics and Psychology in Consumer Markets*, (Oxford University Press, Oxford, 2012), 161–2.
50 FCA, 'General Insurance Pricing Practices Market Study—Consultation Paper, CP20/19', (September 2020), 59, <https://www.fca.org.uk/publication/consultation/cp20-19.pdf>, accessed 19 July 2022.
51 FCA website, 'PS21/11: General Insurance Pricing Practices', (last updated December 2021), <https://www.fca.org.uk/publications/policy-statements/ps21-11-general-insurance-pricing-practices-amendments>, accessed 19 July 2022.
52 Halifax Bank website, 'Switch to Halifax and Get £150', <https://www.halifax.co.uk/bankaccounts/switch-to-halifax.html>, accessed 21 July 2022.
53 Current Account Switch Service, 'Annual Report 2021', 4, <https://www.wearepay.uk/wp-content/uploads/Current-Account-Switch-Service-Annual-Report-2021.pdf>, accessed 19 July 2022.
54 Retail Banker International website, 'UK Current Account Switching: plus ça change, plus c'est la même chose'(8 February 2022), <https://www.retailbanker-international.com/analysis/uk-current-account-switching-winners-losers/>, accessed 19 July 2022.
55 Ibid., (Retail Banker International website).
56 DNB website, 'A Quarter of Dutch Consumers Shared Payment Data in Exchange for Services', <https://www.dnb.nl/en/general-news/2020/a-quarter-of-dutch-consumers-shared-payment-data-in-exchange-for-services/>, accessed 17 July 2022.
57 Ibid., (DNB Survey).
58 OBIE website, Second Impact Report, (2021), <https://openbanking.foleon.com/live-publications/the-open-banking-impact-report-october-2021-ug/appendix/>, accessed 17 July 2022.
59 Ibid., (OBIE Second Impact Report).
60 Ibid., (OBIE Second Impact Report).
61 Tim Waterman, Chief Commercial Officer, Zopa, 'How Do We Grow UK Open Banking Users from 4 Million to 40 Million by 2025', (18 October 2021),

Open Banking Policy in the UK and EU 51

<https://www.altfi.com/article/8425_how-do-we-grow-uk-open-banking-users-from-4-million-to-40-million-by-2025>, accessed 17 July 2022.

62 Yougov website, 'Three Quarters of Britons haven't Heard of Open Banking', (1 August 2018), <https://yougov.co.uk/topics/economy/articles-reports/2018/08/01/three-quarters-britons-havent-heard-open-banking>, accessed 17 July 2022.
63 Ibid., (Yougov website).
64 Ibid., (Yougov website).
65 FT, 'Banks Brace for Next Wave of Digital Shake-up. Open Banking Is Yet to Provide a Flood of Innovation but Its Architects Are Sticking At It', 14 January 2019, <https://www.ft.com/content/8f106e36-15bb-11e9-a581-4ff78404524e> accessed 17 July 2022.
66 Krishan Shah, 'Wealth on the Eve of a Crisis. Exploring the UK's Pre-pandemic Wealth Distribution', (January 2022), Resolution Foundation, 2, <https://www.resolutionfoundation.org/publications/wealth-on-the-eve-of-a-crisis/>, accessed 21 July 2022.
67 Office of National Statistics, 'Distribution of Individual Total Wealth by Characteristic in Great Britain: April 2018 to March 2020', (7 January 2022), <https://www.ons.gov.uk/peoplepopulationandcommunity/personalandhouseholdfinances/incomeandwealth/bulletins/distributionofindividualtotalwealthbycharacteristicingreatbritain/april2018tomarch2020>, accessed 21 July 2022.
68 Katie Evans, 'Playing the Field: Consumers and Competition in Banking', (2015), Social Market Foundation, 10, <https://www.smf.co.uk/wp-content/uploads/2015/07/Social-Market-FoundationPublication-Playing-the-field-Consumers-and-competition-in-banking-160715.pdf>, accessed 21 July 2022.
69 Ibid., (Evans), 40.
70 Ibid., (Evans), 41.
71 Ibid., (Evans), 30.
72 Office of Fair Trading, 'Personal Current Accounts in the UK: An OFT Market Study' (2008).
73 Competition and Markets Authority (CMA) 'Personal Current Accounts – Market Study Update', (July 2014), 121–2, <https://assets.publishing.service.gov.uk/media/53c834c640f0b610aa000009/140717_-_PCA_Review_Full_Report.pdf\>, accessed 21 July 2022.
74 Payment Services Directive I (PSD I) (2007/64/EC), see Recitals on pp. 1–8, <https://ec.europa.eu/info/business-economy-euro/banking-and-finance/consumer-finance-and-payments/payment-services/payment-services_en>, accessed 22 July 2022.
75 Study on the impact of Directive 2007/64/EC on payment services in the internal market and on the application of Regulation (EC) NO 924/2009 on cross-border payments in the Community, Final Report, (February 2013), <https://ec.europa.eu/info/sites/default/files/study-impact-psd-24072013_en.pdf>, accessed 22 July 2022 and Directive on payment services in the internal market (PSD II) (2015/2366/EC), <https://www.eumonitor.eu/9353000/1/j4nvk6yhcbpeywk_j9vvik7m1c3gyxp/vk0vn25mntsj> accessed 22 July 2022.
76 European Commission—Fact Sheet, Payment Services Directive: Frequently Asked Questions, <https://ec.europa.eu/commission/presscorner/detail/de/MEMO_15_5793>, accessed 22 July 2022.
77 Supra n 75 (PSD II), Recital 30.
78 Supra n 75 (PSD II), Art 55.
79 European Central Bank (ECB), 'Card Payments in Europe—Current Landscape and Future Prospects: A Eurosystem Perspective' (17 April 2019), <https://www.ecb.europa.eu/pub/pubbydate/2019/html/ecb.cardpaymentsineu_currentlandscapeandfutureprospects201904~30d4de2fc4.en.html>, accessed 22 July 2022.

80 Ibid., (Card Payments in Europe), Section 2.1.
81 Supra n 75 (PSD II) Recital 4.
82 PSD II Art 62(4).
83 ECB, 'Towards the Retail Payments of Tomorrow: A European Strategy', (26 November 2019), <https://www.ecb.europa.eu/press/key/date/2019/html/ecb.sp191126~5230672c11.en.html>, accessed 23 July 2022.
84 Ibid., (ECB – a European strategy).
85 EU Commission, 'Communication on a Retail Payments Strategy for the EU', (September 2020), <https://eur-lex.europa.eu/legal-content/EN/TXT/PDF/?uri=CELEX:52020DC0592&from=EN>, accessed 25 July 2022.
86 EU Commission, 'Call for Advice to the European Banking Authority (EBA) Regarding the Review of Directive (EU) 2015/2366 (PSD2)', <https://ec.europa.eu/info/sites/default/files/business_economy_euro/banking_and_finance/documents/211018-payment-services-calls-advice-eba_en.pdf>, accessed 25 July 2022.
87 EU Commission website, 'Payment Services—Review of EU Rules', <https://ec.europa.eu/info/law/better-regulation/have-your-say/initiatives/13331-Payment-services-review-of-EU-rules_en>, accessed 25 July 2022.
88 EU Commission, 'Call for Evidence for Evaluation and Impact Assessment', (10 May 2022), Ref. Ares (2022) 3556263, 2.
89 Supra n 85 (EU Commission 'communication'), 21.
90 Supra n 85 (EU Commission 'communication'), 8.
91 Donal Griffin, 'London's Fintech Boom Opens the Door for Dirty Money', (Bloomberg UK, 4 January 2022), <https://www.bloomberg.com/news/features/2022-01-04/fintech-boom-masks-a-shady-side-of-london-s-money-hub>, (accessed 2 July 2022).
92 Supra n 85 (EU Commission 'communication'), 11.
93 Michał Polasika and others, 'The Impact of Payment Services Directive 2 on the PayTech Sector Development in Europe', (2020) 178 Journal of Economic Behavior and Organization, 385–401, 391.
94 Ibid., (Polasika), 397.
95 Jakub Šťastný, 'European Union: Open Banking in Europe in Light Of PSD2 Review', (23 February 2022) Mondaq, <https://www.mondaq.com/financial-services/1165162/open-banking-in-europe-in-light-of-psd2-review>, accessed 25 July 2022.

Part II
Open Banking Regulation

4 Nordic and European Free Trade Association Countries

Introduction

Denmark, Norway, Sweden, Finland and Iceland, as well as the autonomous territories of Faroe Islands, Greenland and Åland, constitute the so-called Nordic region in (northern) Europe. Denmark, Sweden and Finland are among the 27 European Union (EU) countries, and Norway and Iceland are part of the European Free Trade Association (EFTA) along with Switzerland and Liechtenstein. With the exception of Switzerland, Norway, Iceland and Liechtenstein are also European Economic Area (EEA) countries, which means that they are part of the EU's single market and are therefore beneficiaries of the freedom of movement of goods, capital, services and people across the EU.[1] The present analysis considers the development of open banking in the Nordic region and EFTA countries.

The Nordic region

Even though the Nordic region comprises distinctive jurisdictions, it is regarded as one entity because of a history of cross-border synergies and cooperation among its governments.[2] Being part of the EU's internal market, the Nordic countries' financial systems are subject to legislation relating to the single market for financial services. Accordingly, the Revised Payment Services Directive 2 (PSD2) framework is the main instrument involved in the reception and development of open banking across the region.

To begin, in Finland, the PSD2 was transposed into national law in 2018 through the amendment of two acts, namely the 'Payment Institutions Act', which relates to PSD2-specific provisions on payment institutions, and the 'Payment Services Act', which relates to all other PSD2 provisions.[3] In Denmark, the PSD2 framework first required the renewal of the Danish Payments Act. Subsequently, the Danish Financial Supervisory Authority (DFSA) granted payment service providers until March 2021 to comply with the Strong Customer Authentication (SCA) requirements drafted by the European Banking Authority (EBA) and submitted to the European Commission in June 2019.[4] In Sweden, the PSD2 was implemented through a new revised Payment

Services Act in May 2019, and unlike in Denmark, no additional period was granted for complying with the SCA requirements.[5] In Iceland, the 'Act on Payment Services' was issued in November 2021 to enable the operation of the PSD2 and became fully effective in May 2022.[6] Finally, in Norway, the implementation process took longer than in the other Nordic countries. Most of the PSD2 provisions were transposed into the 'Act of 25 June 1999 No 46 on Financial Contract and Financial Assignments' (Financial Contract Act)[7] and the 'Act of 10 April 2015 No 17 on Financial Institutions and Financial Groups'.[8] The remaining parts of the PSD2 concerning consumer rights and protection were then implemented through the passage of the 'Act of 18 December 2022 No 146 on Financial Contract' (the revised Financial Contracts Act), which ultimately entered into force in early 2023.[9]

The PSD2 is a milestone in the development of regulatory-driven open banking approaches in Europe and other jurisdictions. The directive represents either a source for starting an open banking regime from scratch or a necessary tool for facilitating open banking protocols already in place prior to specific legislation. The Nordic context is an example of the second, with authors suggesting the region to be an ideal place for developing a collaborative data-sharing framework for open banking.[10] Open banking is, in fact, welcomed as a significant step in enhancing and consolidating a tradition of digitisation and innovation in almost all jurisdictions. Hence, the PSD2 represents the enabling regulation that Nordic governments, businesses and consumers have been waiting for.[11]

Compared with other European jurisdictions, the countries' digital and technology openness can more strongly help promote the development of open banking under the PSD2 framework. In fact, according to the European Commission's Digital Economy and Society Index (DESI), the Nordic countries have always ranked highest in digital capabilities; Finland is at the forefront for human capital and digital public services, Denmark excels in integrating digital technology and Norway leads the way in Internet use.[12] Recently, Finland, Denmark and Sweden have also come to prominence, in Europe and globally, in the area of digital transformation of businesses.[13] Such leadership results from the Nordic governments' strategies to boost growth through a digitisation and innovation pathway.

The Nordic financial sector is a strong example of this trend, with banks already exhibiting a digital mindset and openness to new technologies in the twentieth century.[14] The crisis that affected the Nordic banking system in the 1980s and 1990s pushed financial institutions even further towards digitalisation and modern technologies as a means for improving the efficiency and security of business operations.[15]

Another critical element facilitating the adoption and development of open banking is the collaborative model that has always characterised Nordic financial institutions. Nordea, the largest financial services group, is a primary example of this—the firm was created through the merger of the Finnish Merita Bank, Swedish Nordbanken, Danish Unibank and Norwegian Christiania Bank.[16] More recently, Nordea and DNB, the largest Norwegian bank, entered into an agreement to create a major Nordic-rooted bank with operations in Baltic countries (Estonia, Latvia and Lithuania).[17] Furthermore, the latest example of cross-jurisdictional cooperation is the 'P27' project aimed at making the region the first area to be able to handle domestic and cross-border payments in multiple currencies. The P27 is owned by the six major Nordic banks: Danske Bank, Handelsbanken, Nordea, OP Financial Group, SEB and Swedbank, all of which have been involved in the creation of a common platform for clearing and settlement in the payment market.[18]

Finally, some important developments have involved all the main open banking players. Since the promulgation of the PSD2, Nordic banks have engaged actively to become agile open banking players. DNB was the first Nordic bank to exploit account aggregation solutions in its mobile banking app in 2018.[19] Then, through a partnership with Nordic API gateway (now Aiia), the service of account-to-account payment from any bank was offered to its customers through DNB's mobile banking.[20] OP Financial Group, the largest Finnish bank, also developed its open banking capabilities through partnerships with API aggregators and FinTech start-ups to promote new products and services to its customers.[21] Synergies between banks and FinTech firms are also relevant in Iceland, where the largest universal banks joined forces with open banking service providers to ensure compliance with the PSD2 access-to-account requirements.[22]

Further, banks and third parties in the Nordic region are strongly connected. The literature indicates the attractiveness of countries such as Sweden, Norway, Denmark and Finland to foreign third parties, which are willing to passport their services in the region.[23] This appeal is explained by the Nordics' high level of digitisation and tech-savviness and the quality of API aggregation services for third parties.

Against this backdrop, Nordic consumers are regarded as ideal open banking practitioners. The digital tradition encouraged by the governments and reflected in every sector of society, including the financial services industry, contributes to creating consumer trust in digital and innovative initiatives. Their trust makes them more amenable to sharing their financial data with third parties, and thus, they are embodying open banking's main aim of giving consumers ownership and control of their data.[24]

In conclusion, the Nordic region is an area where open banking development pursuant to the PSD2 has considerable potential. The so-called Nordic tick[25] to open banking is explained by their digital tradition and openness to advanced technologies, and the Nordic way to open banking is evident in some concrete developments spurred by the promulgation of the PSD2. Such transformative changes are making the region a key open banking hub with promising growth.

EFTA

Norway and Iceland, as well as Liechtenstein and Switzerland, are also signatories of the 1960 'Convention Establishing the EFTA' (EFTA Convention) for the promotion of free trade and economic integration among EFTA States.

Lichtenstein

Like Norway and Iceland, Liechtenstein is also an EEA country and therefore bound by the PSD2. The revised Payment Services Act (Zahlungsdienstegesetz—ZDG) entered into force in 2019 for the implementation of the PSD2.[26] However, the latest data indicate that the country, in terms of the establishment and development of open banking, is still at an early stage. Regulatory sandboxes and further guidance on the use of technology are among the suggested tools for stimulating the development of open banking.[27]

Switzerland

Switzerland is neither a member of the EU nor an EEA country. Unlike the other EFTA states, it has no obligations to implement EU legislation, although it has entered into bilateral agreements with the EU. Like the Nordic region, Switzerland ranks high regarding Internet use, smartphone penetration and e-commerce utilisation.[28] Compared to the Nordics, where the combination of their digital and technological mindset and the implementation of the PSD2 framework has them primed for open banking, Switzerland pursues open banking strategies through market-driven approaches.[29]

Switzerland initially expressed scepticism towards regulatory initiatives—the EU PSD2 framework in particular—for developing open banking. In a 2017 position paper, the Swiss Banker Association (SBA) expressed a firm stance against any legal obligation for financial institutions to share their customers' data with third parties.[30] The SBA contends that such an obligation would result in extra compliance and security costs for financial institutions, which they would have to pass on to their customers.[31] Second, contra the view that access-to-account rules under the PSD2 would enhance competition in the financial services industry, the SBA contended that these rules would distort the Swiss financial markets, which already function perfectly and offer innovative products and services on the basis of strong partnerships between the incumbent banks and the FinTech industry.[32] Accordingly, the Swiss market-driven open banking approach means that banks are free to decide which third parties they will share their customers' data with.

Bank customers, and their right to consent, remain at the centre of the ecosystem. In this context, market-driven open banking developments can be traced as follows. API standardisation is regarded as a decisive factor for the success of open banking as it would guarantee time-to-market implementation, enhanced security and efficient scalability.[33] In this respect, the Swiss open banking scenario is characterised by relevant initiatives such as the 'Swiss FinTech Innovations (SFTI) working group Common API',[34] the SIX b.Link platform (formerly Corporate API)[35] and the openbankingproject.ch.[36]

As for the banks, they are slow in adopting open banking because of several factors. According to a recent study led by the Institute of Financial Services Zug IFZ of the Lucerne School of Business (FZ Open Banking Study 2022), Swiss banking culture is prone to underestimating, if not outright fearing, open banking, and in practice, banks tend to perceive it as an IT compliance issue rather than a strategic tool.[37] Moreover, there is a sense of diffidence towards opening to third parties, with an attendant fear of losing the 'customer interface'.[38] Such fear is also present among bank employers who may be reluctant to pursue novel tools.[39]

Swiss consumers, however, appear to be attracted by the open banking idea. A recent survey from Mastercard showed that even though few interviewed consumers knew about open banking, more than half of those interviewed across Switzerland expressed an interest in open banking services after receiving an explanation of them.[40] Additionally, others advocate for shifting from market-driven to regulatory-driven approaches to achieve the full potential of open banking. This mindset seems to be backed at the policy level, with the 'State Secretariat for International Finance' (SIF) having announced the need for regulation in its 'Digital Finance: Fields of Action 2022+' report.[41] Specifically, the report refers to the transition to open finance amongst other areas and advocates for regulatory approaches in the event that market-driven approaches are insufficient to enable an open finance ecosystem.[42] Further evaluation of the outcomes of the current market-driven approach will dictate whether Swiss open banking stays on its current course or changes direction.

Conclusion

The Nordic region's open banking ethos has been strongly dictated by the enactment of the PSD2, which ultimately positions the region as a promising European open banking hub. Further progress will be made through the issuance of PSD3 and the EU open finance regime. As an EEA country like Norway and Iceland, Liechtenstein is also bound by the PSD2 but the establishment and implementation of an open banking regime are yet to be fully achieved. While observing the transposition of the directive across the EU, representatives of the Swiss financial sector have stated their preference for industry-led approaches to spur the development of open banking nationwide. This view has been dominant until now but has also been opposed by stances advocating regulatory approaches given the banks' slowness in adopting open banking despite the consumers' growing interest.

Notes

1 European Free Trade Association (EFTA), 'The Basic Features of the EEA Agreement' <www.efta.int/eea/eea-agreement/eea-basic-features#6> accessed 7 January 2023.
2 Jussie Laine, 'Nordic Cooperation' in Brite Wassenberg & Bernard Reitel (eds) *Critical Dictionary on Cross Border Cooperation in Europe* (Peter Lang 2020) 615; see also Anna Rosemberg, 'State of the Nordic Region 2022' (2022) Nordic Cooperation <www.norden.org/en/nordicregion2022> accessed 7 January 2023.
3 Financial Supervisory Authority (FIN-FSA) <www.finanssivalvonta.fi/en/banks/payment-service-providers/regulation/> accessed 07 January 2023.
4 Danish Financial Supervisory Authority (DFSA), 'PSD2' (2020) <www.finanstilsynet.dk/Lovgivning/Ny_EU_lovsamling/PSD-2 accessed 8 January 2023>; see also European Banking Authority (EBA), *Final Report on Amending RTS on SCA and CSC under PSD2* (2022) EBA/RTS/2022/03 <www.eba.europa.eu/regulation-and-policy/payment-services-and-electronic-money/regulatory-technical-standards-on-strong-customer-authentication-and-secure-communication-under-psd2> accessed 8 January 2023.
5 Finansinspektionen, 'Payment Services Act' (2010) 2010:751 <www.fi.se/en/> accessed 8 January 2023.
6 Central Bank of Iceland, 'Act No. 114/2021, on Payment Services' (2021) <www.cb.is/library/Skraarsafn—EN/Laws/Act%20No.%20114%202021%20on%20Payment%20Services.pdf> accessed 10 January 2023.
7 Kredittilsynett, 'Act No. 46 on Financial Contracts and Financial Assignments (Financial Contracts Act)' (in force 1 July 2000) <https://app.uio.no/ub/ujur/oversatte-lover/data/lov-19990625-046-eng.pdf> accessed 10 January 2023
8 Kredittilsynett, 'Act No. 40 of 10 June 1988 on Financing Activity and Financial Institutions (Financial Institutions Act)' (1988) <www.imolin.org/doc/amlid/Norway_Financial%20Institutions%20Act.pdf> accessed 15 January 2023.
9 Regjeringen.no, 'Act of 18 December 2022 No. 146 on Financial Contract (the revised Financial Contracts Act)' (2022) <www.regjeringen.no/no/dokumenter/prop.-92-ls-20192020/id2700119/?ch=1> accessed 6 March 2023.
10 Yapily, 'Why Nordic Countries Are Perfectly Positioned to Lead the Way to Open Finance' (25 August 2022) <www.yapily.com/blog/why-nordic-countries-could-unlock-open-finance accessed 6 March 2023>; Baltic, 'Nordic Countries Emerge as Front-Runners in Open Banking Adoption' (21 January 2021) <https://fintech-baltic.com/3555/nordics/open-banking-nordics/> accessed 6 March 2023; James Thorpe, 'UK and Nordics Lead Open Banking in Europe' (*Mastercard*, 17 June 2021) <www.mastercard.com/news/europe/en/newsroom/press-releases/en/2021/june/uk-and-nordics-lead-open-banking-in-europe/> accessed 6 March 2023.
11 Wordline, 'The Nordic Way—A PSD2 Whitepaper from Worldline Nordic' (2017) <https://financial-services.worldline.com/content/dam/equensworldline/documents/whitepaper/Worldline_whitepaper_The_Nordic_Way.pdf> accessed 8 March 2023.
12 Commission, 'Digital Economy and Society Index (DESI) 2022' (2022) Thematic Chapters 2 <https://digital-strategy.ec.europa.eu/en/policies/desi> accessed 08 March 2023.
13 Ibid., 16.
14 Financial Stability Group (FSB) Regional Consultative Group (RCG), 'Nordic Experience of Cooperation on Cross-border Regulation and Crisis Resolution' (2016) Report from an RCG Europe Working Group, 4 <https://www.fsb.org/wp-content/uploads/RCG-Europe-Nordic-experience-of-cooperation.pdf> accessed 10 March 2023.
15 Ibid., 4.

Nordic and European Free Trade Association Countries   61

16 Nordea <www.nordea.com/en/about-us/who-are-we/our-history> accessed 10 March 2023.
17 Richard Milne, 'Nordea and DNB to Combine Baltic Operations' *Financial Times* (25 August 2016) <www.ft.com/content/8feeeb66-6a9b-11e6-a0b1-d87a9fea034f> accessed 10 March 2023.
18 P27 Nordic Payment <https://nordicpayments.eu/> accessed 12 March 2023.
19 Alex Cruickshank, 'Norwegian Banking App Gives Access to Other Banks' Accounts' (*Computerweekly*, 24 March 2020) <www.computerweekly.com/news/252480509/Norwegian-banking-app-gives-access-to-other-banks-accounts> accessed 12 March 2023.
20 Ibid.
21 Ruby Hinchliffe, 'OP Financial Chooses Nordic API Gateway for Open Banking' (*Fintechfutures*, 20 November 2019) <www.fintechfutures.com/2019/11/op-financial-chooses-nordic-api-gateway-for-open-banking/> accessed 12 March 2023.
22 Omar Faridi, 'Open Banking Fintech Salt Edges Teams Up with Landsbankinn, the Largest Icelandic Bank' (*Crowdfundinsider*, 27 November 2021) <www.crowdfundinsider.com/2021/11/183439-open-banking-fintech-salt-edges-teams-up-with-landsbankinn-the-largest-icelandic-bank/> accessed 20 March 2023.
23 Nordic API Gateway, *Accelerating Open Banking. How the Nordics are Driving New Opportunities Across Industries* (White Paper, May 2020) 2 <https://thefintechtimes.com/wp-content/uploads/2020/06/Nordic_API_Gateway_Report_open_banking.pdf> accessed 20 March 2023.
24 Ibid., 17.
25 Louise Basse, 'What Makes the Nordics Tick When It Comes to Open Banking' (*Aiia*, 2020) <https://blog.aiia.eu/what-makes-the-nordics-tick-when-it-comes-to-open-banking> accessed 22 March 2023.
26 'Zahlungsdienstegesetz' (ZDG) (2019) Liechtensteinisches Landesgesetzblatt Nr. 213 <www.gesetze.li/chrono/2019213000> accessed 25 March 2013.
27 Openbankingtracker <www.openbankingtracker.com/country/liechtenstein> accessed 25 March 2023.
28 Daniela Massaro, 'Open Banking in Switzerland' (*Mastercard*, 2021) Part I, 2 <https://mastercardcontentexchange.com/news/media/wxwih35b/2mc20299_mc_ch_whitepaper_part_1_en_vf_31-9.pdf> accessed 25 March 2023.
29 Openbankingproject.ch, <www.openbankingproject.ch/en/resources/news/study-on-open-banking-in-switzerland/> accessed 25 March 2023.
30 Swiss Bankers Association (SBA), 'Open Banking' (February 2020) SBA Position Paper 1 <https://www.swissbanking.ch/_Resources/Persistent/d/8/c/d/d8cd7b-64d64d8034d3d031b227bdfefddcd4fca9/SBA_Position_paper_Open_Banking_EN.pdf> accessed 26 March 2023.
31 Ibid., 3.
32 Ibid.
33 Ibid., 2; see also SBA, 'Open Banking—An Overview for the Swiss Financial Center' (July 2020) 5 <www.swissbanking.ch/_Resources/Persistent/8/8/2/8/88286724aa4fdc3dd8bb8ecd9b9c0d7af659a803/SBA_Overview_OpenBanking_en.pdf> accessed 26 March 2023.
34 Anja Vujovic, 'The New SFTI Working Group OpenPK has Kicked Off!' (*SIFTI*, 16 July 2021) <https://swissfintechinnovations.ch/the-new-sfti-working-group-openpk-has-kicked-off/> accessed 26 March 2023.
35 Six-Group.Com (SIX), 'SIX Launches b.Link—The Central Platform for the Standardized Sharing of Data between Financial Institutions and Third-party Providers' (*SIX*, 19 May 2020) Media Releases <www.six-group.com/en/newsroom/media-releases/2020/20200519-six-blink.html> accessed 26 March 2023.

36 Openbankingproject.ch (n 28).
37 Urs Blattmann and others, *IFZ Open Banking Studie 2022* (2022) Institute of Financial Services Zug IFZ, Hochschule Luzern 1 <https://drive.switch.ch/index.php/s/CXJOVPiTtbUUfGk> accessed 27 March 2023.
38 Ibid., 4.
39 Ibid., 40.
40 Ibid.
41 State Secretariat for International Finance (SIF), 'Digital Finance: Areas of Action 2022+' (*SIF*, 2 February 2022) 5 <https://www.sif.admin.ch/sif/en/home/finanzmarktpolitik/digitalisation-financial-sector/digital-finance-areas-action.html> accessed 27 March 2023.
42 Ibid., 16.

5 The Americas

Introduction

This chapter highlights various levels of progress in the development of open banking. In Canada, open banking plans have been going through significant delays. In the United States of America, the so-called 'open banking rule' will be finalised in 2024. The open banking rule represents an important shift from the prevalent (open banking) market-driven approaches to regulation. Mexico and Chile, instead, provide opportunities for discussion through their respective open banking/open finance legislation. Overall, the chapter offers a diverse picture of strategies and regulation in the Americas.

Canada

The Canadian Department of Finance is leading work on developing open banking in Canada. Work in this area has been slow. In 2018, it set up an Advisory Committee on Open Banking, but this organisation largely limited itself to issues relating to customer data sharing—the so-called 'read-only' form of open banking.[1]

The Department of Finance issued a consultation paper on open banking early in 2019.[2] Its focus, similar to that in Australia, was on data sharing and not on payment initiation.[3] Payments Canada is working on modernising its payment infrastructure which could enable this facility if the government chose to pursue a wider form of open banking.[4] There was little in the consultation on developing fintech and not much on developing competition in financial services. It is possible that the Canadian government does not really see the benefits of competition in financial services. A number of economists see a correlation between banking competition and bank failures in the global financial crisis of 2007/9 with developed economies, with a less competitive banking sector, avoiding the issues experienced by other jurisdictions with more diversified but fragile banking systems.[5]

Payments Canada operates under the Canadian Payments Act 1985. It is funded by both the Bank of Canada and the authorised domestic and foreign banks operating in the country. It is a non-profit making and owns and

DOI: 10.4324/9781003331339-7

operates Canada's payment clearing and settlement infrastructure. There is a very limited amount about open banking in its Corporate Plan and it is vague about the way forward in this area.

'Should the federal government move forward with open banking as it has signaled, this … will offer some exciting opportunities for maximizing the benefits of modern payments for Canadians. Payments Canada is excited to support open banking implementation efforts'.[6]

There have been some initial steps, in the retail payments area, with the Retail Payment Activities Act 2021 which permits authorisation of firms undertaking electronic payment functions (e.g., payment processors, digital wallets, money transfer services and other payment technology companies).[7] However, as mentioned, earlier progress is slow and there is little or no mention of competition as a driving force. The approach appears to be a mixture of government 'top down' development coupled with incumbent bank direction of the development of the payments systems. This cautious approach may be valid based on what happened in the global financial crisis and being a 'follower' may allow Canada to see what works and to select what may be seen as best for the country.

United States of America

The creation and implementation of open banking regulation in Europe and other countries has always been observed with great interest in the US.[8] However, there was scepticism as to the possibility of an *ad hoc* open banking regulation. In this respect, it is worth quoting in full the views expressed by the US Treasury in 2018:

> There are significant differences between the United States and the United Kingdom with respect to the size, nature, and diversity of the financial services sector and regulatory mandates. Given those differences, an equivalent Open Banking regime for the U.S. market is not readily applicable. Nonetheless, as Open Banking matures in the United Kingdom, U.S. financial regulators should observe developments and learn from the British experience.[9]

On the one hand, such an opinion indicates how open banking has developed in the US until now, namely through a hands-off approach by regulators. Market-driven strategies have been the primary tool for the adoption of open banking. On the other hand, the Treasury leaves the way open to regulatory frameworks. Consequently, the main question is whether the US market is ready for significant changes and what progress has been made to date.

Any analysis revolves around the efforts taken by the Consumer Financial Protection Bureau (CFPB) to implement Section 1033 of the Dodd–Frank Act through the 2020 'Advanced Notice on Proposed Rule Making on Consumer Access to Financial Records', and the 2022 'Outline of Proposals and

Alternatives under Consideration'. These documents represent important preliminary stages of rulemaking and a shift from the prevailing industry-led approaches. The following sections review the latest steps toward issuing a rule to apply Section 1033.

CFPB's initiatives

Section 1033 of the Dodd–Frank Act obliges financial institutions offering or providing financial products and services to consumers ('covered persons') to make available, upon consumer request, data relating to the offered products or services, including transaction and account information. The provision also empowers the CFPB to issue rules governing data exchange.[10] So far, the CFPB's initiatives to make Section 1033 work in practice represent an awareness of the existence of an open banking ecosystem in the US and the need to ensure adequate coexistence among the participants.

In 2017, the CFPB issued a set of nonbinding principles (2017 Principles) to protect consumers when authorised third parties access their data to create new financial products and services. The 2017 Principles relate to the nine key areas of data access, data scope and usability, control and informed consent, payment authorisation, security, access transparency, accuracy, unauthorised access and dispute resolution and accountability mechanisms.[11] In line with the open banking philosophy, consumers are at the centre of the data-sharing process through their consent and authorisation.

In parallel with the issuance of the 2017 Principles, the CFPB also published the input received from the main stakeholders regarding the process of sharing data with customer permission (2017 Stakeholder Insights). Significantly, the 2017 Stakeholder Insights document provides a specific categorisation of the main US open banking participants. Different from the specific nomenclature used in the EU, United Kingdom and other open banking systems (AISP, PISP, AIPSP), the main actors (along with consumers) are referred to as 'account data holders' (banks and credit unions), 'data account users' (third parties) and aggregators.[12] All the views expressed by the concerned stakeholders, particularly in relation to the 2017 Principles, converged on the need to create a secure and balanced data-sharing ecosystem in the US financial services industry.

The 2020 CFPB symposium on 'Consumer Access to Financial Records' (2020 Symposium) prefaced the wide discussion of the 2017 Principles as a milestone in enacting the rulemaking process under Section 1033 of the Dodd–Frank Act.[13] The 2020 Symposium considered the underlying technology and highlighted the tendency of banks and aggregators to prefer APIs instead of the predominant 'credential-based access' and 'screen scraping' modes of data accessing.[14] The symposium stressed two key points, namely the participants' interest in open banking and the difficulties in meeting their conflicting views concerning the most critical areas such as the scope of data access, privacy and security, data user rights, role of the aggregators, consumer consent, and the scope of the CFPB's regulatory powers.[15]

Rulemaking developments

The October 2020 'Advanced Notice on Proposed Rule Making (ANPR) on Consumer Access to Financial Records' solicited comments on the optimal framework for implementing Section 1033 of the Dodd–Frank Act.[16] Comments were sought on nine key topics: Benefits and costs of consumer data access, competitive incentives and authorised data access, standard setting, access scope, consumer control and privacy, legal requirements other than Section 1033, data security, data accuracy, and the interaction between Section 1033 and other financial legislative frameworks such as the Gramm–Leach–Bliley Act (GLBA), the Fair Credit Reporting Act (FCRA), the Electronic Fund Transfer Act (EFTA), and their implementing regulations.[17]

The ANPR highlights the link between data sharing and fostering competition and innovation in the financial services industry and the necessity to achieve the latter through legislation on the former.[18] In this respect, further motivation was given in July 2021 when US President Joe Biden signed the 'Executive Order on Promoting Competition in the American Economy' (the Order), with the Order urging, amongst other initiatives, the CFPB to progress in implementing Section 1033 of the Dodd–Frank Act 'to facilitate the portability of consumer financial transaction data so that consumers can more easily switch financial institutions and use new, innovative financial products'.[19]

The 2022 CFPB's 'Outline'

The 'Outline of Proposals and Alternatives under Consideration' (the Outline), issued by the CFPB in October 2022, represents the latest outcome of the rulemaking pathway to implement Section 1033.[20] Procedurally, before issuing any final rule on the implementation of Section 1033, the CFPB must complete a consultative process under the Small Business Regulatory Enforcement Fairness Act of 1996 (SBREFA); in this process, the CFPB receives advice and recommendations from small entities that are likely to be affected by the regulations that the CFPB will issue, namely those entities participating in the open banking ecosystem (data holders, data users and aggregators).[21] To this end, the CFPB must establish and convene the 'Small Business Review Panel' comprising representatives from the CFPB, the Small Business Administration's Chief Counsel for Advocacy, and the Office of Information and Regulatory Affairs in the Office of Management and Budget.[22] Accordingly, the Outline aims to smooth the SBREFA process by pinpointing the proposals and alternatives on which the Review Panel will receive feedback.

To begin, the CFPB proposed to regard as 'covered data providers' those entities meeting the definition of 'financial institutions' under § 1005.2(i) of the CFPB's Regulation E (12 CFR part 1005) or 'card issuer' set forth in § 1026.2(a)(7) of the CFPB's Regulation Z (12 CFR part 1026).[23] The first category would include banks, credit unions, and any other entity providing account services and access devices, including electronic fund transfer, whereas entities issuing credit cards and their agents would fall under the second category.[24] In relation to third-party access, as Section 1033 of the Dodd–Frank Act states, data holders can exchange customer information with third parties acting on consumers' behalf and the CFPB intends to ensure that only third parties authorised by customers can engage in data sharing. In this respect, the Outline proposes considering the authorisation requirement satisfied when third parties are able to do as follows: (1) provide an 'authorisation disclosure' to inform the consumer of key terms of access, (2) obtain the consumer's informed, express consent to the key terms of access contained in the authorisation disclosure and (3) certify to the consumer that it will abide by certain obligations regarding the collection, use and retention of the consumer's information (certification statement).[25]

As to the type of information to be exchanged, Section 1033 refers to information relating to financial products or services consumers obtained by the data holders and transaction and account information. In this context, the Outline identifies the following information to be shared upon request: Periodic statement information for settled transactions and deposits, information regarding prior transactions and deposits that have not yet settled, other information about prior transactions not typically shown on periodic statements or portals, online banking transactions that the consumer has scheduled but that have not yet occurred and account identity information.[26]

The Outline further seeks input on how the proposed categories of information should be exchanged. In the case of 'direct access'—that is, information shared directly with consumers, the CFPB proposes to make information available through financial account management portals and enable consumers to export information in human or machine-readable format.[27] As to third-party access, the proposal is to establish and maintain a 'third-party portal'.[28] Accordingly, the Outline seeks comments on the viability, benefits and costs associated with such a proposal. Finally, inputs are sought regarding the limits to be imposed on third parties with respect to data collection, use, retention and security.[29]

On April 2023, the CFPB released the 'Final Report of the Small Business Review Panel on the CFPB's Proposals and Alternatives Under Consideration for the Required Rulemaking on Personal Financial Data Rights', which summarises the feedback received by the participants and the guidelines and recommendations issued by the Small Business Review Panel.[30] The next step will be drafting the proposed rule prior to the issuance of the final rule, which is likely to be issued in late 2024.

Towards the 'Open Banking Rule'

The US open banking future will therefore be dictated by the final rule implementing Section 1033 of the Dodd–Frank Act, which is also labelled as the 'Open Banking Rule', emphasising the beginning of a new scenario.[31] Prior to the regulatory pathway triggered under Section 1033 of the Dodd–Frank Act, industry-led approaches had shaped the rise of open banking in the US. Significant partnerships were established between banks and data aggregators for the provisions of API gateways to streamline and facilitate the data-sharing process among the involved participants.[32] This trend, in which the API gateway is entirely managed and maintained by the aggregators, was also coupled with the development of open APIs by larger banks themselves.[33] The US financial services industry has clearly embraced the open banking experience. The more open banking is adopted at the industry level, the greater the need to govern and discipline the dynamics associated with the data-sharing framework through regulation.[34] The planned Open Banking Rule testifies to these relevant changes in open banking approaches. The implementation of the final rule will reveal whether it achieves the open banking goal of creating a win-win context for all the participants.

Mexico

When I first wrote about Mexico and open banking in 2020, all the signs were that the country would use FinTech in an innovative way to promote financial inclusion.[35] Mexico's National Council for Financial Inclusion (CONAIF) and the Financial Education Committee (CEF) had developed and published in 2020 a National Financial Inclusion Strategy (PNIF).[36] There was, and remains, an enormous amount of work to be done to improve financial inclusion. For example, only around 43% of households have a bank account compared with 70% or more in both Chile and Brazil.[37] In Mexico, this figure falls to only 6% in rural areas.[38] The International Monetary Fund (IMF) has published similar information.[39]

It was also hoped that the development of Cobro Digital ('CoDi'), Mexico's instant payment system, would widen access to financial services. It is very similar to the much more successful Pix system (see later). However, it appears to have not had a significant take-up even during the COVID-19 period.[40] The Mexican economy remains very heavily dependent on cash transactions.[41] The lack of an adequate financial services infrastructure, especially in rural regions has had an adverse effect on the economy.[42]

The World Bank is supporting the legal and regulatory framework to allow FinTech firms to be authorised and supervised with much of this work focused on 'electronic payment funds institutions (IFPE)'.[43]

Certainly, new firms such as Prometeo and Belvo have entered the open banking market in both Mexico and Brazil.[44] However, while acknowledging the relevance of open banking to aid financial inclusion the focus of, for example, Prometeo is on the growing middle class.[45]

As a further example, Belvo was authorised by both the National Banking and Securities Commission (CNBV) and the Institución de Fondos de Pago Electrónico (IFPE) in 2022.[46] Its website has the look and feel of a European open banking operation with no mention of promoting financial inclusion and with no rural imagery.[47] This is not anyway a criticism of the firms but it may indicate a disconnect between the public policy objectives and the business models of the innovators. There are a number of new internet banks, including Revolut, the largest of which is thought to be Klar.[48] However, the story appears similar, with a focus on the technological astute.

Nevertheless, Mexico which a few years ago led Latin America in digital banking has fallen behind. Juan Carlos Espinosa, Head of digital banking and innovation at HSBC Mexico is quoted as saying that he does not see open banking in Mexico as a success story.[49] It is difficult to explain this. One possibility is that the original strategy originated with the previous government and the current president, Andrés Manuel López Obrador, may see open banking as having a lower priority.

Chile

FinTech trends in Chile

The Chilean FinTech industry has steadily grown since 2016. According to a joint survey from Finnovista, the Chilean Finance Minister and the Inter-American Development Bank, the number of FinTech start-ups increased by 60% between 2019 and 2021.[50] The Chilean FinTech sector is a diversified ecosystem characterised by large, small and medium-size firms. Between domestic and foreign companies, more than 200 FinTech firms have been established.[51] Most of these firms are active in the payment and remittance sector, but others are in the provision of financial management services and technology solutions for banks and other financial institutions.[52]

Even though Brazil, Mexico, Argentina and Colombia have more developed FinTech ecosystems, the Chilean FinTech industry is a dynamic community expanding in key financial services areas. Recent surveys have highlighted the significant presence of FinTech companies in the Chilean lending market, where crowdfunding platforms have been proliferating and positioning themselves as valuable (funding) alternatives to mainstream channels.[53]

The personal finance market is also a notable area where various FinTech start-ups have been reaching lower-income households not usually served by banks.[54] Beyond the banking sector, the Chilean insurance market has also witnessed the establishment and operation of FinTech companies. Numerous 'InsurTech' companies are now based in Chile, offering services ranging from insurance to brokerage, as well as investing in the development of online platforms for facilitating the sale and distribution of insurance products.[55]

Finally, FinTech companies are active in the Chilean savings and investment sector. According to data collected by Finnovista, in this market segment, FinTech firms operate as general fund managers, fund distribution brokers, individual portfolio managers and investment advisors.[56] In this last category, start-ups are also offering personal financial management services through the development of applications to help households have a clear and simplified picture of their financial situation, thus improving their financial understanding, management of resources and investment planning.[57]

The consumer response to the FinTech advent in Chile has been positive. Access to digital solutions facilitated by the highest Internet penetration rate in Latin America and the increasing use of smartphones, as well as consumer adaption to cashless and remote transactions during the COVID-19 pandemic have been the seeds of a spike in FinTech services.[58] To date, Chilean FinTech firms are estimated to have raised more than $100 million in capital.[59] The industry is regarded as a catalyst for enhancing competition in the financial services industry and a gateway for facilitating financial inclusion to the benefit of the unbanked and underserved segments of the Chilean population.[60]

Major reforms and the 'FinTech Ley'

Enhancing competition, promoting innovation and supporting financial inclusion have been the Chilean authorities' long-time objectives. Given the possibilities offered by the FinTech industry in this regard, the country has undertaken a major regulatory reform process to adapt its financial system to new developments and participants. The Financial Portability Law (Law N°21.236), promulgated in September 2020, is a crucial outcome of this process. Law N°21.236 strengthens financial customers' (individuals and micro-small businesses) portability rights by establishing a body of rules that simplifies and expedites the process for switching institutions or financial products and services.[61] In other words, Law N°21.236 intends to reduce the amount of time and the financial burden borne by individuals and micro-small businesses when they change financial service providers or contract new products and services with the same provider.

Banks, insurance companies, managers of endorsable mortgage loans, and savings and loan cooperatives are among the financial entities targeted by Law N°21.236, which also mentions checking accounts, lines of credit, credit and debit cards, consumer loans, mortgage loans and automotive loans as the products and services subject to portability.[62] This legislation is expected to improve transparency, customer experience and access to finance.

Other noteworthy legislation following the issuance of Law N°21.236 includes the 'Market Agents Law' (Law No. 21.314) of April 2021, which reinforces market agents' transparency requirements and responsibilities,[63] and the 'Interchange Rate Law' (Law No. 21.365) of August 2021, which regulates the interchange fees in the Chilean card payment system.[64] Key initiatives also interact with this regulatory reform process, such as the creation of a technology observatory by the Central Bank of Chile for reviewing and assessing the impact of new technologies in the financial services industry, particularly in the retail payment sector.[65]

Further, in November 2020, the 'Financial Market Commission' (Comision Para el Mercado Financiero-CMF), responsible for supervising financial markets and institutions, submitted to the Ministry of Finance the preliminary draft of a FinTech Act for regulating the business and operations of FinTech companies in the Chilean securities market, including alternative finance providers such as crowdfunding platforms.[66] The CMF's preliminary draft was eventually the springboard for larger reforms of the domestic financial services industry and its participants. In fact, the reform process reached its peak in the 'Bill to Promote Financial Competition and Inclusion through Innovation and Technology in the Provision of Financial Services', which was submitted to the Congress in September 2021, approved in October 2022 and finally published in January 2023 (Law No. 21.521, 'FinTech Ley').[67]

The FinTech Ley is a broad piece of legislation aimed at fostering inclusion, competition, financial innovation, financial customer protection, the preservation of financial integrity and stability and the prevention of money laundering and terrorist financing.[68] Against this backdrop, the legal framework covers the main FinTech activities and businesses present in the Chilean financial services industry, including crowdfunding platforms, alternative trading systems, credit and investment advisory services, custodians of financial instruments, order routing and financial intermediation.[69]

All these initiatives and legislative interventions represent relevant steps taken by the government to stimulate economic growth by developing a more diversified financial sector, where more players can operate and improve customer experience by offering a wider range of solutions.

The Chilean open banking/finance framework

The FinTech Ley also governs open banking. The Chilean open banking framework is based on the 2021 report 'Guidelines for the Development of an Open Finance Framework in Chile, with a Focus on Competition and Financial Inclusion', commissioned by the Ministry of Finance in November 2020.[70] The report focuses on the creation of an open finance framework without referring to a gradual transition from an open banking to an open finance system, as seen in other open banking pioneer jurisdictions such as the UK and EU.[71] Nonetheless, it provides guidelines for a regulated financial data-sharing framework, which is clearly premised on the open banking mechanics (customer consent, data-sharing obligation, API, third-party license).[72] Accordingly, an analysis of the specific FinTech Ley provisions helps reveal the evolution of the Chilean open banking/finance system and its future development.

To begin with, Articles 18, 19, and 20 of Title III ('Del Sistema de Finanzas Abierta') of the FinTech Ley clarify the participants of the open banking/finance ecosystem. The financial institutions that are expected to share their customers' data with third parties are denoted as 'information providers' (IPs). This category includes banks, credit card issuers, pay cards with funding provisions, broker-dealers, asset managers, insurance companies, account providers or any other payment service providers licensed by the CMF.[73] As in most of the open banking (regulatory-driven) systems worldwide, FinTech Ley makes it mandatory for IPs to share customers' data upon third parties' request. In this respect, Article 18 also gives the CMF the power to widen the categories of financial institutions subject to the data-sharing obligation, on the basis of their size, customer portfolio, customer data availability and market participation.[74] The CMF shall also identify the type of customer data to be shared.[75]

'Information Based Service Providers' (IBSPs) are the third parties requesting access to IPs' customer data in the interest of providing services. IBSPs may range from FinTech companies to traditional financial service providers.[76] Article 19 requires IBSPs to voluntarily register in the IBSP Register, which the CMF shall establish and maintain.[77] Broadly interpreted, IBSBs also include third parties dealing with payment initiation services for owners of current accounts, savings accounts or sight accounts, which are addressed in Article 20. While Article 19 requires voluntary registration for IBSP accessing customer data, Article 20 makes it mandatory for PISPs to register in the specific 'Payment Initiation Services Providers Register' maintained by the CMF.[78]

Customer consent is always the cornerstone of data-sharing frameworks. To this end, Article 23 refers to the third parties' duty to always obtain explicit and specific consent from customers for accessing information or initiating payments. Customers have the right to revoke their consent at any time.[79] While putting customers at the centre stage of the data-sharing process, Article 23 also demands third parties to have in place an adequate mechanism for customer authentication.[80] IPs are also within the scope of Article 23, as they have the responsibility to implement mechanisms for verifying the third party's status, specifically, that they are properly and thus certified to access information and initiate payments on behalf of IPs' customers.[81]

APIs are also the primary technology enabling the Chilean open banking/finance system. In fact, Article 21 expressly requires the participants to maintain one or more remote and automatic APIs for exchanging information.[82] In line with the UK experience, API standardisation is also promoted by the Chilean regulators. The CMF must determine the standards for the design, implementation, interoperability and safe functioning of the interfaces.[83] Interestingly, the regulators have also followed the approach taken by the EU, UK and Australia in regard to API monetisation. Article 25 prohibits IPs from charging fees to third parties for accessing and exchanging customers' data.[84] Nevertheless, the extent of consultations that third parties can have with IPs is limited. Indeed, Article 25 provides for IPs to charge for the costs of maintaining the system when the volume of requests outnumbers the consultation limit, which the CMF will have to determine.[85] The CMF will also have to elaborate minimum standards for guaranteeing adequate data integrity and confidentiality.

The FinTech Ley entered into force 30 days after its publication in the Official Gazette, whereas Title III, concerning the open finance framework needs to be implemented by the CMF through further regulations to be issued within 18 months from the publication of the FinTech Ley. In turn, these regulations will set implementation plans and deadlines for the involved participants. Title III lays the foundation for the future Chilean open finance ecosystem. Chile has joined Mexico and Brazil as Latin American countries with a specific regulatory framework on open banking/finance. The expected implementing regulations will be crucial for testing the framework's capacity to meet the objectives of promoting competition and financial inclusion.

Conclusion

Canada, USA, Mexico and Chile present wide and diversified degrees of development of open banking strategies and regulation. In Canada, open banking implementation is clearly at a standstill. In the USA, we have witnessed important progress since the consultations for implementing Section 1033 of the Dodd–Frank Act gathered pace. South American countries mirror steadier progress that led to the enactment of specific legislation. Other Latin American countries are expected to join the open banking trend. Much remains to be seen in open banking in the Americas.

Notes

1 Canadian Finance Department website, 'Minister Morneau Launches Advisory Committee on Open Banking', (26 September 2018), <https://www.canada.ca/en/department-finance/news/2018/09/minister-morneau-launches-advisory-committee-on-open-banking.html>, accessed 25 August 2022.
2 Canadian Department of Finance website, 'Consultation Document: Review into the Merits of Open Banking' (January 2019), <https://www.canada.ca/en/department-finance/programs/consultations/2019/open-banking.htm>1, accessed 25 August 2022.
3 Ibid., ('Consultation'), 'Scope and Process'.
4 Ibid., ('Consultation'), 'Scope and Process'.
5 Michael Bordo, Angela Redish and Hugh Rockoff, 'Why Didn't Canada Have a Banking Crisis in 2008 (or in 1930, or 1907, or. . .)', (February 2015), The Economic History Review, Vol. 68, No. 1, 218243, 241.
6 Payments Canada, Corporate Plan 20222026, 14, <https://www.payments.ca/sites/default/files/paymentscanada_corporateplan_2022_en.pdf>, accessed 26 August 2022.
7 Bank of Canada website, Retail payments supervision, <https://www.bankofcanada.ca/core-functions/retail-payments-supervision/>, accessed 26 August 2022.
8 Susan Pandy, *Modernizing U.S. Financial Services with Open Banking and APIs* (Federal Reserve Bank of Boston, Payment Strategy Report, 8 February 2021) 3 <www.bostonfed.org/publications/payment-strategies/modernizing-us-financial-services-with-open-banking-and-apis.aspx>, accessed 6 March 2023.
9 Steven T. Mnuchin and Craig S. Phillips, *A Financial System That Creates Economic Opportunities. Nonbank Financials, Fintech, and Innovation* (US Department of the Treasury, July 2018) Executive Order 13772 on Core Principles

for Regulating the United States Financial System, 29 <https://home.treasury.gov/sites/default/files/2018-08/A-Financial-System-that-Creates-Economic-Opportunities—Nonbank-Financials-Fintech-and-Innovation_0.pdf>, accessed 6 March 2023.
10 Section 1033 'Consumer Rights to Access Information' of 'DoddFrank Wall Street Reform and Consumer Protection Act' (2010) (DoodFrank Act) 124 Stat 1376 Public Law 111203 <https://www.congress.gov/111/plaws/publ203/PLAW-111publ203.pdf>, accessed 6 March 2023.
11 Consumer Financial Protection Bureau (CFPB), 'Consumer Protection Principles: Consumer-Authorized Financial Data Sharing and Aggregation' (CFPB, 18 October 2017) 1 <https://files.consumerfinance.gov/f/documents/cfpb_consumer-protection-principles_data-aggregation.pdf> accessed 5 March 2023.
12 CFPB, 'Consumer-Authorized Financial Data Sharing and Aggregation. Stakeholder Insights That Inform the Consumer Protection Principles' (CFPB, 18 October 2017) 1 <https://s3.amazonaws.com/files.consumerfinance.gov/f/documents/cfpb_consumer-protection-principles_data-aggregation_stakeholder-insights.pdf> accessed 6 March 2023.
13 CFPB, *Bureau Symposium: Consumer Access to Financial Records. A Summary of the Proceedings* (CFPB, 24 July 2020) 1 <https://s3.amazonaws.com/files.consumerfinance.gov/f/documents/cfpb_consumer-protection-principles_data-aggregation_stakeholder-insights.pdf> accessed 6 March 2023.
14 Ibid.
15 Ibid.
16 CFPB, 'Advance Notice of Proposed Rulemaking on Consumer Access to Financial Records' (CFPB, 6 November 2020) <https://s3.amazonaws.com/files.consumerfinance.gov/f/documents/cfpb_section-1033-dodd-frank_advance-notice-proposed-rulemaking_2020-10.pdf> accessed 6 March 2023
17 Ibid.
18 Ibid.
19 Administration of Joseph R. Biden Jr., 'Executive Order 14036—Promoting Competition in the American Economy' (*The White House*, 9 July 2021) <www.whitehouse.gov/briefing-room/presidential-actions/2021/07/09/executive-order-on-promoting-competition-in-the-american-economy/> accessed 10 March 2023.
20 CFPB, 'Outline of Proposals and Alternatives Under Consideration for the Personal Financial Data Rights Rulemaking' (CFPB, 27 October 2022) Small Business Advisory Review Panel for Required Rulemaking on Personal Financial Data Rights 3 <https://files.consumerfinance.gov/f/documents/cfpb_data-rights-rule-making-1033-SBREFA_outline_2022-10.pdf> accessed 15 March 2023.
21 Ibid., Part II, 5.
22 Ibid., 6.
23 Ibid., Part III.A.1, 9.
24 ibid.
25 Ibid., Part III.B.2, 15.
26 Ibid., Part III.C.1, 18.
27 Ibid., Part III.D.1, 28.
28 Ibid., Part III.D.2, 30.
29 Ibid.
30 CFPB, *Final Report of the Small Business Review Panel on the CFPB's Proposals and Alternatives Under Consideration for the Required Rulemaking on Personal Financial Data Rights* (CFPB, 3 April 2023) 2 <https://files.consumerfinance.gov/f/documents/cfpb_1033-data-rights-rule-sbrefa-panel-report_2023-03.pdf> accessed 20 May 2023

31 Jimmy Ma and Stephen Newman, 'The CFPB Open Banking Rule' (*Jdsupra*, 13 March 2023) <www.jdsupra.com/legalnews/the-cfpb-open-banking-rule-8915627/> accessed 7 April 2023.
32 Scarlett Sieber, 'Open Banking: What Does It Mean for the US' (3 May 2021) *Forbes* <https://www.forbes.com/sites/scarlettsieber/2021/03/03/open-banking-what-does-it-mean-for-the-us/> accessed 7 April 2023.
33 Ibid.
34 See Jimmy Chen, 'CFPB Should Protect and Enable the Most Vulnerable in Its Open Banking Rule' (*American Banker*, 23 December 2022) <https://www.americanbanker.com/opinion/cfpb-should-protect-and-enable-the-most-vulnerable-in-its-open-banking-rule> accessed 7 April 2023; see also, Sara C Markov, 'Open Banking: The CFPB Should Follow the European Regulatory Regime' (2022) 26 North Carolina Bank Institute 269.
35 Alan Brener, 'EU Payment Services Regulation and International Developments' in Iris H-Y Chiu and Gudula Deipenbrock (eds), *Routledge Handbook of Financial Technology and Law* (Routledge, Abingdon, 2021), 170.
36 CONAIF, 'National Financial Inclusion Strategy—Mexico', (12 March 2020), <https://www.afi-global.org/publications/national-financial-inclusion-strategy-mexico/>, accessed 16 August 2022.
37 ibid, (National Financial Inclusion Strategy—Mexico), 4.
38 World Bank website, 'Mexico: More Than Half of the Households Don't Have a Bank Account', (12 December 2012), <https://www.worldbank.org/en/news/feature/2012/12/12/mexico-more-than-half-of-households-do-not-have-bank-account>, accessed 16 August 2022.
39 Dmitry Gershenson and others, 'Fintech and Financial Inclusion in Latin America and the Caribbean', (IMF Working Paper, WP/21/221, 2021), 9.
40 Latin America Business Stories website, 'Bad Timing and Cultural Attachment to Ccash: Why Hasn't CoDi, Mexico's Instant Payment System, Taken Off Yet?', (15 December 2020), <https://labsnews.com/en/articles/business/codi-mexican-instant-payment-system/>, accessed 19 August 2022.
41 Reuters website, 'FinTechs Fail to Make a Dent in Mexico as Cash Remains King', (26 May 2022), <https://www.reuters.com/business/finance/fintechs-fail-make-dent-mexico-cash-remains-king-2022-05-26/>, accessed 18 August 2022.
42 World Bank website, 'Expanding Financial Access for Mexico's Poor and Supporting Economic Sustainability', (9 April 2021), <https://www.worldbank.org/en/results/2021/04/09/expanding-financial-access-for-mexico-s-poor-and-supporting-economic-sustainability>, accessed 17 August 2022.
43 Ibid., (World Bank 'Expanding Financial Access').
44 BELatina website 'Prometeo Open Banking, a Latin American Company Leading Financial Services', (22 July 2022), <https://belatina.com/prometeo-open-banking-ximena-aleman/>, accessed 17 July 2022.
45 Ibid., (BELatina).
46 FinTech and Finance News, 'Belvo Receives Authorization to Develop Payment Initiation Solutions in Mexico', (30 June 2022), <https://ffnews.com/newsarticle/belvo-receives-authorization-to-develop-payment-initiation-solutions-in-mexico/>, accessed 17 August 2022.
47 Belvo website, <https://belvo.com/about/>, accessed 17 August 2022.
48 TechCrunch, 'Klar, Believed to be Mexico's Largest Digital Bank, Lands $70M in General Atlantic-led Round', (9 June 2022), <https://techcrunch.com/2022/06/09/klar-believed-to-be-mexicos-largest-digital-bank-lands-70m-in-general-atlantic-led-round/>, accessed 18 August 2022.
49 Iupana website, 'Open Banking in Mexico' (24 June 2022), <https://iupana.com/2022/01/24/open-banking-hsbc-mexico/?lang=en>, (21 August 2022).

76 Open Banking Regulation

50 Inter-America Development Bank (IDB) & Finnovista, 'FinTech Radar Chile 2021' (2021) <www.finnovista.com/wp-content/uploads/2021/05/Fintech-Radar-Chile_Gra%CC%81ficos-1.pdf> accessed 9 September 2022; see also IDB, 'Study: Fintech Industry Doubles in Size in Three Years in Latin America and the Caribbean (*IDB*, 26 April 2022) <www.iadb.org/en/news/study-fintech-industry-doubles-size-three-years-latin-america-and-caribbean> accessed 9 September 2022.
51 See 'FinteChile' (The National FinTech Association) <www.fintechile.org/> accessed 9 September 2022. Most of these firms are established in the capital Santiago, see Statista, 'FinTech in Chile-Statistics and Facts' (*Statista*, 7 June 2022) <www.statista.com/topics/7831/fintech-in-chile/#topicOverview> accessed 9 September 2022.
52 Guillermo Vial and Nicolas Santana, 'Fintech M&A: Latin American and Chilean Fintech Ecosystems in the Global Eye' (*International Bar Association*, 7 October 2021) <www.ibanet.org/latin-american-chilean-fintech-ecosystems> accessed 15 September 2022.
53 Charles Cohen and Miquel Dijkman, 'Chile—Financial Sector Assessment Program: Digital Financial Inclusion' (*World Bank Group*, April 2022) 5 <https://elibrary.worldbank.org/doi/epdf/10.1596/37747> accessed 3 October 2022.
54 Ana Maria Montoya and Rosario Celedon, *Guidelines for the Development of an Open Finance Framework in Chile, with a Focus on Competition and Financial Inclusion* (Ministerio de Hacienda, August 2021) 105 <https://biblioteca.digital.gob.cl/bitstream/handle/123456789/3818/2021.12.06%20-%20Lineamientos%20Informe.pdf?sequence=1&isAllowed=y> accessed 6 October 2022.
55 Ibid., 115.
56 FinTech Radar Chile, 'The Fintech Ecosystem in Chile Grows 49% over the Last 18 Months and Stands as the most Mature in the Latin American Region' (*Finnovista*, 30 July 2019) <www.finnovista.com/en/radar/the-fintech-ecosystem-in-chile-grows-49-over-the-last-18-months-and-stands-as-the-most-mature-in-the-latin-american-region/> accessed 6 October 2022.
57 Ibid.
58 Statista Market Forecast <https://www.statista.com/outlook/dmo/fintech/chile> accessed 8 January 2023.
59 FinteChile (n 51).
60 Cohen and Dijkman (n 53) 5.
61 Ministry of Finance of Chile, 'Financial Portability Law Comes into Effect' (*Ministerio de Hacienda*,14 September 2020) <https://www.hacienda.cl/english/investor-relations-office/newsletter/latest/-financial-portability-law-comes-into-effect> accessed 8 January 2023.
62 Ibid.
63 'Law No. 21.314, Market Agents Law' (2021) Biblioteca del Congreso Nacional de Chile (BCN) <https://www.bcn.cl/leychile/navegar?i=1158144> accessed 10 October 2022.
64 Law No. 21.365 'Interchange Rate Law' (2021) BCN <https://www.bcn.cl/leychile/navegar?idNorma=1163384> accessed 10 October 2022.
65 See Banco Central Chile, 'Observatorio Technologico' <www.bcentral.cl/web/banco-central/areas/observatorio-tecnologico> accessed 10 October 2022.
66 Comision para el Mercado Financiero (CMF), 'CMF Publishes Fintech Act Proposal for the Securities Market' (*CMF*, 9 February 2021) CMF Press Release <www.cmfchile.cl/portal/principal/613/w3-article-46998.html> accessed 16 October 2022, see also <www.cmfchile.cl/portal/principal/613/articles-46983_doc_pdf.pdf> for the complete text of the proposal (in Spanish) accessed 16 October 2022.
67 See Ministry of Finance, 'Law No. 21.521 to Promote Financial Competition and Inclusion through Innovation and Technology in the Provision of Financial Services' ('FinTech Ley') (2023) Diario Oficial de la Republica de Chile

No. 43.442, CVE 2246446 <www.diariooficial.interior.gob.cl/publicaciones/2023/01/04/43442/01/2246446.pdf> accessed 9 January 2023 (Spanish text).
68 FinTech Ley, art 1 ('Disposiciones generales').
69 FinTech Ley, art 2 ('Servicios financieros basados en tecnología').
70 Montoya and Celedon (n 5) 32.
71 While analysing the FinTech Ley framework, some authors use the word 'open banking' and 'open finance' interchangeably. See The World Bank Group, 'Chile. Financial Sector Assessment Programme. Technical Note. Digital Financial Inclusion' (WBG, April 2022), 33. <https://documents1.worldbank.org/curated/en/099440107152219110/pdf/P17202003745650ea0811e02f3df054d83c.pdf> accessed 09 January 2023; Matias Jose Apparcel Carrillo, Maria Consuelo Mackenna Leighton, and Maria Ignacia Valdes Vergara, 'Chile. FinTech' (*The Legal 500*, 2021) Country Comparative Guides, 2 <https://apparcel.cl/en/the-legal-500-presents-the-fintech-comparative-guide-2021-with-the-contribution-of-auv/> accessed 9 January 2023; Valentina Novoa, 'Chile's Fintech Law Project—Advancements Towards Innovation, Competition and Financial Inclusion' (21 November 2021) in María Fernanda Viecens & Esteban Manuel Greco (eds), CPI Columns Latin America, 2 <www.competitionpolicyinternational.com/wp-content/uploads/2021/11/LatAm-Column-November-2021-Full.pdf> accessed 18 January 2023.
72 Ibid.
73 FinTech Ley, art 18 ('Instituciones proveedoras de información').
74 Ibid.
75 Ibid.
76 FinTech Ley, art 19 ('Instituciones Proveedoras de Servicios basados en Información').
77 Ibid.
78 FinTech Ley, art 20 ('Proveedores de servicios de iniciación de pagos').
79 FinTech Ley, art 23 ('Requisitos del consentimiento y autenticación').
80 Ibid.
81 Ibid.
82 FinTech Ley, art 21 ('Medios de entrega e intercambio de información').
83 Ibid.
84 FinTech Ley, art 25 ('Distribución de costos por consultas de información en Sistema de Finanzas Abiertas').
85 Ibid.

6 Far East

Introduction

This chapter reviews the development of open banking in several Far East jurisdictions (Australia, New Zealand, Japan, Taiwan, South Korea, Singapore, China, Hong Kong SAR and Indonesia). These countries have been selected both because of, in many ways, their different approaches and their contrast to what is happening in Europe. Some of the initiatives are aimed at social inclusion where large sections of the population do not have access to banking and payment services. In many jurisdictions, there is less of a drive to increase competition and a much more cooperative approach is evident. This may well be a responsible way forward with the shadow of both the 2007/9 Global Financial Crisis and the 1997 Asian crisis haunting the banking industry.

Australia

Unlike in for example the UK and EU, Australia has not focused on open banking and payment systems. Instead, the regulations have concentrated on the customer's ownership of their own data. The background is the dominance of the four major banks in Australia (the Commonwealth Bank of Australia (CBA), Australia and New Zealand Bank (ANZ), National Australia Bank (NAB) and Westpac). There were concerns about the dominant market power of these banks and their poor record in looking after the interests of their customers. As a consequence, in 2016, the Australian Treasurer asked the Parliament's House of Representative Standing Committee on Economics to undertake an enquiry into the 'performance and conduct' of these banks.[1] The resulting document, known as the 'Coleman Report', advocated increasing competition in banking and it saw customer 'data sharing' with other financial institutions as one way of achieving this.[2]

In parallel, the Australian Treasury asked Professor Ian Harper to undertake a review on competition.[3] The Harper Committee issued its report in March 2015 and recommended, among other things, that consumers should have access to data which facilitates informed choice.[4]

DOI: 10.4324/9781003331339-8

The Australian government followed up on these recommendations with an Issues Paper on open banking in August 2017.[5] However, the focus remained on permitting bank customers to transfer their bank data to facilitate greater competition.[6] The view, in government, was that competition would help to ensure that consumers achieved a 'fair deal' from the banks.[7] The issues went wider than just banking and extended to allowing consumers access to all the data across a range of industries including financial services more generally. It was hoped that with sufficient information consumers would use this knowledge to press for increased competition with a consequent effect on prices and services.

The same perspective can be seen in the Australian Treasury 'Review into Open Banking', (December 2017).[8] The review is focused on data access and sharing. Although the review briefly considers developments in the UK and EU on opening payment services, this is quickly dismissed as a subject for a future review.[9]

As a consequence of these reports in 2019, the government introduced legislation—the Treasury Laws Amendment (Consumer Data Right (CDR)) Bill 2019. This would apply to the banking, energy and telecommunications sectors. The proposed legislation was reviewed by the House of Representatives Standing Committee on Economics.[10] It was broadly supported but it expressed concerns about the issues of data privacy and broader consumer understanding of open data.[11] In due course, the legislation was enacted and new rules were developed for consumer data access and sharing.[12] This element of open banking in Australia has been subsumed within the general area of consumer data protection.[13] It fell under the auspices of the Australian Competition and Consumer Commission (ACCC).

However, there was a change in direction in early 2020. The Treasurer set up an inquiry into 'Future Directions for the CDR' including considering open banking and payment initiation. The inquiry, chaired by Scott Farrell, an Australian lawyer specialising in FinTech, issued its report in October 2020.[14] To some extent, the COVID-19 pandemic accelerated this move as many consumers switched to operating online as the country entered a series of 'lock-downs'.

The Farrell Inquiry reported in October of that year and recommended allowing direct account payment initiation authorised by consumers along the lines operating in the UK at the time.[15] At the end of February 2021, the Treasury took over as lead agency for CDRs from the ACCC and Senator Jane Hume, Minister for Superannuation, Financial Services and the Digital Economy within the Treasury became responsible for making CDR rules.[16]

Immediately following on from his October 2020 report, Scott Farrell was asked to undertake a review of payment systems in Australia. This followed Scott Morrison, the then Australian Prime Minister and the Treasurer, and Josh Frydenberg, announcing at the end of September 2020, a Digital Business Plan which was designed, in part, to help with the country's recovery from the pandemic.[17] A key element of this 'included reviewing the regulatory architecture of the Australian payments system'.[18] The second Farrell report was issued in June 2021 and had several recommendations regarding open banking and payment services. Much of the report covered government and regulatory responsibilities and structures. These aspects included:

- Introducing a tiered payments licensing framework and related regulations (Recommendations 8, 9, 10, 11 and 12).
- Establishing that this new scheme will operate under the Australian financial services licencing regime.
- Giving the Treasury enhanced ministerial powers in the area of payment services regulation.[19]

As part of these changes, Australia merged its three payment systems: BPAY, Eftpos and New Payments Platform Australia (NPPA). The merger was prompted by the central bank, the Reserve Bank of Australia (RBA), with the aim of increasing efficiency, reducing costs and creating a national payments champion able to compete with overseas competition.[20]

These were authorised by the ACCC after obtaining court-enforceable undertakings to protect competition.[21] The RBA is a shareholder in NPPA and may have prompted the merger.[22] The RBA appears to see 'big tech' as a threat and wants to have an Australian national champion able to compete.[23] However, NPPA has still to enable a third-party payment initiation service.

It is not clear why full open banking, as opposed to data sharing, is taking so long to develop in Australia. The Treasury seem to be making most of the running to get Australia closer to catching up with developments in this area. This may be the reason for the minister taking greater powers. The Treasury sees the new rules allowing third-party payment initiation directly from customer accounts to be phased in over a period of time.[24] However, since May 2022, Australia has had a new government with a new Treasurer, and it is not clear what the direction of travel will be and at what speed in the area of open banking. Nevertheless, the Treasury's 'Statutory Review of the CDR', under Elizabeth Kelly is still underway and due to conclude in July 2022.[25]

New Zealand

The development of opening banking in New Zealand is in many ways similar to that in Australia with a focus on customer bank account data sharing. Development in this area is broadly controlled by the Payments NZ Application Programming Interface (API) Council. This organisation was set up in 2017 by participants in the New Zealand payments industry to design API standards. Payments NZ was asked to develop all this on behalf of the industry and launched the new standards in 2019.[26] Payments NZ was set up in 2010 as a not-for-profit organisation owned by the major incumbent New Zealand banks with the support of New Zealand's central bank: The Reserve Bank.

Payment NZ carried out a consumer survey in September 2020 to find out what the public wanted from the payment system. The sample size of over a thousand people was large by New Zealand standards and indicated that very few had heard of open banking.[27] Once explained only 16% said that they would be comfortable with a third party having access to their bank data.[28] Nineteen per cent said that they would be comfortable allowing a third party to take money from their bank account to make payments on their behalf.[29] The key reasons against these arrangements were worries about cybercrime and a general lack of trust.[30]

It was with some frustration that in December 2019, the then Minister for Commerce and Consumer Affairs, Kris Faafoi, sent an open letter to the New Zealand financial services industry expressing his concern at the slow progress with the development of open banking.[31] Towards the end of 2020, Faafoi resigned from this ministerial position and was replaced by David Clark. The latter confirmed the government's intention to introduce CDRs legislation in 2022. This announcement was repeated in July 2021 saying that the aim was to align the New Zealand system with the Australian model announced in 2019.[32] However, the actual proposal was different to that in Australia since it will apply to organisations as well as individuals and the legislation will permit:

> action initiation – the ability for an accredited person to carry out an action with the consent of a consumer. Action initiation will allow consumers to, for example, ask a third-party payment provider to action a bank funds transfer from the consumer's bank account to a business' bank account when paying for a goods or services.[33]

The approach was confirmed by the published minutes of the Cabinet Economic Development Committee meeting on 21 June 2021.[34] After a slow start, the FinTech trade body in New Zealand has great hopes for Open Banking in New Zealand.[35]

Japan

The banking market in Japan is dominated by the big three: MUFG Bank, Sumitomo Mitsui Banking and Mizuho Bank plus Norinchukin Bank.[36] There are also a large number of smaller regional and trust banks.[37]

E-commerce has been slow to develop in Japan and cash usage remains very high compared to other developed countries.[38] In an attempt to encourage open banking, Japan's Banking Act (Act No. 59 of 1981) was amended in 2018. The changes, while similar to the PSD II, are voluntary. It is heavily focused on consumer data access with payment services being assigned a second order of priority.

The Japanese regulator, the Financial Services Authority (JFSA), is trying to encourage cooperation in implementing open banking. In the most recent statement of its strategic priorities, the authority says that it will 'engage in close exchanges of opinions with business operators and industry associations in order to grasp business needs and identify and resolve challenges, including those' that relate to open banking APIs.[39] In relation to intermediary businesses, it will focus on 'the sound development of the businesses and the protection of users'.[40]

As mentioned earlier, in many ways this is a similar approach to that taken by Korea, with a slow methodical path based on cooperation. Competition as an objective is barely mentioned as a JFSA strategic priority in its 2021/2 document mentioned earlier.

Taiwan

The Financial Supervisory Commission (FSC) is responsible for a phased introduction of open banking in Taiwan. Towards the end of 2018, the FSC gave the Taiwan Bankers Association, an industry trade body, and the Financial Information Service Company (FISC), the task of developing an open banking programme. The FISC is responsible for interbank clearing and information exchanges between banks. Taiwan is using Singapore (see later) as its model for open banking. The approach is 'permissive' providing the infrastructure for firms to undertake open banking. In some ways, this is also similar to the strategy adopted in Japan (see later).

There is a three-phase plan. The first phase, set at the end of 2019, was limited to developing an API standard allowing providers to make available basic information on interest rates etc. Under the second phase, banks and other third-party service providers (TSPs) will be able, using APIs, to access customer account information.

The FSC has set out its own open banking plans for 2022, as part of phase 2, including approving 19 cooperation projects involving 14 banks and 2 TSPs.[41] The banks include the South China Commercial Bank, Yuanta Commercial Bank, CTBC Bank, Mega International Commercial Bank, First Commercial Bank, Cathay United Bank and Far Eastern International Bank.[42] The latter bank is working with the Far EasTone Telecommunications Company to allow customers to integrate their bank account, credit card and savings information. The app will use 'artificial intelligence to recommend the most favorable options for customers when making wealth management decisions or choosing banking services'.[43]

The third phase will permit financial transactions initiated by financial services organisations with the customer's consent. This phase has still to get started.

South Korea

In 2019, the Korean Financial Services Commission, the national financial services regulator, set out its plans for open banking.[44] This formed part of the FSC's Financial Policy Roadmap for 2019.[45] Payment systems, including the development and operation of open banking, are controlled and operated by the Korea Financial Telecommunications & Clearings Institute (KFTC).[46] The KFTC is a non-profit organisation controlled primarily by the 'general member banks' in Korea (i.e., the Bank of Korea, the Korea Development Bank, Nonghyup Bank, Shinhan Bank, Woori Bank, Standard Chartered Bank Korea, Hana Bank, Industrial Bank of Korea, Kookmin Bank and Citibank Korea).[47] As part of this centralised structure, the KFTC has a payments fraud detection role ('the KFTC will closely monitor fraudulent activities and automatically shut down suspicious transactions').[48] In addition, the Korean Financial Security Institute (KFSI) will 'examine whether open banking service providers have set up an effective security management system within their firms'.[49]

The Korean strategy for open banking is based on the concept of 'cooperative competition'.[50] It has three stages.[51] The initial phase is based on a voluntary agreement on an open banking system across all banks covering standardised API access and low fees charged by banks to FinTech firms operating these services.

The second phase requires amendments to the Electronic Financial Transaction Act. This will require all to offer payment service providers with a standardised API for money transfers. 'It will also prohibit banks from any discriminatory action against payment service providers using their payment system in processing money transfer and charging fees'.

Finally, the third phase is more conjectural. The FSC will, in the medium to long term, consider permitting certain fintech firms 'direct access to the payment system without relying on banks' services. To be eligible for such direct access, FinTech payment service providers will have to meet certain requirements in financial soundness and digital capabilities'.[52]

It is difficult to determine how much progress has been made in undertaking these three phases. Reading between the lines, there may appear to be some conflicts of opinion between financial companies and FinTech firms in taking open banking forward. These issues were indicated in remarks made by the FSC's, then Vice Chairman, Sohn Byungdoo, at the third consultative body meeting on digital finance in October 2020.

> In order to promote reciprocity between incumbents and new entrants, the government will promote a more balanced "win-win" relationship between financial companies and fintechs by adjusting the scope of data being opened up as well as fee obligations to a reasonable level …
>
> [F]intechs and other new entrants will be required to open up their data to a certain level as well. In addition, fintechs will also share cost burdens for maintaining and operating the open banking network. The government will also set up a joint deliberative body on open banking … to foster discussions and help resolve differences in opinions.[53]

As can be seen, the Korean approach is highly centralised and cautious and requires close coordination and agreement by all participants. It is very different to the focus on increased competition adopted by both the EU and UK.

Singapore

Singapore was close to Europe in initiating its development of open banking. In 2016, the Monetary Authority of Singapore (MAS), Singapore's central bank and integrated financial regulator and the Association of Banks in Singapore (ABS), a banking trade body, published an open banking plan: 'Finance-as-a-Service: API Playbook'.[54] The document provided a full guide to the way forward on FinTech, and open banking, in particular, and it included details on security standards, and FinTech governance and also suggested 'useful' APIs.

The MAS has also published an API register.[55] The open banking APIs are classified into four 'functions':

- 'Product APIs (e.g., to provide information on financial product details and exchange rates).
- Sales & Marketing APIs (e.g., to handle product sign-ups, sales/cross-sales and leads generation).
- Servicing APIs (e.g., to manage customer profile/account details and customer queries/feedback).
- Transaction APIs (e.g., to support customer instructions for payments, funds transfers, settlements, clearing, trade confirmations and trading).'[56]

The broad approach adopted in Singapore may be best described as 'controlled innovation and competition'. The underlying philosophy was best set out by Ravi Menon, Managing Director of MAS in an address in August 2022, discussing crypto-assets.[57] A similar approach applies to other aspects of FinTech such as open banking. He said that 'Singapore wants to be a hub for innovative and responsible digital asset activities that enhance efficiency and create economic value. The development strategy and regulatory approach for digital assets ... go hand-in-hand towards achieving this ... At the same time, MAS evolving regulatory approach makes Singapore one of the most comprehensive in managing the risks of digital assets, and among the strictest in areas ... '.[58]

The key themes continued to be reiterated by MAS: Singapore's reputation for probity, enhancing public trust, good governance in the public interest and social inclusivity.[59] As in Japan and a number of other jurisdictions, adopting and facilitating open banking is optional for banks. The view is, I believe, that competitive and social pressure will ensure that all the major players cooperate to deliver open banking facilities.

As part of this strategy in December 2020, MAS launched the Singapore Financial Data Exchange (SGFinDex). This consolidated all financial information held by the government and banks into one database. It is accessed by using an individual's Singapore's national digital identity known as the Singapore Personal Access (SingPass).

Ng Chee Khern has said that the 'Government can play a role in building the platforms and frameworks for data sharing and digital collaboration'.[60]

Ng was previously an Air Force general and Director of the government's Security and Intelligence Division. This has been taken further by The Ministry of Manpower and GovTech which have developed an online financial planning service, marketed as 'MyMoneySense'. This makes use of SGFinDex data to provide individuals with a comprehensive overview of their finances.[61] 'MoneySense' is run by the MoneySense Council. The latter is co-chaired by the MAS and the Ministry of Manpower and includes 'representatives from various government agencies'.[62]

One option for Singapore is to lead regional cross-border payments using open banking. This is particularly important when citizens of a number of neighbouring countries do not have bank accounts or access to financial services. However, Singapore's approach is rightly cautious and incremental. The role of the state and its agencies is highly facilitative providing encouragement and also encouraging cooperation.[63]

It is interesting to see the different approach taken by Singapore compared with that in Europe. It may be said that the former sees competition as important at the state level underpinned by business and government cooperation towards a common goal. It sees itself as having close economic and cooperative relationships with other states in Southeast Asia often working via ASEAN.[64] It is helped by having a highly educated, IT-literate and financially astute population. Compared, for example, to Europe, cooperation comes first followed by regulation with the organs of the state ever-present.

China

Opening-up reforms, internet finance and FinTech

When reviewing the Chinese open banking experience, authors have emphasised the country's market-driven ethos, which contrasts with the European regulatory-driven approach.[65] In this context, open banking has followed the transformative changes that have occurred in China since the 1970s through the 'reform and opening-up' policy strategy finalised at the Third Plenary Session of the 11th Central Committee of the Chinese Communist Party.[66] This policy embodied the pursuit of economic growth through the injection of foreign capital and technology and was prompted by the necessity of rebuilding the economy and society in the aftermath of the cultural revolution.[67]

New entrepreneurs and business ventures flourished in the wake of the reforms. The country's financial system also changed radically. Prior to the reforms, the People's Bank of China (PBOC) was the only bank that primarily dealt with savings, lending and remittance services. Amid the reform and opening-up policy, the PBOC was designated by the Ministry of Finance as the country's central bank. Between 1979 and 1983, its commercial banking functions were transferred to four state-owned specialised banks: The Industrial and Commercial Bank of China, the Agricultural Bank of China, the China Construction Bank and the Bank of China.[68]

Until 2003, the Chinese banking system underwent a modernisation process motivated by the increased adoption of computer and network technologies, which significantly improved businesses' automation processes and customer experience.[69] For example, in 1996, the Bank of China launched the country's first RMB-denominated debit card as part of the 1993 'Golden Card Project' aimed at increasing credit card purchases. Meanwhile, twelve nationwide joint-stock banks, including CITIC Bank, Hua Xia Bank and Minsheng Bank were entering the financial arena.[70]

The increased use of computers and network technologies by financial institutions laid the groundwork for the present FinTech era, characterised by the extensive use of emerging technologies such as big data, artificial intelligence (AI), blockchain, Internet of things (IoT) and cloud computing throughout the financial services industry.[71]

An intermediary stage between early modernisation and FinTech was 'Internet finance'. In providing a definition of Internet finance, the 2015 Internet Finance Guidelines ('2015 Guidelines') refer to the growth of online platforms for the provision of payment, lending and investment services.[72] The launch of Alipay in 2004, (as the first online payment service) is the example par excellence of the Internet finance phenomenon, which was then followed by the proliferation of other online platforms targeting the lending and money market fund sales services.[73] In a ten-year time period (2004–14), almost all financial services went online.

The Internet finance era also witnessed the creation of privately owned banks in the financial sector, including Internet banks such as Zhejiang E-Commerce Bank and Shenzhen WeBank, respectively founded by the e-commerce giants Alibaba and Tencent.[74] Despite being initiated by non-bank technology companies, Internet finance soon caught the interest of traditional financial institutions, which recognised how the provision of financial services was becoming increasingly Internet-driven; new players were populating the industry, and hence, traditional firms had to keep abreast of the times. Accordingly, Internet finance has been analysed as a business model involving both traditional financial institutions and Internet enterprises.[75]

For these reasons, the 2015 Guidelines are a framework applicable to all the financial services industry players. Although Internet finance and FinTech are sometimes used interchangeably, the latter represents the evolution of the former into a broader space involving the increased use of big data, AI, cloud computing, blockchain and IoT to further innovation and expand the set of players in the Chinese financial system.[76]

Embracing open banking

Given this background, the development of open banking in China relates to the evolution from Internet finance to FinTech. In practice, the digital-only private banks that flourished at the peak of the Internet finance era were the open banking pacesetters by leveraging the data and technology infrastructure

(AI, big data, cloud computing, blockchain) owned by the big tech companies they are affiliated with.[77] For example, as a subsidiary of Alibaba Group's Ant Financial Services, 'MyBank' is a digital-only private bank that provides loans and other financial services by accessing Alibaba's e-commerce ecosystem customer data.[78] Likewise, 'WeBank' (a digital-only bank founded by Tencent, Baiyeyuan Investment Co. and Liye Group) is active in the lending business and has exclusive access to the data generated by the social network and mobile-game platforms owned by Tencent.[79]

Market-driven initiatives continue to promote the development and diffusion of open banking in China. In 2019, WeBank, leveraging Tencent's cloud platform, announced the launch of the Tencent Cloud–WeBank Fintech Innovation Lab, which will pursue 'cooperative research and development of fintech applications directed at open banking scenarios, help financial institutions to create ubiquitous fintech services, and help drive the development of financial inclusion'.[80]

Digital-only banks have had a substantial impact on the Chinese financial services industry. Rightfully, some authors have stressed that open banking in China has been led by disruption instead of regulatory initiatives.[81] Consequently, traditional financial intermediaries have had to embrace the open banking data-sharing trend as an answer to the increased power of big tech companies through their affiliated digital-only banks. Within this 'innovate or perish' environment, Chinese banks have joined the open banking ecosystem either through partnerships with FinTech firms for data sharing and open banking infrastructure or by launching their own open API facilities—this is the case for large state-owned Chinese banks such as the Industrial and Commercial Bank of China, China Construction Bank and Shanghai Pudong Development Bank.[82]

The path to follow

Banking and FinTech experts predict that innovative technologies will foster the transition from the current era of banking 3.0, characterised mainly by mobile banking, to an open banking 4.0 era, spurred by open APIs.[83] Such development raises the question of whether the Chinese open banking experience will still be led by market-driven approaches. At present, the growing interest in open banking by financial institutions goes hand in hand with regulators' concerns regarding data privacy and security. Recently, Alibaba and Tencent have faced regulatory scrutiny and the imposition of fines for antitrust violations.[84] In addition, regulation tackling unauthorised data collection is also under discussion.[85] Attention is being given to the importance of financial data as the driver of firms' digital transformation, with an attendant necessity for appropriate supervision and control to guarantee privacy, security and customer protection.

As a data-sharing framework, open banking is part of this debate. In particular, in its 2019, 'Open Banking Development Research Report', the

Chinese National Internet Finance Association highlighted the deficiencies that the client-end software provided by financial institutions may have in terms of data privacy and security; they thus encouraged the establishment of a regulatory framework to strengthen customer protection and standards for industry self-discipline.[86]

Recently, the PBOC issued the 'FinTech development Plan 2022-2025' (the Plan), which was formulated in accordance with the '14th Five-Year Plan for National Economic and Social Development of the People's Republic of China and the outline of the Vision for 2035'.[87] The Plan points out that it is necessary to adhere to the development principles of 'digital drive, wisdom for the people, green and low carbon, fairness and inclusiveness'.[88] To fulfil these ends, the Plan proposes eight tasks, described in the following table.[89]

1) Strengthen financial technology governance	• Comprehensively shape digital capabilities • Improve the financial technology ethics system with multiparty participation and collaborative governance • Build a digital ecosystem that promotes mutual progress
2) Strengthen the construction of data capacity	• Promote the orderly sharing and comprehensive application of data • Ensure security and privacy • Fully activate the potential of data elements • Effectively improve the quality and efficiency of financial services
3) Build a green and highly accessible data centre	• Build a green and high-availability data centre • Establish a safe and ubiquitous financial network • Deploy an advanced and efficient computing power system • Consolidate the 'digital base' for financial innovation and development
4) Deepen the financial application of digital technology	• Improve the system and mechanism for the application of scientific and technological achievements with equal emphasis on safety and efficiency • Continuously expand the industrial tenets of openness, innovation, and win-win cooperation • Open the 'last mile' of the transformation of scientific and technological achievements

(Continued)

5) Improve the safety and efficiency of the financial technology innovation system	• Build an integrated operation centre that integrates business, technology and data • Establish an intelligent risk control mechanism • Fully activate the new dynamic energy of digital operations
6) Deepen the intelligent reconstruction of financial services	• Build diversified service channels • Strive to create a barrier-free service system • Provide people with more inclusive, green and human-centred digital financial services
7) Accelerate the all-around application of regulatory technology	• Build strong digital regulatory capabilities • Implement carefully tailored regulations on financial technology innovation • Build a risk firewall between finance and technology
8) Cultivate FinTech talent	• Train more FinTech professionals • Promote the construction of standard rules and regulation • Strengthen the implementation of laws and regulations • Safeguard the stable and long-term development of financial technology

Open banking is an aspect of key task No. 2. The Plan does not explain how the tasks will be achieved, but crucially, the seventh and eighth tasks hint that the fulfilment of these objectives will not be left to the market. Implementation of 'carefully tailored' regulation is expected to be a priority. Chinese open banking will be influenced by these strategies and the legislation to be enacted. China may become an exemplar of how the development of open banking can arise first 'by disruption' and then be further shaped and consolidated through regulation.

Hong Kong SAR

The four-phased Open API approach

The rise of open banking and the issuance of specific regulations in the EU, UK and Australia was observed with great interest in Hong Kong, where the 'Open API Framework for the Hong Kong Banking Sector' was finally promulgated by the Hong Kong Monetary Authority (HKMA) on 18 July

2018.[90] The HKMA Open API Framework addresses retail banking operations, but banks are free to apply its provisions to other banking business activities.[91] The framework encourages strong collaboration among banks and third parties for data-sharing purposes. Accordingly, when reviewing the experience of the open banking pioneer countries, the HKMA emphasised that mandatory approaches would be contemplated only if necessary, instead preferring the main actors to develop the open banking ecosystem through bilateral contractual relationships in a four-stage process under the guidelines set in the Open API Framework.[92] A collaborative, risk-based, and four-phased implementation approach is thus the preferred strategy to reinforce the competitiveness of the banking sector, increase synergies between banks and third parties, improve customer experience through new and innovative services and bring Hong Kong in line with the major international trends in the banking sector.[93]

The four-phased approach has so far undergirded the progress in the creation of an Open API ecosystem in the Hong Kong financial services industry. Under phase I (named 'Product and Service Information'), banks were expected to activate open API functions and provide ('read-only') information on products and services relating to deposits, loans, other services considered as 'core banking services', investments and insurance by January 2019.[94] This phase was relatively simple to implement. The 20 participating retail banks were able to activate more than 500 open APIs by July 2019 and offer product and service information to third parties across the mentioned areas.[95] Additionally, phase I has not required complex governance processes to manage the relationship between banks and third-party Services Providers (TSPs) but anticipates that banks should have in place TSP registration processes for consumer protection purposes.[96] Already in March 2019, 800 TSP registrations for accessing the banks' open APIs had been recorded. Phase I resulted in new apps developed by TSPs for mortgage calculation, price comparisons and foreign exchange rate conversions.[97]

Phase II (named 'subscription and new applications for products/services') was completed by the end of October 2019, and within the deposits, loans, other services, investment and insurance categories, it contemplated the deployment of open APIs regarding data concerning customer acquisition processes.[98] In consultation with TSP representatives and other stakeholders, the HKMA instructed the Hong Kong Association of Banks (HKABs) to develop a Common Baseline for streamlining the TSP onboarding process within Phase II, which was finally published in November 2019.[99] The Common Baseline centres on the banks' duties to conduct onboarding checks and ongoing monitoring of TSPs and the need to govern their relationship with TSPs through bilateral contractual arrangements. Specifically, the Common Baseline includes a set of business and risk management considerations to be followed while implementing Phase II. Business and risk management considerations refer to seven areas: TSP information, TSP governance and general risk management policies and procedures, technology risk management and cyber security, data protection, customer care and business practices, business continuity management and outsourcing.[100] The completion of Phase II saw an increase in partnerships between banks and TSPs and brought new apps that improved customer onboarding.[101]

Phase III ('account information') and Phase IV ('transactions') are the most complex, as they entail, respectively, standalone or aggregated viewing of authenticated customer account information and payment transactions.[102] To ensure secure and efficient implementation of Phase III and Phase IV, the HKMA decided to work closely with the involved stakeholders on a specific set of technical standards to be published in 2020 prior to fixing any implementation timetable. The implementation plan was finally announced in May 2021.[103] As of December 2021, 28 participating banks were poised to begin enacting some clusters of API functions relating to deposit account information and online merchant payments between March and June 2022.[104] In the interim, the HKAB refined the Common Baseline document also to include Phases III and IV within the set of business and risk management considerations and to elaborate high-level guidelines on customer authentication and consent management, user experience, data management, information security and operation standards within the account information area covered by Phase III.[105]

Until now, the implementation process of Phase III has progressed as follows. For the account information pertaining to retail customers, 23 out of 28 banks have launched API functions. Of the remaining five, one set March 2023 as a possible Phase III target go-live date, but the others have not provided any implementation plan.[106] As to the account information relating to corporate and small and medium-sized enterprise (SME) customers, 20 out of 28 banks have launched API functions. The others have either not provided plans or engaged with corporate and SME customers.[107] Regarding Phase IV's open API functions on payment transactions, 26 out of 28 participating banks have launched APIs, but the remaining two have not provided implementation plans to date.[108]

Looking ahead

In conclusion, open banking was initially deemed a necessary initiative to enable the so-called 'New Area of Smart Banking in Hong Kong', which also included the six other initiatives of 'Faster Payment System', 'Enhanced FinTech Supervisory Sandbox', 'Promotion of Virtual Banking', 'Banking Made Easy Initiative', 'Closer Cross-Border Collaboration' and 'Enhanced Research and Talent Development'.[109] Being one of the foundations of smart banking, the HKMA Open API framework is also the staple of the 'FinTech 2025' strategy announced by the central bank in June 2021, particularly as a means of meeting the objectives of increasing FinTech adoption, encouraging full digitalisation of banks' operating systems, and building solid infrastructure to enable consent-based data sharing.[110] The current progress in the implementation of the open API framework phases illustrates that important areas remain to

92 Open Banking Regulation

be examined before the results of open banking in the Hong Kong banking sector are clear. The criticality of Phases III and IV will give the HKMA more practical insights into whether the collaborative approach between banks and TSPs stimulates consumer demand for open banking and guarantees adequate security and risk management within the data-sharing ecosystem.

Indonesia

Financial reforms and open banking significance

In Indonesia, open banking is regarded as a fundamental tool in the country's digital transformation. In its 2019, 'Indonesia Payment System (IPS) Blueprint' (the Blueprint), the Central Bank of Indonesia (BI) underscored the nexus between national economic growth and the creation of a sound digital ecosystem.[111] Since then, public interest in digitalisation has gained momentum, particularly in the financial sector, through the burgeoning of FinTech companies and e-commerce platforms.[112]

The Internet market is also growing in size and is anticipated to generate US$100 billion by 2025.[113] Generations Y and Z are the major adherents of the Indonesian digital ethos, as they have been boosting the payment sector by using mobile devices for debit and credit transfers, thereby accelerating disruption in the financial services industry where non-bank players have continued to proliferate.[114]

Digitalisation is seen as a means to greater prosperity and the opportunity to overcome endemic problems of financial exclusion. Recent data highlight how 51% of the Indonesian population is still unbanked and 62.9 million SMEs face significant difficulties in accessing finance.[115] The BI, however, cautions that, as Indonesia enters the digital area, participants must be aware of the associated risks such as cyber risk, customer data abuse, fraud and anti-competitive practices. The policy objective of creating a healthy digital ecosystem thus entails the need to balance advantages and risks.[116]

Given this background, the Blueprint outlines the Indonesian regulators' key strategies to lead the nation into digitalisation. To this end, the Blueprint lists a set of reforms to the domestic payment system, the stability of which is considered the beating heart of the Indonesian economy, along with a robust monetary system.[117] The reforms are planned to be completed by 2025 and are grounded on five key visions.

- 'IPS 2025 Vision 1 reinforces the integration of the national digital economy and finance to ensure the proper functioning of the central bank mandates regarding money circulation, monetary policy and financial system stability as well as financial inclusion'.
- 'IPS 2025 Vision 2 encourages digital transformation within the banking industry to sustain banks' role as a primary institution in the digital economy and finance through the implementation of open banking standards

Far East 93

as well as the deployment of digital technology and data on their financial product and services'.
- 'IPS 2025 Vision 3 assures FinTech and banks are linked as a means of preventing the escalation of shadow banking risk through the regulation of the use of digital technology (e.g., APIs), business relations and business ownership'.
- 'IPS 2025 Vision 4 strikes a balance among innovation, consumer protection, integrity and stability as well as fair competition through the implementation of digital Know Your Customer (KYC) and Anti-Money Laundering/Combating the Financing of Terrorism (AML-CFT) measures, data/information/public business openness and the deployment of RegTech and SupTech for regulatory and supervisory reporting purposes'.
- 'IPS 2025 Vision 5 is to protect the national interest on the cross-border use of components of the digital economy and finance by requiring domestic processing for all onshore transactions and domestic partnerships for all foreign players, guided by the principle of reciprocity'.[118]

The BI expects to fulfil these visions through five initiatives involving the development of open banking, modernising the retail payment system, creating an adequate financial market infrastructure and a robust public infrastructure for data, and strengthening the regulatory, licensing and supervisory landscape.[119]

Open banking is the first initiative necessary to develop a comprehensive financial system and deepen the links between banks and FinTech, as per IPS 2025 Visions 2 and 3. For these objectives, Indonesian regulators are aiming at an open banking ecosystem founded on data reciprocity. The Blueprint clearly explains that openness must occur on both sides to maintain a level playing field, avoid monopolisation and facilitate the exploitation of more granular data to create more inclusiveness.[120] This is a unique feature compared to the majority of jurisdictions in Europe and other parts of the world where data sharing is only a bank prerogative. APIs are again the preferred technology for enabling open banking. The Blueprint emphasises how open banking development needs to be conducted through open API standardisation, including technical standards, security standards and governance standards.[121]

Given the goals of data reciprocity and stronger collaboration among parties, contractual partnerships are pivotal for developing open banking. Regulators intend to provide leeway to the parties to this end, provided that data access is facilitated on both sides.[122] Customer consent remains central, and the Blueprint envisages an appropriate architecture for consumer consent that can guarantee adequate control and ownership, as well as viable security mechanisms.[123]

Open banking progress

In 2021, important regulatory interventions marked the start of implementing the Blueprint initiatives. The BI issued Regulation No. 23/6/2021 governing Payment Service Providers[124] and Regulation No. 23/7/PBI/2021 relating to Payment System Infrastructure Operators.[125] Both regulations complement Regulation No. 22/23/PBI/2020 concerning the Payment System,[126] also known as the 'master regulation' because it represents a consolidation of previous regulations on the elaboration of national standards for the Indonesian payment system with the new Regulation No. 23/11/PBI/2021 concerning the National Payment System Standard ('PBI SNSP').[127]

After the entry into force of PBI SNSP, the 76th Independence Day of the Republic of Indonesia witnessed further significant initiatives. The BI launched the National Open API Payment Standard (SNAP) and sandbox trials of the Quick Response Code Indonesia Standard (QRIS) and Thai QR Payment interconnectivity.[128] SNAP is the result of cooperation between the BI and the Indonesian Payment System Association through the establishment of the 'National Working Group' and was finally enacted through Regulation PBI SNSP and Regulation No 23/15/PADG/2021 on the implementation of National Standards of Payments using Open API ('SNAP Regulation').[129]

As a set of standards aimed at creating a modern, competitive, secure and efficient payment services industry, SNAP is considered a crucial step for advancing the development of open banking in the Indonesian payment industry and thus accelerating digitalisation through the linking of banks and FinTech companies.[130] In fact, SNAP was issued to improve the integration, interconnectivity and interoperability of payment system infrastructures and payment service providers, whether they are banks or FinTech companies.[131]

On the customer side, SNAP is intended to promote financial inclusion by giving customers access to banks and FinTech apps for making payments. Standard consumer protection rules are also set out, with solid security mechanisms and a guarantee of adequate quality of services required.[132]

Article 3 of the SNAP Regulation specifies the areas covered by the regulation, namely interconnection and interoperability, information system safety standards, governance and risk management in the Open API payment.[133] Bank or non-bank payment service providers are denoted 'service providers' while 'service users' are those payment service providers and other institutions that use open API payment for themselves or their customers' benefit.[134]

The implementation process is divided into stages, with the first involving the players who participated in the drafting of SNAP (Mandiri, BNI, BRI, BCA, Nobu, Gopay, OVO, LinkAja, Dana, DOKU, Midtrans, SPOTS, Yokke, BukaLapak, Tokopedia and Shopee); their implementation deadline was in June 2020.[135] Open API providers are expected to implement the SNAP standards by June 2024, and micro enterprises and SMEs must complete implementation by June 2025.[136]

The BI has created the 'SNAP Developer Site' to coordinate and facilitate the implementation process. Accordingly, the site is the venue for the development of the so-called 'SNAP Technical Standards', namely technical and security standards, data standards and technical specifications.[137] Service providers and users, as well as API developers, must register on the SNAP

Developer Site and certify that their own systems comply with the SNAP Technical Standards.[138]

SNAP governance guidelines shall also cover consumer protection, data protection and prudential requirements for service providers and users.[139] Finally, regarding data sharing, the SNAP Regulation refers to the data relating to credit and debit cards, account information, balance inquiries, transaction histories and credit and debit card transfer data.[140]

The way forward

The Blueprint visions are the stepping stones that may enable Indonesia to harness the benefits of a digital economy. Open banking is featured as the first 2025 Blueprint initiative and the engine for sound collaboration between traditional financial intermediaries and FinTech players to the benefit of financial customers, who remain central in the banking scheme through their consent to data sharing. Looking to the future, further action can be taken for achieving a full open banking development. In this respect, some authors suggest that Indonesian open banking is characterised by a lack of consumer knowledge on the meaningfulness of open banking coupled with financial institutions' reluctance to share data with third parties because of privacy and security concerns[141]. Consequently, in accordance with the standardisation strategies pursued by Indonesian regulators, the optimal design of the open banking ecosystem must also reinforce the centrality of consumers by enhancing their (open banking) literacy.

Conclusion

By focussing on the Far East region, this chapter analyses the establishment and implementation of open banking across several jurisdictions. Consumer data ownership and data sharing are the drivers behind the Australian and New Zealander open banking frameworks. In the rest of the region, open banking is instrumental in helping those segments of the population that are underserved and in enhancing digitalisation and innovation programmes. Against this backdrop, open banking is part of reforms led by national central banks. Overall, the Far East is an interesting mixture of regulatory and market-driven (open banking) approaches.

Notes

1 Parliament of Australia, 'Review of the Four Major Banks: First Report', (November 2016), 2, <https://www.aph.gov.au/Parliamentary_Business/Committees/House/Economics/Four_Major_Banks_Review/Report>, accessed 22 August 2022.
2 Ibid., (Review of the Four Major Banks), 37–46.
3 Australian Treasury, Competition Policy Review – Final Report Website ('The Harper Review'), (2015), <https://treasury.gov.au/publication/p2015-cpr-final-report>, accessed 25 August 2022.

96 Open Banking Regulation

4 Ibid., (2015 Report), 5354.
5 Australian Government, 'Review into Open Banking in Australia: Issues Paper', (August 2017), 1, <https://treasury.gov.au/sites/default/files/2019-03/Review-into-Open-Banking-IP.pdf>, accessed 22 August 2022.
6 Ibid., ('Review into Open Banking in Australia'), 2 and 3.
7 Supra (n 1), ('Review of the Four Major Banks'), iii.
8 Australian Treasury, 'Review into Open Banking: Giving Customers Choice, Convenience and Confidence', (December 2017) <https://treasury.gov.au/sites/default/files/2019-03/Review-into-Open-Banking-_For-web-1.pdf>, accessed 16 September 2023.
9 Ibid., ('Open Banking Review'), 109.
10 Australian Parliament website, 'Report by the House of Representatives Standing Committee on Economics, Treasury Laws Amendment (Consumer Data Right) Bill 2019', (21 March 2019), <https://www.aph.gov.au/Parliamentary_Business/Committees/Senate/Economics/TLABConsumerDataRight/Report>, accessed 25 August 2022.
11 Ibid., (2019 Standing Committee Report), 9 and 1317.
12 Competition and Consumer (Consumer Data Right) Rules 2020.
13 Australian Competition and Consumer Commission website, 'Consumer Data Right (CDR)', <https://www.accc.gov.au/focus-areas/consumer-data-right-cdr-0>, accessed 25 August 2022.
14 Australian Treasury, 'Future Directions for the Consumer Data Right', <https://treasury.gov.au/sites/default/files/2021-02/cdrinquiry-final.pdf>, accessed 25 August 2022.
15 Ibid., ('Future Directions'), xivxviii.
16 Supra (n 13), (ACCC website), (Consumer Data Right (CDR) Project).
17 Australian Treasury, 'Payments System Review', (June 2021), vii, <https://treasury.gov.au/sites/default/files/2021-08/p2021-198587.pdf>, accessed 25 August 2022.
18 Ibid., ('Payments System Review'), vii.
19 Ibid., ('Payments System Review'), xixv.
20 ACCC website press release, 'Eftpos, BPAY Group and NPPA Propose to Amalgamate for the Benefit of Australian Consumers and Businesses', (December 2020), <https://www.accc.gov.au/system/files/public-registers/documents/85.%20Media%20Release%20-%20eftpos%2C%20BPAY%20Group%20and%20NPPA%20propose%20to%20amalgamate%20for%20the%20benefit%20of%20Australian%20consumers%20and%20businesses%2C%2015%20December%202020.pdf>, accessed 25 August 2022.
21 ACCC website, 'ACCC Authorises Payment Systems Merger after Undertaking', (9 September 2021), <https://www.accc.gov.au/media-release/accc-authorises-payment-systems-merger-after-undertaking>, accessed 25 August 2022.
22 PYMNTS, 'New Payments Platform Australia Merges with Eftpos, BPAY', (15 December 2020), <https://www.pymnts.com/news/b2b-payments/2020/new-payments-platform-australia-merges-with-eftpos-bpay/>, accessed 25 August 2022.
23 Philip Lowe, Governor of the Reserve Bank of Australia, speech to the Australian Payments Network, 'Innovation and Regulation in the Australian Payments System', 7 December 2020, <https://www.rba.gov.au/speeches/2020/pdf/sp-gov-2020-12-07.pdf>, accessed 25 August 2022.
24 Treasury, 'Government Response to the Inquiry into Future Directions for the Consumer Data Right', (December 2021), 13, 17 and 18, <https://treasury.gov.au/publication/p2021-225462>, accessed 25 August 2022.
25 Treasury website, 'Statutory Review of the Consumer Data Right', <https://treasury.gov.au/review/statutory-review-consumer-data-right>, accessed 25 August 2022.
26 API Centre NZ Payments website, <https://www.apicentre.paymentsnz.co.nz/about/background/>, accessed 25 August 2022.

Far East 97

27 Payments NZ website, 'Research and Reports', <https://www.paymentsnz.co.nz/resources/research-reports/>, accessed 26 August 2022.
28 Ibid., ('Research and Reports').
29 Ibid., ('Research and Reports').
30 Ibid., ('Research and Reports').
31 Kris Faafoi Letter of December 2019, <https://www.mbie.govt.nz/assets/open-letter-to-api-providers-regarding-industry-progress-on-api-enabled-data-sharing-and-open-banking.pdf>, accessed 26 August 2022.
32 Official New Zealand Government website, 'Govt Agrees to Establish a Consumer Data Right', (6 July 2021), <https://www.beehive.govt.nz/release/govt-agrees-establish-consumer-data-right>, accessed 26 August 2022.
33 New Zealand Ministry of Business Innovation and Employment website, 'Consumer Data Rights', <https://www.mbie.govt.nz/business-and-employment/business/competition-regulation-and-policy/consumer-data-right/>, accessed 26 August 2022.
34 Minutes of the Cabinet Economic Development Committee Meeting on 21 June 2021, <https://www.mbie.govt.nz/dmsdocument/15539-establishing-a-consumer-data-right-minute-of-decision-proactiverelease-pdf>, accessed 26 August 2021.
35 FinTech NZ website, 'Open Banking Stimulating NZ Economy', 27 July 2022, <https://fintechnz.org.nz/2022/07/27/open-banking-stimulating-nz-economy/>, accessed 26 August 2022.
36 Nikkei Asia website, 'Where Are Japan's Neo Banks?', (11 May 2021), <https://asia.nikkei.com/Opinion/Where-are-Japan-s-neo-banks>, accessed 30 August 2022.
37 Japanese Bankers Association website, 'Financial Institutions in Japan', <https://www.zenginkyo.or.jp/en/banks/financial-institutions/>, accessed 30 August 2022.
38 Sean Creehan and Paul Tierno, 'The Slow Introduction of Open Banking and APIs in Japan' (2 May 2019), Federal Reserve Bank of San Francisco, <https://www.frbsf.org/banking/asia-program/pacific-exchanges-podcast/open-banking-apis-japan/>, accessed 30 August 2022.
39 The Japanese Financial Services Authority, 'Strategic Priorities July 2021June 2022, Overcoming COVID-19 and Building the Financial System for Greater Vibrancy', 13, <https://www.fsa.go.jp/en/news/2021/20211008/20211008.html>, accessed 30 August 2022.
40 Ibid., (FSA Strategic Priorities).
41 Taiwanese Financial Services Commission website, 'Work Focus for 2022', <https://www.fsc.gov.tw/userfiles/file/2022%20FSC%20press%20release.pdf>, accessed 27 August 2022.
42 FSC website, 'FSC Continues to Promote Phase 2 (Customer Information Inquiries) of Open Banking Initiative', 2 September 2021, <https://www.fsc.gov.tw/en/home.jsp?id=74&parentpath=0,2&mcustomize=multimessage_view.jsp&dataserno=202102090008&dtable=Bulletin>, accessed 27 August 2022.
43 Fintech News website, 'Taiwan Furthers Open Banking Ambitions', 3 February 2021, <https://fintechnews.hk/14698/fintechtaiwan/taiwan-furthers-open-banking-ambitions/>, accessed 27 August 2022.
44 Financial Services Commission (FSC) website, 'Banks' Financial Payment System to Be Open to FinTech Firms', (25 February 2019), <https://www.fsc.go.kr/eng/pr010101/22203>, accessed 30 August 2022.
45 FSC website, 'Financial Policy Roadmap for 2019', (7 March 2019), <https://www.fsc.go.kr/eng/pr010101/22204?srchCtgry=&curPage=&srchKey=&srchText=&srchBeginDt=&srchEndDt=>, accessed 30 August 2022.
46 Korea Financial Telecommunications & Clearings Institute (KFTC) website, <https://www.kftc.or.kr/kftcEn/about/EgovEnDcsMaking.do>, accessed 30 August 2022.
47 Ibid., (KFTC Website).

98 *Open Banking Regulation*

48 FSC website, 'Open Banking', <https://www.fsc.go.kr/eng/po030101>, accessed 30 August 2022.
49 Ibid., (website, 'Open Banking').
50 Ibid., (website, 'Open Banking').
51 Supra (n 44), FSC website ('Banks' Financial Payment System to Be Open to Fintech Firms').
52 Ibid., (FSC Website).
53 FSC website, '3rd Digital Finance Meeting Unveils Ways to Advance Open Banking System', (21 October 2020), <https://www.fsc.go.kr/eng/pr010101/22522>, accessed 30 August 2022.
54 Monetary Authority of Singapore (MAS) and the Association of Banks in Singapore (ABS), 'Finance-as-a-Service: API Playbook', (2016) <https://www.mas.gov.sg/-/media/MAS/Smart-Financial-Centre/API/ABSMASAPIPlaybook.pdf>, accessed 5 September 2022.
55 Monetary Authority of Singapore (MAS) website, 'Financial Industry API Register', <https://www.mas.gov.sg/development/fintech/financial-industry-api-register>, accessed 5 September 2022.
56 Ibid., (MAS website re API Register).
57 Opening Address by Mr Ravi Menon, Managing Director, Monetary Authority of Singapore, at Green Shoots Seminar on 29 August 2022 <https://www.mas.gov.sg/news/speeches/2022/yes-to-digital-asset-innovation-no-to-cryptocurrency-speculation>, accessed 5 September 2022.
58 Ibid., (Menon Address).
59 MAS website, 'Strengthening Trust in Finance', the opening address by Ravi Menon, Managing Director, Monetary Authority of Singapore, at Symposium on Asian Banking and Finance, (3 June 2019), <https://www.mas.gov.sg/news/speeches/2019/strengthening-trust-in-finance>, accessed 5 September 2022.
60 Permanent Secretary (Smart Nation and Digital Government) under the Prime Minister's Office, and the Chairman of Government Technology Agency (GovTech).
61 MoneySense website, <https://www.mymoneysense.gov.sg>, accessed 5 September 2022.
62 MoneySense website, About MoneySense, <https://www.mymoneysense.gov.sg/about-us>, accessed 5 September 2022.
63 For example, see the MAS website, 'Indonesia and Singapore to Pursue Cross-Border QR Code Payments Connectivity and Explore Promoting the Use of Local Currencies for Bilateral Transactions', 'Bank Indonesia and the Monetary Authority of Singapore today announced the commencement of work on a cross-border QR payment linkage between Indonesia and Singapore as part of the ASEAN-wide payments connectivity effort. This linkage, which is targeted to be launched in the second half of 2023, will allow users to make instant, secure and efficient retail payments by scanning the QRIS (Quick Response Code Indonesian Standard)', (29 August 2022), <https://www.mas.gov.sg/news/media-releases/2022/indonesia-and-singapore-cross-border-qr-code-payments-connectivity-and-use-of-local-currencies-for-bilateral-transactions>, accessed 5 September 2022.
64 For example, see the Singapore Ministry of Foreign website, <https://www.mfa.gov.sg/SINGAPORES-FOREIGN-POLICY/Countries-and-Regions/Southeast-Asia/Vietnam>, accessed 5 September 2022.
65 Richard Turrin, 'Open Finance Global Progress Ebook: China: Open Banking by Disruption' (*Open Future World*, 28 April 2022) Open Future World <https://openfuture.world/open-finance-global-progress-ebook-china-open-banking-by-disruption/>, accessed 6 November 2022; Kanika Hope, 'Open Banking and the Rise of Banking-as-a-Service', (*Temenos*, September 2021) 7 <www.temenos.com/wp-content/uploads/2022/06/Open-Banking-and-the-Rise-of-Banking-as-a-Service-V4.

pdf>, accessed 6 November 2022; Adrian Klee, 'Asia Is the Next Frontier in Open Banking', (*RossRepublic*, 2 December 2020) <https://rossrepublic.com/asia-is-the-next-frontier-in-open-banking/>, accessed 6 November 2022.
66 Shigeo Kobayashi, Jia Baobo and Junya Sano, 'The "Three Reforms" in China: Progress and Outlook', (1999) 45 RIM Pacific Business Industry, Japan Research Institute 2 <www.jri.co.jp/english/periodical/rim/1999/RIMe199904three-reforms/>, accessed 15 November 2022; Jacques deLisle and Avery Goldstein, 'China's Economic Reform and Opening at Forty: Past Accomplishments and Emerging Challenges', in Jacques de Lisle and Avery Goldstein (eds.), *To Get Rich Is Glorious: Challenges Facing China's Economic Reform and Opening at Forty* (The Brookings Institution, Washington D.C. 2019) 1.
67 Ibid.
68 Jie Hu and Kai Keller, *At a Crossroads: The Next Chapter for FinTech in China* (White Paper in collaboration with Shanghai Advanced Institute of Finance, March 2021) 5 World Economic Forum <www3.weforum.org/docs/WEF_The_Next_Chapter_for_FinTech_in_China_2021.pdf>, accessed 15 November 2022.
69 Ibid., 6.
70 Ibid., 9.
71 Ibid., 12.
72 People's Bank of China (PBOC), 'Guiding Opinions on Promoting the Sound Development of Internet Finance', (July 2015) <https://uk.practicallaw.thomsonreuters.com/2-617-6285?transitionType=Default&contextData=(sc.Default)&firstPage=true>, accessed 20 November 2022.
73 Hu and Keller (n 68) 10.
74 Wu Hongyuran and Zhang Yuzhe 'China Boots Up an Internet Banking Industry, Tencent and Alibaba Usher in Cyberspace Borrowing', (*ChinaFile*, 27 January 2015) <www.chinafile.com/reporting-opinion/caixin-media/china-boots-internet-banking-industry>, accessed 20 November 2022.
75 Duoqi Xu, John Taylor, and Yuanda Ren, 'Wait-and-See or Whack-a-Mole: What Is the Best Way to Regulate FinTech in China?', (2022) Asian Journal of Law and Society, 1 published online by Cambridge University Press <www.cambridge.org/core/journals/asian-journal-of-law-and-society/article/abs/waitandsee-or-whackamole-what-is-the-best-way-to-regulate-fintech-in-china/D0FB0F29BE4BCD-0B7AF7A19BD4A95345>, accessed 25 November 2022.
76 Xiao Xiang and others, 'China's Path to FinTech Development', (2017) European Economy 143 <https://european-economy.eu/wp-content/uploads/2017/12/China%C3%A2%E2%82%AC%E2%84%A2s-Path-to-FinTech-Development.pdf>, accessed 25 November 2022; see also Xiuping Hua and Yiping Huang, 'Understanding China's FinTech Sector: Development, Impacts and Risks', (2020) University of Nottingham Ningbo China, 1 <https://core.ac.uk/download/pdf/334410228.pdf>, accessed 25 November 2022.
77 Lei Zhou and others, 'Research on the Development of Open Banking in China under the Background of Internet Finance', (*European Union Digital Library*, 13 October 2022) 1 <https://eudl.eu/doi/10.4108/eai.17-6-2022.2322702>, accessed 25 November 2022.
78 Tracey Xiang, 'Open Banking Development Drives Data-sharing in China', (*Miotech*, 16 September 2019) <www.miotech.com/en-US/article/49>, accessed 25 November 2022.
79 Ibid.
80 China Banking News, 'Tencent Cloud and WeBank Launch Fintech Lab to Explore Open Banking in China', (*China Banking News*, 1 April 2019) <www.chinabankingnews.com/2019/04/01/tencent-cloud-and-webank-launch-fintech-lab-to-explore-open-banking/>, accessed 28 November 2022.
81 Turrin (n 65).

82 Ibid.
83 Banking Frontiers, 'China Takes Baby Steps to Bring in Open Banking', (24 December 2020) <https://bankingfrontiers.com/china-takes-baby-steps-to-bring-in-open-banking/>, accessed 25 November 2022.
84 Global Times, 'China's Anti-monopoly Watchdog Fines Alibaba, Tencent for Failing to Report Deals', (10 July 2022) <www.globaltimes.cn/page/202207/1270170.shtml>, accessed 28 November 2022.
85 Banking Frontiers (n 83).
86 Ibid.
87 The State Council, the People's Republic of China, 'The People's Bank of China Issued the FinTech Development Plan (20222025)', (5 January 2022) <www.gov.cn/xinwen/2022-01/05/content_5666525.htm>, accessed 28 November 2022.
88 Ibid.
89 Ibid., English Translation.
90 Hong Kong Monetary Authority (HKMA), 'Open API Framework for the Hong Kong Banking Sector', (18 July 2018) <www.hkma.gov.hk/media/eng/doc/key-information/press-release/2018/20180718e5a2.pdf>, accessed 3 May 2023.
91 Ibid., Title III ('Open API Framework'), para 7 ('Applicability'), 2.
92 Ibid., para 8.2 ('Guiding Principles'), 3.
93 Ibid., para 13 ('A Phased Approach'), 5.
94 Ibid., Annex A ('Open API Functions') A4, 20.
95 International Monetary Fund (IMF), *People's Republic of China-Hong Kong Special Administrative Region* (IMF Country Report No. 21/116, 8 June 2021) Technical Note-Implication of FinTech for the Regulation and Supervision of the Financial Sector, 37 <www.imf.org/en/Publications/CR/Issues/2021/06/04/Peoples-Republic-of-China-Hong-Kong-Special-Administrative-Region-Financial-System-Stability-50197>, accessed 3 May 2023.
96 HKMA (n 90) para 33 ('Phase I'), 11.
97 IMF (n 95) 37.
98 HKMA (n 90) Annex A ('Open API Functions') A8, 22.
99 The Hong Kong Association of Banks (HKAB), 'Open API Framework for the Hong Kong Banking Sector Phase II Common Baseline', (15 November 2019) 2 <https://www.hkab.org.hk/DisplayArticleAction.do?sid=5&ss=32>, accessed 6 May 2023.
100 Ibid., 23.
101 IMF (n 95) 37.
102 HKMA (n 90) Annex A ('Open API Functions') A12 and A13, 23.
103 HKMA, 'The Implementation Plan for Phase III and IV Open Application Programming Interface (Open API)', (2021) <www.hkma.gov.hk/eng/news-and-media/press-releases/2021/05/20210513-3/>, accessed 6 May 2023; the plan is based on the recommendation set in the 2021 HKMA and Accenture joint report, see HKMA and Accenture, *The Next Phase of the Banking Open API Journey* (2021) 8 <www.hkma.gov.hk/media/eng/doc/key-functions/ifc/fintech/The_Next_Phase_of_the_Banking_Open_API_Journey.pdf>, accessed 06 May 2023.
104 HKMA, 'The Four Phases of Open API', (2023) <www.hkma.gov.hk/eng/key-functions/international-financial-centre/fintech/open-application-programming-interface-api-for-the-banking-sector/phase-approach/>, accessed 10 May 2023; see also HKMA, 'The Target Go-live Dates of Phase III and Phase IV Open API Functions of Each Bank', (2023) <www.hkma.gov.hk/eng/key-functions/international-financial-centre/fintech/open-application-programming-interface-api-for-the-banking-sector/target-dates/>, accessed 10 May 2023.

105 HKBA, 'Open API Framework for the Hong Kong Banking Sector Common Baseline', (14 December 2021) 2 <www.hkab.org.hk/DisplayArticleAction.do?sid=5&ss=32>, accessed 10 May 2023.
106 HKMA (n 104).
107 Ibid.
108 Ibid.
109 Norman T. L. Chan, 'A New Era of Smart Banking', (*HKMA*, 28 September 2017) Opening Keynote Speech at HKIB Annual Banking Conference 2017 <www.hkma.gov.hk/eng/news-and-media/speeches/2017/09/20170929-1/>, accessed 10 May 2023.
110 HKMA, 'The HKMA Unveils "Fintech 2025" Strategy', (8 June 2021) Press Release <www.hkma.gov.hk/eng/news-and-media/press-releases/2021/06/20210608-4/>, accessed 10 May 2023.
111 Bank Indonesia, 'Indonesia Payment System Blueprint 2025. Bank Indonesia: Navigating the National Payment System in the Digital Era', (28 November 2019) 1 <www.bi.go.id/en/publikasi/kajian/Documents/Indonesia-Payment-Systems-Blueprint-2025.pdf>, accessed 5 February 2023.
112 Nadiva Aliyya Aryaputri, 'State of Open Banking 2021: Indonesia', (*Fintechnews*, 5 April 2021) <https://fintechnews.sg/50091/openbanking/state-of-open-banking-2021-indonesia/>, accessed 5 February 2023.
113 Bank Indonesia (n 111) 8.
114 Ibid., 6.
115 Ibid.
116 Ibid., 7.
117 Ibid., 16.
118 Ibid., summary table at page 3.
119 Ibid., 3.
120 Ibid., 22.
121 Ibid., 31.
122 Ibid., 32.
123 Ibid., 27: 'The opening of customer data by the bank does not violate the confidentiality of customer data as long as it is initiated by the consent of the consumers who own the data and information'.
124 Bank Indonesia, 'Regulation Number 23/6/PBI/2021 on Payment Services Providers by the Blessings of the Almighty God', (2021) Governor of Bank Indonesia <www.bi.go.id/en/publikasi/peraturan/Documents/PBI_230621_EN.pdf>, accessed 10 February 2023.
125 Bank Indonesia, 'Regulation Number 23/7/PBI/2021 on Payment System Infrastructure Providers by the Blessings of the Almighty God', (2021) Governor of Bank Indonesia <www.bi.go.id/en/publikasi/peraturan/Documents/PBI_230721_en.pdf>, accessed 10 February 2023.
126 Bank Indonesia, 'Regulation Number 23/7/PBI/2020 on Payment System by the Blessing of the Almighty God', (2020) Governor of Bank Indonesia <www.bi.go.id/en/publikasi/peraturan/Documents/PBI_222320.pdf>, accessed 12 February 2023.
127 Bank Indonesia, 'Regulation Number 23/11/PBI/2021 on National Payment System Standard by the Blessing of Almighty God', (2021) <www.bi.go.id/id/publikasi/peraturan/Documents/PBI_231121.pdf>, accessed 15 February 2023.
128 Erwin Haryono, 'Bank Indonesia Launches National Open API Payment Standard and Sandbox Trials of QRIS and Thai QR Payment Interconnectivity', (*Bank Indonesia*, 17 August 2021) <www.bi.go.id/en/publikasi/ruang-media/news-release/Pages/sp_2321121.aspx>, accessed 15 February 2023.

129 Bank Indonesia, 'Board of Governors Regulation Number 23/15/PADG/2021 on the Implementation of the National Open API Payment Standard (SNAP Regulation)', English translation available at <https://legalcentric.com/content/view/167577>, accessed 20 February 2023. See also Bank Indonesia, 'National Open API Standard', (2021) Version 1.0 <www.bi.go.id/id/layanan/Standar/SNAP/Documents/SNAP_Pedoman_Tata_Kelola.pdf>, accessed 20 February 2023.
130 Billiam Billiam, Lastuti Abubakar, and Tri Handayani, 'The Urgency of Open Application Programming Interface Standardization in the Implementation of Open Banking to Customer Data Protection for the Advancement of Indonesian Banking', (2022) 9 Padjajjaran Journal of Law 1, 63. See also, Bank Indonesia (n 129).
131 Ibid.
132 Ibid.
133 SNAP Regulation, art 3.
134 SNAP Regulation, art 1.
135 Bank Indonesia, *Transformation of the Policy Mix and Acceleration of the Digital Economy and Finance* (Economic Report on Indonesia, 2021) ch 6, 113 <www.bi.go.id/en/publikasi/laporan/Documents/8_LPI2021_EN_Chapter_6.pdf#search=snap>, accessed 25 February 2023; see also Fabiola Hutagalung and Nikita Priscila, 'Digital Payment Made Easier Thanks to Cross-Border QRIS and National Open API Standard (SNAP)', (*Dentons HRPR*, 23 June 2022) <https://dentons.hprplawyers.com/en/insights/alerts/2022/june/23/digital-payments-made-easier-thanks-to-cross-border-qris-and-snap>, accessed 25 February 2023.
136 Ibid.
137 SNAP Developer Site <https://apidevportal.bi.go.id/snap/>, accessed 25 February 2023.
138 Ibid.
139 SNAP Regulation, art 3(3) and art 5(2)(3)(4).
140 Billiam, Abubakar, and Handayani (n 130) 76.
141 Brankas Rupertus and Arvinci Ngabut, 'Open Finance Global Progress Ebook: Indonesia' (Open Future World, 17 May 2022) <https://openfuture.world/open-finance-global-progress-ebook-indonesia/>, accessed 27 February 2023.

7 Middle East and North Africa Region

Open banking and FinTech development in Middle East and North Africa countries

Open banking is pivotal to the burgeoning Middle East and North Africa (MENA) region's FinTech ecosystem. With more than 400 million inhabitants, the region encompasses 18 countries divided into three macro areas encompassing the Arab States of the Gulf (Bahrain, Kuwait, Oman, Qatar, the Kingdom of Saudi Arabia [KSA] and the United Arab Emirates [UAE]), the Islamic Republic of Iran and the Near East (Iraq, Israel, Jordan, Lebanon, occupied Palestinian territory, Syria) and North Africa (Algeria, Egypt, Libya, Morocco, Tunisia).[1]

Recent studies have described the MENA region's financial system as heavily bank-based and at different stages of growth depending on the wealth and resources of the countries.[2] Overall, MENA's financial environment faces numerous challenges. Of adult men in MENA, 67% are underserved, and small and medium-sized enterprises (SMEs) struggle to access finance, unlike large firms, which are mainly state-owned or can secure government support.[3] FinTech is regarded as a facilitator of inclusion and economic growth. The latest data provided by the Cambridge Centre of Alternative Finance reveal how MENA regulators have different perceptions of the potential of FinTech compared to other regulators worldwide. Specifically, although they regard FinTech as instrumental in enhancing inclusion and market development and promoting competition and digital financial services, MENA regulators also tend to be concerned about its ability to fulfil consumer protection and financial stability objectives.[4]

Nevertheless, the consensus opinion is that FinTech is booming in the MENA region, although lagging in comparison to the European and Asia–Pacific (APAC) hubs. The rise of FinTech in the MENA region has been nurtured by a combination of factors, the first of which is the increased technology usage by the MENA population. The International Monetary Fund (IMF) has highlighted how the region has the world's second youngest population, who are IT literate and open to digital solutions for their life needs.[5] Consequently, the demand for digital products and services is strong. The young generations' attraction to technology and digital services is also

DOI: 10.4324/9781003331339-9

coupled with a FinTech-supportive regulatory environment, through which MENA governments are intent on developing a powerful ecosystem for attracting investment and global players in the hope of generating substantial economic growth.[6]

Local central banks are currently leading the reforms and transformative processes to shape such an ecosystem. Regulatory sandboxes are widely adopted in Gulf Council Countries (GCCs) and North African countries to test ideas and innovations.[7] Free zones are also fundamental to the rise of FinTech in the MENA region, particularly in GCC countries. Since the creation of the Jebel Ali Free Zone in Dubai in 1985, free zones have proliferated, and there are currently more than 70 free zones across Bahrain, Kuwait, Oman, Qatar, the KSA and the UAE.[8] Through special tax, customs and import regimes and their own regulatory frameworks, free zones offer considerable opportunities and incentives to foreign investors.[9] The UAE is home to the largest number of free zones. The Dubai International Financial Centre (DIFC) is one of the most prominent free zones for financial services,[10] and the DIFC FinTech Hive is the major initiative implemented by the DIFC to connect FinTech, InsurTech, RegTech and Islamic FinTech firms to share ideas, products and services to accelerate innovation in the Middle East–Africa–South Asia region.[11]

The MENA FinTech market is currently developing around the following areas: Money transfers and payments, savings and investments, digital lending and lending marketplaces, online insurance and insurance marketplaces.[12] In the first half of 2022, FinTech investment in the MENA region amounted to $810 million.[13] Eight hundred Fintech start-ups are located in the region, with the UAE having the largest number, followed by Egypt, Jordan and Lebanon.[14] In 2024, the total revenue of the MENA FinTech market is expected to grow to $188 billion and continue to grow at a compound annual growth rate of 8% until 2028.[15]

Open banking is gaining momentum in the MENA region as the force for the development of FinTech markets and an enabler of new business opportunities for participants. At present, however, open banking implementation is rather uneven. Regulatory approaches are in place in some jurisdictions, but others are taking a wait-and-see approach or pursuing market-driven solutions. The following sections examine the latest advancements with a specific focus on GCCs.

Bahrain

Bahrain is regarded as a FinTech leader and open banking pioneer because of the implementation of a specific regulation. In its capacity as the single regulator and supervisor of all the Bahraini financial institutions, the Central Bank of Bahrain (CBB) convened industry consultations and launched the first open banking regulatory sandbox in 2018. Feedbacks and examinations resulted in the issuance of the 'Bahrain Open Banking Framework'

(BOBF) version 1.1.0 in October 2020.[16] Since then, further initiatives have been taken to enable all the participants to adapt to the new ecosystem in an effective and secure manner.

The BOBF builds on the most advanced open banking regimes, particularly the EU Payment Service Directive 2 (EU PSD2), the UK Open Banking Standards and the open banking rules set out in the Australian Consumer Data Rights (CDRs). The BOBF is part of the CBB Rulebook, which is the main source of all financial rules, regulations and standards in Bahrain.[17]

The CBB Rulebook consists of seven volumes, covering conventional bank licensees (Volume 1), Islamic bank licensees (Volume 2), insurance licensees (Volume 3), investment firm licensees (Volume 4), specialised licensees (Volume 5), capital markets (Volume 6) and collective investment undertakings (Volume 7).[18] Each volume is divided into Part A and Part B. Part B provides a glossary, CBB authorisation or reporting forms and supplementary information, whereas Part A divides the rules into chapters called 'Modules'.[19]

The BOBF rules can be analysed in Volumes 1, 2 and 5. Volumes 1 and 2 subject both conventional and Islamic banks to common open banking rules in their General Requirements Module, Licensing Requirement Module and CBB Reporting Requirement Module.[20] The General Requirement Module contains the obligation for conventional and Islamic banks to share their customer data with third parties with customer consent.[21] To date, the data-sharing obligation has only concerned conventional retail banks and Islamic retail banks. Corporate and/or wholesale banks, however, will have to comply with the same requirements at a later stage.

The data-sharing requirement for Bahraini retail banks exhibits some alignments with the major European and Australian open banking frameworks. To start, data sharing is not subject to the imposition of fees by banks. The possibility of charging fees is only contemplated in the case of third-party requests for access to 'Value Added Data' and 'Aggregated Data'.[22] Regarding the type of data that can be accessed by third parties, the General Requirement Module clarifies that the obligation only pertains to information customers have provided (and can be accessed) in digital form. Such information spans transaction data to product/service data, including information on prices and fees.[23] The BOBF then clarifies the type of product/service associated with these data: (a) savings accounts, (b) current accounts, (c) term and call deposits, (d) foreign currency accounts, (e) unrestricted investment accounts, (f) restricted investment accounts, (g) mortgage/housing finance products, (h) auto loans, (i) consumer loans/financing, (j) overdrafts (personal), (k) credit and charge cards, (l) electronic wallets and prepaid cards and (m) other accounts that are accessible to the customer through an e-banking portal or mobile device.[24]

The General Requirement Module demands that conventional and Islamic retail banks provide access to account information and data for the preceding 12 months or 365 days at the time of access.[25] The banks are then required to adhere to the operational guidelines, security standards, strong customer authentication rules, application programming interface (API) specifications and customer journey guidelines set out in the BOBF. To this end, the CBB requires the involved banks to ensure compliance through tests and reviews (even on-site) conducted by independent consultants.[26]

Volume 5 of the CBB Rulebook includes rules on third parties. Titled 'Specialised Licensees', this volume is complex, as it addresses all those financial players performing activities and services not regulated under Volumes 1–4, 6 and 7.[27] In practice, Volume 5 governs the following specialised licensees, each of them the subject of a specific module: Money Changers Licensees, Representative Office Licensees, Financing Companies, Administrators, Trust Service Providers, Microfinance Institutions and Ancillary Service Providers.[28] Account Information Service Providers (AISPs) and Payment Initiation Service Providers (PISPs) are categorised as Ancillary Service Providers and governed under their specific 'Open Banking Module'.[29] Under these rules, AISPs and PISPs can request access to all licensees maintaining a customer account (conventional retail banks, Islamic retail banks and PSPs operating electronic wallets) through APIs.[30]

The Open Banking Module provides strict regulatory standards to ensure that customer data are managed by third parties securely. To this end, the module contemplates provisions on operational risks and internal controls to ensure that business operations are conducted with rigorous safeguards for customers and financial institutions granting data access.[31] As to the interface to be used for data-sharing purposes, the CBB referred to the European experience and demanded that both banks and third parties adopt the UK API standards.[32]

Overall, the Bahraini open banking framework is the answer to the Kingdom's objective to develop a fully digital ecosystem. Despite the implementation of open banking still needing to be completed by extending the data-sharing rules to corporate and wholesale banking, Bahrain can be regarded as the jurisdiction that has paved the way for advancing open banking in the MENA region. The development of open banking is concordant with open finance objectives. Bahrain is therefore considering, like other jurisdictions worldwide, to go beyond the banking sphere. In this respect, the firm FinTech Galaxy was the first to receive an open finance license as an AISP to integrate with bank APIs.[33] Bahrain has forged the open banking pathway, and its framework and implementation progress so far can inspire the region.

Kingdom of Saudi Arabia (KSA)

In the KSA, the design and implementation of an open banking ecosystem must be explained in connection with a set of social and economic reforms aimed at reducing the country's dependence on the oil sector and increasing the role of the private sector. 'Saudi Vision 2030' describes these reforms that aim to make the KSA a global investment powerhouse and an international marketplace linking Asia, Europe and Africa.[34] A robust financial services sector is viewed as the cornerstone to support the long-term goals of Saudi Vision 2030. To this end, the Council of Economic and Development Affairs launched the 'Financial Sector Development Program' (FSDP) in April 2017, with the intention of creating a more heterogeneous and powerful financial services sector through the achievement of financial inclusion, financial stability and digital transformation.[35] Accordingly, the FSDP envisages financial planning and diversification of sources of income, capital market modernisation and the encouragement of domestic financial institutions to be pivotal in private sector growth.[36]

Establishing and consolidating the KSA's leadership in the FinTech market is also crucial for the Saudi Vision 2030 goals. Under the FSDP, the 'FinTech Strategic Implementation Plan' (FinTech Plan) was launched in May 2020 with the goals of making the capital Riyadh a global FinTech hub and hosting FinTech players and operations in the Kingdom.[37] Open banking is central to the Saudi FinTech strategy. As in Bahrain, the development of open banking is under the remit of the national central bank. The Saudi Arabia Monetary Agency (SAMA) established an open banking program to create a framework to enhance innovation and competition in the financial services industry, promote financial inclusion, and improve the Kingdom's banking system productivity through more (and more diversified) products and services for customers.[38]

SAMA structured the creation of the Saudi open banking ecosystem into three stages, namely design, implementation and go-live phases. The go-live phase achieved its most significant outcomes through the issuance of the 'Open Banking Framework' in November 2022.[39] The framework comprises use cases, business rules and KSA standards. Use cases allow for an evaluation of the framework and help set priorities for further improvements; business rules relate to the requirements that banks and FinTech companies must comply with when providing open banking services; and KSA standards include Customer Experience Guidelines, API Specifications, Implementation Requirements and Operational Guidelines.[40]

As for the framework implementation, the KSA appears to be following the UK open banking experience. At present, the open banking framework works with account information services (AISs), and the payment initiation services (PISs) will be enacted subsequently. SAMA continues to monitor the implementation as part of the go-live phase, and it expects the participants to be responsive and ready to provide open banking services. In April 2023, another significant step was taken, with the creation of the 'Open Banking Lab', which is intended to be the major venue for banks and FinTech to create, exchange information and test and ensure that their open banking services comply with the framework.[41]

The Saudi open banking framework is new and going through its development stages. The ecosystem participants will certainly need to familiarise themselves with all the dynamics associated with the data-sharing framework, but like the Bahraini open banking framework, the KSA's framework has good prospects for encouraging the open banking movement in other MENA countries.

United Arab Emirates (UAE)

Currently, open banking market-driven initiatives are prevalent in the UAE. Regulatory approaches are, however, on the agenda of the Central Bank of the UAE (CBUAE). In February 2023, the CBUAE launched its 'Financial Infrastructure Transformation Programme' (FIT Programme), with the aim of promoting digital transformations, competitiveness and innovations in the UAE's financial services sector.[42] The FIT Programme contemplates a series of initiatives to be implemented in two phases, the first of which is concerned with digital payment initiatives driven by the objectives of promoting financial inclusion; enhancing innovation, security and efficiency in payment services; and ensuring a smooth and effective transition to a cashless society.[43] To this end, the first stage provides for the launch of a Card Domestic Scheme, an Instant Payments Platform, and the issuance of a Central Bank Digital Currency (CBDC) for cross-border and domestic use.[44]

The second phase focuses on open banking/finance initiatives. This phase will entail the creation of adequate digital infrastructures, such as a Financial Cloud, Electronic Know Your Customer (eKYC), Supervisory Technology and Open Finance Platforms, to ensure regulatory compliance, reduce costs, improve innovation and customer experience and guarantee security and operational resilience.[45] In line with the country's 'We the UAE 2031 Vision' and 'National Digital Economy Strategy', the FIT Programme is expected to be completed by 2026.

The Open Finance Platform is the enabler of the CBUAE's ambition to create a more data-driven society, where customers are at the centre as the owners and controllers of their data, with its use only permitted through their consent.[46] Presently, the UAE's open finance roadmap includes the following phases: 'Strategy and vision development', 'Release of industry note', 'Stakeholder consultations', 'Regulatory design', 'API prioritisation', 'Design the UAE Open Finance Playbook', 'Develop the digital infrastructure', 'Test and run pilots' and 'Enhance capabilities'.[47]

These initiatives remain at an embryonic stage, and it remains to be seen whether the 2026 deadline will be met. In the meantime, it is worth highlighting how AIS and PIS are already in place through the licenses given by the Dubai Financial Supervisory Authority (DFSA) and Financial Services Regulatory Authority (FSRA).[48] The initial wait-and-see approach taken by the UAE in relation to the open banking movement is now evolving towards an ambitious open finance regulatory framework, which will provide important elements for evaluating open banking/finance progress and significant changes in the MENA region.

The Hashemite Kingdom of Jordan (Jordan)

Jordan has been keeping pace with the trend of interest in open banking in the MENA region. Differently from the countries analysed in the preceding sections, Jordan has been pursuing open finance plans that have been translated into the 'Regulation of Open Finance Services Operations Procedures No. 12/22' (Regulation No. 12/22) issued by the Central Bank of Jordan (CBJ) in November 2022.[49]

Regulation No. 12/22 draws from the UK Open Banking Standard framework but is adapted to local legislation and the characteristics of Jordan's financial services industry. As for the participants of Jordan's open finance ecosystem, the word 'companies' is used in the regulation to designate banks and electronic payments, and transfer of funds companies licensed to operate in the Kingdom under 'Banking Law No. 28 of the year 2000' and the 'Electronic Payment and Money Transfer Bylaw No. (111) of 2017'.[50] These companies are hence required to allow third parties access to their customer data. Customers' explicit consent is again essential to this end. AIS and PIS are the two third-party services contemplated in Regulation No. 12/22.[51] Companies are expected to set their open finance services policies by drawing on international best practices and include governance, API requirements, risk management, security standards and consumer and data protection.[52]

Third parties are also subjected to governance, risk management and security requirements.[53] How the relationship between companies and third parties is organised is a significant element of Jordan's framework. Article 4(B)(4) of Regulation No. 12/22 states clearly that this relationship must be governed through written contractual agreements defining the roles and responsibilities of the parties.[54] Significantly and differently from other frameworks, companies can charge third parties for using their APIs.[55] Overall, the regulation burdens banks and other financial institutions with a series of duties relating to the maintenance of an updated third-party register, providing PISPs with information on the amount of money on a customer's account to initiate a payment and transparency towards their customers regarding commissions and costs for data access and financial transaction execution.[56] Additionally, companies have specific duties relating to APIs, as they are requested under Article 8 to provide, develop and maintain at least one API for data sharing with third parties.[57] Finally, Article 13 sets liability principles by indicating companies' accountability to the CBJ for third-party conduct regarding the open finance services addressed by the regulation.[58] Save extensions, the implementation of Regulation No. 12/22 is expected by November 2023.

The Jordanian open finance services regulation is an innovative framework to the extent that it already moves beyond the scope of open banking and intends to achieve a wider ecosystem in which other financial services are also part of the data-sharing process accomplished through APIs. Some call for improvements and further regulatory standards to address shortcomings such as the lack of a standard formula for calculating the fees for opening/

110   *Open Banking Regulation*

using APIs to reduce bank arbitrariness. Nonetheless, these developments in Jordan demonstrate how openness in the financial services industry is becoming an unstoppable force.

Qatar and rest of the region

In June 2022, Qatar National Bank (QNB) was the first Qatari financial institution to introduce its own open banking platform to enable customers and partners to benefit from core banking services through its API infrastructure.[59] The platform was the first move in creating a wider digital collaborative financial ecosystem to drive innovation in the country and generate better user experience in the financial services domain.[60] The blend of data and technology is recognised as the basic feature for achieving these results and open banking is the prime instrument. In March 2023, Qatar Central Bank (QCB) issued its 'FinTech Sector Strategy Summary' as part of the 'Qatar National Vision 2030', which sets five challenges to be addressed to advance growth in the country by 2030: 'Modernisation and preservation of traditions', 'The needs of the current and future generations', 'Managed growth and uncontrolled expansion', 'The size and quality of the expatriate labour force and the selected path of development' and 'Economic growth, social development and environmental management'.[61] Accordingly, human development, social development, economic development and environmental development are the four areas for regulatory and policy intervention to respond to the identified challenges and facilitate transformative processes in the country.[62]

QCB's FinTech strategy is linked to the 'economic development' pillar of the 2030 Vision, which can be supported through the creation of a diversified, competitive and innovative financial services sector.[63] In this respect, the strategy pursues four key objectives: Hosting investment programmes, consolidating synergies on technologies and innovation with other countries, exploiting technology to strengthen Qatar's leadership in the Islamic finance sector and making Qatar a recognised FinTech hub through leadership and educational programmes to attract the best talents.[64] Among others, FinTech regulation and the build-up of necessary infrastructure are decisive to fulfil the strategy and realise the 2030 National Vision. In this context, the creation of an open banking structure and proper regulation by 2028 are essential elements of QCB's plans.[65] The future Qatar open banking ecosystem will therefore be legislation driven.

Legislative approaches are also expected in Oman and Kuwait. At present, open banking development is at very early stages of consultation. In Oman, an open banking API strategy is under discussion for accelerating the growth of the FinTech sector and innovation across the country's financial sector.[66] In Kuwait, the Central Bank of Kuwait (CBK) has promoted and conducted studies on the need for open banking regulations and API specifications. The CBK open banking working group, involving CBK specialists and Kuwaiti banks, was established to consult on the appropriate framework and development plan.[67] Similarly, consultations are in place in other MENA countries such as Morocco, Tunisia and Egypt.

Conclusion

Even though the MENA region has had less open banking implementation compared to other jurisdictions, it is nonetheless poised to become a future open banking/finance leader. The region has observed the experience of the open banking leaders in Europe and the UK and has finally established its own open banking pathways led by local central banks. Though the development of open banking regulation is rather fragmented across the region, some countries, such as Bahrain, the KSA, the UAE and Jordan, are already expanding into open finance. These countries are either revisiting or creating standalone data protection and cybersecurity laws to reinforce their open banking ecosystems and allow for a safe transition to the wider domain of open finance. Regulatory sandboxes and use cases have also been vital for testing ideas and guiding the development of the current MENA open banking frameworks. The regulators have carved a path in accord with global initiatives towards meeting the final goal of a future open data ecosystem.

Notes

1 Ayman Ismail and others, 'Backgorund to the MENA Region' in Nezameddin Faghih and Mohammad Reza Zali (eds), *Entrepreneurship Education and Research in the Middle East and North Africa (MENA). Perspectives on Trends, Policy and Educational Environment* (Springer 2018) 19.
2 Franklin Allen, 'Globalization of Finance and FinTech in The MENA Region', (*ERF*, September 2021) Working Paper No. 1489, 2 <https://erf.org.eg/app/uploads/2021/09/1634550652_436_521705_1489.pdf> accessed 4 April 2023.
3 Pamela Riley and others, 'Digital Financial Services in the MENA Region', (2020) Rockville, MD: Sustaining Health Outcomes through the Private Sector Plus Project, Abt Associates Inc, 2 <https://shopsplusproject.org/sites/default/files/resources/Digital%20Financial%20Services%20in%20the%20MENA%20Region.pdf> accessed 4 April 2023.
4 Cambridge Centre for Alternative Finance (CCAF), 'FinTech Regulation in the Middle East and North Africa', (2022) University of Cambridge Judge Business School, 17 <www.jbs.cam.ac.uk/wp-content/uploads/2022/02/ccaf-2022-02-fintech-regulation-in-mena.pdf> accessed 4 April 2022
5 International Monetary Fund (IMF), 'MENA in Charts', (8 August 2017) <www.imf.org/en/News/Seminars/Conferences/2017/08/08/morocco-opportunities-for-all/Morocco-Conference-Chart-of-the-Week/chart-of-the-week-1> accessed 4 April 2023.
6 CCAF (n 4) 17.
7 Ibid., 22.
8 Iona Stanley, 'The Free Zone Ecosystem: Triple Mega-drivers - Challenges and Opportunity', (*Gulf News*, 4 May 2023) <https://gulfnews.com/uae/the-free-zone-ecosystem-triple-mega-drivers—challenges-and-opportunity-1.1683186052049> accessed 6 May 2023.

112 Open Banking Regulation

9. Ibid.
10. See Dubai International Financial Centre (DIFC) <www.difc.ae/> accessed 6 May 2023.
11. See DIFC Innovation Hub <https://innovationhub.difc.ae/> accessed 6 May 2023.
12. Mordor Intelligence, *MENA FinTech Market Size and Share Analysis-Growth Trends and Forecasts (2023–2028)* (2023) <www.mordorintelligence.com/industry-reports/mena-fintech-market> accessed 6 May 2023.
13. Ibid.
14. Ibid.
15. Amna Puri-Mirza, 'Fintech in Middle East and North Africa - Statistics & Facts', (*Statista*, 20 December 2022) <www.statista.com/topics/8699/fintech-in-mena/> accessed 06 May 2023.
16. Central Bank of Bahrain (CBB), 'CBB Launches the Bahrain Open Banking Framework', (28 October 2020) Press Release <www.cbb.gov.bh/media-center/cbb-launches-the-bahrain-open-banking-framework/> accessed 10 May 2023.
17. CBB, 'CBB Rulebook: Contents', <https://cbben.thomsonreuters.com/entiresection/500007> accessed 10 May 2023.
18. Ibid.
19. Ibid.
20. Ibid, Volume 1 ('Conventional Banks') and Volume 2 ('Islamic Banks').
21. CBB Rulebook, 'General Requirements Module-Volume 1 Conventional Banks', (GR-6.1/6.5) <https://cbben.thomsonreuters.com/sites/default/files/net_file_store/Vol_1_GR_April_2022.pdf> accessed 10 May 2023; CBB Rulebook, 'General Requirements Module-Volume 2 Islamic Banks' (GR-6.1/6.5), <https://cbben.thomsonreuters.com/sites/default/files/net_file_store/Vol_2_GR_April_2022.pdf> accessed 10 May 2023.
22. GR-6.1.5 Volume 1 ('Conventional Banks') and Volume 2 ('Islamic Banks').
23. Ibid.
24. GR-6.1.8 Volume 1 ('Conventional Banks') and Volume 2 ('Islamic Banks').
25. Ibid.
26. GR-6.4.2 Volume 1 ('Conventional Banks') and Volume 2 (Islamic Banks').
27. CBB Rulebook Volume 5-Specialsed Licensees <https://cbben.thomsonreuters.com/rulebook/central-bank-bahrain-volume-5-specialised-licensees> accessed 10 May 2023.
28. Ibid.
29. CBB Rulebook Volume 5 ('Specialised Licensees'), Type 7-Ancillary Service Providers, Part A, Business Standards, 'Open Banking Module' <https://cbben.thomsonreuters.com/rulebook/ob-open-banking-module> accessed 10 May 2023.
30. Ibid.
31. Ibid.
32. CBB, 'Additional Implementation Guideline', (2019) EDBS/KH/C/34/2019 <https://cbben.thomsonreuters.com/sites/default/files/net_file_store/EDBS_KH_Open_Banking_Additional_Implementation_Guidance_24_April_2019.pdf> accessed 15 May 2023.
33. Ellie Duncan, 'Fintech Galaxy Receives License from Central Bank of Bahrain', (*Openbankingexpo*, 4 November 2022) <www.openbankingexpo.com/news/fintech-galaxy-receives-license-from-central-bank-of-bahrain/> accessed 15 May 2023.
34. Kingdom of Saudi Arabia (KSA), 'Saudi Vision 2030', (2016) 6
35. <https://www.vision2030.gov.sa/media/rc0b5oy1/saudi_vision203.pdf> accessed 18 May 2023.

36 KSA, 'Financial Sector Development Program (FSDP)', (2021) 6 <https://www.vision2030.gov.sa/media/ud5micju/fsdp_eng.pdf> accessed 18 May 2023.
37 Ministry of Finance, 'FSDP Launches FinTech Strategy Implementation Plan', (2022) <www.mof.gov.sa/en/MediaCenter/news/Pages/news_22062022_1.aspx> accessed 18 May 2023.
38 Saudi Central Bank (SAMA), 'Open Banking Policy', (2018) <www.sama.gov.sa/en-US/Documents/Open_Banking_Policy-EN.pdf> accessed 18 May 2023.
39 SAMA, 'SAMA Issues the Open Banking Framework', (2 November 2022) News <www.sama.gov.sa/en-US/News/Pages/news-794.aspx> accessed 18 May 2023.
40 SAMA, 'Open Banking in Saudi Arabia', (2023) <www.openbanking.sa/> accessed 18 May 2023.
41 Ibid.
42 Central Bank of the UAE (CBUAE), 'CBUAE Launches a Financial Infrastructure Transformation Programme to Accelerate the Digital Transformation of the Financial Services Sector', (12 February 2023) 1 <www.centralbank.ae/media/mdupathy/cbuae-launches-a-financial-infrastructure-transformation-programme-to-accelerate-the-digital-transformation-of-the-financial-services-sector-en.pdf> accessed 20 May 2023.
43 Ibid.
44 Ibid.
45 Ibid.
46 CBUAE, 'Open Finance', <www.centralbank.ae/en/our-operations/fintech-digital-transformation/open-finance/> accessed 20 May 2023.
47 Ibid.
48 Nameer Khaan and Hakan Eroglu, 'Embedded Finance in the MENA Region', (*MENA FinTech Association*, November 2022) 1 <https://mena-fintech.org/wp-content/uploads/2022/11/MFTA-Embedded-Finance-Report-NOV2022-FINAL.pdf> accessed 20 May 2023.
49 Central Bank of Jordan, 'Regulating Open Finance Services Procedures Instructions NO. (12/2022)', <www.cbj.gov.jo/EchoBusV3.0/SystemAssets/c0a18148-2e1a-49f0-9bb0-d59286d7a312.pdf> accessed 20 May 2023.
50 Regulation NO. (12/2022), art 2 ('The Term/Expression').
51 Ibid.
52 Regulation NO. (12/2022), arts 5 ('Open Finance Services Policy'), 10 ('Security and Technical Standards for Open Finance Services'), and 11 ('Consumer Protection, Data Privacy and Data Protection').
53 Regulation NO. (12/2022), art 9 ('Third Party Provider (TPP) Standards and Requirements').
54 Regulation NO. (12/2022), art 4(B)4 ('Governance').
55 Regulation NO. (12/2022), art 13 ('General Provisions').
56 Regulation NO. (12/2022), art 6 ('Risk Management').
57 Regulation NO. (12/2022), art 8 ('Application Programming Interface (API) requirements').
58 Regulation NO. (12/2022), art 13 ('General Provisions').
59 QNB, 'QNB the First Bank in Qatar to Launch Open Banking Platform for Clients and FinTechs', (16 June 2022) <https://www.qnb.com/sites/qnb/qnbglobal/en/ennews16june-news> accessed 2 June 2023.
60 Ibid.
61 Qatar Central Bank (QCB), 'Summary of FinTech Sector Strategy in State of Qatar', (March 2023) 3 <www.qcb.gov.qa/Arabic/strategicplan/Documents/%D8%A7%D9%86%D8%AC%D9%84%D9%8A%D8%B2%D9%8A.pdf> accessed 02 June 2023.

62 Ibid.
63 General Secretariat for Development Planning, 'Qatar National Vision 2030', (July 2008) <www.gco.gov.qa/wp-content/uploads/2016/09/GCO-QNV-English.pdf> accessed 2 June 2023.
64 QCB (n 61) 2.
65 Ibid.
66 Dylan Thiam, 'Open Banking in Oman', (9 May 2023) openbankproject <www.openbankproject.com/open-banking-in-oman/> accessed 2 June 2023.
67 Nathan Gore, 'Central Bank of Kuwait Supports Launch of New Open Banking Product', (*The FinTech Times*, 26 August 2022) <https://thefintechtimes.com/central-bank-of-kuwait-supports-launch-of-new-open-banking-product/> accessed 2 June 2023.

Part III
Business Models, Emerging Economies and the Way forward

8 Open Banking and FinTech Business Models in the UK

Challenger banks and e-money firms in the UK

There are some eighty 'challenger banks' and similar firms in the UK. The challenger banks, with the notable exception of Metro Bank, are all largely FinTech-based. Their primary aim is to disrupt, to a greater or lesser extent, the dominant market positions of the major incumbent UK banks. The latter also have FinTech operations but they predominate in the high streets across the country.

In addition, there are a large number of e-money businesses (EMIs). These are not banks and do not take customer deposits but in many ways, they look like banks. They often take advantage of the opportunities provided by Payment Services Directive II (PSD II) which was enacted in UK law by the Payment Services Regulations 2017. There are some two hundred and fifty e-money firms licensed and authorised by the Financial Conduct Authority (FCA) although some 25 of these are shown as having or in the process of going out of business.[1] Some one hundred EMIs are shown as being members of the Electronic Money Association (EMA), described as being a 'trade body for electronic money issuers and innovative payment service providers including payment institutions, banks and payment schemes'.[2]

There are also a number of financial services operations which want to obtain banking authorisation from the Prudential Regulatory Authority (PRA). This will, they hope, increase their credibility and allow them to take deposits from customers.

This chapter considers the broad business models of the FinTech challenger banks and e-money businesses.

This chapter will go on to examine the business strategies of a large sample of current challenger banks and other FinTech operations. It will consider in more detail the approaches taken by some of the largest businesses in these areas including Atom, N26, Monzo, Tide, Starling, Revolut, Klarna and Trustly using publically available information. This review will focus on their balance sheets but will also look at any environmental, social and corporate governance information. The aim is not to undertake some form of business investment analysis but rather to see how these firms are contributing to the society in which they operate.

DOI: 10.4324/9781003331339-11

Finally, traditional, retail and commercial banks have tended to provide support to local communities but with widespread branch closures, some aspects of this are likely to atrophy. Clearly, challenger banks do not have this as an option as a method of contributing to society. This chapter looks at what they are doing and their options. This could include enhancing social inclusion, operating with a widely diverse board and senior management and investing where possible in society and local communities, including staff volunteering and charitable giving. Other aspects include developing socially useful innovation and civic work in schools to develop future generations of IT innovators.

E-money operations

There is a fundamental difference between banks and e-money-authorised institutions. Banks are permitted to accept customer deposits and to make loans using these funds. The customer deposits belong to the bank and the relationship with the customer is one of the debtor/creditor. Banks are subject to onerous capital and liquidity regulatory requirements.

Conversely, e-money institutions are there to help facilitate customer payments. The e-money business can take money from the public, but it must store it safely. In an arrangement similar to the existing 'client money' regulatory requirements, the funds must be kept in a special separate account which cannot be used by the e-money business for any purpose other than making payments on behalf of the customer. Alternatively, the funds can be invested in secure, liquid low-risk assets which have been approved by the FCA and are held in a separate account by a custodian. Finally, there is a third option where an e-money firm acquires a bank guarantee or an insurance bond to safeguard the money if the business fails. If the latter happens the liquidator should be able to pay out the customers without any risk of loss from the segregated funds or assets or by making a claim under the insurance policy or bank guarantee.[3]

In practice the boundary between a bank deposit and the e-money account is a fine one. The FCA is keen to ensure that e-money customers are fully protected since the capital requirements placed on these types of firms are negligible. The FCA will look at a number of factors including 'whether the product is sold as electronic money or as a deposit', 'how long value is allowed to remain on the account, disincentives to keeping value on the account and the payment of interest on it'. Key to all this is whether the customer funds are placed with the firm as a 'means of saving' or a 'means of payment'.[4]

A variety of business models

There are a number of different business approaches in FinTech. These can be broken down into:

- Pure EMIs.
- PSD II account information service providers (AISPs).

- PSD II payment initiation service providers (PISPs).
- Firms that use one or more of these options for a different business purpose (e.g., 'buy-now-pay-later'—BNPL).

It is also worth noting that the UK government's British Business Bank has funded around a dozen of the FinTech firms via its 'Future Fund'.[5]

The main business models are set out below. Many of these are not mutually exclusive and can be used in a variety of combinations. One of these is a business model based on collating and presenting account information.

PSD II AISPs

PSD II has provided a range of opportunities. Provided customer data is well protected the risks involved are limited. However, they need scale to be attractive to firms wishing to purchase this anonymised information. One of these is a business model based on collating and presenting account information. This approach is conceptually attractive since they are relatively easy- and low-cost to set up. They also provide a gateway to sell other services to customers such as investment funds, collective purchases of utility supplies etc. The downside is that account information services are easily replicated and many, if not all, incumbent banks can offer these facilities to existing customers. It also has the immediate advantage of giving them an insight into what other financial assets are held by their customers with switching and transfer opportunities.

The FinTech challenger banks appear to be focused on building market share with profitability, at least in the early stages, coming second. An example of this is Beanstalk, the trading name of KidStart Ltd.[6] It is difficult to understand from its website what it does, but it appears to link various bank accounts into a savings facility aimed at children. It uses a variety of tools including one which rounds shopping payments and transfers the 'rounding' to the investment fund. It appears to fund itself from a 0.5% annual fee on the funds under management. According to the latest set of financial statements to 31 March 2021, it had a retaining deficit of £2.8m (£2.5m for 2021). This in no way is a criticism of this firm. It is put forward as an example of a business operating in a highly competitive market where it is difficult for a firm to distinguish its offering.

Emma Technologies Ltd ('Emma') is another example. This is authorised by the FCA under the Payment Services Regulations and it is also an 'appointed representative' of a number of FCA regulated organisations. 'Appointed representatives' are themselves 'exempt' from the need for authorisation and regulation under s39 Financial Services and Markets Act 2000 ('FSMA 2000') and the FSMA 2000 (Appointed Representative) Regulations 2001 by virtue of a firm which is authorised and regulated taking responsibility for the appointed representative.

The Emma website appears awkward to navigate and provides little information.[7] It does provide consolidated bank account information and allows investment and payments. There are a number of levels of service and features with different charging structures. The company provides almost no financial information legitimately using the micro company reporting arrangements. All that can be said is that according to the very limited data available from Companies House, current assets more than halved to just under £1m between 31 January 2020 and the same date in 2021.

Another example is Money Dashboard which has a well-set-out website.[8] Its services are free to users but it provides a clear explanation of how it makes money on its website:

> Money Dashboard provides insight and market research services to help companies better understand trends in consumer behaviour. We identify shifts in consumer preferences using anonymised spending information from Money Dashboard users. Money Dashboard may offer suggestions for products and services like credit cards, home loan offers or insurance providers that can save you money. If you select a product based on our suggestion, Money Dashboard may receive a fee from the product provider.

The company made a loss of just over £2m in the year to 30 April 2021 and it has been reported that ClearScore, a credit scoring and reporting company, purchased Money Dashboard in May 2022.[9]

PSD II PISPs

There are a number of models that can be operated by payment initiation services. In essence, customers of banks allow third parties such as PISPs to take money directly out of their bank accounts and pay it to someone else. These can take various forms as summarised below.

Embedded finance

A number of firms, particularly in the US, are promoting new finch models based on 'embedded finance'. These are being developed into business propositions by a number of consultancy firms.[10] 'Embedded finance' is often defined very widely and if drawn as a Venn diagram would overlap to a considerable extent with open banking. However, without overstating it, often open banking is seen as a technology while 'embedded finance' is regarded as a business strategy.[11]

Klarna's business model can be seen as a form of 'embedded finance'. Using some very attractive and clever marketing it creates a customer experience introducing customers to its website where goods and services are promoted with material that has the same look and feel using the Klarna house style. Using open banking customers can pay there and then for whatever they want directly from their bank accounts with merchants avoiding credit card fees. Customers, can also, if they want to get ready credit using the mechanism of 'BNPL'. Of course, the lending under these arrangements has yet to be tested in an economic downturn. This model is considered in more detail later.

The concepts behind the 'embedded finance' model, or strategy, are closely related to the 'bank in a box' and 'banking as a service' ('BaaS'). Essentially, a non-bank (e.g., a vehicle manufacturer, hotel group, holiday cruise company) could provide banking-aligned services to customers. The non-bank would leverage its competitive advantage whether this be its brand, existing customer base, non-financial product range and couple this with banking services to increase the value of its offering.

This is not a new idea. It can be found in Lowell Bryan's 'Breaking up the Bank', in 1988.[12] Another model involved 'trusted' brands such as supermarkets providing banking services. Under these arrangements, an authorised bank would provide the services but it would be branded ('white-labelled') with the name of the non-bank. Conceptually, this model appeared strong and it was fashionable to do these types of deals in the 1990s. However, broadly, while not disasters they have not proved nearly as successful as originally expected.[13] There are several problems with this model. Banking is much higher risk than for example, retailing. Much of the lending by both Sainsbury and Tesco banks was unsecured and 'Sainsbury's unsecured book alone, at £4.9bn, equals the grocer's entire market value ... Understandably, the supermarket's new boss Simon Roberts wants out of banking'.[14] There are also likely to be clashes of culture between those working in different industries and banking, as a highly regulated activity probably consumes a considerable amount of senior management and board time.[15]

The Co-op Groups venture into banking proved to be disastrous as the main board operated in a business area it did not fully understand. It ended up damaging both the finances and reputation of the Co-op.[16]

There is a view that 'embedded finance' is different from the older form of 'white label' banking since it is internet-based using API (Application Programming Interface) technology. For example, Klarna currently offers loans to consumers on a BNPL basis. It is planning to do the same for its merchant partners with an arrangement with Liberis. The latter is a UK factoring operation. In its most recent financial statements, it made a loss of some £10m in the year to 31 December 2020 (the previous year's loss was just over £2m and it blames the global pandemic for a substantial reduction in income). Using its API Liberis would be able to see the sales made by Klarna merchants and offer revenue-based finance using actual transaction information. The new element is the access to actual merchant transaction data via the API.[17] From the outside, it is difficult to know where the credit risks might fall. It will also depend on Liberis' access to its own funding to support its factoring business.[18]

Lloyds Bank has recently set up an 'embedded finance' division to diversify its income by targeting online payments.[19] It appears to be partnering with UK-based Satago to provide 'single invoice financing' (SIF).[20] Under 'SIF' the firm providing finance will use IT software to link its operating programme to the merchant's account systems. Rather than factoring a batch of invoices the merchant can select one or more outstanding invoices to be financed. This has the advantage of managing a firm's cash flow without giving away too much value in the debtors' ledger. The payment system IT allows this level of individual invoice selection and very fast debt financing decision making and fundings. It also means that funding cost margins can be much cheaper for merchants. Firms such as Satago provide open banking software and customer management systems for these arrangements. Satago itself made a loss of just over £2m for its last full year accounts to 31 December 2020 and was refinanced in early 2022.

Amsterdam-based Adyen has also announced that it is moving into embedded financial products.[21] Adyen is a very substantial and profitable payment services business with income to the year ended 31 December 2021 of some €6bn. By using embedded finance, it will enable merchants to arrange finance against invoices in multiple currencies and market 'platforms' such as eBay and Etsy to fund end-users. Adyen's target market are the platforms and their client businesses. Adyen has a banking licence in the EU and an overseas bank branch licence in the US. Adyen has the advantage of real-time access to accounts of merchants. This can also be done in the EU using PSD II. It can provide day-to-day finance or longer-term finance by direct payment into the merchant's bank account and it can access its fees and repayments in the same way. Account access privileges allow Adyen to 'pre-qualify' (i.e., pre-approve) lending to the merchant. It can also receive and make payments in foreign currencies and provide value to the merchant in a pre-agreed currency (e.g., US$s, €s). Further, these services can be 'monetised' (i.e., turned into profit) for Adyen. All these facilities tie the merchants and platforms closer to firms such as Adyen—in the jargon, make them 'sticky'.[22]

PSD II business models which leverage the brand

Similarly, Klarna has recently moved into 'embedded finance' with its launch of Klarna Kosma.[23] Using its own PSD II authorisation and its API Klarna Kosma aims to allow firms it partners with to provide, for example, investment services for end-user customers and bank account information. These services can be either presented under the Klarna brand or 'white labelled' using the brand of the Klarna Kosma client.

Clearly, this business model is based on leveraging the Klarna brand which is heavily and cleverly marketed. This importantly helps build trust—especially for end-user customers. The Klarna Kosma client also gets the in-house API and technical support. However, there are lots of firms offering the same in a highly competitive market. Nevertheless, consumer trust is extremely valuable and as mentioned elsewhere consumer distrust of open banking is a key issue in the failure of the technology to attract business.

PSD II and 'BNPL'

Klarna's issues have more to do with the scale of its growth in the context of the various economies in which it operates. The business, although based on open banking, remains heavily focused on BNPL. It has suffered a credit default of SKr4.6bn (more or less the same value in €s) in 2021 (up from SKr2.5bn in 2020). This has increased the full-year losses for 2021 to SKr7.1bn from SKr1.4bn in 2020.[24] In the UK, the FCA estimated that the BNPL market had generated £2.7bn in spending in 2020. However, another estimate said that it had more than doubled to £5.7bn in 2021.[25] Bad debts are almost certain to rise significantly. 'The Centre for Financial Capability', a charity, found that almost a quarter of UK adults who had used BNPL services had failed to pay on time, rising to 35% for people aged between 18 and 34.[26]

BNPL was developed in Australia with a phalanx of FinTech firms such as Afterpay, OpenPay, Zip, Latitude and Douugh. BNPL is not strictly speaking a FinTech product. However, via Klarna and the firms in Australia, it became associated with FinTech businesses. UK regulatory changes are likely to bring BNPL-based models within the full scope of credit regulation.[27] It may go the same way as Wonga and the other digital loan providers.

Salary advance schemes

Australian Beforepay aims at the pre-payday loan market. Here, FinTechs lend to customers in advance of their normal payday. Its business model parallels BNPL. Providers such as Beforepay do 'not conduct traditional credit checks, instead relying on an in-house screening and verification system'.[28] For reasons that are not directly clear, it had significant issues with its floatation on the Australian Securities Exchange (ASX).[29] In its hunt for revenue in the UK, Revolut has also moved into this area.[30] A number of employers have set up these pay advance schemes for their employees in partnership with FinTech firms.[31] This market is well-developed in Australia and the US. In the latter, it is estimated that in 2020 US$9.5bn of wages were accessed in this way.[32]

However, these schemes have been subject to considerable criticism, for example, by the Chartered Institute of Personnel and Development (CIPD), a professional body for those working in human resources.[33] Further, in both the UK and the US, loans in advance of salaries are the subject of close regulatory attention.[34] In the US, the issue is whether these schemes constitute lending and are, hence, subject to legislation.[35]

Open banking and mortgages

Incumbent banks have an inbuilt advantage in mortgage lending. They have lots of information on their account holders and can use this to 'pre-qualify' potential mortgage borrowers. The data also allows them to undertake 'pre-disposition' modelling to work out which customers to offer mortgages to before the customer even approaches the bank. Further, current account customers who have their mortgages with other lenders can be targeted to encourage them to move their mortgages. All this uses existing 'data-mining' and customer management systems. Open banking has the potential to disrupt this—at least to a certain extent.

Lenders have to assess mortgage applications both in credit provision terms and also for affordability. The former assessment aims to protect the lender while the affordability checks are more focused on protecting the borrower.[36] As part of the affordability review process, the potential borrower needs to set out their income and expenditure in considerable detail.[37] These disclosures need to be evidenced. There are a number of ways of doing this but access to the bank accounts of borrowers can be a good source both of data on income and expenditure but can also provide sound evidence. Here the AISP can help. The borrower can provide 'one-off' access and there is no need for a contract. All that is needed is explicit borrower consent to the AISP.

For example, M&S Bank has set up an arrangement with Equifax, a credit referencing business, and AccountScore using its own AISP, 'consent.online', to provide this information for mortgage, credit card and personal loan applications.[38] Equifax has a similar partnership with HSBC.[39]

Other innovative uses for open banking

Checking eligibility for reduced utility charges

In the UK those on various forms of social benefits are eligible for reduced charges by privatised utilities (e.g., electricity, telecoms, water). United Utilities, a water company, has agreed with Equifax to use the latter's AISP to check, in real-time, a customer's bank account to check income levels and to look for evidence of benefit payments.[40] This can be done while the customer is on the utility's website or on a phone call to the business.

Increasing a customer's credit score

Experian, another large Dublin-based credit referencing business, offers customers free of charge, access to a product called 'Boost'. This service uses an API to access the customer's bank account and to analyse the information in the account to see if the Experian algorithms can increase the credit score of the individual.[41]

Payment of UK taxes

In 2021, the UK government allowed firms and individuals to pay their taxes using open banking.[42] It is not immediately clear what the benefits of doing this are for taxpayers. The PISP is a firm called 'Ecospend', a micro-company with one director set up by a Turkish Cypriot, Metin Erkman.[43] Supported by Nordic Capital, a Swedish private equity capital business, Trustly, a Swedish FinTech firm, purchased Ecospend in May 2022.[44]

Using open banking for wealth management

Open banking provides opportunities for financial advisers and wealth management. The open banking fund managers are in many ways similar to the more traditional fund managers but with lower cost models. However, probably operating at the lower end of the wealth management market, financial advisers and wealth management 'platform' operators can use open banking to make customer 'onboarding' easier. Having access to customer bank account information makes the regulatory 'know your customer' ('KYC') process easier with more customers completing the process and hence a higher 'conversion rate'.

Some firms, such as Canadian-based Wealthsimple, focus on crypto assets, while a couple of the larger firms such as Nutmeg and Wealthify, are owned by major conventional fund managers—JP Morgan Asset Managers and Aviva, respectively. Nutmeg is reported to be the largest European digital wealth manager.[45] Other examples include Scalable Capital, based in Munich which is reported to be the second largest digital fund manager in Europe.[46] There is also Moneybox, a UK firm owned by Digital Moneybox. Its most recent financial statements to 31 May 2021 indicate revenue of £5m but with an annual loss of just over £10m. Similarly, Moneyfarm, with strong Italian connections, is the brand of MFM Investments. According to its most recent financial statements to 31 December 2020, it had revenue of almost £6m and a loss of £12m.

The next section considers, by way of example, the different approaches taken by the six largest FinTech operations in the UK using various open banking strategies.

Six of the largest UK FinTech banks and near-banks

This section examines six of the largest UK FinTech banks and near-banks with a particular focus on their business models. These include Atom, Monzo, Revolut, Starling, Klarna and Trustly.

In order to give a measure of the size of these firms, I have used Lloyds Bank, a large incumbent UK bank, as a comparator. It made profits before tax for 2021 of £7bn. Customer deposits stood at £480bn and loans to customers of £459bn.

Atom bank

This digital Durham-based firm was authorised as a bank in 2015. Early in 2022, it successfully undertook another funding round led by Banco Bilbao Vizcaya Argentaria (BBVA), a large Spanish banking group. BBVA owns 39% of Atom. Other large shareholders are asset management firms Toscafund and Infinity Investment Partners. The plan is to float at least part of the Atom in 2023 when the bank expects to make its first full year of profits.[47]

Atom Bank has tended to follow a more traditional banking model compared to its other FinTech competitors. Unlike many competitors, it offers both savings and current accounts and makes loans to both businesses and individuals. It has a well-designed website and along with other digital banks, it uses biometrics to verify customers. The bank employs just over 400 staff.

The bank focuses on taking deposits and lending. It does not seek income from fees and charges. It regards providing the products and services to sustain fees and charges as too costly.[48] The bank has almost £2.2bn in customer deposits. The business continues to make losses (£62m for 2021). The bank has hopes that increased net interest margins, as interest rates rise across the country, will help the bank towards profitability. It has also increased its business lending to almost £700m. Of the latter almost half is unsecured. This is both more profitable and riskier than secured lending.

The bank operates a couple of 'special purpose vehicles'. The bank 'securitises certain loans and advances to customers as a means to source funding and for capital management purposes'.[49] During the course of 2020, the bank transferred almost £450m worth of mortgages to one of its special purpose vehicles at a cost to the bank of £10m. In its financial statements, the bank notes that it 'has an obligation to repurchase mortgage exposures if certain loans no longer meet the programme criteria or representations and warranties'.[50]

Growing mortgage lending is a key Atom Bank strategy. In November 2021, it contracted with Landbay, a buy-to-let (BTL) specialist mortgage originator, to fund £500m lending in this market.

Monzo

Monzo was founded around the same time as Atom Bank, it obtained its full banking authorisation in 2017 and has its headquarters in central London. Monzo, like Atom Bank, has a good website with a similar look and feel.

While the bank is still losing money customer numbers continue to rise year on year and these customers are increasingly more profitable for Monzo, leaving larger amounts on deposit and using their Monzo card more.[51] Prior to 2021, Monzo did not do much by way of marketing but it has redeveloped its 'brand marketing with social media campaigns and launched the first ever Monzo branded London buses' and also launched a reward scheme for customer referrals.[52]

In the most recent financial statements to the end of February 2022, the bank earned £34m in net interest income and £81m in fees and commission revenue. According to the accounts, this was double the sum earned in 2020/1 and 'reflects the higher number of customers spending through Monzo and using our Monzo Plus, Monzo Premium and Monzo Business products'.[53] The amount of customer deposits had also increased substantially over the period to £4.4bn and these deposits were effectively held by the bank in the form of cash (£3.1bn) and Treasury investments (£1.7bn).[54]

A number of the founders of Monzo, including Tom Blomfield, came from Starling Bank. It is reported that the founding Chief Executive Officer of

Monzo, Tom Blomfield, left Starling Bank in less than ideal circumstances.[55] Blomfield stepped down from the CEO role at Monzo in May 2020.

Monzo suffered a customer data security problem in 2019 and had to advise 500,000 customers to change their personal identification number.[56] There is no indication that any customers suffered loss and the two UK data regulators did not apparently take any public action against the bank.

In 2019, the bank started offering a rate of interest significantly higher than that offered by the larger banks (e.g., 8.9% for loans up to £10,000 compared to, for example, HSBC offering the same at 6.7%).[57]

There may other issues with some of Monzo's product offerings. For example, it is reported that Monzo has started to offer OakNorth's tax-incentivised cash savings bonds ('cash ISAs'). OakNorth is another UK challenger bank. It appears that if customers obtain the same 'instant access ISA from OakNorth they would get 1.44 per cent per annum. If they go via Monzo they will only get 1.14 per cent'.[58] It is also noted that the gap between the two banks is 'even bigger for other products: there are 40 basis points between OakNorth's six-month fixed-term savings account and the same account accessed via the Monzo app'.[59]

It is difficult to know how effective Monzo's business strategy is. There may be a distinction that can be drawn between those that 'bank with Monzo' and those that simply hold a Monzo card. This point was clearly highlighted by a Financial Times journalist when they wrote that they and their colleagues who own Monzo cards 'think of Monzo as a kind of add-on; a secondary service that we use to pay friends quickly, to buy stuff abroad, and to set weekly budgets. Where do our salaries go? Where do we pay our bills out of? The traditional banks, still'.[60]

The impression given is that Monzo, and others, are scratching around for profitable income. This includes moves into offering 'premium' current accounts and its own version of BNPL borrowing with its 'Monzo Flex'.

The newish CEO TS Anil in an interview for the Financial Times confirmed that Monzo continues to be careful with its lending practices and that cryptocurrencies were not part of its future plans.[61] However, the bank hopes to launch an investment platform in the near future (Revolut launched one in 2019 including offering cryptocurrencies).[62]

MONZO AND CUSTOMER COMPLAINTS

For a small bank Monzo appears to have a significantly large number of customer complaints about its banking products. Based on the most recent FCA data for the second half of 2022, Monzo received 3.61 complaints per thousand accounts.[63] This compares with, for example, 2.55 for Lloyds Bank, 4.56 for HSBC and 1.86 for Atom Bank.[64] In absolute numeric terms is this over twenty-seven thousand complaints. This compares with over eighty-two thousand and one hundred and fourteen thousand for Lloyds and HSBC Banks, respectively.[65] Equivalent complaints, for example, for both Atom and Starling Banks are significantly lower at less than four hundred and under five thousand, respectively.[66]

It is difficult to know for certain why Monzo has received so many complaints. However, many of these could relate to many of its customers being shut out of their bank accounts by Monzo. Accounts have been frozen for long periods without notice. It has led to the creation of a Facebook group 'Monzo Stole Our Money' with some thirteen thousand members. Some of these customer complaints have ended up with the Financial Ombudsman Service (FOS). The latter published its adjudication on one complaint in which a Ms A complained 'that Monzo Bank Ltd repeatedly blocked and then closed her account without explanation' in the latter part of 2018.[67] The FOS adjudicator found for the bank saying that it was within its rights to do so and was not obliged to give any reasons. It may have happened as a result of Monzo complying with the UK's anti-money laundering regulations. Monzo has said in the past 'it has to sometimes freeze accounts in order to stop criminals using Monzo for illegal activities'.[68]

All this may relate to the continuing FCA investigation into Monzo and its anti-money laundering arrangements disclosed in the latter's financial statements in the period 'between 1 October 2018 to 30 April 2021. This ongoing investigation is looking into both potential civil and criminal liability'.[69]

Additionally, in October 2021, it was reported that after 'conversations with the Office of the Comptroller of the Currency (OCC), Monzo has made the decision to withdraw its application for its US operations. The decision was made after regulators told the digital bank that its application was unlikely to be approved'.[70]

FRAUD

The latest financial statements to the end of February 2022 state that the bank has paid £16m for the year in compensation to customers who have fallen victim to financial crime.[71] The cost has risen 32% compared to the previous year.[72]

MONZO AND US PLANS

In 2019, Monzo decided to launch its services in the US which is seen as somewhat behind in open banking. However, it was warned that this would be very difficult. The FT reported that while the US 'to outsiders looks like this massive opportunity, a big market … the challenges tend to be much harder than new entrants expect'.[73] This prediction turned out to be correct and Monzo withdrew its application for a US banking licence in October 2021 after the OCC, the relevant US regulator, apparently said that it was likely to be declined.[74] It is not known what concerns the OCC.

This is probably a good point to consider current UK regulatory issues specifically relating to the 'challenger banks'.

Bank of England concerns about challenger bank growth

The Bank of England's PRA is concerned that the challenger banks have not developed their risk and control arrangements in line with the growth and increased complexity of their businesses.[75] The PRA wants to make significant investments in these areas including improved corporate governance. What may have been appropriate for a start-up is not sustainable. The PRA is keen that these banks develop business models which 'focus on reaching profitability and the ability to achieve organic capital generation [i.e., not dependent on regular funding rounds] within a reasonable time period following authorisation'.[76] The PRA views dependence for too long on venture capital funding to contain too many risks.

In the view of the PRA, while novel and untested business models may be acceptable the regulator intends to keep these firms subject to a 'high degree of scrutiny' to ensure that risks are properly managed and that risk controls and governance are appropriate.[77]

The PRA expects within three years of authorisation 'banks to have more clarity over their path to profitability. By five years post-authorisation, banks should either be profitable or have a credible strategy to achieve profitability, with definite capital support to achieve this'.[78]

The new banks need to keep the Bank of England informed in advance of material changes to their business plans. They must also 'produce more realistic business plans as they mature; the PRA expects banks to be able to produce more accurate forecasts by approximately two to three years post-authorisation and have realistic forecasts within five years of authorisation. Banks should ensure they factor investment in governance and controls into their financial projections'.[79] Finally, in this area the PRA wanted the new banks to move as soon as possible towards having conventional bank levels of capital. Until the key test of sustainable profitability was achieved the challengers had to 'have a credible capital plan which will ensure new capital is injected' before the bank risked breaching capital trigger points.[80] The Regulator threatened that if there was a delay in achieving profitability there would be 'no delay in transitioning to the PRA buffer on a stress test basis'.[81]

The 'stress tests' are designed to ensure that even in the event of changing circumstances banks have sufficient capital to meet these contingencies. The particular concern of the regulators, as mentioned above, was that investors would lose patience with a bank that took too long to become profitable. The challenger bank without these further injections of funding would risk entering a downward spiral towards financial collapse. Consequently, it was important that this possibility was addressed at an earlier stage before the contingent event crystallised. These aspects are addressed in some detail in Section 6 of the Supervisory Statement. It is possible that these issues were behind the Bank of England's request for Monzo to increase its capital under what is known as 'Pillar 2' of the Basel capital requirements.[82]

FCA review of anti-money laundering controls and procedures: Challenger banks

In 2021, the FCA reviewed anti-money laundering and terrorism financing controls and procedures at several challenger banks.[83] The review was based on the Treasury and Home Office's 'National risk assessment of money laundering and terrorist financing 2020'.[84] The specific risk raised in the latter report was that 'criminals may be attracted to the fast onboarding process challenger banks advertise, particularly when setting up money mule networks. In addition, where banks promote the ability to open accounts very quickly to attract customers, there is a risk that information gathered at the account opening stage is insufficient to identify higher risk customers'.[85]

The FCA review found broad control weakness which 'create an environment for more significant risks of financial crime to occur both when customers are onboarded and throughout the customer journey'.[86] More specifically, 'most challenger banks did not obtain details about customer income and occupation, resulting in an incomplete assessment of the purpose and intended nature of a customer's relationship with the bank'.[87] Additionally, some of these businesses were not consistently applying enhanced due diligence (e.g., for politically exposed persons).[88] The FCA also found that some of these banks had failed to implement customer risk assessment processes or if they had, these were not well developed.[89] Even more worryingly, the FCA 'found ineffective management of transaction monitoring alerts. For example, inconsistent or inadequate rationale is used for discounting alerts'. Further, The FCA highlighted 'that the challenger banks' control frameworks were not able to keep up with changes to the business models'.[90]

There were also concerns regarding the volume and quality of the statutory 'suspicious activity reports' (SARs) to the UK Financial Intelligence Unit (UKFIU) within the UK's National Crime Agency (NCA). Finally, the FCA is critical of challenger banks failing to comply with Principle 11 of the FCA rulebook. This is probably the single most important rule which requires regulated firms to be open and honest with their regulator.

Starling bank

Starling Bank, founded by Anne Boden, was authorised as a bank by the regulators in 2016. The COVID-19 pandemic has provided it with an opportunity to substantially increase its balance sheet in 2020, 2021 and in the first part of 2022. Between 2021 and 2022, it turned a loss of £31m before tax into a profit of £32m for the year to 31 March 2022.[91] In many ways, this puts it ahead of its competitors.

Presciently, Starling Bank has deliberately kept clear of crypto assets and services and described them as too high risk.[92]

Besides becoming profitable, the increase in a number of related measures has been remarkable in the year to 31 March 2022 compared to the previous

16-month accounting period. Net interest income rose from £59 m to £122m and fees and commission income increased from £34m to £58m. The latter largely comes from customer card transaction fees.

The changes in the balance sheet are even more extraordinary. Debt securities rose over 50% from £1.5bn to £2.3bn. This figure consists largely of government and supranational bodies' securities and covered bonds issued by other banks.

Cash at the Bank of England almost doubled from £3.2bn to £6.1bn. Customer loans rose by over 40% from £2.2bn to £3.2bn. Over 40% of this related to mortgages while the rest was large to loans made to businesses under various government-backed COVID-19 lending schemes. The advantage of this lending is that almost all of it is guaranteed by the government's British Business Bank. The funding for this lending can be seen in the liabilities side of the balance sheet with £2.2bn in funding provided by the Bank of England (note 21 to the financial statements). Approximately, 20% of the mortgage book is to finance 'BTL' properties.

There has been almost a 50% increase in small and medium-sized company deposits with Starling (from £3.4bn to £5.0bn) and an over 60% increase in personal customer deposits £2.4bn to £3.9bn) (note 20 to the financial statements).

These substantial changes appear to reflect a more aggressive push to grow the business. For example, the increase in mortgage lending from zero in the period to the end of March 2021 is the result of buying existing mortgage books, acquiring Fleet Mortgages a mortgage originator in the BTL market, and what is described as 'forward flow agreements with third-party mortgage originators'.[93] There are no details provided regarding these latter funding arrangements. Starling bought Fleet Mortgages from West Hill Capital in August 2021 for £50m. Fleet Mortgages is described as a firm which originates, sells and services first 'charge buy-to-let mortgage loans, primarily to professional and semi-professional landlords'.[94] Going forward Starling Bank will be the sole funder of the Fleet Mortgage business.[95]

Starling's acquisition of the Masthaven mortgage book for a reported £500m came after the latest accounts were published.[96] Masthaven was another FinTech challenger bank that decided to withdraw from the banking market early in 2022.[97] Masthaven's business focused on bridging loans and 'loans for homebuyers who may not meet conventional banks' requirements'.[98]

In parallel, Starling Bank is marketing the services of its subsidiary Engine. The latter is a 'BaaS business'.[99] This will allow Starling Bank to enter into partnerships with firms, in both the US and EU, to develop modular banking services. This will include customer ID verification and onboarding as well as 'card issuance and management ... Engine is designed as a "bank in a box" that will help financial service providers build tools and apps rapidly ... [included in] a ready-to-use toolkit for a range of banking and payment processing applications'.[100] Of course, the concept of a 'bank in a box' has been around for some time. Peter Burt, then CEO of Bank of Scotland in 1999, put forward the concept on the eve of the 'dotcom boom'.

In July 2022, Starling Bank reversed its EU banking strategy and withdrew its application for an Eire banking licence which would have given it banking access across the EU.[101] The reasons for this change in direction are not clear.

The revised strategy may be driven by the new investors who came in in Spring 2021: Fidelity, Qatar Investment Authority and Goldman Sachs and there is talk of flotation in the near future.[102]

Trustly

Trustly Group AB ('Trustly') is a Swedish FinTech payments business. It is authorised under the Swedish Payment Services Act 2010 and supervised by the Swedish Financial Supervisory Authority (SFSA) (Finansinspektionen). As a business authorised in accordance with PSD II, it can provide cross-border payment services within the EU/EEA. Trustly is also 'deemed' authorised and regulated by the FCA under the Temporary Permissions Regime. This status allows EEA-based firms to operate in the UK for a limited period while seeking full authorisation. Since 2018, Trustly has been majority-owned by Nordic Capital, a Swedish private equity fund.

Trustly operates a relatively straightforward business model fully focused on providing payment services. As a privately owned company, it provides relatively few details about its operations and finances. However, in the latest figures available for the calendar year 2020, Trustly reported net revenue of 1,974m SEK and earnings before interest, taxes, depreciation and amortisation ('EBITDA') of 821m SEK. The exchange rate for Swedish Krona (SEK) and US$s is near enough one for one. The business has almost five hundred full-time equivalent employees.

Trustly was planning a $9bn flotation but this has been deferred since it is reported that the Swedish regulator has raised concerns regarding the firm's compliance with 'money laundering and terrorist financing prevention rules'.[103] The payments business reported that 'the review is ongoing and the SFSA has not yet communicated any assessment or conclusion'.[104] It is reported that Trustly is currently undertaking due diligence on its end-user customers.[105]

Finally, Trustly continues to expand by acquisition with the purchase of Ecospend in the UK mentioned earlier.

Klarna Bank AB

Klarna, a Swedish bank, has focused on coupling access to short-term credit via 'BNPL' and creating a business model which removes the need for card payments. The former BNPL approach is easily replicated, and many have followed Klarna. Additionally, using PSD II to develop new markets is also,

Open Banking and FinTech Business Models in the UK 133

now, well-travelled ground. However, Klarna has gone further with a business model which relies heavily on its unique branding.

'Rather than project the business as simply an on-line payment services firm able to offer credit Klarna seeks to use its brand based around the products of its merchant partners to engage the emotions of its customers.'[106]

'Our tonality adapts, mirroring where the customer is in our model. For example, in the attract phase we grab their attention with our smooth products, while further down into the engage phase, we guide them more, explaining why our product is smooth. This process ensures that we create a natural flow from a consumer first hearing about Klarna, all the way to them joining the Klarna ecosystem'.[107]

Klarna Bank AB is authorised and regulated by the SFSA. This gives it passporting rights across the EU. In addition, like Trustly, it is deemed authorised by the Prudential Regulation Authority and it is subject to regulation by the FCA under the 'Temporary Permissions Regime, which allows EEA-based firms to operate in the UK for a limited period while seeking full authorisation'.[108]

Klarna is also experimenting with taking customer deposits. It is 'soft-launching' this in Germany with a select number of customers to get user feedback before initiating a wider roll-out. This may, in due course, be linked to Klarna savings accounts which are already available to its Swedish customers.[109] It is unclear, if this is being done to allow Klarna to access funding more cheaply or as part of a broader customer engagement and retention strategy.

FINANCIAL FOUNDATIONS OF THE BUSINESS MODEL

The business is largely dependent on commission paid to Klarna by retailers. In the calendar year 2021, commission income in total was 11.3m SEK compared to only 3.2m SEK net interest income. Costs were significantly up in 2020 producing a loss of 7.1m SEK compared to a loss of 1.4m SEK for the previous year.[110]

The balance sheet at the end of 2021 was dominated by the 25m SEK held in cash at the central banks and government securities; 62m SEK in short-term loans to customers and 58m SEK deposited with Klarna by customers.[111]

As can be seen this is a very different model to other challenger banks.

CHALLENGES TO THE KLARNA MODEL GOING FORWARD

Systems and controls relating to data security In recent years Klarna had been subject to a number of allegations regarding its data security. For example, in 2021, after undertaking a system update for around 30 minutes just 10000 Klarna app users had access to other user account information although no bank or card information was compromised.[112] in 2020 a number of UK residents complained to the data protection regulator about being marketed Klarna services sent by email to their personal email addresses although never having previously been Klarna customers.[113] Klarna apologised and said that the emails were 'sent to Klarna consumers who have recently used one of Klarna's products or services including Klarna's checkout technology'.[114]

In terms of fraud, apparently criminals are keen on BNPL systems.[115] The assertion is that the latter have weaker fraud controls than other banks and credit card companies. Klarna denies that its arrangements are any more lax than other banks.[116]

In Spring 2022, the Integritetsskyddsmyndigheten (IMY), the Swedish Authority for Privacy Protection, fined Klarna 7.5 SEK. IMY stated that:

> During the investigation, Klarna has continuously changed the information provided on how the company handles personal data...IMY states that Klarna did not then provide information on the purpose for which... personal data was processed in one of the company's services. The company also provided incomplete and misleading information about who were the recipients of different categories of personal data when data was shared with Swedish and foreign credit information companies.[117]

Klarna has announced that it is appealing the decision.[118]

The regulation of BNPL

Currently, short-term interest-free credit, better known as BNPL arrangements are exempt from credit and other financial services regulation in the UK. Following the growth of this market, primarily lead by Klarna in the UK, the government consulted on bring this area of credit under credit and financial services regulatory control. As a result, the government announced 'that lenders will be required to carry out affordability checks, ensuring loans are affordable for consumers...that advertisements are fair, clear, and not misleading'. Lenders offering the product will need to be authorised and supervised by the FCA and borrowers will be able to complaint to the Financial Ombudsman Service (FOS).[119]

The new regime will need to be enacted via secondary legislation and new rules made by the FCA. This is likely to take well into 2024.

Similarly, the EU is also proposing to amend its Consumer Credit Directive.[120] It will ensure that consumers are provided with all the necessary information and that lenders undertake borrower affordability checks.[121]

It is not clear how these measures will affect Klarna's, and others, business model and how this may affect its costs, for example, for improved data protection arrangements, affordability assessments and compensation payments for successful customer complaints. All that can be said is that Klarna's valuation has fallen dramatically, along with that of other tech stocks.[122]

Revolut

Revolut has been described as attempting to be 'the everything store of internet banking'.[123] The firm is authorised as a bank by the Central Bank of Lithuania. This gives it banking passporting rights across the EU. The business is currently seeking banking licences in both the UK and the US (see below). The business is London based and in the UK Revolut is authorised by the FCA under the e-money regulations. This information along with other regulatory material is provided at the foot of its website in very faint and small text. The regulatory information is similarly displayed on its Spanish and Singaporean websites. The Estonian website is only set out in Russian while the US and Australian websites cannot be viewed from the UK.

The website has a similar look and feel to many other FinTech firms.

US and UK banking licence applications

As mentioned above in Spring 2021, Revolut applied for a UK banking licence, and it submitted a similar application to the California Department of Financial Protection and Innovation as well as the Federal Deposit Insurance Corporation (FDIC).[124] Currently, if a customer adds funds to their Revolut account in the US, they are credited to a parallel customer account with Metropolitan Commercial Bank.[125] The latter also issue cards on behalf of Revolut. Savings made by a customer to their 'Revolut Vault' US product are credited to a customer account at Sutton Bank.[126] Both Metropolitan Commercial Bank, New York and Sutton Bank, Attica, Ohio, are FDIC insured. It is unclear why both applications are being delayed.

Business areas/model

Revolut provides its customers with a range of services 'including electronic money and payments through a prepaid card via a free and tiered subscription model, peer-to-peer payments, foreign currency exchange services, junior accounts, exposure to precious metal commodity prices, the ability to buy and sell certain shares and fractional shares in listed companies and cryptocurrencies through the Group's trading partners'.[127]

Financials

Revolut's financial statement for the year to the end of December 2020 (the latest available) shows revenue of over £222m largely derived from card and interchange fees and customer subscriptions for Revolut services. This is a 34% increase from the previous year. Losses for the year are £206m compared with £107m for the previous year.

The balance sheet shows that by far the largest asset is just over £5bn of cash or cash equivalents and liabilities to customers are £4.6bn. This largely represents customer e-money accounts.

136 Business Models, Emerging Economies and the Way forward

Revolut's corporate culture

Culture within a firm can be measured using a number of metrics. These include staff morale and engagement; how customers are treated; the firm's attitude towards its regulators and the spirit, as well as the letter, of the rules and how well corporate governance operates.

Attitude towards its staff

There have been persistent reports of poor staff practices at Revolut, including allegations of recruitment methods that were effectively quashed by the financial services regulators in the early 1990s.[128] This was broadly confirmed by the Revolut CEO in a blog in 2019.[129] It is difficult to say, from the outside, whether the culture has improved. The information provided in the latest annual report is very generic and bland.

Attitude to its customers

How customer complaints are treated is another indicator of corporate culture. The FCA does not publish customer complaints information on Revolut, but a Financial Times Freedom of Information request in 2019 found that in the recent past Revolut, in relation to its size, has received more customer complaints compared to its competitors.[130] Unfortunately, there is no more recent data available.

This leaves anecdotal information. There are two cases in the public domain relating to 'authorised push payment ('APP') frauds. Unfortunately, Revolut has not signed up to the industry's voluntary 'The Contingent Reimbursement Model Code (CRM Code)'.[131] The case of Miss N was decided in favour of the customer by the Financial Services Ombudsman in September 2021.[132] The Ombudsman was critical of Revolut's fraud detection and prevention arrangements and also the way the firm communicated with the customer during the course of the fraud and subsequently in handling her complaint.[133] There was a similar complaint reported in The Guardian newspaper.[134] Here the customer lost all her savings for her wedding, and Revolut refused to reimburse her. In response to being contacted by the journalist, Revolut responded by saying that while 'Revolut is not a signatory to the CRM … it relies on the spirit of it'. Based on the newspaper article it is questionable whether this last statement by Revolut is correct.[135]

Issues with the regulators

In the Lithuanian parliament concerns about the country's ability to supervise banks such as Revolut have been raised by Stasys Jakeliunas, head of the Lithuanian parliament's budget and finance committee.[136] The Bank of Lithuania fined two Revolut companies in Lithuania a total of €200,000 for anti-money laundering failures.[137]

It has also had problems with some of its marketing in the UK.[138] The central issue is that much of regulatory compliance requires the regulated firm to internalise the need for it to comply with both the spirit and the letter of the regulations. Much of the UK's rule book is written using broad objectives and principles (e.g., 'treat customers fairly'). This will become even more important with the advent of the new FCA 'Consumer Duty' which came into force in 2023.[139] Regulated firms without the right culture and ethics are likely to fail to comply with the regulatory objectives.[140]

In May 2019, Revolut contacted the FCA to report that its suspicious activity identification system had been deactivated for three months towards the end of 2018.[141] The issue came to light after a 'whistleblower' 'contacted the company's board over serious failings in its transaction approval system'.[142] This followed Revolut reporting 'a spate of suspected money laundering on its digital payments system' to the FCA in 2018.[143]

Improving corporate governance

The firm appears to be dominated by its two founders. In the banking sector, and in other areas, this can be a significant issue. To address these concerns, Revolut appointed Richard Davies as its chief operating officer.[144] Mr Davies has a long history in UK mainstream banking. Unfortunately for Revolut, he left after a year to become CEO of Allica, a newly authorised bank.[145]

Martin Gilbert, founder of Aberdeen Asset Management, became chair of Revolut towards the end of 2019.[146] This was followed in March 2020 by the appointment of Bill Rattray as the interim chief financial officer.[147] Rattray had worked with Gilbert at Aberdeen Asset Management for many years.[148] He replaces David MacLean, who had joined Revolut from Metro Bank in 2019.[149] In the autumn of 2020, Richard Holmes was appointed by Revolut to oversee its banking license application.[150] Holmes had previously been Standard Chartered's European businesses CEO.

Other key non-executive appointments included Caroline Britton, who is hugely experienced in financial services as a former partner at Deloitte. In March 2020, Revolut appointed two new non-executive directors to its board: Michael Sherwood, former Goldman Sachs International CEO and Ian Wilson, a retail banking risk expert who formerly worked a Royal Bank of Scotland, Santander and Tesco Bank.[151]

This is a strong board, but the question continues whether any board can effectively rein in a dominant CEO. These are issues that the Bank of England will be considering when assessing the firm's banking licence application. Revolut's cause may not be helped by Revolut's marketing stunt to appoint a dog to the C-suite as part of its pet insurance launch.[152] There may also be questions regarding the firm's apparent strategy to enter into markets which raise concerns whether these be cryptocurrencies or offering customers advances on their wages.[153]

138 *Business Models, Emerging Economies and the Way forward*

There have been a large number of senior risk and compliance staff departures. The executive responsible for global affairs including expansion, authorisations, regulatory affairs, etc.[154]; the UK's chief risk officer; the UK's head of regulatory compliance; the UK's money laundering reporting officer; the UK's data protection officer and the UK's deputy money laundering reporting officer have all resigned.[155] This is clearly very unusual and it is not clear what has caused these departures.

Open banking in the UK—The future?

Almost none of the open banking challenger firms are profitable and the worry is that we have been here before. In the late 1990s, a number of innovative internet banks were established (e.g., Egg Bank, Smile Bank, Intelligent Finance, Cahoot). They are almost all founded by existing large banks or insurance companies but were generally run independently with their own management and 'style'. They used innovative marketing and product offerings to attract internet customers. They were seen as the future as the stodgy 'bricks and mortar' banks closed branches.

However, none of these banks or neo-banks really prospered. Some like Egg Bank were sold on several times as their value eroded. Others became shadows of when they were in their pomp often subsumed within their funding organisations.

Will it be different this time? The new open banking firms remain dependent on continuing funding from various types of investment businesses. It is unclear how much longer the cash spigots will remain open. Some, such as Adyen in Amsterdam, are already highly successful with a clear and focused business model. However, with the exception of Klarna and a few others, the vast majority have failed to distinguish themselves. They have relatively high-cost bases in relation to their income.

The market identified by, for example, Adyen, can probably only sustain a relatively small number of firms. A number of others are trying, to a greater or lesser extent, to move into the field of internet banking. This means taking on the full rigour of banking regulation. This is both onerous and costly compared to the more lightly regulated e-money and payment services regimes. Their main sources of income will depend on lending and on fees and charges. Lending to any great extent means incurring risk and will consumer regulatory capital. '"Egg thought they'd invented alchemy, but soon found it's fine lending money out—getting it back is the difficult bit"'.[156] It is possible that a change in the economic climate may threaten the funding and value of the current crop of firms.[157]

A business model which develops a reliance on fees and charges income will expose these firms to conduct business regulation. All this will be in highly competitive markets setting limits on pricing strategies. Finally, UK-based businesses with any pretensions to scale will need to set up EU-authorised firms to allow them to have access to the much larger EU financial services markets and significantly greater numbers of consumers.

Finally, the next section is both an elegy but also a suggested way forward.

What might be lost

Before moving on, it may be worth reflecting on what may be lost. In the UK, the total number of bank and building society branches fell from 13,345 in 2012 to 8,810 in 2021, a fall of 4,535 or 34%. A certain number of these closures is enviable as technology and customer demand change. However, something important is lost if this goes too far.

The high-street bank, as the name suggests, is embedded in its community. Its presence on the high street, in each town engenders a high level of stability and familiarity in the area. Each branch closed, along with well-known retail shops, post offices etc., helps destroy another piece of a sense of community.

We cannot turn back the clock, nor should we try to, but a place that loses its sense of community may fall into the 'slough of despond'. The online banks provide important functions, but they have no special identity within each local community.

As each branch closes the bank's links with a place slips. They employ no local staff and they have no presence. They only know their customers as bits of data. The children of their staff are absent from local schools and they have no engagement with local festivals and celebrations. The people go with the branch closures and the bank has nothing to contribute to that particular community.

Online banks and payment service firms need to build themselves into their local community. If they grow to any size, they need to consider opening regional offices and training and employing local people. They need to be more than short-term tenants; they need to be embedded in a 'place' with a sense of local identity.

Notes

1 TheBanks.eu, 'List of EMIs in the UK', <https://thebanks.eu/list-of-emis/United-Kingdom>, accessed 26 July 2022.
2 Electronic Money Association website, <https://e-ma.org/about>, accessed 26 July 2022.
3 The Electronic Money Regulations 2011, provisions 21 and 22.
4 FCA Handbook, 'Perimeter Guidance (PERG) 3A.3. The Definition of Electronic Money'.
5 British Business Bank website, 'Companies in Which the Future Fund Has a Shareholding', <https://www.british-business-bank.co.uk/ourpartners/coronavirus-business-interruption-loan-schemes/future-fund/future-fund-companies/>, accessed 15 August 2022.
6 Beanstalk website, <https://beanstalkapp.co.uk>, accessed 27 July 2022.
7 Emma website, <https://emma-app.com/about-us>, accessed 27 July 2022.

8. Money Dashboard website, <https://www.moneydashboard.com/features>, accessed 27 July 2022.
9. Daily Business, 'ClearScore Buys Budgeting Platform Money Dashboard', 20 May 2022.
10. McKinsey website, 'What the Embedded-Finance and Banking-as-a-Service Trends Mean for Financial Services', (1 March 2021), <https://www.mckinsey.com/industries/financial-services/our-insights/banking-matters/what-the-embedded-finance-and-banking-as-a-service-trends-mean-for-financial-services>, accessed 31 July 2022.
11. Forbes website, 'Why Open Banking Could Usher in a New Era of Growth in 2022', (10 March 2022) <https://www.forbes.com/sites/forbesfinancecouncil/2022/03/10/why-open-banking-could-usher-in-a-new-era-of-growth-in-2022/>, accessed 31 July 2022.
12. Lowell Bryan, *Breaking Up the Bank*, (Dow Jones Irwin, Homewood, Illinois, 1988), 94 and following.
13. For example, FT, 'Co-op's Big Adventure May Turn Sour', (18 March 2012), <https://www.ft.com/content/4879ad2c-6e90-11e1-a82d-00144feab49a>.
14. FT, 'UK Banking: Mixing Mediocrity', (20 November 2020).
15. FT, 'Sainsbury's Considers Sale of Banking Arm', (1 November 2020).
16. Sir Christopher Kelly, 'Failings in Management and Governance—Report of the Independent Review into the Events Leading to the Co-operative Bank's Capital Shortfall', (30 April 2014), <https://assets.ctfassets.net/5ywmq66472jr/3LpckmtCnuWiuuuEM2qAsw/9bc99b1cd941261bca5d674724873deb/kelly-review.pdf>, accessed 28 July 2022.
17. FT, 'Worldpay to Provide Loans to Small Businesses', (4 December 2015).
18. altfi website, 'Embedded Finance: Klarna Partners with Liberis for Revenue-Based Finance', (29 June 2021), <https://www.altfi.com/article/8051_embedded-finance-klarna-partners-with-liberis-for-revenue-based-finance>, accessed 28 July 2022.
19. FT, 'Lloyds Reshuffles Bankers as Part of Chief's New Strategy', (29 June 2022).
20. Crowdfund Insider, 'Satago, a Provider of Invoice Financing, Teams Up with Sage, Lloyds Bank', (10 June 2022), <https://www.crowdfundinsider.com/2022/06/192134-satago-a-provider-of-invoice-financing-teams-up-with-sage-lloyds-bank/>, accessed 27 August 2022.
21. Adyen website, 'Adyen Expands beyond Payments, Announces Embedded Financial Products', 30 March 2022, <https://www.adyen.com/press-and-media/2022/adyen-expands-beyond-payments-announces-embedded-financial-products>, accessed 29 July 2022.
22. Adyen website, 'Capital Markets Day', (31 March 2022), <https://www.adyen.com/investor-relations/events/capital-markets-day-2022>, accessed 29 July 2022.
23. Klarna website, 'Klarna Launches 'Klarna Kosma' Sub-Brand and Business Unit to Harness Rapid Growth of Open Banking Platform', (31 March 2022), <https://www.klarna.com/international/press/klarna-launches-klarna-kosma-sub-brand-and-business-unit-to-harness-rapid-growth-of-open-banking-platform/>, accessed 29 July 2022.
24. FT, 'Klarna's Widening Losses Driven by Rapid Expansion', (28 February 2022).
25. FT, '"Buy Now Pay Later" Boom Fuels Consumer Debt Concerns as Transactions Soar', (12 February 2022).
26. Ibid., (FT article on BNPL, 12 February 2022).
27. HM Treasury, 'Regulation of Buy-Now Pay-Later: Response to Consultation', (June 2022), <https://assets.publishing.service.gov.uk/government/uploads/system/uploads/attachment_data/file/1083547/BNPL_consultation_response__Formatted_.pdf>, accessed 30 July 2022.

28 Australian Payroll Association, 'Sharper Lending Algorithms and "More Affluent" Users Turning Beforepay to Profitability, CEO Says', (1 May 2022), <https://www.austpayroll.com.au/sharper-lending-algorithms-and-more-affluent-users-turning-beforepay-to-profitability-ceo-says/>, accessed 30 July 2022.
29 Sidney Morning Herald website, 'Beforepay Shares Sink 44% on Debut', (17 January 2022), <https://www.smh.com.au/business/companies/beforepay-shares-sink-44-per-cent-on-debut-20220117-p59ovd.html>, accessed 30 July 2022.
30 Revolut website, 'On-Demand Pay—Get Your Pay Any Day', <https://www.revolut.com/legal/on-demand-pay/>, accessed 30 July 2022.
31 FT, 'Beware the Promise of Salary Advance Schemes', (17 May 2022).
32 Aite-Novarica website, 'Making Ends Meet: On-Demand Pay and Employer-Based Loans', (24 February 2021), <https://aite-novarica.com/report/making-ends-meet-demand-pay-and-employer-based-loans>, accessed 30 July 2022.
33 Chartered Institute of Personnel and Development website, 'Policy Position on Employer Salary Advance Schemes', (28 June 2021), <https://www.cipd.co.uk/news-views/cipd-voice/Issue-29/policy-position-employer-salary-advance-schemes#gref>, accessed 30 July 2022.
34 FCA website, 'FCA Sets Out Views on Employer Salary Advance Schemes', 30 July 2020, <https://www.fca.org.uk/news/statements/fca-sets-out-views-employer-salary-advance-schemes>, accessed 30 July 2022.
35 Bloomberg website, 'Earned-Wage Access Products Face Fresh Scrutiny From CFPB, States', (3 January 2022), <https://news.bloomberglaw.com/banking-law/earned-wage-access-products-face-fresh-scrutiny-from-cfpb-states>, accessed 30 July 2022.
36 Alan Brener, *Housing and Financial Stability*, (Routledge, Abingdon, Oxfordshire, 2020), 105–6.
37 Ibid., (Brener), 117–8.
38 Equifax website, 'M&S Bank Enables Faster Mortgage Applications with Open Banking', <https://www.equifax.co.uk/about-equifax/press-releases/en_gb/-/blog/m-s-bank-enables-faster-mortgage-applications-with-open-banking/>, accessed 30 July 2022.
39 consent.online website, <https://consents.online>, accessed 30 July 2022.
40 Equifax website, 'United Utilities and Equifax UK Deliver First Real Time Open Banking Product for Water Industry: Platform Accelerates Social Tariff Application Process', (7 July 2021), <https://www.equifax.co.uk/about-equifax/press-releases/en_gb/-/blog/united-utilities-and-equifax-uk-deliver-first-real-time-open-banking-product-for-water-industry-2>, accessed 30 July 2022.
41 Experian website, 'Open Banking and Experian Boost', <https://www.experian.co.uk/consumer/experian-boost-open-banking.html>, accessed 30 July 2022.
42 UK Government website, 'Open Banking Privacy Notice', (23 March 2021), <https://www.gov.uk/government/publications/open-banking-privacy-notice/open-banking-privacy-notice>, accessed 30 July 2022.
43 Ecospend website, <https://ecospend.com/our-mission/>, accessed 30 July 2022.
44 Nordic Capital website, 'Trustly, Backed by Nordic Capital, Acquires Ecospend, Further Strengthening Position in the UK', (30 May 2022), <https://www.nordiccapital.com/news/trustly-backed-by-nordic-capital-acquires-ecospend-further-strengthening-position-in-the-uk/>, accessed 30 July 2022.
45 altfi website, 'Nutmeg Reportedly Overtakes Scalable Capital to Become Europe's Largest Digital Wealth Manager', 31 January 2020, <https://www.altfi.com/article/6140_nutmeg-reportedly-overtakes-scalable-capital-to-become-europes-largest-digital-wealth-manager>, accessed 30 July 2022.
46 altfi website, 'Here are the UK's 6 Leading Digital Wealth Managers', (17 June 2020), <https://www.altfi.com/article/6714_here-are-the-uks-6-leading-digital-wealth-managers>, accessed 30 July 2022.

142 *Business Models, Emerging Economies and the Way forward*

47 FT, 'Atom Bank Valued at £435mn as It Targets Market Listing Next Year', (16 February 2022).
48 Chief Executive Officer report in the 2021 Financial Statements, 11, <https://www.atombank.co.uk/~/docs/annual-report-20-21.pdf>, accessed 4 August 2022.
49 Ibid., (Atom), 97.
50 Ibid., (Atom), 97.
51 Monzo Financial Statements for the period to 28 February 2022, 7, <https://monzo.com/static/docs/monzo-annual-report-2022.pdf>, accessed 5 August 2022.
52 Ibid., (Financial Statements), 21.
53 Ibid., (Financial Statements), 24.
54 Ibid., (Financial Statements), 106.
55 The Guardian, '"I Suffered Anxiety": Monzo Founder on the Pressures of Running a Digital Bank', (30 January 2021).
56 FT, 'Monzo Tells Almost 500,000 Customers to Change Pin', (5 August 2019).
57 Monzo website, 'Get a loan that treats you right. Ditch hidden fees, confusing terms and waiting around. Achieve your goals and feel in control with a Monzo loan. If you're eligible, our representative APR is 8.9% for loans more than £10,000, up to £25,000. For loans up to £10,000 it's 23.9%', (accessed 4 August 2022). HSBC website, '3.9% APR representative. This rate is available for loans between £7,000 and £15,000.', <https://www.hsbc.co.uk/loans/products/personal/>, accessed 4 August 2022.
58 FT, 'How Monzo is Banking on Customer Apathy', (23 April 2019).
59 Ibid., ('Customer Apathy').
60 FT, 'FinTech Users Just Can't Get Enough of Traditional Banks', (7 January 2020).
61 FT, 'Monzo Chief Vows to Scale up Business despite FinTech Turmoil', (14 July 2022).
62 Ibid., ('Monzo Chief').
63 FCA website, 'Firm-Level Complaints Data Sortable Table: 2022 H2', <https://www.fca.org.uk/data/firm-level-complaints-data-sortable-table>, accessed 16 September 2023.
64 Ibid., (FCA Complaints).
65 Ibid., (FCA Complaints).
66 Ibid., (FCA Complaints).
67 Financial Services Ombudsman publication—Ref: DRN1029460, <https://www.financial-ombudsman.org.uk/decision/DRN1029460.pd>, accessed 5 August 2022.
68 FT, 'The Virus Has Crushed the Challenger Bank Dream', (2 November 2020).
69 Supra (n 51), (Monzo Financial Statements)168.
70 altfi website, 'Monzo Withdraws US Banking Licence Application', (4 October 2021), <https://www.altfi.com/article/8385_monzo-withdraws-us-banking-licence-application>, accessed 5 August 2022.
71 Supra (n 51), (Monzo Financial Statements).
72 Supra (n 51), (Monzo Financial Statements).
73 FT, 'Monzo takes a step into the US digital banking fray', quoting Ronit Ghose, head of banks analysis for Citigroup, (13 June 2019).
74 altfi website, 'The US Regulator Told Monzo That Its Banking Licence Was Unlikely to Be Approved', 4 October 2021, <https://www.altfi.com/article/8385_monzo-withdraws-us-banking-licence-application>, accessed 6 August 2022.
75 PRA, 'Non-systemic UK Banks: The Prudential Regulation Authority's Approach to New and Growing Banks', (Supervisory Statement SS3/21), April 2021, <https://www.bankofengland.co.uk/-/media/boe/files/prudential-regulation/supervisory-statement/2021/ss321-april-2021.pdf?la=en&hash=026DEAE7DDDEA5A80DC4BFDFF12821E5DF033E71>, accessed 5 August 2022.

76 Ibid., (SS3/21), 3.4.
77 Ibid., (SS3/21), 3.6.
78 Ibid., (SS3/21), 3.4.
79 Ibid., (SS3/21), 3.5.
80 Ibid., (SS3/21), 3.4.
81 Ibid., (SS3/21), 3.4.
82 FT, 'BoE Hit Monzo with Tougher Capital Demands during Fundraising', (6 August 2020), <https://www.ft.com/content/ca53305d-e44f-4f1c-a74e-dd2583b7c26b>, accessed 5 August 2022.
83 FCA website, 'Financial Crime Controls at Challenger Banks', (22 April 2022), <https://www.fca.org.uk/publications/multi-firm-reviews/financial-crime-controls-at-challenger-banks>, accessed 7 August 2022.
84 HM Treasury and Home Office, 'National Risk Assessment of Money Laundering and Terrorist Financing 2020', (December 2020), <https://assets.publishing.service.gov.uk/government/uploads/system/uploads/attachment_data/file/945411/NRA_2020_v1.2_FOR_PUBLICATION.pdf>, accessed 7 August 2022.
85 Ibid., (HMT and Home Office report), 55.
86 Supra (n 83), (FCA 'Financial Crime Controls').
87 Supra (n 83), (FCA 'Financial Crime Controls').
88 'A politically exposed person (PEP) is someone who's been appointed by a community institution, an international body or a state, including the UK, to a high-profile position within the last 12 months', (e.g., a head of state, a judge, a manager of a state-owned enterprise). It also includes family members, business associates etc. Law Society website, 'Politically exposed persons', (19 December 2019), <https://www.lawsociety.org.uk/topics/anti-money-laundering/peps>, accessed 7 August 2022.
89 Supra (n 83), (FCA 'Financial Crime Controls').
90 Supra (n 83), (FCA 'Financial Crime Controls').
91 Starling Bank, 'Annual Report & Consolidated Financial Statements 2022', 111, <https://www.starlingbank.com/docs/annual-reports/Starling-Bank-Annual-Report-2022.pdf>, accessed 8 August 2022.
92 PYMNTS website, 'Why Starling Bank CEO Said No to Crypto', (9 June 2022), <https://www.pymnts.com/digital-first-banking/2022/why-starling-bank-ceo-said-no-to-crypto/>, accessed 9 August 2022.
93 Supra (n 91), (Starling Financial Statements), 12.
94 West Hill Capital website, 'Exit Announcement – Starling Bank Acquires Fleet Mortgages for £50 million', <https://westhillcapital.co.uk/exit-announcement-starling-bank-acquires-fleet-mortgages-for-50-million-2-5m-capital-subscribed-on-launch-by-west-hill-investors-and-management/>, accessed 9 August 2022.
95 Ibid., (West Hill).
96 FT, 'Starling Bank Faces Questions over Reliance on State-Backed Funding', (1 August 2022).
97 Masthaven Bank website, 'Important Announcement about Masthaven Bank', (January or February 2022), https://www.masthaven.co.uk, accessed 9 August 2022.
98 FT, 'Masthaven Launches Digitally-Focused UK Bank', (28 November 2016).
99 PYMNTS website, '5 Things to Know About Starling's Banking-as-a-Service Product, Engine', <https://www.pymnts.com/news/banking/2022/5-things-to-know-about-starlings-banking-as-a-service-product-engine/>, (21 July 2022), accessed 9 August 2022.
100 Ibid., ('5 Things').
101 Retail Banker International website, 'Starling Bank Shelves Plans to Secure Irish Banking Licence', (19 July 2022), <https://www.retailbankerinternational.com/news/starling-bank-withdraws-licence-application/>, accessed 9 August 2022.

144 *Business Models, Emerging Economies and the Way forward*

102 FT 'Starling Bank Matures from Digital Upstart to Mainstream Lender', (8 November 2021).
103 Trustly, 'Year-end Summary', (January–December, 2020), 8, <https://site.trustly.net/site/binaries/content/assets/verticals/press/trustly-year-end-summary-2020-in-english-only.pdf>, accessed 9 August 2022.
104 Ibid., (Trustly Year-end Summary).
105 FT, 'Trustly Postpones $9bn Flotation after Regulator Flags Concerns', (3 May 2021).
106 Alan Brener, 'EU Payment Services Regulation and International Developments', in Iris H-Y Chiu and Gudula Deipenbrock (eds), *Routledge Handbook of Financial Technology and Law*, (Routledge, Abingdon, 2021), 167.
107 Cited in Brener, 'EU Payment Services Regulation and International Developments', 167.
108 Klarna website, 'Terms and Conditions', <https://www.klarna.com/uk/terms-and-conditions/>, accessed 10 August 2022.
109 Klarna website, 'Klarna Launches Bank Account in Germany', (10 February 2021), <https://www.klarna.com/international/press/klarna-launches-bank-account-in-germany/>, accessed 10 August 2022.
110 Klarna Report and Accounts for 2021, 25, <https://www.klarna.com/assets/sites/15/2022/03/28054307/Klarna-Bank-AB-Annual-report-2021-EN.pdf>, accessed 11 August 2022.
111 Ibid., (Klarna accounts) 26.
112 Klarna website, 'Klarna Comment: Statement on App Bug', (27 May 2021), <https://www.klarna.com/uk/blog/written-statement-on-app-bug/>, accessed 11 August 2022.
113 BBC New website, 'Privacy Watchdog to Probe Klarna after Email Backlash', 13 October 2020), <https://www.bbc.co.uk/news/business-54521820>, accessed 11 August 2022.
114 Ibid., (BBC website).
115 CNBC website, '"Criminals Love Buy Now, Pay Later": How Fraudsters Exploit Popular Interest-Free Payment Plans', (18 November 2021), <https://www.cnbc.com/2021/11/18/criminals-exploit-buy-now-pay-later-services-like-klarna-and-afterpay.html>, accessed 11 August 2022.
116 Ibid., (CNBC website).
117 IMY website, 'Administrative Fine against Klarna after Investigation', (31 March 2022), <https://www.imy.se/en/news/administrative-fine-against-klarna-after-investigation/>, accessed 11 August 2022.
118 Klarna website, 'Klarna Comment: SDPA's Conclusion of Their Audit', 29 March 2022, <https://www.klarna.com/uk/blog/klarna-comment-sdpas-conclusion-of-their-audit/>, accessed 11 August 2022.
119 UK government website, 'Regulation of Buy-Now-Pay-Later Set to Protect Millions of People', (20 June 2022), <https://www.gov.uk/government/news/regulation-of-buy-now-pay-later-set-to-protect-millions-of-people>, (accessed 11 August 2022).
120 EU website, 'Proposed Consumer Credit Directive', COM(2021) 347 final 2021/0171(COD), <https://eur-lex.europa.eu/legal-content/EN/TXT/?uri=CELEX%3A52021PC0347&qid=1655282823416>, accessed 11 August 2022.
121 EU website on Consumer Credit, <https://ec.europa.eu/info/business-economy-euro/banking-and-finance/consumer-finance-and-payments/retail-financial-services/credit/consumer-credit_en>, accessed 11 August 2022.
122 FT, 'Klarna's Valuation Crashes to under $7bn in Tough Funding Round [From over $46bn Just over a Year Ago]', (11 July 2022).
123 Bloomberg website, 'Revolut's $33 Billion Bank App Hits a Roadblock in Britain', (6 May 2022), <https://www.bloomberg.com/news/articles/2022-05-06/

revolut-33-billion-banking-app-wants-to-play-in-the-big-league>, accessed 12 August 2022.
124 Techcrunch website, 'Revolut Applies for Bank Charter in the US', (22 March 2021), <https://techcrunch.com/2021/03/22/revolut-applies-for-bank-charter-in-the-us/>, accessed 13 August 2022.
125 Revolut website, 'Welcome to US Revolut', <https://blog.revolut.com/us-welcome-to-revolut/>, accessed 13 August 2022.
126 Revolut website, 'Where Can I Find the Terms and Conditions for My Savings Vaults?', <https://www.revolut.com/en-US/help/wealth/savings-vaults/using-savings-vaults/where-can-i-find-the-terms-conditions-for-my-savings-vaults>, accessed 13 August 2022.
127 'Revolut Report and Financial Statements for the year to 31 December 2020', 11, <https://assets.revolut.com/pdf/Revolut%20Ltd%20Annual%20Report%20YE%202020.pdf>, accessed 12 August 2022.
128 For example, Wired website, 'Revolut Insiders Reveal the Human Cost of a FinTech 'Unicorn's' Wild Rise', (28 February 2019), <https://www.wired.co.uk/article/revolut-trade-unions-labour-fintech-politics-storonsky>, accessed 14 August 2022.
129 Revolut website, 'Revolut's Culture: The Past, Present and the Future', (3 April 2019), <https://blog.revolut.com/weve-made-mistakes-but-were-learning/>, accessed 14 August 2022.
130 FT, 'Revolut Leads Fintechs in Complaints to Ombudsman', (26 May 2019).
131 Lending Standards Board website, 'The Contingent Reimbursement Model Code (CRM Code)', <https://www.lendingstandardsboard.org.uk/crm-code/#firms-that-have-signed-up-to-the-code>, accessed 14 August 2022.
132 Financial Services Ombudsman (FOS), 'Reference: DRN-2868209', (September 2021), <https://www.financial-ombudsman.org.uk/decision/DRN-2868209.pdf>, accessed 14 August 2022.
133 Ibid., (FOS Adjudication).
134 The Guardian, 'Scammers Took £20,000 of My Wedding Savings but Revolut Won't Pay Me Back', (10 August 2022).
135 'Contingent Reimbursement Model Code for Authorised Push Payment Scams', (28 April 2022). In particular, sections SF 1(2) (a)-(e), <https://www.lendingstandardsboard.org.uk/wp-content/uploads/2022/04/LSB-CRM-Code-V3.0-28-April-2022.pdf>, accessed 14 August 2022.
136 FT, 'Revolut's Russian Founder Stirs up Lithuania's Fintech Debate', (20 February 2019).
137 Bank of Lithuania website, 'Regulatory Measures on Revolut Group Companies', (18 March 2022), <https://www.lb.lt/en/news/sanctions-on-revolut-group-companies>, accessed 14 August 2022.
138 FT, 'City Watchdog to Probe Revolut's 'Spoof' Takeaway Ad Campaign Fintech Firm Attracts Ire of Regulators after It Admits Using Falsified Data', (8 February 2019).
139 FCA website, 'The FCA's Consumer Duty Will Lead to a Major Shift in Financial Services', (27 July 2022), <https://www.fca.org.uk/news/press-releases/fca-consumer-duty-major-shift-financial-services>, accessed 14 August 2022.
140 Alan Brener, *Strategies for Compliance*, (Routledge, Abingdon, Oxfordshire, 2021), 146 and following.
141 Freshbusinessthinking website, 'Revolut in Money Laundering Controversy', (1 March 2019), <https://www.freshbusinessthinking.com/purpose/revolut-in-money-laundering-controversy/46468.article>, (accessed 14 August 2022).
142 Ibid., (freshbusinessthinking).
143 FT, 'Revolut Reports Suspected Money Laundering on Its System', (17 July 2018).
144 FT, 'Revolut's New Hire Pledges to Improve Governance', (15 July 2019).

145 FT, 'Banking Veteran Departs Revolut after One Year', (27 July 2020).
146 Reuters, 'Martin Gilbert Joins Fintech Revolut as Chairman', (12 November 2019), <https://www.reuters.com/article/revolut-chairman-idUSL4N27R3AB>, accessed 14 August 2022.
147 Finance Magnate's website, 'Bill Rattray Becomes Interim CFO at Revolut', (18 March 2020), <https://www.financemagnates.com/executives/moves/bill-rattray-becomes-interim-cfo-at-revolut/>, accessed 14 August 2022.
148 Ibid., (Finance Magnate).
149 Ibid., (Finance Magnate).
150 Sifted website, 'Revolut Nominates City Veteran to Lead UK Bank Bid, Hoping "White Hairs" Will Woo Regulators', (October 2020), <https://sifted.eu/articles/revolut-chairman/>, accessed 14 August 2022.
151 Revolut website, 'Revolut Further Strengthens Its Board, with City Veterans Michael Sherwood and Ian Wilson', (5 March 2022), <https://www.revolut.com/news/revolut_further_strengthens_its_board_hiring_city_veterans_michael_sherwood_and_ian_wilson>, accessed 14 August 2022.
152 FT, 'Revolut Offers Dog Tricks as Bank of England Licence Talks Drag on', (4 February 2022).
153 FT Lex, 'Revolut: Loans for Paydays after Their Heyday May Prompt Naysay', (19 August 2021) and FT, 'Revolut: Bitcoin Hype-Merchant or Bank?', (27 January 2021).
154 altfi website, 'Revolut's Only Female EXEC Becomes Latest to Leave the Company', (11 July 2022), <https://www.altfi.com/article/9522_revoluts-only-female-exec-becomes-latest-to-leave-the-company>, accessed 14 August 2022.
155 altfi website, 'Revolut UK Regulatory and Risk Bosses Quit as FinTech Giant Awaits UK Banking Licence Decision', (25 July 2022), <https://www.altfi.com/article/9586_revolut-uk-regulatory-and-risk-bosses-quit-as-revolut-awaits-uk-banking-licence-decision>, accessed 14 August 2022.
156 FT, 'Lessons from the UK's First Fintech Failures', (21 March 2021).
157 FT, 'Half a Trillion Dollars Wiped from Once High-Flying FinTechs', (18 July 2022).

9 Open Banking, Financial Inclusion and Economic Growth in Developing Countries

Economic growth in developing countries

"I always wanted to run a small shop," she says. "But I wasn't allowed to have money of my own, I didn't have the resources to be an entrepreneur."[1]

The subject of economic growth and developing countries is one which is wide and vast. This chapter looks at a narrow element of the issue and considers the different approaches taken by Brazil and India, two large developing countries, that have taken very active steps to promote and develop open banking, albeit in very different ways.

Economic growth is dependent on many factors. One of these is the ability of individuals to engage directly in the economy.[2] This includes selling goods and services including their labour and being able to cheaply and easily recirculate the proceeds back through the economy. Empirical research undertaken in India suggests that 'financial inclusion is a driver of economic growth ...Therefore, the government and policymakers must look to address policy issues to foster economic growth through financial inclusion'.[3]

There is a close link between financial inclusion and financial literacy. Here the combination of easy and affordable access to the financial system combined with financial understanding or literacy 'facilitates the flow of funds from savers to borrowers. This efficient flow of funds largely leads to a sustainable, efficient and effective financial system'.[4] The empirical evidence has demonstrated a close relationship between financial inclusion and economic development influenced by a number of other factors including 'income, inequality, literacy, urbanization, and physical infrastructure'.[5]

It helps empower those disadvantaged sections of the population to engage in the wider economy and to move away from a hand-to-mouth existence. With financial information and access to digital payment systems, there are opportunities to generate more employment and to reduce poverty and income disparities. Empirical research has established 'a significant correlation between higher financial inclusion and lower poverty rates for both full and developing Asian' states.[6] There is also a 'significant relationship between higher financial inclusion and lower income inequality'.[7] The empirical

DOI: 10.4324/9781003331339-12

research goes further finding that 'financial inclusion removes the obstructions such as poverty, income inequality and unemployment to a great extent and leads to a sustainable economic growth'.[8]

The appreciation of the importance of financial inclusion and economic growth dates back to the 1960s in India.[9] In a non-traditional central bank role, the Reserve Bank of India (RBI) advocated for the importance of financial inclusion and worked with the central government to start to set up the necessary infrastructure.[10]

However, much of the work to promote financial inclusion has been focused on access to bank branches and ATMs. It is only more recently with the rise of online banking and digital access to payments that the focus moved to open banking.[11]

In both case studies in this chapter, the approach taken in both jurisdictions is very much top-down. The private sector has been given important parts to play but they are heavily guided and controlled by the state and its agencies, including the central bank. Unlike in, say, the UK or Europe, there is no mention of competition. In many ways, the latter is perceived as having failed. Large sections of the population are financially excluded both by having little or no access to financial institutions and by high costs. The incumbent banks do not act competitively, and the market has not worked. Moreover, the failure of competition has muzzled innovation. Direct intervention by the government was seen as the solution. All the indications are of success.

As a result, both Brazil and India provide considerable insights into how open banking may be used by developing economies to increase financial inclusion both as a tool of social engineering and as a part of a strategy of economic growth. India's approach to open banking has been part of a much wider series of projects aimed at giving everyone access to government services via individual digital identities. This certainly reflects the vast population of India and its, otherwise, highly diffused system of government. An intended consequence of this approach in India has been a reduction in corruption and inordinate bureaucratic complexity.

Brazil

The position prior to the introduction of open banking

Brazil is an ideal jurisdiction for launching open banking. The country is dominated by the five big banks: The private institutions of Itaú, Bradesco and Santander Brasil, and the state-controlled Banco do Brasil and Caixa Econômica Federal. It has been described as a 'small club of institutions' which dominate 'the high street in Latin America's largest economy, long notorious for its costly banking fees and borrowing rates, with their fat margins often the source of public anger'.[12] Credit has traditionally been very expensive and difficult to obtain, partly due to the habitual high levels of inflation and the lack of competition. For a long time, the banks made easy returns by investing customer deposits in high-yielding government debt.[13]

The big five banks have an 80% share of commercial banking assets and the 'rigidity and oligopolistic nature of Brazil's banking sector' is described as constraining the Brazilian economy and 'leaving too many Brazilians unbanked and consumers looking for better and more convenient options'.[14]

The military government in the late 1960s encouraged consolidation of the banking sector in Brazil. Following the ending of the army's rule in Brazil in 1985, the central bank continued this process of concentration. This was reinforced by the banking crisis in 1994 which aimed to reduce the 'excessive participation of state-owned banks and their politically guided objectives'.[15] In 2008, two of the leading banks merged to form the largest private bank in Brazil when Itaú and Unibanco combined. 'The share of total lending of the top four banks rose from 60% to 70% between mid-2008 and mid-2009, and this level has increased steadily to 75% by the end of 2015. These levels place Brazil's banks as one of the most concentrated banking sectors in Latin America, together with Mexico's, where the top three banks have retained nearly 70% of total lending since 2002'.[16]

About a third of the country's adult population is unbanked (some 55 million).[17] Almost 50% of transactions are in cash.[18] 'Central Bank statistics show that nearly 30% of all municipalities have no bank branch ...There are seven states (out of twenty-seven), mostly in the North, where more than 70% of municipalities have no bank branch. In the country as a whole, about 1,680 of 5,600 municipalities have no bank branches.'[19]

There is no interbank direct-debit scheme and credit transfers are slow, expensive and limited to business hours.[20] Debit and credit cards are not widely accepted since the fees charged to merchants are high and they are reimbursed slowly.[21] The credit card market in Brazil is dominated by the usual international duopoly of MasterCard and Visa. Fees for credit cards in Brazil are around 2.2% compared to 1.7% in the USA, 1.5% in Canada and 0.3% in the European Union.[22]

Since 1993, Brazil has operated what is described as its 'official payments system': The boleto bancário.[23] It is operated by Federação Brasileira de Bancos (FEBRABAN), the Brazilian Federation of Banks, a trade body with 126 member banks. It accounts for some 3.7 billion transactions each year or 25% of all online transfers.[24] It operates both in a paper and online format. In the case of the former, the merchant gives the customer a pre-filled payment authorisation form issued by the merchant's bank. The customer can initiate the payment by taking it to a bank branch or authorised payment outlet such as a post office or supermarket. Customers can also initiate payments via the ATM network. For merchants, the process can be slow. Confirmation of the payment to the merchant can take two to three business days. However, there is Boleto Flash which can confirm the payment in less than two hours on business days.

150   *Business Models, Emerging Economies and the Way forward*

Banks charge a fee to the merchant for every payment made by the customer using boleto bancário. The fee varies between 1 and 12 Brazilian Reals (12 Reals is approximately US$2.40) depending on the bank.

Merchants can opt for registered and unregistered boleto bancário payments. The former is more expensive and requires the merchant to pre-notify its bank of its customer invoice which can then be matched to the customer's payment when it is received. The bank can then generate various reports for its merchant customers. Registration was compulsory for boletos worth more than Brazilian Reals 2,000 (around 3.7% of all issued boletos).

In recent years, there have been increasing concerns about the boleto payments system being used for fraud including payments for cryptocurrencies and issues with international payments. As a result, Federação Brasileira de Bancos now requires that all its banking members register all boletos.[25] Previously, anyone could issue a boleto and the issuing bank would first become aware of the boleto only when it was presented for payment. Registration requires fiscal data (i.e., their personal Cadastro de Pessoas Físicas (CPT) fiscal number) from both the merchant and the customer.

There were several issues with the boleto system. These included delays in processing and confirming payments; the cost to merchants; the 'closed shop', anti-competitive element which restricted it to only those who were members of the Brazilian banking federation. This excluded other non-member banks and fintech operations.

Introduction of open banking

In 2013, responsibility for regulating the payments industry was devolved to Brazil's central bank. The aim, among others, was to improve access to credit and develop better financial inclusion in the payments system.[26]

Open banking was seen by the Brazilian government as a means of social engineering to increase access to affordable payments for everyone including the large percentage of the population without bank accounts. This is in addition to the more usual open banking objectives of increasing competition, innovation and payment efficiency.[27] This approach was supported by the International Monetary Fund which advocated 'allowing authorized third parties to develop services and tools for customers to facilitate the development of new entrants and new business models, as well as a specific FinTech framework to stimulate innovations'.[28] It is possible that this approach was in response to research which demonstrated a correlation between the expansion of access to banking services and economic growth. Based on bank branch penetration, data research has found 'that higher financial development fosters firm growth, higher labor demand, and higher average wages, especially for cities initially in banking deserts'.[29]

In addition, customer preference was moving to more modern and cheaper payment services based on more smartphones. This assisted in what some also consider as 'a well-ingrained culture of instalment payments in Brazil.

Open Banking, Financial Inclusion and Economic Growth 151

The widespread use of payments for purchases both large and small began in the 1950s with the popularisation of "crediários", whereby consumers could register with a store to purchase items but then pay for them over a series of months. This culture of instalment payments lent itself to increased digital finance'.[30]

Further, the government has singled out a number of changes in banking services over recent years. For example, it tried to introduce more competition in the credit card market in 2010 and 2013 trying to increase access to credit and encourage the development of more financial products.

The Brazilian central bank, Banco Central do Brasil (BCB) has taken open banking a long way forward and a considerable amount has been published on these developments.[31] The BCB and the National Monetary Council (CMN) have been working together to develop open banking. The CMN is in 'charge of formulating monetary and credit policies, aiming to preserve Brazilian monetary stability, and to promote economic and social development'.[32] In many ways, the aim of the BCB and the CMN is focused on the customer. Within this central perspective, there are multiple objectives. The stated aims are 'to enhance the efficiency in credit and payments markets by promoting a more inclusive and competitive business environment, as well as preserving the security of the National Financial System'.[33]

Both the central bank and the CMN see open banking as key to promoting innovation and competition and in this, they mirror developments in both the UK and EU. However, as mentioned earlier, they also have a wider objective to promote 'financial citizenship'.[34] They see open banking as favouring 'new forms of relationship among the participating entities, their customers, and partners... [and this would allow a] proper understanding and anticipation capabilities regarding the demands of customers, which have been changing at a significant pace'.[35]

This aligns with the BCB's mission statement: 'to ensure the stability of the currency purchasing power, to foster a sound, efficient and competitive financial system, and to promote the economic well-being of society'.[36]

In a Communiqué issued in Spring 2019, the central bank set out four elements to its open banking plan. This would include institutions regulated by the BCB providing:

I 'data on products and services offered by participating institutions (location of branches and other access channels, product characteristics, contractual terms and conditions, financial costs, among others);
II customer personal data (name, address, among others);
III customer transactional data (data related to deposit accounts, credit operations and other products and services contracted by customers, among others); and
IV payment services (initialization of payments, transfers of funds, payments of products and services, among others)'.[37]

Implementing open banking

The BCB subsequently carried out a public consultation in 2019 on implementing these plans.[38] The implementation plan was issued in May 2020 with new regulations requiring the four elements mentioned above to be implemented in a series of phases and completed by December 2021.[39] The May 2020 joint statement and the BCB Circular set out a range of requirements including the importance of non-discriminatory access to the open banking system.[40] The joint statement also sets out the governance structure to oversee the implementation process and the arrangements to agree on technology standards, operational procedures, system security etc.

Most of the implementation will be undertaken by the BCB 'coordinating the initial self-regulatory efforts of the regulated firms'.[41] The BCB will control this by defining the open banking rules, approving decisions and revisions and retaining veto power if necessary.

Governance is subject to the 'Deliberative Council' which decides on implementation and it will, from time to time, put forward technical standard proposals for the BCB to agree. The Deliberative Council has a balanced membership of six independent directors and six other directors who are representatives of organisations providing open banking services.[42]

Pix

Having announced its plans in 2019, in November 2020 the Central Bank of Brazil set up the highly successful e-payment system known as Pix. It has come to dominate retail payments in the country.

The 36 large and medium banks in Brazil, defined as those with more than 500,000 accounts, are required to offer Pix. However, such is the popularity of Pix most banks and FinTech firms in Brazil joined Pix. As of January 2023, more than 120 million Brazilians use Pix for transactions (nearly 60% of the population).[43]

In contrast to the older payment systems Pix payments are instantaneous and it operates continuously. It works for all types of accounts including savings and current accounts. It is cheap to use.[44] Payments are initiated by scanning a QR code or keying in a Pix password (e.g., a telephone number, email address or tax reference number). There is no intermediary, and the process is simpler and faster than boleto bancário. It also operates round the clock and not just on 'business days'. It has 'payment finality' so that the merchant is certain of being paid once the transaction is initiated and confirmation is received.

In line with open banking more generally, progress has also been made on customers authorising the disclosure of their banking transactions, and the open banking system is moving towards permitting the transmission of information about customer investments, pension and insurance arrangements.

While Pix has been highly successful, as elsewhere, fintech firms are dependent on funding rounds and may face severe difficulties in Brazil since interest rates have risen from 2% in Spring 2021 to over 13% in June 2022.[45]

Customer acquisition costs remain high so many fintech models in Brazil may not be financially viable. Additionally, the social inclusivity agenda has still some way to go since customers need to have a bank account to operate Pix.

Effect of open banking on incumbent banks

There were concerns that open banking would erode the earnings of incumbent banks. '"There's a big debate going on in Brazil [on] what's going to happen to the profitability of the big banks", Bank of America analyst Mario Pierry told the FT'.[46] Fees account for about 30% of bank earnings and Moody's estimated the banks could lose Brazilian Reals 16bn ($2.9 bn) of payment fees (almost 10%).[47] The average return on equity for banks in Brazil was 17.2% in 2019.[48] This compares with 10.6% in the US, 8.8% in Asia-Pacific and 5.8% in Europe.[49]

The Financial Times has reported that incumbent banks have been cutting costs, closing branches and sacking staff.[50] These banks are also responding to the rise of Nubank, seen as 'Brazil's internet banking unicorn'. The latter was listed on the New York Stock Exchange in December 2021 but its value has since halved.[51] NuBank claims to be the fifth-largest financial institution in Latin America by number of active customers with 85 million customers in Brazil, Mexico and Colombia.[52] It is, in turn being challenged by Neon and C6. Neon claims to have some 15 million customers.[53] In its latest funding round BBVA, a global Spanish bank raised its stake to just under 30%.[54] C6 bank claims to have some 25 million customers.[55] In June 2021 JP Morgan Chase took a 40% stake in the bank.[56]

Pix—Lesson from the approach taken

The Brazilian central bank has adopted a highly centralised approach to implement open banking. It is important to understand that open banking forms part of the central bank's medium-term working agenda known as Agenda BC#. This agenda includes:

'The Dimension **Education** aims at raising citizen awareness so that everyone can participate in the financial markets and strengthen their habit of saving,
The '**Inclusion** Dimension' brings about non-discriminatory access to the market,
The '**Transparency** Dimension' aims at improving the price formation process,
The '**Competitiveness** Dimension' seeks to promote adequate pricing by favouring competitive access to markets. There are several innovations—driven by technology—that encourage competition. On the other hand, challenges related to reducing barriers, simplifying procedures and managing risks still prevail.

The agenda also includes excellence and sustainability'.[57]

This included having only one option for open banking and mandating that all the large banks should use this. Rule-making and policy setting were not delegated, and governance was centralised.[58] There are a range of possible reasons for this, none of which are mutually exclusive. In part, it may be because the aims of the central banks were not congruent with those of the large incumbent banks. The latter are likely to be more focused on maintaining their high revenue and profits from existing payment arrangements. Without mandated encouragement, mere exhortations would have been ineffective. Additionally, the central bank had as its highest priority user access as part of its socio-economic policy objectives. Consequently, the payment process had to be easy to use, all-encompassing and robust.

With all this in mind the central bank has taken a very interventionist role. It is the rule maker, the 'operator and manager' of the clearing and 'settlement infrastructure' and the coordinator of the various parts of the market.[59] This includes corralling all the large banks into participating.[60] There is a consultative 'Pix Forum'. This has some two hundred members and has a purely advisory role.[61] As mentioned above the central bank both manages and operates Pix. There are two infrastructures needed for this. These are the: 'The Transaction Accounts Identifier Directory—database that links 'aliases' (e.g., telephone number, email addresses etc.) and users' account information and The Instant Payments System—a real-time gross settlement (RTGS) infrastructure that settles transactions between different institutions in few seconds'.[62]

While competitiveness features as a policy 'dimension' there is a much greater emphasis on socio-economic objectives. This is in sharp contrast to the approach taken in more developed economies such as the EU and UK. The Brazilian policy objectives seem to be entirely appropriate for the country and the success of Pix has been outstanding.

India

Context

India has taken a range of policy steps to promote financial inclusion. This has been led by the RBI's committee on financial inclusion which in 2015 stated that saw financial inclusion as providing 'convenient access to a set of basic formal financial products and services that should include savings, remittance, credit, government-supported insurance and pension products to small and marginal farmers and low-income households at reasonable cost with adequate protection progressively supplemented by social cash transfer besides increasing the access for micro and small enterprises to formal finance with greater reliance on technology to cut costs and improve service delivery, such that by 2021 over 90% of the hitherto underserved sections of society become active stakeholders in economic progress empowered by formal finance. Thus, the financial inclusion initiative as envisaged by the

Committee is much broader in scope, going beyond the traditional domain of the Reserve Bank'.[63] Included in this policy was the need to develop easy and cheap access to the payments and financial information system. The Committee's 2015 report set out the strategy to achieve this.[64]

This was not an isolated initiative but was woven into a much wider government digital strategy. India's approach is different to that taken by other jurisdictions including developing economies such as Brazil. In many ways, it is a 'gesamtwerk' conceived as a whole but implemented in stages and amended as it proceeds. In many ways, it can be seen as a piece of socio-economic engineering.

The India Stack is at its centre. This contains three main layers of digital infrastructure rolled over the years.[65] These are:

- The Aadhaar digital ID system allows for identity verification and the mapping of information across datasets.
- Unified Payments Interface (UPI) interoperable payments system and the work of the role of the National Payments Corporation of India (NPCI).
- The network of regulated account aggregators. These firms have been described as 'operation of data fiduciaries that act as intermediaries between individuals and financial companies'.[66]

This is coupled with a series of parallel initiatives which include:

- Pradhan Mantri Jan-Dhan Yojana (PMJDY) (Prime Minister's People Wealth Project).
- The provision of cheap mobile phone handsets.

Open banking fits within these programmes and to understand the development of open banking in India, and, as mentioned above, we first need to understand the term "Indian Stack". As part of the financial inclusion mission to allow the citizens of the country to access several important services digitally, the government of India introduced the Indian Stack. The latter is based on 'a set of digital identity products centered around Aadhaar, India's national identity program. More than 1.31bn (95%) Indians possess an Aadhaar number'. Their digital identity is based on biometric information together with information on their age, gender, mobile number etc. It enables users to access a range of documents and information including driver licenses, educational diplomas, insurance policies etc.[67] Its foundations are a set of open standard APIs and an infrastructure to provide services safely and digitally to the citizens.[68] As with other jurisdictions safety and the prevention of fraud are crucial to the success of online commerce in general and open banking specifically.[69]

In common with many other developing countries much of the population of India lacks easy access to financial services. The International Monetary Fund Financial Access Survey for 2022 uses two measures for financial access: ATMs and commercial bank branch access per 100,000 people.[70] For example, in 2022 India had 14.31 commercial bank branches per 100,000 people. This compares with 16.55 in Brazil and, as a benchmark, 19.77 in Canada.[71] The contrast is even greater when it comes to ATMs. India has 24.64 per 100,000 people compared with 97.94 in Brazil and over two hundred in Canada.[72]

The drive towards greater financial inclusion

The key factors behind this move to increase access to financial services were explained in 2011 by K C Chakrabarty, Deputy Governor of the RBI.[73] These include, first, financial inclusion to lead the transformation of the economy and banking. 'It will change the way banking for the masses would be done. By doing so banks would be addressing not only the banking and several other financial services needs of the low-income population, but they also would be increasing the base for value-added banking services in times to come. Partnering in poverty and unemployment reduction and growth acceleration should not only be an altruistic objective for the banks, but a self-serving one'.[74]

Second, 'there has been an increasing recognition that finance is important for growth. Countries with better functioning banks and financial markets grow faster ... Finance also matters for income distribution, and poverty alleviation as it reduces information and transactions costs'.[75] More inclusive finance will enable the country to access the savings of its citizens and so increase domestic investment. Often a key motive behind the move to financial inclusion is the need to mobilise the savings of the unbanked or underbanked.[76]

In 2016 the RBI issued its Master Direction re account aggregators. Under this Direction, the account aggregator network was introduced as a financial data-sharing system. The aim was to 'facilitate investing and credit', to give 'consumers access and control over their financial records' and to 'expand the potential pool of customers for financial sector entities and fintech companies'.[77] In outline, through using an account aggregator individuals and businesses can share their financial data with the financial information users (FIUs). When the FIU need to access the data, they request consent from the users through the account aggregator. Once the latter receives the necessary consent from the user, they will share the data with the FIU through the Unified Payment Interface (UPI) application.[78]

The account aggregator performed an intermediary role between all Financial Information Providers (FIPs) (for example, banks, insurance companies, non-bank financial companies, etc.). Via the account aggregators, the customers are able to share their financial information. The existing regulation allows the FIU to submit a request to access consumer data. Once consent from the customer is received the account aggregators can facilitate information sharing from the FIP to the FIU. Sharing the data through account aggregators is safe as the account aggregators are legally not allowed to see the data and cannot store any financial information of the customer shared by the FIPs. The account aggregators are regulated by the RBI, the Security Exchange Board of India, the Pension Fund Regulatory and Development Authority, and also the Insurance Regulatory and Development Authority of India.

Interestingly, the Goods and Services Tax Network (GSTN) is allowed to act as a FIP through the system of account aggregator.[79] The GSTN was set up to facilitate the introduction of a unitary tax system across all the states.[80] The indirect tax platform assists taxpayers in India to prepare and file their returns and also to make their tax payments. The GSTN is allowed to share the GST information as a FIP using the account aggregator framework.

With the introduction of a secured framework for account aggregators, the Indian government has allowed over a hundred million people to digitally access and digitally share their own financial data across entities with confidence through a secure channel.[81] In addition, the account aggregator allows individuals to have control over their personal financial data and gives them the power to approach any financial institution user (FIU) when they need credit.

As of September 2023, the RBI had approved thirteen account aggregators in India.[82]

Sandboxes

In India, the government has introduced regulatory 'sandboxes' to aid the safe development of digital financial services including open banking. There are three main financial regulators in India: the RBI, the Insurance Regulatory and Development Authority of India, and the Securities Exchange Board of India. All three have sandbox schemes but the RBI is the most developed and the most relevant to the open banking initiative and the testing of account aggregator systems.[83]

The role of the NPCI

The NPCI is a 'not for profit' company which acts as 'umbrella organisation for operating retail payments and settlement systems in India, is an initiative of Reserve Bank of India (RBI) and Indian Banks' Association (IBA) under the provisions of the Payment and Settlement Systems Act 2007, for creating a robust Payment and Settlement Infrastructure in India'.[84] The NPCI aims to bring 'innovations in the retail payment systems through the use of technology for achieving greater efficiency in operations and widening the reach of payment systems'.[85]

In 2016 the NPCI introduced the UPI system to enable participating organisations to transfer payments securely in real-time. This includes transfers involving banks and between, for example, suppliers.[86] There remains the question of whether the UPI system creates arrangements that deter new entrants into open banking. For example, it is claimed that the State Bank of

India (SBI) has combined UPI with its own 'shopping app, Yono, which offers discounts on selected top brands through using SBI services'. The power of SBI may be too great for others to compete successfully.[87] Other major banks in India, such as HDFC and ICICI, also offer online shopping with multiple discounts and offers using UPI systems.[88]

PMJDY (Prime Minister's people wealth project)

Alongside the Indian Stack, there are a number of other government initiatives. These include the PMJDY (the Prime Minister's People Wealth Project), Government E-Marketplace (GeM) and the Goods and Service Tax mentioned earlier. The PMJDY, launched by the Indian government in 2014, aims to provide access to financial services to the unbanked and underbanked population of the country. Specially, PMJDY aims to ensure that everyone has access to affordable basic savings and deposits bank accounts, insurance and pension.[89] By the end of August 2023, it is claimed that some 500 million people have benefited from PMJDY.[90]

This initiative has been praised by, for example, the Financial Times.[91] Besides favourable comments some in the media have been more cautious, '[b]eyond enabling account ownership and the use of financial services, the PMJDY also facilitated financial inclusion for a variety of demographics. While the program has made significant headway towards genuine financial inclusion, it is clear that improving policy communication, widening and deepening progress in low-income states, and ironing out the kinks in the bank-agent model will be crucial if these hard-fought gains are to prove sustainable'.[92] From the perspective of this book, these types of initiatives emphasise the importance of considering access to the payment infrastructure and economic growth as part of the wider issues of financial exclusion. It is possible to view the Indian government's GeM initiative in a similar light. This gives all types of businesses, large and small, equal digital access to accessing the government's procurement services.[93] This includes, importantly, ready access to online payment systems.

The important role of access to cheap internet-enabled mobile phones in India

The success of the various government schemes to develop financial inclusion has been greatly aided by the provision of cheap mobile internet-enabled handsets. This has had the effect of empowering not just the urban middle classes but the full range of the population including illiterate tribal communities.

'I never attended school', says Mallika, a member of an indigenous nomadic tribe in southern India. 'I can sign my name, guess where a bus goes, or what a road sign says, but not much beyond that'. (She believes she is 38 but doesn't have a proper birth record.)... Mallika, like 200 million other women in India, is illiterate. In the past few years though, millions of Indian women have gone online thanks to cheaper smartphones and mobile data, and apps that let them communicate using sounds and images. Anecdotal evidence suggests the phones are empowering many women to access information, build networks, and participate in markets'.[94]

This can be seen in the level of smartphone penetration in India which has risen from almost zero in 2009 to over 70% in 2023 and is forecast to rise to around 95% by 2028.[95] This compares with 85% currently in Japan, a much more economically developed country.[96] By way of comparison, the smartphone generation level in Brazil is 67% in 2023.[97]

The leap in smartphone access in India has been aided by the low cost of handsets. For example, an internet-enabled Jio (a Reliance company) Bharat V2 handset is available for 1600 Indian Rupees (approximately US $19).[98]

Conclusion

Broadly, jurisdictions such as the UK and EU have focused on setting up a legal framework to promote open banking. It has then been left to competition to work to deliver innovation and lower prices.

The challenges faced by developing countries are immense, including large remote and illiterate populations, very limited access to digital technology or even electricity, and often little to no engagement with either central or regional governments or with markets for goods and services. It is almost certainly a correct assessment both for the Brazilian and Indian central governments that, in this circumstance, competition will not aid increased financial inclusion and economic growth.

While both India and Brazil appreciate the importance of financial inclusion and economic growth, the approach taken by India is much more comprehensive and balanced with a strategy aimed at each person having their own digital identity. With this they are able, among other things, to access the open banking elements of the payment systems and engage in the financial economy. This includes the mobilisation of savings put to use for the wider economy.

There are many similarities between the Brazilian and Indian approaches. This includes not placing much, if any, reliance on competition to increase financial inclusion. Both also employ the central government and its agencies, including the central bank, for societal as well as economic and regulatory purposes. Both have embraced innovation where traditional financial institutions appeared to have been too complacent and lacking in innovation. As already mentioned, direct intervention by the government was seen as the solution and all the indications demonstrate success. They show how open banking may be used for a variety of purposes including facilitating economic inclusion and growth, engaging all citizens in a productive economy and helping governments to reduce, if not defeat, endemic corruption.

These two case studies are useful in showing what can be done and achieved in societies facing considerable challenges.

Notes

1. Wired website, 'In India, Smartphones and Cheap Data Are Giving Women a Voice', <https://www.wired.com/story/india-smartphones-cheap-data-giving-women-voice/>, accessed 11 September 2023.
2. Ebenezer Anarfo and others, 'Financial Inclusion and Financial Sector Development in Sub-Saharan Africa: A Panel Var Approach', (April 2019), International Journal of Managerial Finance 15(3), 444–463, 445.
3. Dipasha Sharma, 'Nexus between Financial Inclusion and Economic Growth', (2016), Journal of Financial Economic Policy 8(1), 13–36, 32.
4. Ibid., (Sharma), 16.
5. Loan Thi-Hong Van, 'Financial Inclusion and Economic Growth: An International Evidence', (2021), Emerging Markets, Finance and Trade, Vol 57, No. 1, 239–263, 244
6. Cyn-Young Park and Rogelio Mercado, 'Financial Inclusion, Poverty, and Income Inequality', (2018) Singapore economic review 63(1), 185–206, 204.
7. Ibid., (Park and Mercado), 204.
8. Ibid., (Park and Mercado), 186.
9. Suman Dahiya, Manoj Kumar and Radha, 'Linkage between Financial Inclusion and Economic Growth: An Empirical Study of the Emerging Indian Economy', (2020), Vision 24(2), 184–193, 186.
10. See speech by Raghuram Rajan, Governor of the Reserve Bank of India, 'The changing paradigm for financial inclusion' at the National Seminar on 'Equity, Access, and Inclusion—Transforming Rural India through Financial Inclusion', organised by the National Institute of Rural Development and Panchayat Raj, Hyderabad, 18 July 2016, <https://www.bis.org/review/r160719a.htm>, accessed 9 September 2023.
11. Ibid., (Rajan speech).
12. FT, 'Brazil's Biggest Banks Battle for Reinvention in Digital Era', (4 April 2021).
13. Ibid., (FT).
14. OMFIF website, Kate Jaquet, 'Brazil Is Undergoing a Fintech Revolution', (24 January 2023), <https://www.omfif.org/2023/01/brazil-is-undergoing-a-fintech-revolution/>, accessed 17 August 2023.
15. Gustavo Cortes and Renato Marcondes, 'The Evolution of Brazil's Banking System', (chapter 10) in Edmund Amann, Carlos Azzoni, and Werner Baer (eds), *The Oxford Handbook of the Brazilian Economy*, Oxford Handbooks (OUP, 2018), 207.
16. Ibid., (Cortes and Marcondes), 212.
17. PagBrasil website, 'Cash Is Still King in Brazil', (4 July 2019), <https://www.pagbrasil.com/insights/cash-still-king-brazil/>, accessed 17 August 2023.
18. Ibid., (PagBrasil).
19. World Bank website, 'Access to Financial Services in Brazil' A study led by Anjali Kumar, (2005), 3, <https://documents1.worldbank.org/curated/pt/738461468743954483/pdf/30858.pdf>, accessed 17 August 2023.
20. European Payments Council website, 'Pix: The Rapid Development of Instant Payments in Brazil', (14 April 2002), <https://www.europeanpaymentscouncil.eu/news-insights/insight/pix-rapid-development-instant-payments-brazil>, accessed 18 September 2022.
21. Ibid., (European Payments Council).

Open Banking, Financial Inclusion and Economic Growth   161

22 Angelo Duarte and others, Bank of International Settlement's Bulletin No.52, (23 March 2022), 7, <https://www.bis.org/publ/bisbull52.pdf>, accessed 17 August 2023.
23 PagBrasil website, 'boleto bancário', <https://www.pagbrasil.com/payment-methods/boleto-bancario/>, accessed 17 August 2023.
24 Ibid., (PagBrasil website).
25 PPRO website, 'Registered Boleto Bancário: the impact for clients and merchants', (12 October 2017), <https://www.ppro.com/insights/registered-boleto-bancario-the-impact-for-clients-and-merchants/#:~:text=The%20new%20registered%20Boleto%20Banc%C3%A1rio,fraud%20and%20boost%20payment%20rates>, accessed 17 august 2023.
26 Provisional Measure No. 615 dated 17 May 2013 ('MP 615').
27 Banco Central do Brasil website, 'Open Finance', <https://www.bcb.gov.br/en/financialstability/open_finance>, accessed 17 August 2023.
28 IMF, 'IMF Country Report No. 18/339 Brazil Financial System Stability Assessment', (November 2018), 33, <https://www.imf.org/en/Publications/CR/Issues/2018/11/30/Brazil-Financial-System-Stability-Assessment-46411>, accessed 17 August 2023.
29 Julia Fonseca and Adrien Matray, 'The Real Effects of Banking the Poor: Evidence from Brazil', (March 2022), Griswold Center for Economic Policy Studies Working Paper No. 293, <https://gceps.princeton.edu/wp-content/uploads/2022/04/wp293_Matray_Fonseca.pdf>, accessed 18 August 2023.
30 Supra (n 14) (OMFIF).
31 Julia Vicente, 'Fintech Disruption in Brazil: A Study on the Impact of Open Banking and Instant Payments in the Brazilian Financial Landscape', (2020). Social Impact Research Experience (SIRE), 86 and Gabriel Quatrochi, Ana Lucia G. da Silva and José Eduardo Cassiolato, 'Banks 4.0 in Brazil: Possibilities to Ensure Fintechs Financing Role through Its Market Positioning, Innovation and Development', (2022), published online by Taylor and Francis, https://www.tandfonline.com/doi/full/10.1080/2157930X.2022.2086336, accessed 13 September 2022.
32 'The CMN created by Law 4.595, dated 31 December 1964—National Financial System', <https://www.bcb.gov.br/content/about/legislation_norms_docs/Law%204.595%2C%20dated%2012_31_1964%20-%20National%20Financial%20System.pdf>, accessed 17 September 2022.
33 Banco Central do Brasil website, 'Open Banking', <https://www.bcb.gov.br/en/financialstability/open_banking>, accessed 17 September 2022.
34 Ibid., (BCB website).
35 Ibid., (BCB website).
36 BCB website, 20202023 Strategic Map, <https://www.bcb.gov.br/content/publicacions/rig_2020_en/info_pag_09a.jpg>, accessed 18 September 2022.
37 BCB Communiqué 33,455 (24 April 2019), <https://www.bcb.gov.br/content/config/Documents/BCB_Open_Banking_Communique-April-2019.pdf>, accessed 18 September 2022.
38 BCB Public Consultation 73/2019, BCB, Open Banking, 9, <https://www.amf.org.ae/sites/default/files/publications/2022-01/centrab-bank-of-brazil-session-3.pdf>, (accessed 18 September 2022).
39 BCB website, 'New Regulation on Open Banking in Brazil', (8 May 2020), <https://www.bcb.gov.br/en/pressdetail/2330/nota>, accessed 18 September 2022.
40 Circular N° 4.015, de 4 de Maio de 2020, <https://www.in.gov.br/web/dou/-/circular-n-4.015-de-4-de-maio-de-2020-255164763>, accessed 18 September 2022.
41 Ibid., (Circular N° 4.015).
42 BCB website, 'Agenda BC#—Regulation of the Initial Governance Framework for the Open Banking Implementation', (24 June 2020), <https://www.bcb.gov.br/en/pressdetail/2338/nota>, accessed 18 September 2022.

162 *Business Models, Emerging Economies and the Way forward*

43 Sergey Sarkisyan, 'Instant Payment Systems and Competition for Deposits', (June 2023), Jacobs Levy Equity Management Center for Quantitative Financial Research Paper, SSRN, 12: <http://dx.doi.org/10.2139/ssrn.4176990>, accessed 17 August 2023.
44 BCB website, 'Pix', <https://www.bcb.gov.br/en/financialstability/pix_en>, accessed 18 September 2022.
45 FitchRatings website, 'Rising Interest Rates Test Brazilian Fintechs' Rapid Growth', (17 June 2022), <https://www.fitchratings.com/research/banks/rising-interest-rates-tests-brazilian-fintechs-rapid-growth-17-06-2022>, accessed 18 September 2022.
46 PYMNTS website, 'FinTech Competition Pressures Brazil's Biggest Banks', 4 April 2021, <https://www.pymnts.com/news/banking/2021/fintech-competition-pressures-brazil-biggest-banks/>, accessed 29 June 2023.
47 Supra (n 12) (FT April 2021).
48 Supra (n 12) (FT April 2021).
49 Supra (n 12) (FT April 2021).
50 Supra (n 12) (FT April 2021).
51 FT, 'SoftBank's LatAm Fund Co-head Commits to Further Investments despite Losses', (26 March 2023).
52 Nubank website, 'About Nu', <https://international.nubank.com.br/about/#:~:text=Nu%20was%20born%20in%202013,Brazil%2C%20Mexico%2C%20and%20Colombia>, accessed 18 August 2023.
53 Neon Bank website, 'Nossa história', <https://neon.com.br/conheca-a-neon>, accessed 18 August 2023.
54 Fintech Nexus website, Brazilian Unicorn Neon Raises $64 Million', (7 February 2023), <https://www.fintechnexus.com/brazilian-unicorn-neon-raises-64-million/>, accessed 18 August 2023.
55 C6 bank website, 'Get to Know the Bank of Your Life in Brazil and the World', <https://www.c6bank.com.br/quem-somos>, accessed 18 August 2023.
56 JP Morgan Chase Website, 'JPMorgan Chase Takes 40% Stake in Brazil's C6 Bank', (28 June 2021), <https://www.jpmorganchase.com/news-stories/jpmorgan-chase-takes-40-percentage-stake-in-brazils-c6-bank>, accessed 18 August 2023.
57 Banco Central do Brasil website, BC# agenda, <https://www.bcb.gov.br/en/about/bcbhashtag>, accessed 20 August 2023.
58 Breno Lobo and Carlos Eduardo Brandt, 'Pix: The Brazilian Fast Payment Scheme', (2022), Journal of Payments Strategy and Systems 15(4), 367–375, 369.
59 Ibid., (Lobo and Brandt), 370.
60 Law 12,865 of 9 October 2013, SPB (Sistema de Pagamentos Brasileiro).
61 Banco Central do Brasil website, 'Pix: BCB role', <https://www.bcb.gov.br/en/financialstability/pixcentralbanksrole>, accessed 20 August 2023.
62 Ibid., (BCB website).
63 'Report of the Committee on the Medium-term Path on Financial Inclusion', vii, <https://rbidocs.rbi.org.in/rdocs/PublicationReport/Pdfs/FFIRA27F4530706A41A0BC394D01CB4892CC.PDF>, accessed 5 September 2023.
64 Ibid., (RBI Financial Inclusion report), 56–62.
65 IMF Working Paper, Yan Carrière-Swallow, Vikram Haksar, and Manasa Patnam 'India's Approach to Open Banking: Some Implications for Financial Inclusion', (February 2021), 16, <file:///N:/Downloads/wpiea2021052-print-pdf.pdf>, accessed 9 September 2023.
66 Ibid., (IMF paper), 16.
67 India Stack website, 'Identity', <https://indiastack.org/identity.html>, accessed 4 September 2023.
68 Reserve Bank of India website, 11 November 2020, 'FinTech: The Force of Creative Disruption' (2020) RBI Bulletin 75, <https://rbi.org.in/Scripts/BS_ViewBulletin.aspx?Id=19899> accessed 4 September 2023.

69 Sudiksha Shree and others, 'Digital Payments and Consumer Experience in India: A Survey based Empirical Study' (2021), Journal of Banking and Financial Technology 5, 2, <file:///N:/Downloads/Digital_Payments_and_Consumer_Experience_in_India.pdf>, accessed 6 September 2023.
70 IMF website, 'Financial Access Survey', <https://data.imf.org/?sk=e5dcab7e-a5ca-4892-a6ea-598b5463a34c>, accessed 4 September 2023.
71 Ibid., (IMF FAS).
72 Ibid., (IMF FAS).
73 Special address by Dr K C Chakrabarty, Deputy Governor of the Reserve Bank of India, at BANCON 2011, Chennai, 4 November 2011, 'Gearing Up for the Competitive Impulse in the Indian Banking in Its Defining Decade', <https://www.bis.org/review/r111108a.pdf>, accessed 4 September 2023.
74 Ibid., (Chakrabarty).
75 Ibid., (Chakrabarty).
76 Taruna Gautam and Kapil Garg, 'Union Bank of India: Initiatives Towards IT-Enabled Financial Inclusion', (2014), *Sage Business Cases*. SAGE Publications.
77 Ministry of Finance website, Financial Institutions Onboarded on Account Aggregator (AA) Platform as Financial Information User (FIU), 12 December 2022, <https://pib.gov.in/PressReleaseIframePage.aspx?PRID=1882868#:~:text=Giving%20background%20information%2C%20the%20Minister,was%20introduced%20as%20a%20financial>, accessed 4 September 2023.
78 Sahamati website, 'Account Aggregators Are the Future of Data Sharing', <https://sahamati.org.in/what-is-account-aggregator/>, accessed 4 September 2023.
79 GST website, <https://www.gstn.org.in/home>, accessed 4 September 2023.
80 FT, 'Unity at Midnight Beckons with India's Tax Reform', 28 June 2017.
81 Times of India, Yogesh Kabirdoss, 'Indian Bank Activates Account Aggregator System', 18 July 2022, <https://timesofindia.indiatimes.com/business/india-business/indian-bank-activates-account-aggregator-system/articleshow/92955639.cm>, accessed 4 September 2023.
82 Sahamati website, 'Help Shape the Future of Data Empowerment in India', <https://sahamati.org.in/signatories-of-aa-participation-terms/#>, accessed 4 September 2023.
83 Economic Times website, 'Regulatory Sandbox Explained: How RBI Is Moderating FinTechs' Disruption in BFSI [Banking, financial services and insurance]', <https://bfsi.economictimes.indiatimes.com/news/policy/regulatory-sandbox-explained-how-rbi-is-moderating-fintechs-disruption-in-bfsi/87098591>, accessed 5 September 2023.
84 The National Payments Corporation of India (NPCI) website, <https://www.npci.org.in/who-we-are/about-us>, accessed 6 September 2023.
85 Ibid., (NPCI).
86 NPCI website, 'UPI Product Overview', <https://www.npci.org.in/what-we-do/upi/product-overview>, accessed 6 September 2023
87 Pinar Ozcan, 'Blurred Lines: How Open Banking is Facilitating Big Tech's Creep into Finance' (Saïd Business School, 26 January 2023), <https://www.sbs.ox.ac.uk/oxford-answers/blurred-lines-how-open-banking-facilitating-big-techs-creep-finance>, accessed 6 September 2023.
88 For example, HDFC and ICICI: HDFC website, 'Open Skies, Open Banking, HDFC Bank's APIs Power One of India's Leading Airlines to Maximise Revenue and Accelerate Growth', <https://developer.hdfcbank.com/>; ICICI's website, 'ICICI Bank Net Offers on Food, Groceries, Apparels, Travel and Many More', https://www.icicibank.com/offers/categories/category-listing/net-banking>, accessed 6 September 2023.
89 Ministry of Finance, Department of Financial Services website, 'Pradhan Mantri Jan-Dhan Yojana', <https://pmjdy.gov.in/about>, accessed 5 September 2023.
90 Ibid., (PMJDY), <https://pmjdy.gov.in/account>, accessed 5 September 2023.

91 FT, 'Emerging Markets 'Leapfrog' the West in Digital Payments Race', (30 November 2021).
92 The Mint website, 'The Admirable Success of the Jan Dhan Yojana', (28 August 2017), <https://www.livemint.com/Opinion/wfertnZlyGRTmGiyGnJLrI/The-admirable-success-of-the-JanDhan-Yojana.html>, accessed 5 September 2023.
93 Times of India website, 'The GeM in What Govt Buys: Commerce & Industry Minister Argues a Transition to GoI's Online Platform for Procurement Led to Savings by Departments & Transparency and Fair Competition for Vendors', (20 April 2023), <https://timesofindia.indiatimes.com/blogs/toi-edit-page/the-gem-in-what-govt-buys-commerce-industry-minister-argues-a-transition-to-gois-online-platform-for-procurement-led-to-savings-by-departments-transparency-and-fair-competition-for-vendo/>, accessed 5 September 2023.
94 Wired website, 'In India, Smartphones and Cheap Data Are Giving Women a Voice About 200 Million Women in the Country Are Illiterate. But Voice Memo and Image-Sharing Apps Make It Easier to Connect, Communicate, and Run Businesses', 4 January 2021, <https://www.wired.com/story/india-smartphones-cheap-data-giving-women-voice/>, accessed 5 September 2023.
95 Statista website, 'Smart Phone Penetration in India', <https://www.statista.com/statistics/1229799/india-smartphone-penetration-rate/>, accessed 5 September 2023.
96 Statista website, 'Share of the Population Owning a Smartphone in Japan', <https://www.statista.com/statistics/275102/share-of-the-population-to-own-a-smartphone-japan/#:~:text=It%20was%20estimated%20that%20more,than%2069%20percent%20in%202018>, accessed 5 September 2023.
97 Statista website, 'Smartphone Penetration in Brazil', <https://www.statista.com/forecasts/625406/smartphone-user-penetration-in-brazil>, accessed 5 September 2023.
98 Smartprix website, 'Jio Mobile Phones Price List in India', <https://www.smartprix.com/mobiles/jio-brand>, accessed 5 September 2023.

10 The Road Ahead

Introduction

The Habsburg Empire of Charles V was historically known as 'the empire on which the sun never sets'.[1] There is a rough similarity between this phrase and open banking if we think about its worldwide development. The sun never sets on open banking; it is a global phenomenon across continents and characterised by different drivers, approaches and degrees of implementation. The previous chapters demonstrated that open banking is an irreversible trend in the financial services industry. Consequently, there is and always will be something to discover and review in this domain.

On the one hand, there has always been enthusiasm for the potential disruptions and benefits of open banking.[2] On the other hand, there are critical points common to all the countries on the open banking journey that represent what must be enhanced or solved to make open banking a concrete global ecosystem rather than a phenomenon developed across countries but substantially confined within each jurisdiction's borders. As the title of this chapter hints, the road ahead is a reflection on the future of open banking and whether there is the possibility of creating alignments and fostering exchanges of experiences among open banking adopters through the lens of common issues such as security, consumer education and financial inclusion.

Against this background, this chapter refers to 'open banking participants' with a different connotation than in the introductory chapters. While in Chapter 2, the word 'participants' was limited to the main open banking players, in this chapter, it widely refers to all the jurisdictions participating in the open banking movement. Accordingly, it is to be questioned whether common open banking issues can be exploited to see togetherness as a global phenomenon.

Building on this insight, this chapter first reflects on whether we can measure the success or failure of open banking at this stage. Then, it discusses issues such as security, consumer education and financial inclusion, which are part of the open banking debate worldwide, as critical areas that elicit wide, cross-jurisdictional dialogue to make the benefits of open banking more global. Before concluding, the chapter briefly reflects on the transition from open banking to open finance.

DOI: 10.4324/9781003331339-13

Success or failure?

In October 2021, at a hearing before the UK House of Commons Treasury Select Committee, Anne Boden, founder and (now former) CEO of Starling Bank, criticised open banking. Boden argued that open banking was unsuccessful for three reasons: (1) it did not incentivise account switching among users; (2) there were no business models to pay for and exploit data suitably; and (3) its implementation was burdensome.[3] Boden's final words sounded like an epitaph on open banking: 'I would be very careful, and we cannot just keep pushing on at this because we think it is going to get us somewhere... [O]pen banking is a lesson in us trying to make something work when, halfway through the project, we realised it was not going to work'.[4]

The FinTech world did not echo Boden's criticism. Fifty members of the 'FinTech Founders Group' signed a letter to the Treasury Select Committee in which they decried her views as anti-competitive[5] and a distortion of the real value and results brought by open banking since the nine largest UK banks were mandated to 'open' to third parties.[6] Amid this controversy, Boden later softened her stance by stating that she intended to trigger a debate on issues to be fixed within open banking, of which she is 'one of the biggest advocates'.[7]

Nonetheless, Boden was not the first to express scepticism. In March 2020, Monzo's founder, Tom Blomfield, claimed that open banking did not bring innovation to the financial services industry but resulted in significant implementation costs.[8] Failure, unsuccess or flop were the words that characterised the debate triggered by Boden's and Blomfield's comments. Representatives of the FinTech industry again put up a strong defence of open banking.[9] Even though these disagreements are confined to the UK open banking experience, they stimulate important reflections.

The main question is whether it is possible to measure the success or failure of open banking. Such a measure could be made by considering open banking in its global dimension (i.e., as an idea happening worldwide) or by focusing on selected jurisdictions. For the former consideration, recent surveys predict that the number of open banking users worldwide will reach 132.2 million by 2024.[10] Further surveys look at the potentiality of open banking and the volume of business it can generate and conclude that global open banking payments will exceed $116 billion in 2026.[11] These data are encouraging but still inconclusive regarding the success of open banking. For the latter consideration, some countries are at a more advanced stage of developing and implementing open banking than others. The subdivision of jurisdictions into pioneers, followers and beginners made by commentators when open banking spread worldwide[12] is still useful, though it needs to be regularly updated to reflect the progress jurisdictions have made or will make. At the country level, slowness in implementation or stakeholders' dissatisfaction can be noted, but, again, these elements would not amount to a failure of open banking. Accordingly, any answer as to whether open banking has succeeded or failed is premature.

Another significant question is whether there is an open banking leader among the jurisdictions that have embraced this idea and are contributing to its development through appropriate frameworks and market strategies. The fact that some jurisdictions are regarded as open banking pioneers implies that a milestone for worldwide adoption was set, but currently, we have a patchwork of open banking philosophies. Part II of the book highlighted how domestic open banking regimes have diametrically opposed stances on issues such as data reciprocity or charging fees for data access. It is, therefore, more realistic if we say that some countries, like the EU and UK, are the early open banking influencers, but there is no open banking leader. This argument can be supported by the fact that some countries are now pushing the development and implementation of their own open banking at a faster pace than the early adopters.[13]

Open banking is here to stay, but its global dimension requires countries to look beyond their borders. Different open banking approaches should not mean that countries develop 'isolated' open banking. Global development should mean cross-jurisdictional data sharing, namely, a global open banking ecosystem. There is no need for an open banking leader within this ecosystem, but instead, common efforts, experience sharing and dialogue. It, therefore, makes no sense to discuss success or failure. Reviewing common issues and obstacles should be the starting point for creating a wider alignment towards a global open banking ecosystem.

A safe open banking ecosystem

Opening APIs to third parties to share customer financial information is the open banking paradigm that drives initiatives worldwide. Despite different drivers and approaches across jurisdictions, every advocate for open banking needs to deal with security risks. Guaranteeing a safe open banking ecosystem is even more pressing given the circulation of customer data between diverse actors. Information exchange, experience sharing and dialogue among jurisdictions are vital to open banking security. Several angles are the subject of this discussion.

API risk

Since the rise and development of open banking, most of the narrative has been based on the advantages of deploying open APIs versus other practices for accessing financial data. Chapter 2 delves into the primacy that APIs have gained as opposed to screen-scraping and reverse engineering practices.

The API hierarchy derives from regulation or industry consensus. The UK and the EU, as the pioneers of open banking, have exerted significant influence in this matter. In the UK, the FCA oversees third parties under the Payment Services Regulations 2017 (PSRs), which transposed part of the

EU PSD2.[14] Banks were mandated to establish (open) APIs in line with certain specifications and standards. The Open Banking Implementation Entity (OBIE) was created to develop common standards banks had to implement to start open banking, including API standards.[15] The UK Open Banking Standard version 3.0, published in 2018, consists of four components: API Specifications, Customer Experience Guidelines, Operational Guidelines and Security Profiles.[16] API Specifications explain APIs' design philosophy, functionality, behaviour and interaction with other APIs. Within the UK framework, API specifications are divided into read/write API,[17] open data API,[18] open banking directory,[19] dynamic client registration[20] and management information (MI) reporting[21] specifications. The UK Open Banking Standard became a model other jurisdictions followed, with regulatory frameworks developing standards on API specifications akin to the UK standards.[22]

In the EU, regulatory approaches are based on technology neutrality, and unlike in the UK, they do not mandate API technical standards. The PSD2 requires data access through the financial institutions' online interfaces without naming or requesting an API as the primary interface. Article 98 of the PSD2 mandated the European Banking Authority (EBA) to develop draft regulatory technical standards (RTS) for specifying, inter alia, requirements relating to customer authentication and security measures.[23] The final draft RTS translated into Regulation No 389/2018 does not prescribe APIs either.[24] Moreover, screen-scraping practices appear to survive as 'contingency mechanisms' in case the financial institution's 'dedicated interface' (which can be APIs even though they are not mandated) fails.[25]

Nonetheless, EU regulators do not deny the importance and wide use of APIs at the industry level.[26] Within the EU context, API primacy revolves around industry consensus, particularly through the initiatives of industry groups that formed to create API standards.[27] Consequently, as discussed in Chapter 2, we can reiterate the worldwide acknowledgement of API as the underlying technology of open banking.

However, this recognition does not come without security risks. Apart from the costs financial institutions may face for equipping themselves with an adequate API structure and governance, recent studies highlighted how sensitive parameters (e.g., client ID, API key, password, OAuth Client secret) were exposed in the Uniform Resource Locator (URL) of banks' APIs and websites.[28] There is, therefore, an API vulnerability[29] that must be addressed as a common issue for all open banking adopters, no matter the variations in policies and frameworks across jurisdictions.

Designing and having proper APIs is hard, especially when security risks come into play. As API technical standards appear to be widespread in open banking jurisdictions, borrowing from each other must become the source of dialogue beyond simply looking at what the others are doing. The sharing of experience among open banking participants is necessary and crucial, as trust in open banking-enabled products and services will also depend on the security of the underlying technology. API primacy within the open banking world, therefore, requires API dialogue among open banking participants.

Third-party security

The third-party world is largely populated by FinTech companies. As most are start-ups or middle-size companies, the adequateness of their security mechanisms against external attacks is a key issue. Third parties will ask to access bank customers' financial information. Despite regulatory frameworks setting specific limits on data processing, storage, management and transmission, third parties could be vulnerable to cyber-attacks when downloading bank data. Some studies describe this phase as critical because it is outside the control of anti-fraud bank teams or much more difficult to detect.[30]

Within the third-party context, security also concerns the products they can develop through open banking. Most solutions put forward by third parties are on the market as mobile applications that operate on the user's behalf, thus creating more potential for phishing.[31] These risks inevitably raise questions about the robustness of third parties' anti-fraud systems. As important players within the open banking ecosystem, third parties must build a proper security culture. Accordingly, open banking adopters must remain vigilant and responsive to the evolution of the technological and digital landscape to develop software secured by design and checked through appropriate internal or external audits.

Finally, the identity of third parties is another security concern in the open banking world. In most jurisdictions, third parties are licensed or authorised by competent authorities. However, in EU open banking, recent studies stress the need to improve control mechanisms over third parties after they enter the market as licensed or authorised players.[32] Banks are supposedly overburdened with verifying that the third parties asking to access their customer data are who they say they are and, thus, are still fully licensed.[33]

The third-party registers adopted in some countries would not be helpful either, as they work as a mere list of third parties, with authorities simply filling in these registers but declining any responsibility as to information veracity.[34] The dialogue and experience sharing in the third-party security subject must be developed through the lens of their governance and adequate ex-post registration controls.

Customer authentication

Through their consent, consumers interact with new actors in addition to the banks. They are clearly affected by security issues. Recent open banking surveys show that their main concerns pertain to fraud and privacy issues. In Chapter 2, we sketched the contours of the stages preceding consumer consent. Looking at the EU experience under the PSD2 and then integrated by the draft RTS, we can see the introduction of strong customer authentication (SCA) requirements on financial institutions when payers access their accounts online, initiate payments or, more generally, perform any other action through remote channels that entail fraud or abuse risks.[35] At the heart of these requirements lies a multi-factor authentication (MFA) process that banks should perform by using at least two of the following three elements: Knowledge—Something only the user knows, such as passwords and security questions; Possession—Something only the user possesses, such as a phone, token or card reader; Inherence—Something unique or inherent to the user, such as biometrics (fingerprint, voice or face).[36] The three elements are independent in that failure in one should not compromise the applicability of the others.[37]

Moreover, the PSD2 introduced the 'dynamic linking' concept, which adds further layers of security within the authentication process to have certainty that the transaction is linked to a specific payer and for a specified amount.[38] The PSD2 SCA has become the model other jurisdictions implementing an open banking framework follow.[39]

Despite consumer protection mechanisms and requirements, data breaches and cyber-attacks are always at stake. The critical issue to face in this context is the loss of consumer trust in open banking, which would finally undermine its development. This loss of trust is another problem that can have repercussions on the global development of open banking. If open banking is deemed unsafe, there will be no interest. It is another area where common dialogue must be enhanced: guaranteeing a secure ecosystem to make it trustworthy and solid in its borderless development.

Overall, all the selected issues are not confined to specific jurisdictions. They represent the need for more coordination at the global level, in line with the fact that open banking is a global movement. Global reach should not exclusively be interpreted as the development of open banking worldwide (which is a tangible fact) but also with the cross-border implications that the business it generates entails. For these reasons, the security subject imposes a more aligned and coordinated dialogue among the open banking participants.

Consumer education on open banking

Security is fundamental to shore up the open banking ecosystem, but the actors, particularly consumers, also need to know about important changes. Ensuring adequate open banking education should be among the top priorities to concretise the benefits of promoting and implementing open banking. There are numerous calls to give this matter proper consideration.[40] The open banking/open finance goal of giving financial customers ownership and control of their data raises questions about their knowledge, readiness and capability.

As anticipated in Chapter 2, bank customer consent to the sharing of data between financial institutions and third parties makes them central (if not the most important) actors within the open banking process and is pivotal to expanding into larger data-sharing ecosystems such as open finance or open data.[41] Consequently, it is natural to wonder whether consumers have open banking knowledge and awareness that it is the beginning of a new era in the financial services industry and whether they are ready to become decisive actors in progressing to a fully data-driven society.

Knowledge and readiness are both imperative in the sense that a lack of the former would nullify the latter. The need for open banking knowledge is always of capital importance when the debate turns to 'consumer education'. Open banking knowledge, however, has more than one meaning. Since the inception and spread of open banking, commentators have emphasised that consumers have no clue what open banking is. For example, in Canada, where the creation of an open banking framework is still embryonic, some surveys showed that only 9% of Canadians knew about open banking.[42] These figures should be taken with a pinch of salt as they are limited to selected respondents.[43] However, the striking aspect of these investigations is that among those respondents identified as having an awareness of the existence of open banking, some demonstrated significant misunderstandings relating to how open banking works and its implications.[44] Lack of open banking knowledge should, therefore, be construed as the absence of open 'banking know-how', ranging from unawareness of its existence ('never heard about it') to misunderstanding of how it works and its implications.

Canada is not the only example. With specific reference to the UK, this book brought to attention the reasons behind consumers' lack of engagement with open banking. Once again, lack of awareness and lack of trust are pervasive.[45] In 2018, data from Cardlytics revealed that 26% of the targeted consumers confirmed that they had heard about open banking, but only 8% used it. Nonetheless, 72% of the respondents had never heard of open banking.[46] By comparison, 2023 marked relevant improvements. As of July 2023, the number of payment users had reached 4.2 million, thus showing steady growth.[47] According to the UK Open Banking Limited, 'this robust growth signals a clear preference among consumers using open banking solutions to manage their finances effectively'.[48]

All jurisdictions have been debating the issue of open banking education, no matter whether they have an advanced, early-stage or planned open banking regime. Consumers' lack of open banking knowledge undermines its adoption. Educating consumers about the meaning and use of open banking is vital for its concrete development and functioning.[49] Within this context, it is important to address the following points.

Part 2 shows how some jurisdictions have young populations who are familiar with digital and technological solutions. Clearly, open banking is potentially appealing to young generations of consumers, who are more tech-savvy than older generations. However, consumer education about open banking cannot neglect generational disparities and the vulnerabilities of those who are not digitally literate. Open banking is thought to benefit all categories of consumers. Education initiatives need to target all categories of consumers to avoid open banking becoming an exclusive dialogue between tech-savvy advisers and tech-savvy customers.[50] This negative outcome would increase the risk of limited adoption of open banking and financial exclusion.[51]

Talking about education initiatives brings forward another important point: who is responsible for open banking education? There are different stances on this issue, with some commentators assigning this task to financial institutions[52] while others encourage regulators' proactiveness:

> Open Banking promises to put consumers in control of their data by providing them with a secure, government-regulated way to use it. All the ingredients to deliver on this promise are available, except one: Consumers don't know about Open Banking. And after years of being told not to share their financial information, they're understandably cautious. With the initial roll-out complete, businesses launching use cases and consumers showing real interest, now is the time for the government to start educating consumers about the secure, government-regulated alternative to sharing banking passwords.
> (Tony Thrassis, CEO Frollo)[53]

This division may be explained in connection with the approaches characterising the development of open banking across jurisdictions. The dichotomy between market-driven and government-led approaches may dictate responsibilities regarding education. It would be logical to give tasks to banks when the development of open banking is left to market strategies and, vice versa, to governments or regulators when legislative approaches are in place.

In reality, efforts need to be taken carefully and always with the involvement of consumer representatives in any open banking consultation. If open banking aims at revolutionising the financial services industry by eliciting new data-sharing methods, the starting point is that, for bank customers, it represents the opposite of what they have always been told: 'Do not share your information with anybody'. For this reason, a lack of knowledge determines a lack of trust in open banking and a reluctance to make their data accessible outside the banking domain.[54] Consequently, educating users is imperative if we believe that open banking is an irreversible trend. All the involved stakeholders must play a role in open banking education initiatives.

The last issue is how to educate. Some advocate launching educational campaigns. This stance is particularly strong in countries like Australia, where open banking is embedded in wider open data regulation.[55] Nonetheless, the focus of education campaigns should be questioned. There seem to be different opinions on whether consumers should be educated on the outcomes or the practicalities of open banking.[56] They are both important given the twofold meaning of 'lack of open banking knowledge' (i.e., not knowing versus misunderstanding). Overall, with open banking being the milestone to open finance and open data, education initiatives need to aim at the outcome of giving consumers the tools to feel secure and in control within a complex ecosystem founded on their consent.

Open banking and financial inclusion

A secure, well-functioning and widely known open banking system is the ecosystem for everyone. Financial inclusion has a strong relationship with open banking. As seen in the previous chapters, financial reforms and FinTech regulations in several countries are also driven by the objective of reaching those segments of the population not served by the financial services system.[57] Within this context, open banking is unanimously regarded as a valuable tool for inclusionary purposes.[58]

Financial inclusion is a complex concept originating from research that brought to attention the difficulties experienced by individuals in accessing credit services because of geographical, race and gender prejudices.[59] Recent studies have shed light on the correlation between financial inclusion, poverty reduction and economic growth, particularly in developing countries.[60] Nonetheless, Reis argues that financial inclusion has undefined contours: There is no consensus on its scope, categories affected by exclusion or responsibilities for delivering inclusion.[61] These drawbacks, coupled with different interpretations of the concept, would result in misalignments between financial inclusion aims and implementation strategies.[62] For these reasons, the author stresses the necessity of a plain definition of financial inclusion.[63]

This debate shows that interest in financial inclusion is constantly rising among researchers and financial stakeholders and how the concept evolves in connection with the radical changes affecting the financial services industry, inter alia, digitalisation and technological innovation. Accordingly, it is worth starting with a basic understanding of financial inclusion, which means the possibility for individuals to access and use suitable financial services.[64] Within this general definition, bank account ownership is considered the beginning of financial inclusion and the gateway to various services or products spanning credit and insurance.[65] Significantly, the impossibility of accessing financial services determines financial exclusion, which results in individuals being 'unbanked' or 'underbanked'. These two categories are a recurring theme within the financial inclusion and open banking narratives, with the former designating those individuals unable to get access to (even basic) bank accounts and the latter those individuals having access to bank accounts but ultimately unable to obtain other financial products and services.[66] Unbanked individuals carry a more negative connotation than underbanked individuals, but they are both united by the fact that they suffer limitations in the financial services industry.

Since its inception and development, worldwide open banking has been strongly associated with the underserved, so boosting financial inclusion is among the drivers behind the creation of open banking frameworks.[67] Through the sharing of financial data in a collaborative ecosystem, open banking would facilitate accessibility to more competitive and customised financial services and products for all consumer categories.[68]

Recent studies highlight advantages for small and medium enterprises (SMEs), which are also underserved by banks. For example, with reference to the UK financial sector, Gardner and Leong point out how open banking technology is valuable in giving SMEs more options to access credit.[69] In this respect, the authors refer to leveraging open banking technology for 'Open Accounting' solutions, which allow SMEs to link their accounting platforms with their bank accounts. There is a faster flow of transactional data into the SMEs' accounting systems that can give banks a wider and more accurate picture of accounting data, thus accelerating lending decisions for SMEs.[70]

From the perspective of individuals, other UK-related studies claim benefits for the so-called on the margins of financial services (with no unsecured borrowing and little or no financial buffer) and overstretched (included but overindebted) segments. Open banking would help them manage their financial lives better and pay fewer fees by using open banking-enabled services.[71] These prospects are also echoed in countries where the adoption of open banking is nascent and strongly encouraged to achieve inclusion.[72]

Against this backdrop, the financial inclusion theme has greatly influenced the design and adoption of open banking. Scholars even explicitly mention the financial inclusion goal within those open banking regulations, driven by enhancing competition and innovation in the retail banking and payment sectors.[73] However, the potential of open banking to boost financial inclusion is not unanimously accepted. Naturally, there are always counterarguments when advantages and benefits are brought forward. The correlation between open banking and financial inclusion is challenged by opposite views, according to which the data-sharing model fostered by open banking will not be a determinant of financial inclusion. Again, security issues, a lack of trust and open banking education are at the heart of conflicting opinions.[74] At present, there is no confirmation of where the balance tilts. On the one hand, whilst it is recognised that the literature on the connection between open banking and financial inclusion is still nascent, on the other hand, specific results on the open banking potential for inclusion or exclusion are still missing, and they should constitute the aims of future research.[75]

The worldwide debate and initiatives to spur financial inclusion will act as catalysts for optimally framing the correlation between open banking and financial inclusion. It is important to have certainty about the concrete value that open banking gives consumers. Some commentators call for a change of narrative in the open banking movement or, in other words, to give more consideration to creating (through open banking) products and services that meet consumers' needs.[76] The possibilities of making open banking a financial inclusion booster lie in the awareness of what all consumer segments, from the so-called on the margins to the so-called asset-rich, expect from open banking and what it can deliver to them.[77] A significant challenge for the global open banking movement is, therefore, how to respond effectively to the needs of underserved categories and work against its image of being suitable only for digitally literate segments.

From open banking to open finance

Today is open banking; tomorrow is open finance; and next is open data. As mentioned in Chapter 2, this is not a mere prediction but the shape of things to come. The financial services industry is where radical and innovative changes are already in place, tested and improved to be the benchmark for other key social sectors. Technically, open finance means extending the open banking data-sharing model to other financial areas such as mortgages, insurance or pensions.[78] Claiming that open finance is not simply widening the scope of open banking is a valid argument.[79] Open finance reinforces the vision of an increasingly data-driven financial environment characterised by collaborations among diversified players and where consumers fully control their financial information.[80]

Part 2 of the book showed how some countries have already framed, been planning or are working towards a gradual transition from open banking to open finance. Once again, ideas are observed and borrowed but then adapted to different purposes and needs at the country level. Countries developing open finance regimes start with observing open banking frameworks in other jurisdictions, while countries moving from open banking to open finance test this possibility by looking at the outcomes of their open banking regimes. In either case, the data-sharing model underlying open banking (e.g. consumer consent, API technology, collaborative data-sharing between financial institutions and third parties) is always the point from which to start.[81]

Chapter 9 reviews the significant progress that Brazil has made until now in consolidating its open banking/open finance ecosystem and how its outcomes, as they unfold, can be inspirational to all those countries aiming to make the same move. There have been plans in the UK to expand open banking into open finance, but there are ongoing discussions about the optimal governance and implementation of open banking.[82] It is worth noting the open finance pathway commenced at the EU level. In June 2023, the European Commission issued a legislative 'Proposal for a Framework for Financial Data Access'.[83] The proposal aims at establishing a more solid and secure data-sharing ecosystem in the financial services industry by referring to the principles that guided the PSD2, the GDPR and the recent (draft) Data Act: Customers should be able to authorise their service providers to share their data with third parties securely and efficiently.[84] Significantly, 'Financial Data Access' extends beyond the payment accounts area under the PSD2 to cover categories of data to be available spanning mortgage credit agreements, savings, pension rights and non-life insurance products, crypto-assets and real estate.[85] Authorised financial institutions and non-financial institutions ('Financial Information Service Providers') can obtain data access (though further rules are still needed as to modalities and methods to obtain access).[86] An electronic third-party register to be developed, operated and maintained by EBA is contemplated, along with the possibility of financial institutions 'opening' ('data holders') to third parties along with the possibilities for data holders to claim compensation for making customer data available to third parties. Governance and security requirements are also drafted to make the open finance ecosystem work effectively and securely.[87] The proposal is under consultation before being directed to the European Parliament and the EU Council of Ministers for completing the last stages of the legislative process, which will be completed in a (estimated) two-year time frame.

Within this brief description, it is to be questioned whether open banking under the PSD2 framework will evolve into this wider financial data access regime so that the same rules will be applied within the payment account area. Interestingly, the EU Commission put forward on the same day the proposal for amending and modernising the PSD2 (which will become PSD3)[88] and establishing a PSR. As stated by the Commission, one of the fundamental pillars of the proposed reforms is to 'Improve the functioning of open banking, by removing remaining obstacles to providing open banking services and improving customers' control over their payment data, enabling new innovative services to enter the market'.[89] There is still much to be seen and said about the EU open finance framework-to-be. However, it appears clear that there are no similar changes applied to the future PSD3, particularly regarding the possibility of charging for data access. Accordingly, open banking in the EU will continue to be regulated under the PSD2 (then the PSD3). At present, we could say that the EU has two frameworks for governing the access and sharing of data in the financial services industry: Open banking and open finance.

These examples demonstrate the pivotal role that open finance is playing. An open finance debate is being carried out in parallel with the open banking debate. This debate appears to be premised on the same issues and doubts affecting open banking.[90] Open finance is not the subject of this book, but it is hard to neglect its importance. Some scholars pointed out that evolving from open banking to open finance would first require revisiting the progress in implementing open banking and then addressing all the ongoing issues within the former.[91] Such arguments are based on the recognition of open banking as the milestone of the wider evolutionary plans towards an open data society, and thus, they conclude that it would be hard to think bigger without first fixing the issues that may prevent open banking from functioning properly.[92]

As discussed in the previous section, it may be easily claimed that it is pointless to discuss whether open banking has failed, but at the same time, every open banking regime faces issues of security, consumer education and slowness in implementation. Consequently, it is sensible to conclude that the issues that can be identified in open banking and how they may be addressed greatly help in designing the proper open finance ecosystem. Any discussion on open finance is forward-thinking because open finance is still nascent while open banking has become a global movement. Open banking must be the benchmark for assessing and building open finance readiness. The EU is only one example of how the open banking journey is not over and is likely not to be over even when open finance regimes agree in place.

It is not premature to discuss open finance, but the main argument is that open banking has not finished teaching lessons because it is central to the financial world. Open finance is on the regulator's agenda but is not yet a movement like open banking. The voice of this movement needs to be listened to build a larger data-sharing ecosystem in the financial services sector.

Conclusion

Open banking is not and never will be a fad. There are different stages of progression in implementing open banking among participating jurisdictions, but there is no open banking leader. Inspirers are needed more than leaders. However, the consolidation of the meaning of open banking as a global phenomenon goes through the willingness of participants to look beyond their own territory, not simply to observe what others do but also to dialogue with participants. This is the road ahead. Common open banking issues constitute the ideal basis to this end.

Notes

1 Lambert M Surhone, Miriam T Timpledon, and Susan F Marseken, *The Empire on Which the Sun Never Sets* (VDM Publishing 2010).
2 The Paypers, *Report 2022: The Enablers of Open Banking, Open Finance, and Open Data* (2022) <https://thepaypers.com/reports/report-2022-the-enablers-of-open-banking-open-finance-and-open-data/r1258969> accessed 18 August 2023; Ritesh Jha and others, 'Open Banking. Unleashing the Power of Data and Seizing New Opportunities', (2021), 3 Deloitte <www2.deloitte.com/content/dam/Deloitte/in/Documents/financial-services/in-fs-open-banking-report-noexp.pdf> accessed 18 August 2023; KPMG, 'Open Banking Opens Opportunities for Greater Customer Value. Reshaping the Banking Experience', (2019), 1 <https://assets.kpmg.com/content/dam/kpmg/xx/pdf/2019/05/open-banking-opening-opportunities-for-customer-value.pdf> accessed 18 August 2023; TransUnion, 'The Evolution of Open Banking: Adoption, Benefits and Consent', (White Paper, 2020), 1 <www.openbankingexpo.com/wp-content/uploads/2020/11/Open-Banking-whitepaper.pdf> accessed 18 August 2023.
3 House of Commons, 'Oral Evidence: Future of Financial Services', (2021), Treasury Committee HC 147, 18 <https://committees.parliament.uk/oralevidence/2889/pdf/> accessed 22 August 2023.
4 Ibid.
5 'Typical of banks trying to thwart the future of innovation in financial services', see Oliver Smith, 'In Full: Here's the Fintech Founders Letter Criticising Anne Boden's Select Committee Comments' *AltFi* (29 December 2021) <www.altfi.com/article/8664_in-full-heres-the-fintech-founders-letter-criticising-anne-bodens-select-committee-comments> accessed 22 August 2023.
6 Ibid., 'There Are Now over 2.5 Million Open Banking Payments a Month, Compared to Just 320,000 in the Whole of 2018'.
7 Louisa Clarence-Smith, 'Fintech Bosses Accuse Starling Bank's Anne Boden of Stifling Innovation' *The Times* (29 December 2021) <www.thetimes.co.uk/article/

fintech-bosses-accuse-starling-banks-anne-boden-of-stifling-innovation-rgd6jhhdj> accessed 22 August 2023.
8 Matthew Field, 'Monzo Boss Warns Open Banking Reforms Have "Zero Benefit"' *The Telegraph* (7 March 2020) <www.telegraph.co.uk/technology/2020/03/07/monzo-boss-warns-open-banking-reforms-have-zero-benefit/> accessed 22 August 2023.
9 Eric Johansson, 'TrueLayer CEO Accuses Monzo Founder Blomfield of Trashing Open Banking' *Verdict* (14 April 2021) <https://www.verdict.co.uk/truelayer-ceo-monzo/> accessed 22 August 2023.
10 This is noteworthy compared to the 24.4 million in 2020, see Statista, 'Number of Open Banking Users Worldwide in 2020 with Forecasts from 2021 to 2024, by Region (in Millions)', (2023), <www.statista.com/statistics/1228771/open-banking-users-worldwide/> accessed 22 August 2023.
11 Roland Selmer, 'Insight: Why Momentum Tells the True UK Open Banking Success Story' *OpenBankingExpo* (1 March 2022) <www.openbankingexpo.com/insights/insight-why-momentum-tells-the-true-uk-open-banking-success-story/> accessed 22 August 2023.
12 Alice Prahmann and others, *Open Banking APIs Worldwide* (White Paper, 2021) <https://ndgit.com/en/open-banking-api-status-whitepaper/> accessed 22 August 2023.
13 Helen Thomas, 'The UK Led the World in Open Banking—and Then Got Left Behind' *Financial Times* (26 January 2023) <www.ft.com/content/219ac7fd-28b7-4709-883c-eba308b7f573> accessed 22 August 2023.
14 The Payment Services Regulations 2017 <www.legislation.gov.uk/uksi/2017/752/contents/made> accessed 4 September 2023.
15 Chapter 3, 'Open Banking Policy in the UK and EU'.
16 See <www.openbanking.org.uk/> accessed 4 September 2023.
17 Ibid., Read/write API specifications allow third parties to connect securely and through customer consent for accessing information and initiate payments.
18 Ibid., Open data API specifications relate to the creation of API endpoints where third-party developers can build mobile and web applications for bank customers.
19 Ibid., Open banking directory specifications relate to the purpose of the Open Banking Director and the roles of each participant.
20 Ibid., Dynamic client registration specifications relate to the process financial institutions must follow for registering third parties as 'OpenID Connect' (OIDC) clients without the need for a manual process.
21 Ibid., MI reporting specifications relate to the information financial institutions and third parties must report to the implementation entity (Open Banking Limited).
22 See Part 2, 'Open Banking Regulation' (Bahrain), (KSA), (Indonesia).
23 PSD2 art 98 ('Regulatory technical standards on authentication and communication').
24 There is a generic reference to 'dedicated interface' to be used for account access and payment initiation purposes, see 'Commission Delegated Regulation (EU) 2018/389 of 27 November 2017 supplementing Directive (EU) 2015/2366 of the European Parliament and of the Council with regard to regulatory technical standards for strong customer authentication and common and secure open standards of communication', (2017), OJEU L69/23.
25 See Regulation 2018/389 art 33 ('Contingency measures for a dedicated interface').
26 European Banking Authority (EBA), 'Draft Regulatory Technical Standards on Strong Customer Authentication and Common and Secure Communication under Article 98 of Directive 2015/2366 (PSD2)', (2017) Final Report, 118: 'The EBA requires the ASPSPs to offer at least one interface for TPPs to access the information needed. The RTS do not mandate APIs although the EBA appreciates that the industry may agree that they are suitable'.

27 See Chapter 2, 'Open Banking World', (API).
28 Feike Hacquebord and others, 'Ready or Not for PSD2: The Risks of Open Banking' (*Trend Micro Research*, 17 September 2019) 8 <www.trendmicro.com/vinfo/de/security/news/cybercrime-and-digital-threats/the-risks-of-open-banking-are-banks-and-their-customers-ready-for-psd2> accessed 4 September 2023.
29 For a detailed list of API weaknesses, see Urs Zurbuchen, Michael Doujak, and Christoph Lutz, 'API Security—Limiting Factor Or Accelerator of an Open Banking Strategy', (White Paper, 2020) 6 <www.airlock.com/fileadmin/content/07_Airlock-PDFs/Whitepaper_API_Security_v3.pdf> accessed 4 September 2023.
30 Hacquebord and others (n 28).
31 Ibid.
32 Kristian T Sørensen and others, *The Tricky Encounter* (White Paper, 2020), 6 <www.konsentus.com/wp-content/uploads/The_Tricky_Encounter_2020_final.pdf> accessed 4 September 2023.
33 Ibid.
34 See, for example, the EBA Payment Institutions Register disclaimer: 'The present Register has been set up by the EBA solely on the basis of information provided by national competent authorities of the EEA Member States. Therefore, unlike national registers under PSD2, this Register has no legal significance and confers no rights in law. If an unauthorised institution is inadvertently included in the Register, its legal status is in no way altered; similarly, if an institution has inadvertently been omitted from the Register, the validity of its authorisation will not be affected... The European Banking Authority is responsible only for the accurate reproduction of the information received by competent authorities for each natural or legal person included in the register, while responsibility for the accuracy of that information lies with the competent authorities at national level'. <https://euclid.eba.europa.eu/register/pir/disclaimer> accessed 4 September 2023.
35 PSD2 art 97 ('Authentication').
36 Regulation 2018/389 art 4 ('Authentication Code').
37 PSD2 art 4(30) ('Definitions').
38 PSD2 art 97; Regulation 2018/389 art 5 ('Applications for Authorisation').
39 Part 2 'Open Banking Regulation', (MENA region).
40 Roderick Simons, Bronwyn Boy, and Koen Mol, *Data Security and Open Banking, Dispelling Myths and Misconceptions* (White Paper, 2021) 10 <https://yts.yolt.com/images/logos/YTS_Whitepaper_Data-Security-1.pdf>, accessed 31 August 2023; Faith Reynolds and others, 'Consumer Priorities for Open Banking', (*Open Banking*, 2018) <www.openbanking.org.uk/wp-content/uploads/2021/04/Consumer-Priorities-for-Open-Banking-report-June-2019.pdf#:~:text=The%20consumer%20manifesto%20for%20open%20banking&text=People%20and%20small%20businesses%20should,the%20market%20thinks%20about%20consumers> accessed 31 August 2023; ECOMMPAY, 'Beyond the Pandemic: The Outlook for Open Banking', (White Paper, 2021), 5 <https://ecommpay.com/uploads/2021/08/19/beyond-the-pandemic-whitepaper.pdf> accessed 31 August 2023.
41 Chapter 2, 'The Open Baking World ('Consumer Consent')'.
42 Financial Consumer Agency of Canada, 'Open Banking and Consumer Protection: Canadian's Awareness and Expectations', (2023), 4 <www.canada.ca/en/financial-consumer-agency/programs/research/open-banking-consumer-protection.html> accessed 1 September 2023.
43 Ibid.
44 Ibid.
45 Chapter 3, 'Open Banking Policy in the UK and EU'.
46 Cardlytics, 'Open Banking in the UK. Finding the Tipping Points', (2018), 3 <https://www.cardlytics.com/blog/open-banking-in-the-uk-finding-the-tipping-points> accessed 2 September 2023.

47 'Showcasing a Substantial 10.5% Rise from June 2023 and an Impressive 68.2% Surge from July 2022', see Open Banking, 'Open Banking Reaches 11 Million + Payments Milestone', (2023), <www.openbanking.org.uk/news/open-banking-reaches-11m-payments-milestone/#:~:text=In%20July%202023%2C%20the%20number,to%20manage%20their%20finances%20effectively> accessed 1 September 2023.
48 Ibid.
49 Francesco De Pascalis, 'The Journey to Open Finance: Learning from the Open Banking Movement', (2022), 33 European Business Law Review 3, 397
50 Ibid.
51 Ibid.
52 Mariane ter Veen, 'Open Banking Consumer Education: Fear of Fun?', (*The Paypers*, 16 December 2019) <https://thepaypers.com/expert-opinion/open-banking-consumer-education-fear-of-fun–1239920> accessed 2 September 2023.
53 Frollo, 'It's Time for a Consumer Awareness Campaign as More Businesses Embrace Open Banking', (10 November 2022) <https://frollo.com.au/blog/open-banking-consumer-awareness/> accessed 2 September 2022. See also Jessica Bayley, 'Who Is Driving Open Banking Education and Adoption in the UK?' (*Finextra*, 9 November 2021) <www.finextra.com/blogposting/21227/who-is-driving-open-banking-education-and-adoption-in-the-uk> accessed 2 September 2023.
54 See Suela Bylykbashi, Virginie Fitamant, and Ji-Yong Lee, 'Consumers' Fears about Open Banking: How Banks can Overcome Them?', (20th International Marketing Trends Conference, 2021) 1 <http://archives.marketing-trends-congress.com/2021/pages/PDF/034.pdf> accessed 2 September 2023.
55 Natalia Jevglevskaja and Ross P Buckley, 'The Consumer Data Right: How to Realise this World-Leading Reform', (2022), 45 UNSW Law Journal 4, 1621: 'The potential of a consumer education campaign by government to alert consumers to the potential benefits of directing the sharing of data about them to potential new providers of banking, energy and other services is very large indeed. It is understandable and probably right, given how early we are in the data-sharing journey, that government is yet to undertake such a campaign, but certainly once data sharing is available across more than one sector, the time will be ripe for such a campaign'. See also Frollo, 'The State of Open Banking 2023: A Pulse Check of the Industry Packed with Research, Insights, Case Studies and Interviews', (2023), <https://blog.frollo.com.au/> accessed 2 September 2023.
56 Darcy Ammerman and others, 'Canadians Awareness of Open Banking Is Low—But Does It Matter?' (*McMillan*, 29 June 2023) <https://mcmillan.ca/insights/publications/canadians-awareness-of-open-banking-is-low-but-does-it-matter/> accessed 2 September 2023.
57 Part 2 'Open Banking Regulation'.
58 Open Banking, 'Financial Inclusion and Open Banking with TechUK and the OBIE', (2021), <www.openbanking.org.uk/insights/financial-inclusion-and-open-banking-with-techuk-and-the-obie/> accessed 5 September 2023.
59 It is acknowledged that the concept of financial inclusion dates back to the research disseminated in the 1990s. See Andrew Leyshon and Nigel Thrift, 'Access to Financial Services and Financial Infrastructure Withdrawal: Problems and Policies', (1994), 26 Area 3, 268; Andrew Leyshon and Nigel Thrift, 'The Restructuring of the UK Financial Services Industry in the 1990s: A Reversal of Fortune?', (1993), 9 Journal of Rural Studies 3, 223; Andrew Leyshon and Nigel Thrift, 'Geographies of Financial Exclusion: Financial Abandonment in Britain and the United States', (1995), 20 Transactions of the Institute of British Geographers, New Series 3, 312; Gary Arthur Dymski and James M Veitch, 'Financial Transformation and the Metropolis: Booms, Busts, and Banking in Los Angeles', (1996), 28 Environment and Planning A: Economy and Space 7, 1233; Elaine Kempson

and Claire Whyley, *Kept Out Or Opted Out? Understanding and Combating Financial Exclusion* (The Policy Press 1999) 1.
60 Sami Ben Naceur and Samir Ghazouani, 'Stock Markets, Banks, and Economic Growth: Empirical Evidence from the MENA Region', (2007), 21 Research in International Business and Finance 2, 297; Mandira Sarma and Jesim Pais, 'Financial Inclusion and Development', (2011), 23 International Development 5, 613; Jamel Boukhatem, 'Assessing the Direct Effect of Financial Development on Poverty Reduction in a Panel of Low- and Middle-Income Countries', (2016), 37 Research in International Business and Finance, 214; Douglas Pearce, 'Financial Inclusion in the Middle East and North Africa: Analysis and Roadmap Recommendations', (2011), World Bank Group Policy Research Working Papers No. 5610, 4 <https://papers.ssrn.com/sol3/papers.cfm?abstract_id=1794915> accessed 5 September 2023.
61 Thereza Balliester Reis, 'What Is Financial Inclusion? A Critical Review', (2021), Working Paper No. 246 SOAS Department of Economics, 1 <www.soas.ac.uk/sites/default/files/2022-10/economics-wp246.pdf> accessed 5 September 2023.
62 Ibid.
63 Ibid.
64 World Bank, *Global Financial Development Report 2014: Financial Inclusion* (2014) 15 <https://elibrary.worldbank.org/doi/abs/10.1596/978-0-8213-9985-9> accessed 5 September 2023.
65 Asli Demirguc-Kunt, Leora Klapper, and Dorothe Singer, 'Financial Inclusion and Inclusive Growth. A Review of Recent Empirical Evidence', (2017), Policy Research Working Paper 8040, World Bank Group, 2 <https://openknowledge.worldbank.org/entities/publication/b90d407a-b789-5cbd-9f43-6e6f5438b8da> accessed 5 September 2023.
66 Emma Leong and Jodi Gardner, 'Open Banking in the UK and Singapore: Open Possibilities for Enhancing Financial Inclusion', (2021), 5 Journal of Business Law, 424.
67 Ariadne Plaitakis and Stefan Staschen, 'Open Banking: How to Design for Financial Inclusion', (2020), Consultative Group to Assist the Poor' (CGAP) Working Paper, 1 <https://www.cgap.org/research/publication/open-banking-how-to-design-for-financial-inclusion> accessed 5 September 2023.
68 Reynolds and others (n 40).
69 Leong and Gardner (n 66).
70 Ibid.
71 Equal, respectively, to 0.8% and 2.5% of their income. See Reynolds and others (n 39).
72 Nasim Shah Shirazi, Ahmet Faruk Aysan, and Zhamal Nanaeva, 'Open Banking for Financial Inclusion: Challenges and Opportunities in Muslim Majority Countries' in Zul Hakim Jumat, Saqib Hafiz Khateeb and Syed Nazim Ali (eds), *Islamic Finance, FinTech, and the Road to Sustainability Reframing the Approach in the Post-Pandemic Era* (Palgrave Macmillan 2023) 259.
73 Magda Bianco and Maria Iride Vangelisti, 'Open Banking and Financial Inclusion', (2022), European Economy Banks, Regulation, and the Real Sector <https://european-economy.eu/2022/open-banking-and-financial-inclusion/> accessed 5 September 2023.
74 Michal Polasick and Radoslaw Kotkowski, 'The Open Banking Adoption Among Consumers in Europe: The Role of Privacy, Trust, and Digital Financial Inclusion', (2022), <https://papers.ssrn.com/sol3/papers.cfm?abstract_id=4105648> accessed 5 September 2023; See also Greg Chen and Xavier Faz, 'Open Data and the Future of Banking', (2019), Consultative Group to Assist the Poor (CGAP) CGAP Leadership Essay Series <www.cgap.org/blog/open-data-and-future-of-banking> accessed 5 September 2023.

182 *Business Models, Emerging Economies and the Way forward*

75 Leong and Gardner (n 66).
76 Reynolds and others (n 40).
77 Ibid.
78 Financial Conduct Authority (FCA), 'Call for Input: Open Finance', (2019), 1 <www.fca.org.uk/publication/call-for-input/call-for-input-open-finance.pdf> accessed 6 September 2023.
79 Finextra, 'The Future of Regulation: From Innovation to Execution', (2022), 4 <www.finextra.com/researcharticle/238/the-future-of-regulation-2022> accessed 6 September 2023.
80 Ibid.
81 Part 2 'Open Banking Regulation'.
82 Joint Regulatory Oversight Committee, 'Recommendations for the Next Phase of Open Banking in the UK', (2023), 3 <https://assets.publishing.service.gov.uk/government/uploads/system/uploads/attachment_data/file/1150988/JROC_report_recommendations_and_actions_paper_April_2023.pdf> accessed 6 September 2023.
83 Commission, 'Proposal for a Regulation of the European Parliament and of the Council on a Framework for Financial Data Access and Amending Regulations (EU) No. 1093/2010, (EU) No. 1094/2010, (EU) No 1095/2010 and (EU) 2022/2554' (2023) COM(2023) 360 Final <https://eur-lex.europa.eu/legal-content/EN/TXT/PDF/?uri=CELEX:52023PC0360> accessed 6 September 2023.
84 Commission, 'Framework for Financial Data Access', (2023), <https://finance.ec.europa.eu/digital-finance/framework-financial-data-access_en> accessed 6 September 2023.
85 Commission, 'Proposal for a Regulation of the European Parliament' (n 82).
86 Ibid.
87 Ibid.
88 Commission, 'Modernising Payment Services and Opening Financial Services Data: New Opportunities for Consumers and Businesses', (2023), <https://ec.europa.eu/commission/presscorner/detail/en/ip_23_3543> accessed 6 September 2023.
89 Ibid.
90 Dan Awrey and Joshua Macey, 'The Promise and Perils of Open Finance', (May 2022), Law Working Paper No. 632/2022 ECGI, 2 <https://www.ecgi.global/sites/default/files/working_papers/documents/openfinancefinal.pdf>
91 De Pascalis (n 49).
92 Ibid.

11 Conclusion

The open banking world

Open banking is a catch-all term signifying the large-scale changes occurring in our digitalised world. Data and technology have disrupted social relationships and revolutionised how we interact, work and communicate.

These developments are most tangible in the financial services industry. Encounters between financial institutions and potential customers trigger exchanges of information that make the sector one of the most data-intensive. Advances in technologies such as artificial intelligence, cloud computing and the Internet of Things also improve the collection, storage and flow of information.

Through this lens, open banking is the result of data-driven finance. In other words, it is the answer to making the financial sector an open place where data are shared among the participants. Consequently, the basic understanding of open banking is a data-sharing process pursued through the interaction of three key players: The banks, third parties and bank customers.

Through customer consent and the use of API technology, customer data are accessed by third parties (mainly FinTech companies) for the development of new products and services, enabling, for instance, bank account aggregation or the initiation or payment transactions. From this perspective, open banking reflects the diversification of the financial services industry, now populated by incumbent and challenger firms.

By giving consumers the right to consent to the data-sharing process, open banking clarifies who is at the centre of the relationship between banks and third parties. Open banking is thus the catalyst of a new vision of using data in finance. Data are no longer collected to be kept in the banks' walls but to be opened to other service providers through customer consent. New dynamics and paradigmatic shifts are happening because of open banking.

However, the interaction among the open banking players creates an ecosystem. One fundamental question the open banking ecosystem poses is what the benefits are for its participants. Open banking has undeniably generated large enthusiasm as a win-win situation for all its main actors. Banks can rethink their business models, generate new revenue streams and offer

DOI: 10.4324/9781003331339-14

customers a broader range of products and services. Consumers will benefit from more personalised solutions and ultimately improve their financial well-being. Finally, third parties will be crucial for making the financial sector more competitive and inclusive by changing how individuals understand and manage their finances. These expectations have fostered an open banking world.

The idea has spread worldwide and made open banking a cross-jurisdictional data-sharing phenomenon. There are approaches, regulations, visions and strategies that characterise the open baking world and flourish because of its potential benefits to the financial industry. Against this backdrop, the last meaning of open banking looks at the future of an open data society. Open banking is the basis and the test for developing an open data society: Today, open banking; tomorrow, open finance; and in the future, open data.

Key concepts behind open banking in the UK and EU

Several key concepts underpin open banking in the UK and EU and, to a certain extent, in the US. The central point is that competition will solve everything. The incumbent banks and credit card companies were seen as too comfortable in the payment services market and too slow to innovate. Concomitant with this is the belief that the current arrangements are driven by a number of market failures. There is a view, certainly in the UK and EU, that regulation can and should be used to change and develop new business models.

There is a strong view that the customer's financial data belongs to the customer and not just to the incumbent financial institution. Open banking regulation aims to ensure that customers have proprietary rights over this information, which they can market for value. This data and new technologies will allow new businesses to develop and produce new value propositions to benefit customers.

Regulation is often seen as controlling and limiting. However, the objectives of regulation can also be seen as necessary to promote key public policy aims. For example, regulation is used to correct market imperfections or failures. However, open banking and Payment Services Directive II (PSD2) are much more dirigiste. Regulation can be seen as a re-emergence of high-tech colbertism, encouraging and guiding innovation and competition.

In part, the EU's approach is directed at the incumbent credit card companies. For example, the European Central Bank (ECB) focuses on payment systems subject to European controls. There is a strong element of European protectionism in the EU's open banking initiatives. There is talk of having a European retail payments strategy with a pan-European vision. It would support a common brand and logo and foster a European identity, with Europeans controlling the strategy and direction of payment systems to benefit European customers.

The UK tends to sound triumphalist in open banking and payment services. While it is true that the UK is a leader in this area, other states, such as the Baltics, are developing fast. Part of the challenge is the shift from open banking to open finance. Whatever way it is perceived, it is probably fair to say that the open banking project is still a work in progress. It is too early to trumpet its success.

Open banking regulation

Nordic and European Free Trade Association (EFTA) countries

Nordic and EFTA countries are interesting cases of open banking development in Europe. Their choice permits us to contrast regulatory-driven versus market-driven approaches and evaluate further progress. Whereas some of the examined Nordic countries are also EFTA countries (i.e., Norway and Iceland), there are relevant differences in the development of open banking compared with the other jurisdictions that are part of the free trade area (i.e., Liechtenstein and Switzerland). Accordingly, the dichotomy between regulatory-driven and market-driven strategies addressed in this part of the book ('Open Banking Regulation') has involved the whole Nordic group vis-à-vis Switzerland and Liechtenstein.

In this context, Chapter 4 highlighted opposite views on implementing the PSD2 to enable open banking. In the Nordic region, the PSD2 was well-awaited. Finland, Norway, Denmark and Sweden enacted this directive through relevant legislative reforms. It may be argued that this is in line with the European Commission's implementation deadlines set in the directive, and, thus, there would be no difference with the other European jurisdictions that are subject to the same obligations. However, the most important aspect that justifies the choice of the Nordic region is the so-called Nordic attitude towards open banking.

The region has a distinguished tradition of digitisation and innovation that makes it the ideal place for revolutionary ideas like open banking. The financial sector best represents the Nordic digital and technology mindset through synergies and collaborations among the major banks across the whole region.

Financial players have proactively embraced open banking since the promulgation of PSD2. Partnerships with FinTech companies have been growing to ensure the optimal development of open banking capabilities. Foreign third parties are also interested in passporting their services in the region, while local consumers appear to trust open banking initiatives thanks to new products and services that have been launched.

Overall, the Nordic region's open banking ethos has been strongly dictated by the enactment of the PSD2, which ultimately positions the region as a promising European open banking hub. Further progress will be made through the issuance of PSD3 and the EU open finance regime.

As an EEA country like Norway and Iceland, Liechtenstein is also bound by the PSD2, but the establishment and implementation of an open banking regime are yet to be fully achieved. Like the Nordic countries, Switzerland also ranks high in digitalisation and technological adoption. However, implementing the PSD2 is not a requirement for Swiss regulators. While observing the transposition of the directive across the EU, representatives of the Swiss financial sector have stated their preference for industry-led approaches to spur the development of open banking nationwide. This view has been dominant until now but has also been opposed by stances advocating regulatory approaches, given the banks' slowness in adopting open banking despite the consumers' growing interest. Consequently, the open banking scenario in Switzerland may be turning to legislative approaches in the future.

The analysis of Nordic and EFTA countries provides a thought-provoking example of opposing views on expanding open banking in Europe. These jurisdictions are at the forefront of digitalisation, innovation and technological advancements. As such, open banking appeals to them, but they have different strategies. In conclusion, PSD2 followers and supporters of different approaches dictate the open banking development in Europe. This division is not the final image of the European open banking scene. Ongoing EU reforms and upcoming legislation may be influential across Europe and set new open banking/open finance scenarios.

The Americas

The selected American jurisdictions (Canada, the USA, Mexico and Chile) present wide and diversified degrees of development of open banking strategies and regulations. In Canada, open banking implementation is clearly at a standstill. The benefits that open banking and payment modernisation would bring to the country are highly recognised and debated. Even though open banking is on the regulatory agenda, frustration has been growing because of slowness and continuous delays. Some of the largest FinTech companies have launched a public action campaign to urge the federal government to take more concrete steps. The minister of finance assured that the implementation plans are set in stone, but, at present, Canada is the only G7 country without an open banking system.

In the USA, we have witnessed important progress since the consultations for implementing Section 1033 of the Dodd–Frank Act gathered pace. The finalisation of the so-called 'US open banking rule' is expected by late 2024. The open banking rule will generate significant attention in the US open banking system as it marks the evolution from market-driven approaches, which are still prevalent in the USA, to regulation. Within this context, the advocates of open banking also push for a more harmonised federal data protection legislation, which is still lacking in the USA and will be necessary to complement the open banking rule.

By comparison, South American countries mirror steadier progress that led to the enactment of specific legislation. Mexico can be regarded as the country that pioneered open banking in Latin America through the 2018 FinTech Law. The main drivers of this legislation were the promotion of innovation and the enhancement of financial inclusion. Even though the Mexican open banking framework has facilitated the entrance of new FinTech players, the proposed goals are yet to be concretely achieved, particularly financial inclusion. There appear to be discrepancies between the public policy objective of reaching inclusion through open banking and the business models of these firms, which do not mention financial inclusion or seem to target middle-class customers.

As argued in Chapter 5, the current open banking progress in Mexico is controversial. It would be more appropriate to discuss whether the interest in open banking is the same as when the 2018 Fintech Law was passed. Mexico started with relevant open banking strategies that are currently taking second place. A plausible explanation is that open banking is less prioritised in the new government's agenda.

Chile has recently issued its open banking framework as part of the 'FinTech Ley' published in January 2023. Promoting competition and inclusion in the financial services sector through innovation and technology is the rationale behind this legislation, which explains the incorporation of open banking rules. These rules interplay with other legislation on data protection as part of the legislation packages the national Financial Market Commission submitted to the Chilean government. Additional implementing acts are awaited to test the capacity of the open banking regime to meet its goal.

In conclusion, other Latin American countries are expected to join the open banking trend that spread in Mexico, Brazil and Chile, while in Canada and the USA, the work is still in progress for setting proper regulations. Much remains to be seen in open banking in the Americas.

Far East

This is the largest chapter in Part II of the book, as it includes numerous jurisdictions with open banking regimes. In many ways, the path to open banking taken in many Far Eastern jurisdictions differs from and can be contrasted with that in, for example, Europe. While the latter is focused on driving increased competition, in many other jurisdictions, the aims are greater social inclusion and cohesion, with many lacking access to banking and payment services. In some countries, such as Japan, the process is much more cooperative. This may be due to cultural perspectives and a belief that avoiding excessive competition was key to escaping the worst effects of the 2007/09 Global Financial Crisis.

This is also evident in jurisdictions such as Singapore, Taiwan, South Korea and Hong Kong, which have adopted a more statist competitive approach through centralised bank cooperation. For instance, the Hong Kong Monetary Authority (HKMA) published its Open API framework in July 2018. Open banking develops through a four-phased approach under which banks are expected to develop APIs, but they can pose restrictions to third parties regarding data access.

In Indonesia, the development of open banking is strictly connected to the payment system, which is considered the beating heart of the Indonesian economy. Open banking standards have been planned as part of a radical reform of the domestic payment system set out in the '2019 Indonesia Payment System Blueprint'. Under the aegis of the Central Bank of Indonesia, a new regulation was issued to enact the reforms, along with a set of standards to enable open banking. Nonetheless, the lack of consumer knowledge and financial institutions' reluctance to share financial data need to be tackled to further enhance open banking.

Finally, open banking industry-led approaches have always been prevalent in China. Digital-only banks have played a major role in a wave of open banking-enabled products. However, as of 2021, the development of open banking has been scrutinised by the Chinese government in connection with data privacy and security issues. Data protection regulation is under discussion, and, therefore, it is to be questioned whether and to what extent market-driven approaches will still underpin the Chinese open banking system.

Other states in the Far East have focused on consumer interests and protection. For example, Australia and New Zealand prioritise consumer data ownership and data sharing. Australia issued the Consumer Data Right (CDR) in 2019. The CDR is a wide-scope open data framework covering the banking, energy and telecommunications sectors. Data-sharing rules have been rolled out in stages. The banking sector was first tested, followed by the energy and non-bank lending sectors. Significantly, the CDR is a broader framework than Europe and other countries have produced until now. It covers more products and services and expands beyond banking. The CDR allows to list Australia among the countries that pioneered open banking/open data frameworks.

However, implementing the open banking part of the CDR underwent several delays. Concrete results are still debatable. Open banking awareness among consumers is also low. Accordingly, the launch of educational campaigns in Australia is envisaged to ensure better consumer knowledge and capabilities.

Middle East and North Africa (MENA)

This chapter has analysed the development of open banking in Gulf Council Cooperation (GCC) countries. The FinTech market has grown considerably worldwide thanks to a population that is IT literate and open to digital solutions. Moreover, MENA governments promote a FinTech-supportive regulatory environment to fulfil inclusion and economic growth objectives and finally develop an ecosystem able to attract foreign investments.

Open banking is considered an essential instrument to reach these goals. Despite its patchy development across the region, central banks have been leading important changes. Bahrain, the Kingdom of Saudi Arabia (KSA), the United Arab Emirates (UAE) and the Hashemite Kingdom of Jordan (Jordan) have been active in creating open banking frameworks.

Bahrain has been at the forefront since issuing the Bahrain Open Banking Framework (BOBF) in 2020. The BOBF results from consultations between the Central Bank of Bahrain (CBB) and the main industry stakeholders. This open banking framework builds significantly on the EU, UK and Australian open banking experiences. However, its fast creation and incorporation into the CBB Rulebook governing the Bahraini financial system have made it a model for designing open banking frameworks in other GCC jurisdictions. Though the BOBF has not been fully implemented, Bahrain also aims to move towards open finance frameworks. They have, therefore, traced an important path in the region.

Similarly, the Saudi Arabian Monetary Agency (SAMA) has divided the creation of an open banking ecosystem into 'design, implementation and go-live' phases. The go-live phase was attained in November 2022 by issuing the Open Banking Framework, consisting of use cases, business rules and KSA standards. The creation of the framework is a crucial step in realising a set of social and economic reforms highlighted in the 'Saudi Vision 2030' aimed at making the Kingdom a recognised international marketplace. The Saudi open banking framework is new, and its potential remains to be evaluated. However, like the Bahraini open banking framework, it can be inspirational for stimulating and strengthening open banking trends in other MENA countries.

Jordan is also part of this group of GCC countries that pursued open banking legislative approaches. In November 2022, the Central Bank of Jordan (CBJ) issued Regulation of Open Finance Services Operations Procedures No. 12/22, which follows the UK Open Banking Standard framework but is adapted to local legislation and the characteristics of Jordan's financial services industry. This regulation is innovative to the extent that, like in some Latin American countries (e.g., Brazil and Chile), it shifted from the typical open banking (payment account) perimeter to other financial services. Being a very recent framework, it still needs further implementation. Nonetheless, this regulation is another example of how the data openness philosophy spurred by open banking is a borderless phenomenon.

Market-driven initiatives are finally being pursued in the UAE, though regulatory approaches are on the Central Bank of the UAE's agenda through the Financial Infrastructure Transformation Programme. In the rest of the region (Qatar, Oman and Kuwait), the open banking debate is live, and development steps are contemplated. Overall, there has been an important buildout in the analysed jurisdictions. They started by observing other jurisdictions' open banking experiences, and they are now earmarked as faster open banking adopters.

Open banking and challenger financial service businesses in the UK

In recent years, there has been a surge in the number of challenger banks and e-money businesses in the UK. Their primary aim is to disrupt and take market share from the major incumbent UK banks. Electronic money institutions (EMIs) are not banks and do not accept customer deposits; yet, they look like banks in many ways. Most of these firms take advantage of the open banking opportunities provided by PSD2, enacted in UK law by the Payment Services Regulations 2017. The Financial Conduct Authority (FCA) has licensed and authorised approximately 250 EMIs.

The challenger financial institutions pursue a wide array of innovative business models. Almost none of those relying on open banking are profitable. In many ways, the situation mirrors the 'dotcom bubble' when a number of innovative internet banks were established (e.g. Egg, Smile, Intelligent Finance, Cahoot). The latter were almost all founded by existing large banks or insurance companies but were generally run independently with their own management and style. They used innovative marketing and product offerings to attract internet customers. With large marketing budgets, they presented themselves as the future of banking. However, none prospered and either failed or were absorbed by the incumbents.

The cry is that this time, it will be different. Much will depend on how successful future funding rounds are and how they can manage their relatively high-cost bases in relation to their income. Even highly successful companies, such as Adyen, have seen their share price fall steeply in 2023, and they face high employee recruiting costs and strong competition in the US. Finally, UK-based businesses with any hope of large-scale growth will need to set up EU-authorised firms to access the much larger EU financial services markets and significantly greater numbers of consumers.

Finally, we are seeing some loss in community with the growth of open banking and more online access to financial services in developed countries. This may be inevitable. The traditional bank branch largely operated in the high street and was the foundation of its community. *Dad's Army*, a British comedy series from the late 1960s and 1970s, was about a fictitious 1940s Home Guard unit formed by the local bank manager and two of his staff. While a work of fiction, the plot was based on truth, as the bank's presence in each town represented stability and cohesion. As economic forces, including online challenger businesses, lead to bank branch closures, a portion of each community dies.

This is no mere threnody for a disappearing world. It is a call to challenger financial services firms and others to help rebuild and enhance local communities. Being the mechanism for transferring money cheaply and efficiently is great, but something more is needed. Online banks and payment service firms need to build themselves into their local communities. If they grow to any size, they need to train and employ local people. They need to be embedded in a 'place' and develop a sense of local identity.

Open banking and social inclusion and economic growth in developing countries

There is a close link between financial inclusion, increased financial literacy and economic growth. The basic premise is that too many people, for example, in Brazil and India, operate in the subsistence economy. Among other issues, they are deterred from contributing to the wider economy by a lack of access to affordable credit and payment services and by the lack of safe places to store any surplus funds. This is particularly an issue for women and those who are illiterate. There is a close link between financial inclusion and financial literacy. Consequently, those who may be socially and financially excluded must be able to sell their goods and services, including their labour, and cheaply and easily recirculate the proceeds back through the economy. This may also allow them to borrow on competitive terms and store their cash safely. All these factors are important, particularly for women.

To address this, in recent years, central governments in these states have developed easily accessible technology to allow individuals to engage directly in the economy. This theme has run through the work of the Indian government since the 1960s. In a non-traditional role for a central bank, the Reserve Bank of India has taken the lead in many aspects of setting up the necessary infrastructure to promote and enhance financial inclusion.

Developing nations faced with a plethora of problems, unlike the UK and EU, do not see competition as the answer. Indeed, as seen in many developing countries, the incumbent financial businesses may have blocked or delayed financial innovation.

Both India and Brazil focus on financial inclusion and economic growth. However, India's approach is much more comprehensive and balanced, with a strategy aimed at each person having their own digital identity. With this, people are able, among other things, to access the open banking elements of the payment systems and engage in the financial economy.

Unlike the incumbent financial institutions, the governments and agencies of both countries have embraced innovation. In the case of India, the aim has been to engage directly with citizens to reduce intermediation and, as far as possible, endemic corruption.

These two case studies help show what can be achieved by open banking when coupled with other financial inclusion strategies.

Looking to the future

The road ahead is not simple, but it is worth starting with what the book establishes. In line with its objectives, the book captures the global reach of open banking. Its global dimension is a concrete fact, though it is not possible to measure its size and impact because everything is in flux across countries, even in jurisdictions designated as open banking pioneers. Looking at the whole picture, the open banking world is a patchwork of approaches going through different stages of implementation.

Within this context there are open banking adopters rather than open banking leaders. Among them, some jurisdictions were early adopters of open banking and wielded influence over others. However, open banking regimes are finally the result of each nation's growth strategies. There are various drivers behind open banking frameworks that also dictate approaches and progress. Accordingly, the open banking world is diversified, where the adopters move at different speeds. If, for these reasons, there are no leaders, it is also not sensible to draw conclusions on whether open banking has failed or succeeded. At present, we can say that open banking exists and is here to stay as a global phenomenon.

This argument, however, is not the endpoint. If its global dimension cannot be called into doubt, it should be questioned where we can move from this outcome. In other words, whether there can be room for achieving a global open banking ecosystem. It may sound unrealistic in the first place, but it is important to give things the right meaning.

Amid the different drivers behind open banking adoption, it would be utopian to think about a unique and global open banking ecosystem made of common rules for all the participants, but there should be a communion of intentions to make the benefits of open banking global. This objective should be down to the jurisdictions deciding to embrace open banking. Until now, there has been recognition of the spread of open banking worldwide, but things have remained within jurisdictional walls.

To overcome this limit, dialogue and sharing experiences should occur more concretely. Even though the observation and review of countries' open banking experiences have been the input for developing open banking worldwide, now it is time to talk to each other as open banking adopters. This aspect needs to be strengthened. Open banking as a global phenomenon exists because (currently) eighty nations have pursued implementation programmes and, thus, an open banking system exists. The participants in this system now need to move from observation to interaction.

Common open banking issues such as security, inclusion and consumer education have been identified as the keys to getting the participants closer. These issues are crucial to making open banking work and achieving its benefits, no matter the drivers behind the adoption of open banking. Dialogue will also be necessary once data sharing is expanded into open finance. Some jurisdictions are already moving to an open finance framework or planning such a transition. If open banking is the test to move to an open data society, it is time for the participants in this global phenomenon to meet. This is what we hope to capture beyond this book.

Bibliography

Books and reports

Australian Government, 'Review into Open Banking in Australia: Issues Paper', (August 2017), 1, https://treasury.gov.au/sites/default/files/2019-03/Review-into-Open-Banking-IP.pdf

Australian Treasury, Competition Policy Review – Final Report Website' ('The Harper Review'), (2015), https://treasury.gov.au/publication/p2015-cpr-final-report

Australian Treasury, 'Review into Open Banking: Giving Customers Choice, Convenience and Confidence', (December 2017)

Bank Indonesia, 'Indonesia Payment System Blueprint 2025. Bank Indonesia: Navigating the National Payment System in the Digital Era', (28 November 2019), www.bi.go.id/en/publikasi/kajian/Documents/Indonesia-Payment-Systems-Blueprint-2025.pdf

Bank Indonesia, 'Transformation of the Policy Mix and Acceleration of the Digital Economy and Finance', (2021), Economic Report on Indonesia 2021, www.bi.go.id/en/publikasi/laporan/Documents/8_LPI2021_EN_Chapter_6.pdf#search=snap

Bar-Gill O, *Seduction by Contract, Law, Economics and Psychology in Consumer Markets*, (Oxford University Press, Oxford, 2012)

'Blattmann U et al., 'IFZ Open Banking Studie 2022', (2022), Institute of Financial Services Zug IFZ, Hochschule Luzern 1, https://drive.switch.ch/index.php/s/CXJOVPiTtbUUfGk

Brener A, *Housing and Financial Stability*, (Routledge, Abingdon, Oxfordshire, 2020)

Brener A, 'EU Payment Services Regulation and International Developments', in Iris H-Y Chiu and Gudula Deipenbrock (eds), *Routledge Handbook of Financial Technology and Law*, (Routledge, Abingdon, 2021a)

Brener A, *Strategies for Compliance*, (Routledge, Abingdon, Oxfordshire, 2021b)

Bryan L, *Breaking Up the Bank*, (Dow Jones Irwin, Homewood, Illinois, 1988)

Chakrabarty, K C, special address, Deputy Governor of the Reserve Bank of India, at BANCON 2011, Chennai, 4 November 2011, 'Gearing up for the competitive impulse in the Indian banking in its defining decade', https://www.bis.org/review/r111108a.pdf

Chesbrough H, 'Open Services Innovation: Rethinking Your Business to Grow and Compete in a New Era' in Cooksey B (eds), *An Introduction to APIs*, (Jossey-Bass, San Francisco, California, 2011) (Zapier, Inc 2014)

Cortes G and Marcondes R, 'The Evolution of Brazil's Banking System' (chapter 10) in Edmund Amann, Carlos Azzoni, and Werner Baer (eds), *The Oxford Handbook of the Brazilian Economy*, (Oxford Handbooks, OUP, Oxford, 2018)

deLisle J and Goldstein A, 'China's Economic Reform and Opening at Forty: Past Accomplishments and Emerging Challenges' in Jacques de Lisle and Avery Goldstein (eds), *To Get Rich Is Glorious: Challenges Facing China's Economic Reform and Opening at Forty* (The Brookings institution, Washington, D.C., 2019)

Duarte A et al., 'Bank of International Settlement's Bulletin No. 52', (23 March 2022), 7, https://www.bis.org/publ/bisbull52.pdf

EBA, 'Draft Regulatory Technical Standards on Strong Customer Authentication and Common and Secure Communication under Article 98 of Directive 2015/2366 (PSD2)', (2017) Final Report

EBA, 'Final Report on Amending RTS on SCA and CSC under PSD2', (2022) EBA/RTS/2022/03

EU, 'Study on the Impact of Directive 2007/64/EC on Payment Services in the Internal Market and on the Application of Regulation (EC) NO 924/2009 on Cross-border Payments in the Community, Final Report', (February 2013), https://ec.europa.eu/info/sites/default/files/study-impact-psd-24072013_en.pdf

Financial Stability Group and Regional Consultive Group, 'Nordic Experience of Cooperation on Cross-border Regulation and Crisis Resolution', (2016) Report from a RCG Europe Working Group, https://www.fsb.org/wp-content/uploads/RCG-Europe-Nordic-experience-of-cooperation.pdf

General Secretariat for Development Planning, 'Qatar National Vision 2030', (July 2008), www.gco.gov.qa/wp-content/uploads/2016/09/GCO-QNV-English.pdf

HKBA, 'Open API Framework for the Hong Kong Banking Sector Phase II Common Baseline', (2019), https://www.hkab.org.hk/DisplayArticleAction.do?sid=5&ss=32

HKBA, 'Open API Framework for the Hong Kong Banking Sector Common Baseline', (2021), www.hkab.org.hk/DisplayArticleAction.do?sid=5&ss=32

HKMA, 'Open API Framework for the Hong Kong Banking Sector', (18 July 2018), www.hkma.gov.hk/media/eng/doc/key-information/press-release/2018/20180718e5a2.pdf

IMF, 'IMF Country Report No. 18/339 Brazil Financial System Stability Assessment', (November 2018), 33, https://www.imf.org/en/Publications/CR/Issues/2018/11/30/Brazil-Financial-System-Stability-Assessment-46411

IMF, 'People's Republic of China-Hong Kong Special Administrative Region', (8 June 2021), www.imf.org/en/Publications/CR/Issues/2021/06/04/Peoples-Republic-of-China-Hong-Kong-Special-Administrative-Region-Financial-System-Stability-50197

Investigation of Open Banking Limited, 'Independent report by Alison White', 28, https://assets.publishing.service.gov.uk/government/uploads/system/uploads/attachment_data/file/1022451/Independent_report.pdf

Ismail A et al., 'Backgorund to the MENA Region' in Nezameddin Faghih and Mohammad Reza Zali (eds), *Entrepreneurship Education and Research in the Middle East and North Africa (MENA). Perspectives on Trends, Policy and Educational Environment* (Springer, 2018), 19–31.

Japanese Financial Services Authority, 'Strategic Priorities July 2021June 2022, Overcoming COVID-19 and Building the Financial System for Greater Vibrancy', 13, https://www.fsa.go.jp/en/news/2021/20211008/20211008.html

Kalifa Review of UK Fintech, (2022), 105, https://assets.publishing.service.gov.uk/government/uploads/system/uploads/attachment_data/file/978396/KalifaReviewofUKFintech01.pdf

Kelly, Chrisopher, 'Failings in Management and Governance - Report of the Independent Review into the Events Leading to the Co-operative Bank's Capital Shortfall',

(30 April 2014), https://assets.ctfassets.net/5ywmq66472jr/3LpckmtCnuWiuuuE M2qAsw/9bc99b1cd941261bca5d674724873deb/kelly-review.pdf

Kempson E and Whyley C, *Kept Out or Opted Out? Understanding and Combating Financial Exclusion*, (The Policy Press, Bristol University, Bristol, 1999)

Kingdom of Saudi Arabia (KSA), 'Saudi Vision 2030', (2016), https://www.vision2030.gov.sa/media/rc0b5oy1/saudi_vision203.pdf

Kitchin R, *The Data Revolution: Big Data, Open Data, Data Infrastructures and Their Consequences*, (Sage Publication, London, 2014)

Laine J, 'Nordic Cooperation' in Brite Wassenberg & Bernard Reitel (eds), *Critical Dictionary on Cross Border Cooperation in Europe*, (Peter Lang, Brussels, 2020)

Littlejohn G, Boskovich G, and Prior R, 'United Kingdom: The Butterfly Effect' in Linda Jeng (ed), *Open Banking* (Oxford University Press, New York, 2022)

Lowe, Philip, Governor of the Reserve Bank of Australia, speech to the Australian Payments Network, 'Innovation and Regulation in the Australian Payments System', (7 December 2020), https://www.rba.gov.au/speeches/2020/pdf/sp-gov-2020-12-07.pdf

Mazzucato Marina, *The Entrepreneurial State*, (Public Affairs, New York, NY, 2015)

Mnuchin St and Phillips S C, 'A Financial System That Creates Economic Opportunities. Nonbank Financials, Fintech, and Innovation', (July 2018), https://home.treasury.gov/sites/default/files/2018-08/A-Financial-System-that-Creates-Economic-Opportunities—Nonbank-Financials-Fintech-and-Innovation_0.pdf

Montoya A M and Rosario Celedon R, 'Guidelines for the Development of an Open Finance Framework in Chile, with a Focus on Competition and Financial Inclusion' (2021) Ministerio de Hacienda, https://biblioteca.digital.gob.cl/bitstream/handle/123456789/3818/2021.12.06%20-%20Lineamientos%20Informe.pdf?sequence=1&isAllowed=y

New Zealand, 'Kris Faafoi letter of December 2019', https://www.mbie.govt.nz/assets/open-letter-to-api-providers-regarding-industry-progress-on-api-enabled-data-sharing-and-open-banking.pdf

New Zealand, 'Minutes of the Cabinet Economic Development Committee meeting on 21 June 2021', https://www.mbie.govt.nz/dmsdocument/15539-establishing-a-consumer-data-right-minute-of-decision-proactiverelease-pdf

Nuffield Politics Research Centre, 'Red Wall: Red Herring? Economic Insecurity and Voting Intention in Britain', (May 2022), 35–6, https://politicscentre.nuffield.ox.ac.uk/media/5142/nprc-econ-insecurity-report_bridges_final.pdf

Office of Fair Trading, 'Personal Current Accounts in the UK: An OFT Market Study' (2008)

Oxera and the Nuffield Centre for Experimental Social Sciences, 'Increasing Consumer Engagement in the Annuities Market: Can Prompts Raise Shopping Around?' (June 2016). Research prepared for the Financial Conduct Authority, 17, https://www.oxera.com/wp-content/uploads/2018/07/consumer-engagement-in-annuities-market-1.pdf-1.pdf

Pandy S, 'Modernizing U.S. Financial Services with Open Banking and APIs', (10 February 2021), *Payment Strategy Report*, Federal Reserve Bank of Boston, www.bostonfed.org/publications/payment-strategies/modernizing-us-financial-services-with-open-banking-and-apis.aspx

Parliament of Australia, 'Review of the Four Major Banks: First Report', (November 2016), 2, https://www.aph.gov.au/Parliamentary_Business/Committees/House/Economics/Four_Major_Banks_Review/Report

Rajan, Raghuram speech, Governor of the Reserve Bank of India, 'The changing paradigm for financial inclusion' at the National Seminar on 'Equity, Access, and Inclusion - Transforming Rural India through Financial Inclusion', organised by the National Institute of Rural Development and Panchayat Raj, Hyderabad, 18 July 2016, https://www.bis.org/review/r160719a.htm

Report of the Committee on the Medium-term Path on Financial Inclusion', vii, https://rbidocs.rbi.org.in/rdocs/PublicationReport/Pdfs/FFIRA27F4530706A41A0BC394D01CB4892CC.PDF

Riley P et al., 'Digital Financial Services in the MENA Region', *Sustaining Health Outcomes through the Private Sector Plus Project* (Abt Associates Inc, Rockville, MD, 2020), https://shopsplusproject.org/sites/default/files/resources/Digital%20Financial%20Services%20in%20the%20MENA%20Region.pdf

Sharples M, 'An Introduction to Human Computer Interaction' in Margaret Boden (ed), *Artificial Intelligence* (Academic Press, San Diego, 1996)

Shirazi N S, Aysan A F, and Nanaeva Z, 'Open Banking for Financial Inclusion: Challenges and Opportunities in Muslim Majority Countries' in Zul Hakim Jumat, Saqib Hafiz Khateeb and Syed Nazim Ali (eds), *Islamic Finance, FinTech, and the Road to Sustainability Reframing the Approach in the Post-Pandemic Era* (Palgrave Macmillan, Cham, 2023) 259–74

Social Market Foundation and Evans Katie, 'Playing the Field: Consumers and Competition in Banking', (2015), Social Market Foundation, 10, https://www.smf.co.uk/wp-content/uploads/2015/07/Social-Market-FoundationPublication-Playing-the-field-Consumers-and-competition-in-banking-160715.pdf

Stiglitz, Joseph, 'Government Failure vs. Market Failure: Principles of Regulation' in Edward Balleisen and David Moss (eds), *Government and Markets: Toward a New Theory of Regulation* (Cambridge University Press, Cambridge, 2010) 13–51

Surhone L M, Timpledon M T, and Marseken S F, *The Empire on Which the Sun Never Sets* (VDM Publishing, Riga, Latvia, 2010)

The Paypers, 'Report 2022: The Enablers of Open Banking, Open Finance, and Open Data', (November 2022), https://thepaypers.com/reports/report-2022-the-enablers-of-open-banking-open-finance-and-open-data/r1258969

Treasury Committee Oral Evidence: Lessons from Greensill Capital, HC 151 Thursday 27 May 2021, https://committees.parliament.uk/oralevidence/2293/pdf/

Treasury Select Committee, 'Formal Meeting (Oral Evidence Session): HM Treasury's Role in Combating Fraud', https://committees.parliament.uk/event/13079/formal-meeting-oral-evidence-session/

Treasury Select Committee (TSC), 'Lessons from Greensill Capital: Sixth Report of Session 2021–22 Report', (14 July 2021), 46, https://committees.parliament.uk/publications/6800/documents/72205/default/

Wilkes M, Wheeler D, and Gill S, *The Preparation of Programs for an Electronic Digital Computer. With Special Reference to the EDSAC and the Use of a Library of Subroutines* (Cambridge, MA, Addison-Wesley Press, Inc., 1951)

World Bank, 'Global Financial Development Report 2014: Financial Inclusion', (November 2014), https://elibrary.worldbank.org/doi/abs/10.1596/978-0-8213-9985-9

Articles

Anarfo E et al., 'Financial Inclusion and Financial Sector Development in Sub-Saharan Africa: A Panel VAR Approach', (April 2019), International Journal of Managerial Finance 15(3), 444–63, 445

Bianco M and Vangelisti M I, 'Open Banking and Financial Inclusion', (2022) European Economy Banks, Regulation, and the Real Sector, https://european-economy.eu/2022/open-banking-and-financial-inclusion/

Billiam B, Abubakar L, and Handayani T, 'The Urgency of Open Application Programming Interface Standardization in the Implementation of Open Banking to Customer Data Protection for the Advancement of Indonesian Banking', (2022) 9, Padjajjaran Journal of Law 1, 63

Bordo M, Redish A, and Rockoff H, 'Why didn't Canada Have a Banking Crisis in 2008 (or in 1930, or 1907, or …)', (February 2015), The Economic History Review 68(1), 218–43, 241

Boukhatem J, 'Assessing the Direct Effect of Financial Development on Poverty Reduction in a Panel of Low- and Middle-Income Countries' (2016), Research in International Business and Finance 37, 214

Briones de Araluze G K and Cassinello Plaza N, 'Open Banking: A Bibliometric Analysis-Driven definition' (2022), PLoS ONE 17(10), 1

Carrière-Swallow Y, Haksar V, and Patnam M, (IMF Working Paper) 'India's Approach to Open Banking: Some Implications for Financial Inclusion', (February 2021), 16, file:///N:/Downloads/wpiea2021052-print-pdf.pdf

Cohen E, 'Industrial Policies in France: The Old and the New', (2007), Journal of Industry, Competition and Trade 7, 213–27, 226

Dahiya S, Kumar M, and Radha, 'Linkage between Financial Inclusion and Economic Growth: An Empirical Study of the Emerging Indian Economy', (2020), Vision 24(2), 184–93, 186

De Pascalis F, 'The Journey to Open Finance: Learning from the Open Banking Movement', (2022), 33, European Business Law Review 3, 397

Dymski G A and Veitch J M, 'Financial Transformation and the Metropolis: Booms, Busts, and Banking in Los Angeles' (1996) 28, Environment and Planning A: Economy and Space 7, 123

Fonseca J and Matray A, 'The real effects of banking the poor: evidence from Brazil', (March 2022), Griswold Center for Economic Policy Studies Working Paper No. 293, https://gceps.princeton.edu/wp-content/uploads/2022/04/wp293_Matray_Fonseca.pdf

Gautam T and Garg K, 'Union Bank of India: Initiatives Towards It-Enabled Financial Inclusion', (2014) South Asian Journal of Business and Management Cases, 3(2), 149–156

Gershenson D et al., 'Fintech and Financial Inclusion in Latin America and the Caribbean', (IMF Working Paper, WP/21/221, 2021), 9

Jevglevskaja N and Buckley R P, 'The Consumer Data Right: How to Realise this World-Leading Reform', (2022), 45 UNSW Law Journal 4, 1621

Leong E and Gardner J, 'Open Banking in the UK and Singapore: Open Possibilities for Enhancing Financial Inclusion', (2021), Journal of Business Law 5, 424

Leyshon A and Thrift N, 'Access to Financial Services and Financial Infrastructure Withdrawal: Problems and Policies', (September 1994), Area, 26(3), 268–275

Leyshon A and Thrift N, 'Geographies of Financial Exclusion: Financial Abandonment in Britain and the United States', (1995), Transactions of the Institute of British Geographers, New Series 20(3), 312

Leyshon A and Thrift N, 'The Restructuring of the U.K. Financial Services Industry in the 1990s: A Reversal of Fortune? (1993) 9, Journal of Rural Studies 3, 223

Lobo B and Brandt C, 'Pix: The Brazilian Fast Payment Scheme', (2022), Journal of Payments Strategy and Systems 15(4), 367–75, 369.

Markov S C, *Open Banking: The CFPB Should Follow the European Regulatory Regime* (Vol. 26), (North Carolina Bank Institute, 269, 2022).

Naceur S B and Ghazouani S, 'Stock Markets, Banks, and Economic Growth: Empirical Evidence from the MENA Region', (2007), Research in International Business and Finance 21(2), 297

Park C and Mercado R, 'Financial Inclusion, Poverty, and Income Inequality', (2018), Singapore Economic Review 63(1), 185–206, 204

Polasika M et al., 'The Impact of Payment Services Directive 2 on the PayTech Sector Development in Europe', (2020), Journal of Economic Behavior and Organization 178, 385–401, 391

Sarma M and Pais J, 'Financial Inclusion and Development', (2011), International Development 23(5), 613

Sharma D, 'Nexus between Financial Inclusion and Economic Growth', (2016), Journal of Financial Economic Policy 8(1), 13–36, 32

Shree S et al., 'Digital Payments and Consumer Experience in India: A Survey based Empirical Study', (2021), Journal of Banking and Financial Technology 5, 2, file:///N:/Downloads/Digital_Payments_and_Consumer_Experience_in_India.pdf

Simon Jean P, 'API, the Glue under the Hood. Looking for the "API Economy"', (2021), Digital Policy Regulation and Governance 23(5), 498

Thi-Hong Van L, 'Financial Inclusion and Economic Growth: An International Evidence', (2021), Emerging Markets, Finance and Trade 57(1), 239–263, 244

Vicente J, 'Fintech Disruption in Brazil: A Study on the Impact of Open Banking and Instant Payments in the Brazilian Financial Landscape', (2020), Social Impact Research Experience (SIRE), 86 and Gabriel Quatrochi, Ana Lucia G. da Silva and José Eduardo Cassiolato, 'Banks 4.0 in Brazil: Possibilities to Ensure Fintechs Financing Role through Its Market Positioning, Innovation and Development', (2022), published online by Taylor and Francis, https://www.tandfonline.com/doi/full/10.1080/2157930X.2022.2086336

Xiang X et al., 'China's Path to FinTech Development' (2017) European Economy 2, 143

Xu D, Taylor J, and Ren Y, 'Wait-and-See or Whack-a-Mole: What Is the Best Way to Regulate Fintech in China?', (2022), Asian Journal of Law and Society 10(3), 433–462.

Websites

ABS website, 'Finance-as-a-Service: API Playbook', (2016), https://abs.org.sg/docs/library/abs-api-playbook.pdf

ACCC website, 'Competition and Consumer (Consumer Data Right) Rules 2020', (2020), www.accc.gov.au/by-industry/banking-and-finance/the-consumer-data-right

ACCC website, 'ACCC authorises payment systems merger after undertaking', (9 September 2021), https://www.accc.gov.au/media-release/accc-authorises-payment-systems-merger-after-undertaking

ACCC website, 'Consumer Data Right – Proposed Timetable for Participation of Non-major Authorised Deposit-taking Institutions (ADIs) in the CDR', (2020) www.accc.gov.au/system/files/CDR%20-%20Proposed%20timetable%20for%20participation%20of%20non-major%20ADIs%20in%20the%20CDR_0.pdf

ACCC website press release, 'eftpos, BPAY Group and NPPA Propose to Amalgamate for the Benefit of Australian Consumers andBusinesses', (December 2020), https://

www.accc.gov.au/system/files/public-registers/documents/85.%20Media%20 Release%20-%20eftpos%2C%20BPAY%20Group%20and%20NPPA%20propose%20to%20amalgamate%20for%20the%20benefit%20of%20Australian%20consumers%20and%20businesses%2C%2015%20December%202020.pdf

Adyen website, 'Adyen Expands beyond Payments, Announces Embedded Financial Products', (30 March 2022a), https://www.adyen.com/press-and-media/2022/adyen-expands-beyond-payments-announces-embedded-financial-products

Adyen website, 'Capital Markets Day', (31 March 2022b), https://www.adyen.com/investor-relations/events/capital-markets-day-2022

Aiia website, 'What Makes the Nordics Tick When it Comes to Open Banking', (2020), https://blog.aiia.eu/what-makes-the-nordics-tick-when-it-comes-to-open-banking

Airlock, 'API Security – Limiting Factor or Accelerator of an Open Banking Strategy', (2020), www.airlock.com/fileadmin/content/07_Airlock-PDFs/Whitepaper_API_Security_v3.pdf

Aite-Novarica website, 'Making Ends Meet: On-Demand Pay and Employer-Based Loans', (24 February 2021), https://aite-novarica.com/report/making-ends-meet-demand-pay-and-employer-based-loans

altfi website, 'Here Are the UK's 6 Leading Digital Wealth Managers', (17 June 2020a), https://www.altfi.com/article/6714_here-are-the-uks-6-leading-digital-wealth-managers

altfi website, 'Nutmeg Reportedly Overtakes Scalable Capital to Become Europe's Largest Digital Wealth Manager', (31 January 2020b), https://www.altfi.com/article/6140_nutmeg-reportedly-overtakes-scalable-capital-to-become-europes-largest-digital-wealth-manager

altfi website, 'Embedded finance: Klarna partners with Liberis for revenue-based finance', (29 June 2021a), https://www.altfi.com/article/8051_embedded-finance-klarna-partners-with-liberis-for-revenue-based-finance

altfi website, 'In Full: Here's the Fintech Founders Letter Criticising Anne Boden's Select Committee Comments', (29 December 2021b), www.altfi.com/article/8664_in-full-heres-the-fintech-founders-letter-criticising-anne-bodens-select-committee-comments

altfi website, 'Monzo Withdraws US Banking Licence Application', (4 October 2021c), https://www.altfi.com/article/8385_monzo-withdraws-us-banking-licence-application

altfi website, 'The US Regulator Told Monzo That Its Banking Licence Was Unlikely to Be Approved', (4 October 2021d), https://www.altfi.com/article/8385_monzo-withdraws-us-banking-licence-application

altfi website, 'Open Banking. State of the Market Report', (29 March 2022a), https://www.altfi.com/research/open-banking-state-of-the-market-report-2022

altfi website, 'Revolut's Only Female Exec Becomes Latest to Leave the Company', (11 July 2022b), https://www.altfi.com/article/9522_revoluts-only-female-exec-becomes-latest-to-leave-the-company

altfi website, 'Revolut UK Regulatory and Risk Bosses Quit as Fintech Giant Awaits UK Banking Licence Decision', (25 July 2022c), https://www.altfi.com/article/9586_revolut-uk-regulatory-and-risk-bosses-quit-as-revolut-awaits-uk-banking-licence-decision

American Banker website, 'CFPB Should Protect and Enable the Most Vulnerable in its Open Banking Rule', (23 December 2022), https://www.americanbanker.com/opinion/cfpb-should-protect-and-enable-the-most-vulnerable-in-its-open-banking-rule

200 Bibliography

API Centre NZ Payments website, https://www.apicentre.paymentsnz.co.nz/about/background/

API Metrics website, 'UK Open Banking APIs Performance Analysis: 2018. An Analysis of the Quality and Cloud Service Performance of the UK's CMA9 Group of Open Banking APIs in 2018', (May 2019), https://apimetrics.io/wp-content/uploads/2020/06/finextra_apimetrics_cma9_report_2018.pdf

Australian Competition and Consumer Commission website, 'Consumer data right (CDR)', (1 August 2019), https://www.accc.gov.au/focus-areas/consumer-data-right-cdr-0

Australian Parliament website, 'Report by the House of Representatives Standing Committee on Economics, Treasury Laws Amendment (Consumer Data Right) Bill 2019', (21 March 2019), https://www.aph.gov.au/Parliamentary_Business/Committees/Senate/Economics/TLABConsumerDataRight/Report

Australian Payroll Association, 'Sharper Lending Algorithms and "More Affluent" Users Turning Beforepay to Profitability, CEO Says', (1 May 2022), https://www.austpayroll.com.au/sharper-lending-algorithms-and-more-affluent-users-turning-beforepay-to-profitability-ceo-says/

Australian Treasury, 'Future Directions for the Consumer Data Right', (October 2020), https://treasury.gov.au/sites/default/files/2021-02/cdrinquiry-final.pdf

Australian Treasury, 'Payments System Review', (June 2021), vii, https://treasury.gov.au/sites/default/files/2021-08/p2021-198587.pdf

Axway website, 'Open Banking. The Art of the Possible in 10 Use Cases', (2022), https://resources.axway.com/financial-services-doc/checklist-open-banking-10-use-cases-en

Baltic website, 'Nordic Countries Emerge as Front-Runners in Open Banking Adoption', (21 January 2021), https://fintechbaltic.com/3555/nordics/open-banking-nordics/

Banco Central Chile website, 'Observatorio Technologico', www.bcentral.cl/web/banco-central/areas/observatorio-tecnologico

Banco Central do Brasil website, 'BC# agenda', https://www.bcb.gov.br/en/about/bcbhashtag

Banco Central do Brasil website, 'Open Banking', https://www.bcb.gov.br/en/financialstability/open_banking

Banco Central do Brasil website, 'Open Finance', https://www.bcb.gov.br/en/financialstability/open_finance

Banco Central do Brasil website, 'Pix: BCB Role', https://www.bcb.gov.br/en/financialstability/pixcentralbanksrole

Bank of Canada website, 'Retail Payments Supervision', https://www.bankofcanada.ca/core-functions/retail-payments-supervision/

Bank of Lithuania website, 'Regulatory Measures on Revolut Group Companies', (18 March 2022), https://www.lb.lt/en/news/sanctions-on-revolut-group-companies

Banking Frontiers website, 'China Takes Baby Steps to Bring in Open Banking', (24 December 2020), https://bankingfrontiers.com/china-takes-baby-steps-to-bring-in-open-banking/

BBC New website, 'Privacy Watchdog to Probe Klarna after Email Backlash', (13 October 2020), https://www.bbc.co.uk/news/business-54521820

BCB Communiqué, 33,455 (24 April 2019), https://www.bcb.gov.br/content/config/Documents/BCB_Open_Banking_Communique-April-2019.pdf

BCB Public Consultation, 73/2019, BCB, Open Banking, 9, https://www.amf.org.ae/sites/default/files/publications/2022-01/centrab-bank-of-brazil-session-3.pdf

Bibliography 201

BCB website, '20202023 Strategic Map', https://www.bcb.gov.br/content/publications/rig_2020_en/info_pag_09a.jpg

BCB website, 'Agenda BC# - Regulation of the Initial Governance Framework for the Open Banking Implementation', (24 June 2020a), https://www.bcb.gov.br/en/pressdetail/2338/nota

BCB website, 'New Regulation on Open Banking in Brazil', (8 May 2020b), https://www.bcb.gov.br/en/pressdetail/2330/nota

BCB website, 'Pix', https://www.bcb.gov.br/en/financialstability/pix_en

BCB Public Consultation 73/2019, BCB, Open Banking, 9, (2019), https://www.amf.org.ae/sites/default/files/publications/2022-01/centrab-bank-of-brazil-session-3.pdf

BCBS website, 'Report on Open Banking and Application Programming Interfaces', (November 2019), www.bis.org/bcbs/publ/d486.pdf

BELatina website 'Prometeo Open Banking, a Latin American Company Leading Financial Services', (22 July 2022), https://belatina.com/prometeo-open-banking-ximena-aleman/

Beanstalk website, https://beanstalkapp.co.uk

Belvo website, https://belvo.com/about/

BI Communication Department, 'Bank Indonesia Launches National Open API Payment Standard and Sandbox Trials of QRIS and Thai QR Payment Interconnectivity', (17 August 2021), www.bi.go.id/en/publikasi/ruang-media/news-release/Pages/sp_2321121.aspx

Bloomberg website, 'Earned-Wage Access Products Face Fresh Scrutiny From CFPB, States', (3 January 2022a), https://news.bloomberglaw.com/banking-law/earned-wage-access-products-face-fresh-scrutiny-from-cfpb-states

Bloomberg website, 'Revolut's $33 Billion Bank App Hits a Roadblock in Britain', (6 May 2022b), https://www.bloomberg.com/news/articles/2022-05-06/revolut-33-billion-banking-app-wants-to-play-in-the-big-league

British Business Bank website, 'Companies in Which the Future Fund Has a Shareholding', https://www.british-business-bank.co.uk/ourpartners/coronavirus-business-interruption-loan-schemes/future-fund/future-fund-companies/

C6 Bank website, 'Get To Know the Bank of Your Life in Brazil and the World', https://www.c6bank.com.br/quem-somos

Canadian Department of Finance website, 'Consultation Document: Review into the Merits of Open Banking', (January 2019), https://www.canada.ca/en/department-finance/programs/consultations/2019/open-banking.html

Canadian Finance Department website, 'Minister Morneau Launches Advisory Committee on Open Banking', (26 September 2018), https://www.canada.ca/en/department-finance/news/2018/09/minister-morneau-launches-advisory-committee-on-open-banking.html

Cardlytics, 'Open Banking in the UK. Finding the Tipping Points', (2018), https://www.cardlytics.com/blog/open-banking-in-the-uk-finding-the-tipping-points

CBB website, 'CBB Launches the Bahrain Open Banking Framework', (2020), www.cbb.gov.bh/media-center/cbb-launches-the-bahrain-open-banking-framework/

CBUAE website, 'CBUAE Launches a Financial Infrastructure Transformation Programme to Accelerate the Digital Transformation of the Financial Services Sector', (2023), www.centralbank.ae/media/mdupathy/cbuae-launches-a-financial-infrastructure-transformation-programme-to-accelerate-the-digital-transformation-of-the-financial-services-sector-en.pdf

Bibliography

CCAF website, 'FinTech Regulation in the Middle East and North Africa', (2022), www.jbs.cam.ac.uk/wp-content/uploads/2022/02/ccaf-2022-02-fintech-regulation-in-mena.pdf

CFPB website, 'Bureau Symposium: Consumer Access to Financial Records. A summary of the Proceedings', (18 October 2017a), https://s3.amazonaws.com/files.consumerfinance.gov/f/documents/cfpb_consumer-protection-principles_data-aggregation_stakeholder-insights.pdf

CFPB website, 'Consumer-Authorized Financial Data Sharing and Aggregation. Stakeholder Insights that Inform the Consumer Protection Principles', (18 October 2017b), https://s3.amazonaws.com/files.consumerfinance.gov/f/documents/cfpb_consumer-protection-principles_data-aggregation_stakeholder-insights.pdf

CFPB website, 'Consumer Protection Principles: Consumer-Authorized Financial Data Sharing and Aggregation', (18 October 2017c), https://files.consumerfinance.gov/f/documents/cfpb_consumer-protection-principles_data-aggregation.pdf

CFPB website, 'Advance Notice of Proposed Rulemaking on Consumer Access to Financial Records' (2020), https://s3.amazonaws.com/files.consumerfinance.gov/f/documents/cfpb_section-1033-dodd-frank_advance-notice-proposed-rulemaking_2020-10.pdf

CFPB website, 'Outline of Proposals and Alternatives Under Consideration', (27 October 2022), https://files.consumerfinance.gov/f/documents/cfpb_data-rights-rulemaking-1033-SBREFA_outline_2022-10.pdf

CFPB website, 'Final Report of the Small Business Review Panel on the CFPB's Proposals and Alternatives Under Consideration for the Required Rulemaking on Personal Financial Data Rights', (30 March 2023), https://files.consumerfinance.gov/f/documents/cfpb_1033-data-rights-rule-sbrefa-panel-report_2023-03.pdf

CGAP website, 'Open Data and the Future of Banking', (23 October 2019), www.cgap.org/blog/open-data-and-future-of-banking

CGAP website, 'Open Banking: How to Design for Financial Inclusion' (2020) Consultative Group to Assist the Poor', (2020), https://www.cgap.org/research/publication/open-banking-how-to-design-for-financial-inclusion

Chartered Institute of Personnel and Development website, 'Policy Position on Employer Salary Advance Schemes', (28 June 2021), https://www.cipd.co.uk/news-views/cipd-voice/Issue-29/policy-position-employer-salary-advance-schemes#gref

Chief Executive Officer Report in the 2021 Financial Statements, 11, https://www.atombank.co.uk/~/docs/annual-report-20-21.pdf

China Banking News website, 'Tencent Cloud and WeBank Launch Fintech Lab to Explore Open Banking in China', (1 April 2019), www.chinabankingnews.com/2019/04/01/tencent-cloud-and-webank-launch-fintech-lab-to-explore-open-banking/

ChinaFile website, 'China Boots Up an Internet Banking Industry, Tencent and Alibaba Usher In Cyberspace Borrowing', (27 January 2015), www.chinafile.com/reporting-opinion/caixin-media/china-boots-internet-banking-industry

Circular N° 4.015, de 4 de Maio de 2020, https://www.in.gov.br/web/dou/-/circular-n-4.015-de-4-de-maio-de-2020-255164763

CMA 'Personal Current Accounts - Market Study Update', (July 2014), 121–2, https://assets.publishing.service.gov.uk/media/53c834c640f0b610aa000009/140717_-_PCA_Review_Full_Report.pdf\

CMA, 'Retail Banking Market Investigation', (2017), https://assets.publishing.service.gov.uk/media/63bed8958fa8f513b40f866c/BANKING_PROVIDERS_Roadmap_Completion_Decision_.pdf

CMA, 'Retail Banking Market Investigation - Provisional Decisions on Remedies', (May 2016), https://www.openbanking.org.uk/wp-content/uploads/2021/04/retail_banking_market_pdr.pdf

CMA, 'The Retail Banking Market Investigation Order 2017, 64 and following', https://assets.publishing.service.gov.uk/government/uploads/system/uploads/attachment_data/file/600842/retail-banking-market-investigation-order-2017.pdf

CMA, 'Update on Open Banking', (5 November 2021), www.gov.uk/government/publications/update-governance-of-open-banking/update-on-open-banking

CMA, 'The Future Oversight of the CMA's Open Banking Remedies Response to Consultation', (24 March 2022), 2, https://assets.publishing.service.gov.uk/government/uploads/system/uploads/attachment_data/file/1063319/Consultation_response.pdf

CMF website, 'CMF Publishes Fintech Act Proposal for the Securities Market', (2021), www.cmfchile.cl/portal/principal/613/w3-article-46998.html

CNBC website, '"Criminals Love Buy Now, Pay Later": How Fraudsters Exploit Popular Interest-Free Payment Plans', (18 November 2021), https://www.cnbc.com/2021/11/18/criminals-exploit-buy-now-pay-later-services-like-klarna-and-afterpay.html

Competition and Markets Authority, 'Making Banks Work Harder for Customers', (August 2016), 1–2, https://www.gov.uk/government/publications/retail-banking-market-investigation-overview

Competition Policy International website, 'Chile's Fintech Law Project – Advancements Towards Innovation, Competition and Financial Inclusion', (November 2021), www.competitionpolicyinternational.com/wp-content/uploads/2021/11/LatAm-Column-November-2021-Full.pdf

Computerweekly website, 'Norwegian Banking App Gives Access to Other Banks' Accounts', (24 March 2020), www.computerweekly.com/news/252480509/Norwegian-banking-app-gives-access-to-other-banks-accounts

CONAIF, 'National Financial Inclusion Strategy – Mexico', (12 March 2020), https://www.afi-global.org/publications/national-financial-inclusion-strategy-mexico/consent.online website, https://consents.online

'Contingent Reimbursement Model Code for Authorised Push Payment Scams', (28 April 2022). In particular, sections SF 1(2) (a)(e), https://www.lendingstandardsboard.org.uk/wp-content/uploads/2022/04/LSB-CRM-Code-V3.0-28-April-2022.pdf

Core website, 'Understanding China's Fintech Sector: Development, Impacts and Risks', (27 August 2020), https://core.ac.uk/download/pdf/334410228.pdf

Crowdfund Insider, 'Open Banking Fintech Salt Edges Teams Up with Landsbankinn, the Largest Icelandic Bank', (27 November 2021), www.crowdfundinsider.com/2021/11/183439-open-banking-fintech-salt-edges-teams-up-with-landsbankinn-the-largest-icelandic-bank/

Crowdfund Insider, 'Satago, a Provider of Invoice Financing, Teams Up with Sage, Lloyds Bank', (10 June 2022), https://www.crowdfundinsider.com/2022/06/192134-satago-a-provider-of-invoice-financing-teams-up-with-sage-lloyds-bank/

Crown Commercial Court website, 'How Payment Initiation Service Providers Are Changing the Way Citizens Pay Online', (24 December 2021), www.crowncommercial.gov.uk/news/how-payment-initiation-service-providers-are-changing-the-way-citizens-pay-online

Current Account Switch Service, 'Annual Report 2021', 4, https://www.wearepay.uk/wp-content/uploads/Current-Account-Switch-Service-Annual-Report-2021.pdf

Deloitte website, 'Open Banking. Unleashing the Power of Data and Seizing New Opportunities', (January 2021), www2.deloitte.com/content/dam/Deloitte/in/Documents/financial-services/in-fs-open-banking-report-noexp.pdf

Dentons HPRP website, 'Digital Payment Made Easier Thanks to Cross-Border QRIS and National Open API Standard (SNAP)', (23 June 2022), https://dentons.hprplawyers.com/en/insights/alerts/2022/june/23/digital-payments-made-easier-thanks-to-cross-border-qris-and-snap

DFCI website, https://innovationhub.difc.ae/

Directive on Payment Services in the Internal Market (PSD II) (2015/2366/EC), https://www.eumonitor.eu/9353000/1/j4nvk6yhcbpeywk_j9vvik7m1c3gyxp/vk0vn25mntsj

DNB website, 'A Quarter of Dutch Consumers Shared Payment Data in Exchange for Services', https://www.dnb.nl/en/general-news/2020/a-quarter-of-dutch-consumers-shared-payment-data-in-exchange-for-services/

Donal Griffin, 'London's Fintech Boom Opens the Door for Dirty Money', (Bloomberg UK, 4 January 2022), https://www.bloomberg.com/news/features/2022-01-04/fintech-boom-masks-a-shady-side-of-london-s-money-hub

ECB, 'Card Payments in Europe – Current Landscape and Future Prospects: A Eurosystem Perspective', (17 April 2019), https://www.ecb.europa.eu/pub/pubbydate/2019/html/ecb.cardpaymentsineu_currentlandscapeandfutureprospects201904~30d4de2fc4.en.html

ECB, 'Towards the Retail Payments of Tomorrow: A European Strategy', (26 November 2019), https://www.ecb.europa.eu/press/key/date/2019/html/ecb.sp191126~5230672c11.en.html

ECGI website, 'The Promise and Perils of Open Finance', (2022), https://www.ecgi.global/sites/default/files/working_papers/documents/openfinancefinal.pdf

ECOMMPAY website, 'Beyond the Pandemic: The Outlook for Open Banking', (2021), https://ecommpay.com/uploads/2021/08/19/beyond-the-pandemic-whitepaper.pdf

Economic Research Forum website, 'Globalization of Finance and FinTech in The MENA Region', (September 2021), https://erf.org.eg/app/uploads/2021/09/1634550652_436_521705_1489.pdf

Economic Times website, 'Regulatory Sandbox Explained: How RBI Is Moderating FinTechs' Disruption in BFSI [Banking, financial services and insurance]', https://bfsi.economictimes.indiatimes.com/news/policy/regulatory-sandbox-explained-how-rbi-is-moderating-fintechs-disruption-in-bfsi/87098591

Ecospend website, https://ecospend.com/our-mission/

EFTA website, 'The Basic Features of the EEA Agreement', www.efta.int/eea/eea-agreement/eea-basic-features#6

Electronic Money Association website, https://e-ma.org/about

Emma website, https://emma-app.com/about-us

EPDP website, 'Guidelines 06/2020 on the Interplay of the Second Services Directive and the GDPR' https://edpb.europa.eu/our-work-tools/our-documents/guidelines/guidelines-062020-interplay-second-payment-services_en.

Equifax website, 'M&S Bank Enables Faster Mortgage Applications with Open Banking', https://www.equifax.co.uk/about-equifax/press-releases/en_gb/-/blog/m-s-bank-enables-faster-mortgage-applications-with-open-banking/

Equifax website, 'United Utilities and Equifax UK Deliver First Real Time Open Banking Product for Water Industry: Platform Accelerates Social Tariff Application

Bibliography 205

Process', (7 July 2021), https://www.equifax.co.uk/about-equifax/press-releases/en_gb/-/blog/united-utilities-and-equifax-uk-deliver-first-real-time-open-banking-product-for-water-industry-2

EU Commission, 'Call for Advice to the European Banking Authority (EBA) Regarding the Review of Directive (EU) 2015/2366 (PSD2)', https://ec.europa.eu/info/sites/default/files/business_economy_euro/banking_and_finance/documents/211018-payment-services-calls-advice-eba_en.pdf

EU Commission, 'Communication from the Commission to the European Parliament, the Council, the European Economic and Social Committee, and the Committee of the Regions on a Digital Finance Strategy for the EU', (2020), COM (2020) 591 final https://eur-lex.europa.eu/legal-content/EN/TXT/PDF/?uri=CELEX:52020DC0591&from=EN

EU Commission, 'Communication on a Retail Payments Strategy for the EU', (September 2020), https://eur-lex.europa.eu/legal-content/EN/TXT/PDF/?uri=CELEX:52020DC0592&from=EN

EU Commission, 'Call For Evidence for Evaluation and Impact Assessment', (10 May 2022a), Ref. Ares (2022)3556263, 2 https://ec.europa.eu/info/law/better-regulation/have-your-say/initiatives/13331-Payment-services-review-of-EU-rules_en

EU Commission, 'Payment Services – Review of EU Rules', (2022b), https://ec.europa.eu/info/law/better-regulation/have-your-say/initiatives/13331-Payment-services-review-of-EU-rules_en

EU Commission – Fact Sheet, 'Payment Services Directive: Frequently Asked Questions', (2018), https://ec.europa.eu/commission/presscorner/detail/de/MEMO_15_5793

EU website, 'Proposed Consumer Credit Directive', COM(2021) 347 final 2021/0171(COD), https://eur-lex.europa.eu/legal-content/EN/TXT/?uri=CELEX%3A52021PC0347&qid=1655282823416

EU website, 'Digital Economy and Society Index (DESI) 2022', (2022), https://digital-strategy.ec.europa.eu/en/policies/desi

EU website, 'Framework for Financial Data Access', (2023a), https://finance.ec.europa.eu/digital-finance/framework-financial-data-access_en

EU website, 'Modernising Payment Services and Opening Financial Services Data: New Opportunities for Consumers and Businesses', (2023b), https://ec.europa.eu/commission/presscorner/detail/en/ip_23_3543

EU website, 'Proposal for a Regulation of the European Parliament and of the Council on a Framework for Financial Data Access and Amending Regulations (EU) No 1093/2010, (EU) No 1094/2010, (EU) No 1095/2010 and (EU) 2022/2554', COM(2023c) 360 Final https://eur-lex.europa.eu/legal-content/EN/TXT/PDF/?uri=CELEX:52023PC0360

EU website on Consumer Credit, https://ec.europa.eu/info/business-economy-euro/banking-and-finance/consumer-finance-and-payments/retail-financial-services/credit/consumer-credit_en

European Payments Council, 'Pix: The Rapid Development of Instant Payments in Brazil', (14 April 2002), https://www.europeanpaymentscouncil.eu/news-insights/insight/pix-rapid-development-instant-payments-brazil

European Union Digital Library website, 'Research on the Development of Open Banking in China under the Background of Internet Finance', (13 October 2022), https://eudl.eu/doi/10.4108/eai.17-6-2022.2322702

Experian website, 'Open Banking and Experian Boost', https://www.experian.co.uk/consumer/experian-boost-open-banking.html

FCA website, 'Thematic Review of Annuities', (2014), TR 14/2, 29, https://www.fca.org.uk/publication/thematic-reviews/tr14-02.pdf
FCA website, 'The Financial Lives of Consumers across the UK', (2017), 68–72, https://www.fca.org.uk/publication/research/financial-lives-consumers-across-uk.pdf
FCA website, 'Call for Input: Open finance', (December 2019), www.fca.org.uk/publication/call-for-input/call-for-input-open-finance.pdf
FCA website, 'FCA Sets Out Views on Employer Salary Advance Schemes', (30 July 2020a), https://www.fca.org.uk/news/statements/fca-sets-out-views-employer-salary-advance-schemes
FCA website, 'General Insurance Pricing Practices Market Study - Consultation Paper, CP20/19', (September 2020b), 59, https://www.fca.org.uk/publication/consultation/cp20-19.pdf
FCA website, 'FCA Handbook', (2021a), www.handbook.fca.org.uk/handbook/PERG/15/3.html
FCA website, 'FS21/7: Open Finance – Feedback Atatement', (March 2021b), https://www.fca.org.uk/publications/feedback-statements/fs21-7-open-finance-feedback-statement
FCA website, 'PS21/11: General Insurance Pricing Practices', (last updated December 2021c), https://www.fca.org.uk/publications/policy-statements/ps21-11-general-insurance-pricing-practices-amendments
FCA website, 'Financial Crime Controls at Challenger Banks', (22 April 2022a), https://www.fca.org.uk/publications/multi-firm-reviews/financial-crime-controls-at-challenger-banks
FCA website, 'Firm Specific Complaints Data', (28 April 2022b), https://www.fca.org.uk/data/complaints-data/firm-level
FCA website, 'The FCA's Consumer Duty Will Lead to a Major Shift in Financial Services', (27 July 2022c), https://www.fca.org.uk/news/press-releases/fca-consumer-duty-major-shift-financial-services
FDIC website, 'Customer Data Access and Fintech Entry: Early Evidence from Open Banking', (21 April 2022), www.fdic.gov/analysis/cfr/bank-research-conference/annual-21st/papers/gornall-paper.pdf
FDTA website, 'Opportunities in Open Banking', (April 2019), https://fdata.global/north-america/wp-content/uploads/sites/3/2019/04/FDATA-Open-Banking-in-North-America-US-version.pdf
Federal Reserve Bank of Kansas City website, 'Data Aggregators: The Connective Tissue for Open Banking', (24 August 2022), www.kansascityfed.org/Payments%20Systems%20Research%20Briefings/documents/9012/PaymentsSystemResearch-Briefing22AlcazarHayashi0824.pdf
Finance Magnate's website, 'Bill Rattray Becomes Interim CFO at Revolut', (18 March 2020), https://www.financemagnates.com/executives/moves/bill-rattray-becomes-interim-cfo-at-revolut/
Financial Consumer Agency of Canada, 'Open Banking and Consumer Protection: Canadian's Awareness and Expectations', (June 2023), www.canada.ca/en/financial-consumer-agency/programs/research/open-banking-consumer-protection.html
Financial Services Ombudsman (FOS), reference: DRN-2868209, (September 2021), https://www.financial-ombudsman.org.uk/decision/DRN-2868209.pdf
Financial Services Ombudsman Publication - Ref: DRN1029460, https://www.financial-ombudsman.org.uk/decision/DRN1029460.pd

Bibliography 207

Finextra website, 'Who Is Driving Open Banking Education and Adoption in the UK?', (9 November 2021), www.finextra.com/blogposting/21227/who-is-driving-open-banking-education-and-adoption-in-the-uk

Finextra website, 'The Future of Regulation: From Innovation to Execution', (2022), www.finextra.com/researcharticle/238/the-future-of-regulation-2022

Finnovista website, 'The Fintech Ecosystem in Chile Grows 49% Over the Last 18 Months and Stands as the Most Mature in the Latin American Region', (2019), www.finnovista.com/en/radar/the-fintech-ecosystem-in-chile-grows-49-over-the-last-18-months-and-stands-as-the-most-mature-in-the-latin-american-region/

Finnovista website, 'FinTech Radar Chile 2021', (2021), www.finnovista.com/wp-content/uploads/2021/05/Fintech-Radar-Chile_Gra%CC%81ficos-1.pdf

FinTechFuture website, 'OP Financial Chooses Nordic API Gateway for Open Banking', (20 November 2019), www.fintechfutures.com/2019/11/op-financial-chooses-nordic-api-gateway-for-open-banking/

FinTech Magazine website, 'FinTech Timeline: The History of Open Banking in Europe', (1 September 2022), https://fintechmagazine.com/banking/fintech-timeline-the-history-of-open-banking-in-europe

FintechNZ website, 'Open Banking Stimulating NZ Economy', 27 July 2022, https://fintechnz.org.nz/2022/07/27/open-banking-stimulating-nz-economy/

FinTech News website, 'State of Open Banking 2021: Indonesia', (5 April 2021a), https://fintechnews.sg/50091/openbanking/state-of-open-banking-2021-indonesia/

FinTech News website, 'Taiwan Furthers Open Banking Ambitions', (3 February 2021b), https://fintechnews.hk/14698/fintechtaiwan/taiwan-furthers-open-banking-ambitions/

Fintech Nexus website, 'Brazilian Unicorn Neon Raises $64 Million', (7 February 2023), https://www.fintechnexus.com/brazilian-unicorn-neon-raises-64-million/

FirstPartner website, 'Why Open Banking Payments Need Chargeback', (5 October 2021), www.firstpartner.net/blog/why-open-banking-payments-need-chargebacks/

FitchRatings website, 'Rising Interest Rates Test Brazilian Fintechs' Rapid Growth', 17 June 2022, https://www.fitchratings.com/research/banks/rising-interest-rates-tests-brazilian-fintechs-rapid-growth-17-06-2022

Forbes website, 'The History and Rise of API', (23 June 2020), https://www.forbes.com/sites/forbestechcouncil/2020/06/23/the-history-and-rise-of-apis/

Forbes website, 'Open Banking: What Does it Mean for the US', (3 March 2021), https://www.forbes.com/sites/scarlettsieber/2021/03/03/open-banking-what-does-it-mean-for-the-us

Forbes website, 'Why Open Banking Could Usher in a New Era Of Growth in 2022', (10 March 2022), https://www.forbes.com/sites/forbesfinancecouncil/2022/03/10/why-open-banking-could-usher-in-a-new-era-of-growth-in-2022/

Freshbusinessthinking website, 'Revolut in Money Laundering Controversy', (1 March 2019), https://www.freshbusinessthinking.com/purpose/revolut-in-money-laundering-controversy/46468.article

Frollo website, 'It's Time for a Consumer Awareness Campaign as More Businesses Embrace Open Banking', (10 November 2022), https://frollo.com.au/blog/open-banking-consumer-awareness/

Frollo website, 'The State of Open Banking 2023: A Pulse Check of the Industry Packed with Research, Insights, Case Studies and Interviews', (2023), https://blog.frollo.com.au/

FSC website, 'Banks' Financial Payment System to Be Open to Fintech Firms', (25 February 2019a), https://www.fsc.go.kr/eng/pr010101/22203

FSC website, 'Financial Policy Roadmap for 2019', (7 March 2019b), https://www.fsc.go.kr/eng/pr010101/22204?srchCtgry=&curPage=&srchKey=&srchText=&srchBeginDt=&srchEndDt=

FSC website, '3rd Digital Finance Meeting Unveils Ways to Advance Open Banking System', (21 October 2020), https://www.fsc.go.kr/eng/pr010101/22522

FSC website, 'FSC Continues to Promote Phase 2 (Customer Information Inquiries) of Open Banking Initiative', (2 September 2021), https://www.fsc.gov.tw/en/home.jsp?id=74&parentpath=0,2&mcustomize=multimessage_view.jsp&dataserno=202102090008&dtable=Bulletin

FSC website, 'Open Banking', https://www.fsc.go.kr/eng/po030101

Future of Privacy Forum website, 'Development in Open Banking. Key Issues from a Global Perspective', (March 2022), https://fpf.org/wp-content/uploads/2022/08/FPF-Open-Banking-Report-R2-Singles.pdf

Global Times website, 'China's Anti-monopoly Watchdog Fines Alibaba, Tencent for Failing to Report Deals', (10 July 2022), www.globaltimes.cn/page/202207/1270170.shtml

Glory Global website, 'The Future of Banking - Why Traditional Banks Are Embracing Open Banking', (2021), www.glory-global.com/-/media/GloryGlobal/Downloads/EN_GB/Thought-leadership_EN_GB/Glory-Open-Banking-White-Paper-Thought-Leadership-EN-V1-0.pdf

Gocardless website, 'Open Banking Apps Explained', (May 2022), https://gocardless.com/guides/posts/open-banking-apps-explained

GOVCN website, 'The People's Bank of China Issued the Fintech Development Plan (20222025)', (5 January 2022), www.gov.cn/xinwen/2022-01/05/content_5666525.htm

GOV.UK website, 'Recommendations for the Next Phase of Open Banking in the UK', (17 April 2023), https://assets.publishing.service.gov.uk/government/uploads/system/uploads/attachment_data/file/1150988/JROC_report_recommendations_and_actions_paper_April_2023.pdf

GST website, https://www.gstn.org.in/home

Gulf News website, 'The Free Zone Ecosystem: Triple Mega-drivers - Challenges and Opportunity', (4 May 2023), https://gulfnews.com/uae/the-free-zone-ecosystem-triple-mega-drivers—challenges-and-opportunity-1.1683186052049

Halifax Bank website, 'Switch to Halifax and Get £150', https://www.halifax.co.uk/bankaccounts/switch-to-halifax.html

HDFC website, 'Open Skies, Open Banking, HDFC Bank's APIs Power One of India's Leading Airlines to Maximise Revenue and Accelerate Growth', https://developer.hdfcbank.com/

HKMA website, 'A New Era of Smart Banking', (29 September 2017), www.hkma.gov.hk/eng/news-and-media/speeches/2017/09/20170929-1/

HKMA website, 'The HKMA Unveils "Fintech 2025" Strategy', (2021a), www.hkma.gov.hk/eng/news-and-media/press-releases/2021/06/20210608-4/

HKMA website, 'The Implementation Plan for Phase III and IV Open Application Programming Interface (Open API)', (13 May 2021b), www.hkma.gov.hk/eng/news-and-media/press-releases/2021/05/20210513-3

HKMA website, 'The Next Phase of the Banking Open API Journey', (2021c), www.hkma.gov.hk/media/eng/doc/key-functions/ifc/fintech/The_Next_Phase_of_the_Banking_Open_API_Journey.pdf

HKMA website, 'The Four Phases of Open API', (2023a), www.hkma.gov.hk/eng/key-functions/international-financial-centre/fintech/open-application-programming-interface-api-for-the-banking-sector/phase-approach/

HKMA, 'The Target Go-live Dates of Phase III and Phase IV Open API Functions of Each Bank', (2023b), www.hkma.gov.hk/eng/key-functions/international-financial-centre/fintech/open-application-programming-interface-api-for-the-banking-sector/target-dates/

HM Treasury, 'Payments Landscape Review: Response to the Call for Evidence', (October 2021), https://assets.publishing.service.gov.uk/government/uploads/system/uploads/attachment_data/file/1024174/HMT_Payments_Landscape_Review_-_The_Government_s_Response__October_2021_.pdf

HM Treasury, 'Regulation of Buy-Now Pay-Later: Response to consultation', (June 2022), https://assets.publishing.service.gov.uk/government/uploads/system/uploads/attachment_data/file/1083547/BNPL_consultation_response__Formatted_.pdf

HM Treasury and Home Office, 'National Risk Assessment of Money Laundering and Terrorist Financing 2020', (December 2020), https://assets.publishing.service.gov.uk/government/uploads/system/uploads/attachment_data/file/945411/NRA_2020_v1.2_FOR_PUBLICATION.pdf

HSBC website, '3.9% APR Representative. This Rate Is Available for Loans between £7,000 and £15,000', https://www.hsbc.co.uk/loans/products/personal/

ICICI's website,' ICICI Bank Net Offers on Food, Groceries, Apparels, Travel and Many More', https://www.icicibank.com/offers/categories/category-listing/net-banking

IMF website, 'Financial Access Survey', (2022), https://data.imf.org/?sk=e5dcab7e-a5ca-4892-a6ea-598b5463a34c

IMF website, 'MENA in Charts', (2017), www.imf.org/en/News/Seminars/Conferences/2017/08/08/morocco-opportunities-for-all/Morocco-Conference-Chart-of-the-Week/chart-of-the-week-1

IMY website, 'Administrative Fine against Klarna after Investigation', (31 March 2022), https://www.imy.se/en/news/administrative-fine-against-klarna-after-investigation/

India Stack website, 'Identity', https://indiastack.org/identity.html

Inter-America Development Bank website, 'Study: Fintech Industry Doubles in Size in Three Years in Latin America and the Caribbean', (26 April 2022), https://www.iadb.org/en/news/study-fintech-industry-doubles-size-three-years-latin-america-and-caribbean

International Bar Association website, 'Fintech M&A: Latin American and Chilean Fintech Ecosystems in the Global Eye', (7 October 2021), www.ibanet.org/latin-american-chilean-fintech-ecosystems

Iupana website, 'Open Banking in Mexico', (24 June 2022), https://iupana.com/2022/01/24/open-banking-hsbc-mexico/?lang=en

Jakub Šťastný, 'European Union: Open Banking in Europe in Light Of PSD2 Review', (23 February 2022), Mondaq, https://www.mondaq.com/financial-services/1165162/open-banking-in-europe-in-light-of-psd2-review

Japanese Bankers Association website, 'Financial Institutions in Japan', https://www.zenginkyo.or.jp/en/banks/financial-institutions/

Japan Research Institute website, 'The "Three Reforms" in China: Progress and Outlook', (September 1999), www.jri.co.jp/english/periodical/rim/1999/RIMe199904threereforms/

Jdsupra, 'The CFPB Open Banking Rule', (13 March 2023), www.jdsupra.com/legalnews/the-cfpb-open-banking-rule-8915627/

JP Morgan Chase Website, 'JPMorgan Chase Takes 40% Stake in Brazil's C6 Bank', (28 June 2021), https://www.jpmorganchase.com/news-stories/jpmorgan-chase-takes-40-percentage-stake-in-brazils-c6-bank

Klarna website, 'Klarna Comment: Statement on App Bug', (27 May 2021a), https://www.klarna.com/uk/blog/written-statement-on-app-bug/

Klarna website, 'Klarna Launches Bank Account in Germany', (10 February 2021b), https://www.klarna.com/international/press/klarna-launches-bank-account-in-germany/

Klarna website, 'Report and Accounts for 2021', 25, https://www.klarna.com/assets/sites/15/2022/03/28054307/Klarna-Bank-AB-Annual-report-2021-EN.pdf

Klarna website, 'Klarna Comment: SDPA's Conclusion of Their Audit', (29 March 2022a), https://www.klarna.com/uk/blog/klarna-comment-sdpas-conclusion-of-their-audit/

Klarna website, 'Klarna Launches 'Klarna Kosma' Sub-Brand and Business Unit to Harness Rapid Growth of Open Banking platform', (31 March 2022b), https://www.klarna.com/international/press/klarna-launches-klarna-kosma-sub-brand-and-business-unit-to-harness-rapid-growth-of-open-banking-platform/

Klarna website, 'Terms and Conditions', https://www.klarna.com/uk/terms-and-conditions/

Konsentus website, 'The Tricky Encounter', (2020), www.konsentus.com/wp-content/uploads/The_Tricky_Encounter_2020_final.pdf

Konsentus website, 'Open Banking in Review: Trends and Progress', (22 December 2021), www.konsentus.com/insights/articles/open-banking-in-review-trends-and-progress/

Korea Financial Telecommunications & Clearings Institute (KFTC) website, https://www.kftc.or.kr/kftcEn/about/EgovEnDcsMaking.do

KPMG website, 'Open Banking Opens Opportunities for Greater Customer Value. Reshaping the Banking Experience', (May 2019), https://assets.kpmg.com/content/dam/kpmg/xx/pdf/2019/05/open-banking-opening-opportunities-for-customer-value.pdf

Krishan Shah, 'Wealth on the Eve of a Crisis. Exploring the UK's Pre-pandemic Wealth Distribution', (January 2022), Resolution Foundation, 2, https://www.resolutionfoundation.org/publications/wealth-on-the-eve-of-a-crisis/

KSA website, 'Open Banking Policy', (2018), www.sama.gov.sa/en-US/Documents/Open_Banking_Policy-EN.pdf

KSA website, 'Financial Sector Development Program (FSDP)', (2021), https://www.vision2030.gov.sa/media/ud5micju/fsdp_eng.pdf

KSA website, 'FSDP Launches FinTech Strategy Implementation Plan', (22 June 2022a), www.mof.gov.sa/en/MediaCenter/news/Pages/news_22062022_1.aspx

KSA website, 'SAMA Issues the Open Banking Framework', (2022b), www.sama.gov.sa/en-US/News/Pages/news-794.aspx

KSA website, 'Open Banking in Saudi Arabia', (2023), www.openbanking.sa/

Latin America Business Stories website, 'Bad Timing and Cultural Attachment to Cash: Why Hasn't CoDi, Mexico's Instant Payment System, Taken off Yet?', (15 December 2020), https://labsnews.com/en/articles/business/codi-mexican-instant-payment-system/

Law Society website, 'Politically Exposed Persons', (19 December 2019), https://www.lawsociety.org.uk/topics/anti-money-laundering/peps

Legal500 website, 'Chile. FinTech', (30 November 2021), https://apparcel.cl/en/the-legal-500-presents-the-fintech-comparative-guide-2021-with-the-contribution-of-auv

Lending Standards Board website, 'The Contingent Reimbursement Model Code (CRM Code)', https://www.lendingstandardsboard.org.uk/crm-code/#firms-that-have-signed-up-to-the-code

Marketing Trends website, 'Consumers' Fears about Open Banking: How Banks can Overcome Them?', (2021), http://archives.marketing-trends-congress.com/2021/pages/PDF/034.pdf

MAS website, 'Strengthening Trust in Finance', the opening address by Ravi Menon, Managing Director, Monetary Authority of Singapore, at Symposium on Asian Banking and Finance, (3 June 2019), https://www.mas.gov.sg/news/speeches/2019/strengthening-trust-in-finance

MAS website, 'Indonesia and Singapore to Pursue Cross-border QR Code Payments Connectivity and Explore Promoting the Use of Local Currencies for Bilateral Transactions', 'Bank Indonesia and the Monetary Authority of Singapore today announced the commencement of work on a cross-border QR payment linkage between Indonesia and Singapore as part of the ASEAN-wide payments connectivity effort. This linkage, which is targeted to be launched in the second half of 2023, will allow users to make instant, secure, and efficient retail payments by scanning the QRIS (Quick Response Code Indonesian Standard)', (17 November 2023), https://www.mas.gov.sg/news/media-releases/2023/launch-of-cross-border-qr-payments-linkage-between-indonesia-and-singapore

Mastercard website, 'Open Banking in Switzerland', (2021a), https://mastercardcontentexchange.com/news/media/wxwih35b/2mc20299_mc_ch_whitepaper_part_1_en_vf_31-9.pdf

Mastercard website, 'UK and Nordics Lead Open Banking in Europe', (17 June 2021b), www.mastercard.com/news/europe/en/newsroom/press-releases/en/2021/june/uk-and-nordics-lead-open-banking-in-europe/

Masthaven bank website, 'Important Announcement about Masthaven Bank', (January or February 2022), https://www.masthaven.co.uk

McKinsey website, 'Data Sharing and Open Banking', (5 September 2017), www.mckinsey.com/industries/financial-services/our-insights/data-sharing-and-open-banking#/

McKinsey website, 'Financial Data Unbound: The Value of Open Data for Individuals and Institutions', (24 June 2021a), https://www.mckinsey.com/industries/financial-services/our-insights/financial-data-unbound-the-value-of-open-data-for-individuals-and-institutions

McKinsey website, 'Financial Services Unchained: The Ongoing Rise of Open Financial Data', (11 July 2021b), https://www.mckinsey.com/industries/financial-services/our-insights/financial-services-unchained-the-ongoing-rise-of-open-financial-data

McKinsey website, 'What the Embedded-Finance and Banking-as-a-Service Trends Mean for Financial Services', (1 March 2021c), https://www.mckinsey.com/industries/financial-services/our-insights/banking-matters/what-the-embedded-finance-and-banking-as-a-service-trends-mean-for-financial-services

McMillan website, 'Canadians Awareness of Open Banking Is Low—But Does It Matter?', (29 June 2023), https://mcmillan.ca/insights/publications/canadians-awareness-of-open-banking-is-low-but-does-it-matter/

MENA FinTech Association website, 'Embedded Finance in the MENA Region', (November 2022), https://mena-fintech.org/wp-content/uploads/2022/11/MFTA-Embedded-Finance-Report-NOV2022-FINAL.pdf

Ministry of Finance, Department of Financial Services website, 'Pradhan Mantri Jan-Dhan Yojana', https://pmjdy.gov.in/about

Ministry of Finance of Chile website, 'Financial Portability Law Comes into Effect', (14 September 2020), https://www.hacienda.cl/english/investor-relations-office/newsletter/latest/-financial-portability-law-comes-into-effect

Ministry of Finance website, 'Financial Institutions Onboarded on Account Aggregator (AA) Platform as Financial Information User (FIU)', 12 December 2022, https://pib.gov.in/PressReleaseIframePage.aspx?PRID=1882868#:~:text=Giving%20background%20information%2C%20the%20Minister,was%20introduced%20as%20a%20financial

Miotech website, 'Open Banking Development Drives Data-sharing in China', (16 September 2019), www.miotech.com/en-US/article/49

Monetary Authority of Singapore (MAS) website, 'Financial Industry API Register', https://www.mas.gov.sg/development/fintech/financial-industry-api-register

Monetary Authority of Singapore (MAS) and the Association of Banks in Singapore (ABS), 'Finance-as-a-Service: API Playbook', (2016), https://www.mas.gov.sg/-/media/MAS/Smart-Financial-Centre/API/ABSMASAPIPlaybook.pdf

Money Dashboard website, https://www.moneydashboard.com/features

MoneySense website, https://www.mymoneysense.gov.sg

MoneySense website, 'About MoneySense', https://www.mymoneysense.gov.sg/about-us

Monzo Financial Statements for the period to 28 February 2022, 7, https://monzo.com/static/docs/monzo-annual-report-2022.pdf

Monzo website, 'Get a loan that treats you right. Ditch hidden fees, confusing terms and waiting around. Achieve your goals and feel in control with a Monzo loan. If you're eligible, our representative APR is 8.9% for loans more than £10,000, up to £25,000. For loans up to £10,000 it's 23.9%', https://monzo.com/loans/#

Mordor Intelligence website, 'MENA FinTech Market Size and Share Analysis-Growth Trends and Forecasts (20232028)', (2023), www.mordorintelligence.com/industry-reports/mena-fintech-market

NACHA website, 'Afinis: Advancing Financial Services Through API Standardization', (30 October 2018), https://cloud.google.com/blog/products/api-management/afinis-advancing-financial-services-through-api-standardization

Nationwide Building Society, 'Savings Accounts Explained', www.nationwide.co.uk/savings/help/savings-accounts-explained/

Ndgit website, 'Open Banking APIs Worldwide', (2021), https://ndgit.com/en/open-banking-api-status-whitepaper/

Neon bank website, 'Nossa história', https://neon.com.br/conheca-a-neon

New Zealand Ministry of Business Innovation and Employment website, 'Consumer Data Rights', https://www.mbie.govt.nz/business-and-employment/business/competition-regulation-and-policy/consumer-data-right/

Nikkei Asia website, 'Where Are Japan's neo banks?', (11 May 2021), https://asia.nikkei.com/Opinion/Where-are-Japan-s-neo-banks

Nordea website, www.nordea.com/en/about-us/who-are-we/our-history

Norden webiste, 'State of the Nordic Region 2022', (2022), Nordic Cooperation www.norden.org/en/nordicregion2022

Nordic APIs AB website, 'Developing the API Mindset. A Guide to Using Private, Partner, & Public APIs', (2015), https://nordicapis.com/ebooks/developing-the-api-mindset/

Nordic APIs AB website, 'The API Economy. Disruption and the Business of APIs', (2016), https://nordicapis.com/ebooks/the-api-economy/

Nordic API Gateway website, 'Accelerating Open Banking. How the Nordics are Driving New Opportunities Across Industries', (May 2020), https://thefintechtimes.com/wp-content/uploads/2020/06/Nordic_API_Gateway_Report_open_banking.pdf

Nordic Capital website, 'Trustly, Backed by Nordic Capital, Acquires Ecospend, Further Strengthening Position in the UK', (30 May 2022), https://www.nordiccapital.

com/news/trustly-backed-by-nordic-capital-acquires-ecospend-further-strengthening-position-in-the-uk/

NPCI website, 'UPI Product Overview', https://www.npci.org.in/what-we-do/upi/product-overview#:~:text=Unified%20Payments%20Interface%20(UPI)%20is,merchant%20payments%20into%20one%20hood (accessed 14 January 2024)

Nubank website, 'About Nu', https://international.nubank.com.br/about/#:~:text=Nu%20was%20born%20in%202013,Brazil%2C%20Mexico%2C%20and%20Colombia

OBIE website, https://www.openbanking.org.uk/about-us/

OBIE website, 'Second Impact Report', (2021), https://openbanking.foleon.com/live-publications/the-open-banking-impact-report-october-2021-ug/appendix/

OECD website, 'Digital Disruption in Banking and its Impact on Competition', (2020a), www.oecd.org/competition/digital-disruption-in-banking-and-its-impact-on-competition-2020.pdf

OECD website, 'Personal Data Use in Financial Services and the Role of Financial Education: A Consumer-centric Analysis', (2020b), 5 www.oecd.org/daf/fin/financial-education/Personal-Data-Use-in-Financial-Services-and-the-Role-of-Financial-Education.pdf

Office of National Statistics, 'Distribution of Individual Total Wealth by Characteristic in Great Britain: April 2018 to March 2020', (7 January 2022), https://www.ons.gov.uk/peoplepopulationandcommunity/personalandhouseholdfinances/incomeandwealth/bulletins/distributionofindividualtotalwealthbycharacteristicingreatbritain/april2018tomarch2020

Official New Zealand Government website, Govt Agrees to Establish a Consumer Data Right', (6 July 2021), https://www.beehive.govt.nz/release/govt-agrees-establish-consumer-data-right

OMFIF website, Kate Jaquet, 'Brazil Is Undergoing a Fintech Revolution', (24 January 2023), https://www.omfif.org/2023/01/brazil-is-undergoing-a-fintech-revolution/

Openbanking website, 'Open Banking. A Consumer Perspective', (January 2017), www.openbanking.org.uk/wp-content/uploads/Open-Banking-A-Consumer-Perspective.pdf

Openbanking website, 'Open Banking Apps in Action', www.openbanking.org.uk/how-open-banking-can-help-consumers/

Openbanking website, 'Open Banking Customer Experience Guidelines', (30 November 2018a), www.openbanking.org.uk/wp-content/uploads/Customer-Experience-Guidelines-V1-1.pdf

Openbanking website, 'Open Banking Guidelines for Read/Write Participants', (May 2018b), www.openbanking.org.uk/wp-content/uploads/Guidelines-for-Read-Write-Participants.pdf

Openbanking website, 'Open Banking, Preparing for Lift Off', (June 2019), www.openbanking.org.uk/wp-content/uploads/open-banking-report-150719.pdf

Openbanking website, 'Financial Inclusion and Open Banking with TechUK and the OBIE', (15 July 2021), www.openbanking.org.uk/insights/financial-inclusion-and-open-banking-with-techuk-and-the-obie/

Openbanking website, 'Open Banking Reaches 11 Million + Payments Milestone', (30 August 2023), www.openbanking.org.uk/news/open-banking-reaches-11m-payments-milestone/#:~:text=In%20July%202023%2C%20the%20number,to%20manage%20their%20finances%20effectively

Openbankingexpo website, 'Fintech Galaxy Receives License from Central Bank of Bahrain', (4 November 2022a), www.openbankingexpo.com/news/fintech-galaxy-receives-license-from-central-bank-of-bahrain/

Openbankingexpo website, 'Insight: Why Momentum Tells the True UK Open Banking Success Story', (1 March 2022b), www.openbankingexpo.com/insights/insight-why-momentum-tells-the-true-uk-open-banking-success-story/

Openbankingexpo, 'OBIE Appoints Henk Van Hulle as Its New CEO to Strengthen Governance', (3 February 2022), https://www.openbankingexpo.com/news/obie-appoints-henk-van-hulle-as-its-new-ceo-to-strengthen-governance/

Openbankingexpo website, 'The Evolution of Open Banking: Adoption, Benefits and Consent', (2020), www.openbankingexpo.com/wp-content/uploads/2020/11/Open-Banking-whitepaper.pdf

Openbankingtracker website, www.openbankingtracker.com/country/liechtenstein

Openbankingproject website, www.openbankingproject.ch/en/resources/news/study-on-open-banking-in-switzerland/

Openbankproject website, 'Open Banking in Oman', (9 May 2023), www.openbankproject.com/open-banking-in-oman/

Open Banking Exchange website, 'How Many TPPs in Europe?', (26 July 2019), www.openbanking.exchange/europe/resources/insights/how-many-tpps-in-europe/

Open Future World website, 'Open Finance Global Progress Ebook: China: Open Banking by Disruption', (28 April 2022a), https://openfuture.world/open-finance-global-progress-ebook-china-open-banking-by-disruption/

Open Future World website, 'Open Finance Global Progress Ebook: Indonesia', (17 May 2022b), https://openfuture.world/open-finance-global-progress-ebook-indonesia/

Open Future World website, 'Open Finance Global Progress Ebook: Singapore Special Editorial Focus', (16 May 2022c), https://openfuture.world/open-finance-global-progress-ebook-singapore-special-editorial-focus/

Opening Address by Mr Ravi Menon, Managing Director, Monetary Authority of Singapore, at Green Shoots Seminar on 29 August 2022, https://www.mas.gov.sg/news/speeches/2022/yes-to-digital-asset-innovation-no-to-cryptocurrency-speculation

P27 website, https://nordicpayments.eu/

PagBrasil website, 'boleto bancário', https://www.pagbrasil.com/payment-methods/boleto-bancario/

PagBrasil website, 'Cash is Still King in Brazil', (4 July 2019), https://www.pagbrasil.com/insights/cash-still-king-brazil/

Payments NZ website, 'Research and Reports', https://www.paymentsnz.co.nz/resources/research-reports/

Payment Services Directive I (PSD I) (2007/64/EC), see Recitals on pp. 1–8, https://ec.europa.eu/info/business-economy-euro/banking-and-finance/consumer-finance-and-payments/payment-services/payment-services_en

Payments Canada, 'Corporate Plan 20222026', 14, https://www.payments.ca/sites/default/files/paymentscanada_corporateplan_2022_en.pdf

PBOC, 'Guiding Opinions on Promoting the Sound Development of Internet Finance', (July 2015), https://uk.practicallaw.thomsonreuters.com/2-617-6285?transitionType=Default&contextData=(sc.Default)&firstPage=true

Pinar Ozcan, 'Blurred Lines: How Open Banking Is Facilitating Big Tech's Creep Into Finance', (Saïd Business School, 26 January 2023), https://www.sbs.ox.ac.uk/oxford-answers/blurred-lines-how-open-banking-facilitating-big-techs-creep-finance

PPRO website, 'Registered Boleto Bancário: The Impact for Clients and Merchants', (12 October 2017), https://www.ppro.com/insights/registered-boleto-bancario-the-impact-for-clients-and-merchants/#:~:text=The%20new%20registered%20Boleto%20Banc%C3%A1rio,fraud%20and%20boost%20payment%20rates

PRA, 'Non-systemic UK Banks: The Prudential Regulation Authority's Approach to New and Growing Banks', (Supervisory Statement SS3/21), April 2021, https://www.bankofengland.co.uk/-/media/boe/files/prudential-regulation/supervisory-statement/2021/ss321-april-2021.pdf?la=en&hash=026DEAE7DDDEA5A80DC4BFDFF12821E5DF033E71

PWC website, 'The Future of Banking is Open. How to Seize the Open Banking Opportunity', (2018), www.pwc.co.uk/financial-services/assets/open-banking-report-web-interactive.pdf

PYMNTS, 'New Payments Platform Australia Merges With Eftpos, BPAY', (15 December 2020), https://www.pymnts.com/news/b2b-payments/2020/new-payments-platform-australia-merges-with-eftpos-bpay/

PYMNTS website, 'FinTech Competition Pressures Brazil's Biggest Banks', (4 April 2021), https://www.pymnts.com/news/banking/2021/fintech-competition-pressures-brazil-biggest-banks/

PYMNTS website, '5 Things to Know About Starling's Banking-as-a-Service Product, Engine', (21 July 2022a), https://www.pymnts.com/news/banking/2022/5-things-to-know-about-starlings-banking-as-a-service-product-engine/

PYMNTS website, 'Why Starling Bank CEO Said No to Crypto', (9 June 2022b), https://www.pymnts.com/digital-first-banking/2022/why-starling-bank-ceo-said-no-to-crypto/

QNB website, 'Summary of FinTech Sector Strategy in State of Qatar', (March 2023), www.qcb.gov.qa/Arabic/strategicplan/Documents/%D8%A7%D9%86%D8%AC%D9%84%D9%8A%D8%B2%D9%8A.pdf

Researchgate website, 'Data Sharing Fundamentals: Characteristics and Definitions', (January 2023), www.researchgate.net/publication/363769417_Data_Sharing_Fundamentals_Characteristics_and_Definition

Reserve Bank of India website, 'FinTech: The Force of Creative Disruption' (2020) RBI Bulletin 75', (11 November 2020), https://rbi.org.in/Scripts/BS_ViewBulletin.aspx?Id=19899

Retail Banker International website, 'Starling Bank Shelves Plans to Secure Irish Banking Licence', (19 July 2022a), https://www.retailbankerinternational.com/news/starling-bank-withdraws-licence-application/

Retail Banker International website, 'UK Current Account Switching: plus ça change, plus c'est la même chose', (8 February 2022b), https://www.retailbankerinternational.com/analysis/uk-current-account-switching-winners-losers/

'Revolut Report and Financial Statements for the year to 31 December 2020', 11, https://assets.revolut.com/pdf/Revolut%20Ltd%20Annual%20Report%20YE%202020.pdf

Revolut website, 'On-Demand Pay – Get Your Pay Any Day'.

Revolut website, 'Revolut's Culture: The Past, Present and the Future', (3 April 2019), https://blog.revolut.com/weve-made-mistakes-but-were-learning/

Revolut website, 'Revolut Further Strengthens Its Board, with City Veterans Michael Sherwood and Ian Wilson', (5 March 2022), https://www.revolut.com/news/revolut_further_strengthens_its_board_hiring_city_veterans_michael_sherwood_and_ian_wilson

216 Bibliography

Revolut website, 'Welcome to US Revolut', https://blog.revolut.com/us-welcome-to-revolut/

Revolut website, 'Where Can I Find the Terms and Conditions for My Savings Vaults?', https://www.revolut.com/en-US/help/wealth/savings-vaults/using-savings-vaults/where-can-i-find-the-terms-conditions-for-my-savings-vaults

Reuters website, 'Martin Gilbert Joins Fintech Revolut as Chairman', (12 November 2019), https://www.reuters.com/article/revolut-chairman-idUSL4N27R3AB

Reuters website, 'Fintechs Fail to Make a Dent in Mexico as Cash Remains King', (26 May 2022), https://www.reuters.com/business/finance/fintechs-fail-make-dent-mexico-cash-remains-king-2022-05-26/

Rossrepublic website, 'Asia is the Next Frontier in Open Banking', (2 December 2020), https://rossrepublic.com/asia-is-the-next-frontier-in-open-banking/

Sahamati website, 'Account Aggregators Are the Future of Data Sharing', 'https://sahamati.org.in/what-is-account-aggregator/

Sahamati website, 'Help Shape the Future of Data Empowerment in India', https://sahamati.org.in/signatories-of-aa-participation-terms/#

Santander website, 'Using Open Banking to Link Financial Accounts You Hold with Other Providers', www.santander.co.uk/personal/support/help-with-managing-my-money/open-banking

Sarkisyan S, 'Instant Payment Systems and Competition for Deposits', (June 2023). Jacobs Levy Equity Management Center for Quantitative Financial Research Paper, SSRN, 12, http://dx.doi.org/10.2139/ssrn.4176990

Sean Creehan and Paul Tierno, 'The Slow Introduction of Open Banking and APIs in Japan', (2 May 2019), Federal Reserve Bank of San Francisco, https://www.frbsf.org/banking/asia-program/pacific-exchanges-podcast/open-banking-apis-japan/

'Services Directive and the GDPR', (15 December 2020), https://edpb.europa.eu/our-work-tools/our-documents/guidelines/guidelines-062020-interplay-second-payment-services_en

Sidney Morning Herald website, 'Beforepay Shares Sink 44 per cent on Debut', (17 January 2022), https://www.smh.com.au/business/companies/beforepay-shares-sink-44-per-cent-on-debut-20220117-p59ovd.html

Sifted website, 'Revolut Nominates City Veteran to Lead UK Bank Bid, Hoping 'White Hairs' Will Woo Regulators', (October 2020), https://sifted.eu/articles/revolut-chairman/

Singapore Ministry of Foreign website, https://www.mfa.gov.sg/SINGAPORES-FOREIGN-POLICY/Countries-and-Regions/Southeast-Asia/Vietnam

Six-Group.Com website, 'SIX Launches b.Link – The Central Platform for the Standardized Sharing of Data Between Financial Institutions and Third-party Providers', (19 May 2020), www.six-group.com/en/newsroom/media-releases/2020/20200519-six-blink.html

Slaughter and May, 'Independent Review Following TSB's Migration onto a New IT Platform in April 2018', (October 2019), 206–8, https://www.tsb.co.uk/news-releases/slaughter-and-may/

Smartprix website, 'Jio Mobile Phones Price List in India', (5 September 2023), https://www.smartprix.com/mobiles/jio-brand

SMIT website, 'The Concept of Open Banking: From a Remedy to an Ecosystem', (8 March 2021), https://smit.vub.ac.be/policy-brief-44-the-concept-of-open-banking-from-a-remedy-to-an-ecosystem

SNAP Developer Site (2023), https://apidevportal.bi.go.id/snap

Bibliography 217

SOAS website, 'What Is Financial Inclusion? A Critical Review', (December 2021), www.soas.ac.uk/sites/default/files/2022-10/economics-wp246.pdf

SSRN website, 'Financial Inclusion in the Middle East and North Africa: Analysis and Roadmap Recommendations', (1 March 2011), https://papers.ssrn.com/sol3/papers.cfm?abstract_id=1794915

SSRN website, 'Open Banking and Customer Data Sharing: Implications for FinTech Borrowers', (29 November 2022a), https://papers.ssrn.com/sol3/papers.cfm?abstract_id=4278803#

SSRN website, 'Open Banking: Credit Market Competition When Borrowers Own the Data', (23 November 2022b), https://papers.ssrn.com/sol3/papers.cfm?abstract_id=3735686

SSRN website, 'The Open Banking Adoption Among Consumers in Europe: The Role of Privacy, Trust, and Digital Financial Inclusion', (30 April 2022c), https://papers.ssrn.com/sol3/papers.cfm?abstract_id=4105648

Starling Bank website, 'Annual Report & Consolidated Financial Statements 2022', 111, https://www.starlingbank.com/docs/annual-reports/Starling-Bank-Annual-Report-2022.pdf

State Secretariat for International Finance website, 'Digital Finance: Areas of Action 2022+', (2 February 2022), https://www.sif.admin.ch/sif/en/home/finanzmarktpolitik/digitalisation-financial-sector/digital-finance-areas-action.html

Statista website, 'FinTech in Chile-Statistics and Facts', (7 June 2022a), www.statista.com/topics/7831/fintech-in-chile/#topicOverview

Statista website, 'Fintech in Middle East and North Africa - Statistics & Facts', (20 December 2022b), www.statista.com/topics/8699/fintech-in-mena/

Statista website, 'Number of Open Banking Users Worldwide in 2020 with Forecasts from 2021 to 2024, by Region (in Millions)', (2023a), www.statista.com/statistics/1228771/open-banking-users-worldwide/

Statista website, 'Share of the Population Owning a Smartphone in Japan', (5 September 2023b), https://www.statista.com/statistics/275102/share-of-the-population-to-own-a-smartphone-japan/#:~:text=It%20was%20estimated%20that%20more,than%2069%20percent%20in%202018

Statista website, 'Smartphone Penetration in Brazil', (5 September 2023c), https://www.statista.com/forecasts/625406/smartphone-user-penetration-in-brazil

Statista website, 'Smartphone Penetration in India', (5 September 2023d), https://www.statista.com/statistics/1229799/india-smartphone-penetration-rate/

Swiss Bankers Association website, 'Open Banking', (February 2020a), https://www.swissbanking.ch/_Resources/Persistent/d/8/c/d/d8cd7b64d64d8034d3d031b227bdfefddcd4fca9/SBA_Position_paper_Open_Banking_EN.pdf

Swiss Bankers Association website, 'Open Banking - An Overview for the Swiss Financial Center', (July 2020b), www.swissbanking.ch/_Resources/Persistent/8/8/2/8/88286724aa4fdc3dd8bb8ecd9b9c0d7af659a803/SBA_Overview_OpenBanking_en.pdf

Swiss FinTech Association website, 'The New SFTI Working Group OpenPK Has Kicked Off!', (16 July 2021), https://swissfintechinnovations.ch/the-new-sfti-working-group-openpk-has-kicked-off/

Taiwanese Financial Services Commission website, 'Work Focus for 2022', https://www.fsc.gov.tw/userfiles/file/2022%20FSC%20press%20release.pdf

TechCrunch website, 'Revolut Applies for Bank Charter In the US', (22 March 2021), https://techcrunch.com/2021/03/22/revolut-applies-for-bank-charter-in-the-us/

218 Bibliography

TechCrunch website, 'Klar, Believed to Be Mexico's Largest Digital Bank, Lands $70M in General Atlantic-Led Round', (9 June 2022), https://techcrunch.com/2022/06/09/klar-believed-to-be-mexicos-largest-digital-bank-lands-70m-in-general-atlantic-led-round/

Temenos website, 'Open Banking and the Rise of Banking-as-a-Service', (September 2021), www.temenos.com/wp-content/uploads/2022/06/Open-Banking-and-the-Rise-of-Banking-as-a-Service-V4.pdf

'TheBanks.eu, List of EMIs in the UK', https://thebanks.eu/list-of-emis/United-Kingdom

The CMN created by Law 4.595, dated 31 December 1964 - National Financial System, https://www.bcb.gov.br/content/about/legislation_norms_docs/Law%204.595%2C%20dated%2012_31_1964%20-%20National%20Financial%20System.pdf

The Economist Intelligent Unit website, 'Whose Customer Are You? The Reality of Digital Banking', (2018), https://impact.economist.com/perspectives/sites/default/files/Global%20Retail%20Banking%20%282%29.pdf

The FinTech Times website, 'Central Bank of Kuwait Supports Launch of New Open Banking Product', (26 August 2022), https://thefintechtimes.com/central-bank-of-kuwait-supports-launch-of-new-open-banking-product/

The Mint website, 'The Admirable Success of the Jan Dhan Yojana', (28 August 2017), https://www.livemint.com/Opinion/wfertnZlyGRTmGiyGnJLrI/The-admirable-success-of-the-JanDhan-Yojana.html, (accessed 5 September 2023)

The National Payments Corporation of India (NPCI) website, https://www.npci.org.in/who-we-are/about-us, (accessed 6 September 2023)

The Paypers website, 'Open Banking Consumer Education: Fear of Fun?', (16 December 2019), https://thepaypers.com/expert-opinion/open-banking-consumer-education-fear-of-fun–1239920

The White House website, 'Executive Order 14036—Promoting Competition in the American Economy', (9 July 2021), www.whitehouse.gov/briefing-room/presidential-actions/2021/07/09/executive-order-on-promoting-competition-in-the-american-economy/

Tim Waterman, Chief Commercial Officer, Zopa, 'How Do We Grow UK Open Banking Users from 4 Million to 40 Million by 2025', (18 October 2021), https://www.altfi.com/article/8425_how-do-we-grow-uk-open-banking-users-from-4-million-to-40-million-by-2025

Times of India website, 'The GeM in What Govt Buys: Commerce & Industry Minister Argues a Transition to GoI's Online Platform for Procurement Led to Savings by Departments & Transparency and Fair Competition for Vendors', (20 April 2023), https://timesofindia.indiatimes.com/blogs/toi-edit-page/the-gem-in-what-govt-buys-commerce-industry-minister-argues-a-transition-to-gois-online-platform-for-procurement-led-to-savings-by-departments-transparency-and-fair-competition-for-vendo/, (accessed 5 September 2023)

Traefiklabs website, 'The History and Evolution of API', (7 February 2023), https://traefik.io/blog/the-history-and-evolution-of-apis/

Treasury, 'Government Response to the Inquiry into Future Directions for the Consumer Data Right', (December 2021), 13, 17 and 18, https://treasury.gov.au/publication/p2021-225462

Treasury website, 'Statutory Review of the Consumer Data Right', (2022), https://treasury.gov.au/review/statutory-review-consumer-data-right

Trend Micro Research website, 'Ready or Not for PSD2: The Risks of Open Banking', (17 September 2019), www.trendmicro.com/vinfo/de/security/news/cybercrime-and-digital-threats/the-risks-of-open-banking-are-banks-and-their-customers-ready-for-psd2

Trustly, 'Year-end Summary', (January–December, 2020), 8, https://site.trustly.net/site/binaries/content/assets/verticals/press/trustly-year-end-summary-2020-in-english-only.pdf

UK Finance website, 'The Rise of Mobile Payments in 2020', based on research on the UK payments market in 2021, https://www.ukfinance.org.uk/news-and-insights/blogs/rise-mobile-payments-2020

UK Government website, 'Open Banking Privacy Notice', (23 March 2021), https://www.gov.uk/government/publications/open-banking-privacy-notice/open-banking-privacy-notice

UK Government website, 'Regulation of Buy-Now-Pay-Later Set to Protect Millions of People', (20 June 2022), https://www.gov.uk/government/news/regulation-of-buy-now-pay-later-set-to-protect-millions-of-people

UK HM Treasury 'Joint Statement by HM Treasury, the CMA, the FCA and the PSR on the Future of Open Banking', (25 March 2022), https://www.gov.uk/government/publications/joint-statement-by-hm-treasury-the-cma-the-fca-and-the-psr-on-the-future-of-open-banking/joint-statement-by-hm-treasury-the-cma-the-fca-and-the-psr-on-the-future-of-open-banking

UK Parliament website, "Oral Evidence: Future of Financial Services', (25 October 2021), https://committees.parliament.uk/oralevidence/2889/pdf/

Visa, 'Unlocking the Opportunity of Open Banking', (2022), https://navigate.visa.com/na/money-movement/unlocking-the-opportunities-of-open-banking/

Wavestone website, 'The API Economy. Why Public APIs Are So Important', (October 2017), www.wavestone.com/app/uploads/2017/10/Api-Economy-2017.pdf

Wavestone website, 'Open Banking, an Opportunity for Banks to Rethink Their Business Models', (November 2021), www.wavestone.com/app/uploads/2021/11/Wavestone-Report-2021_26112021.pdf

West Hill Capital website, 'Exit Announcement – Starling Bank Acquires Fleet Mortgages for £50 million', (August 2021), https://westhillcapital.co.uk/exit-announcement-starling-bank-acquires-fleet-mortgages-for-50-million-2-5m-capital-subscribed-on-launch-by-west-hill-investors-and-management/

Wired website, 'Revolut Insiders Reveal the Human Cost of a Fintech 'Unicorn's' Wild Rise', (28 February 2019), https://www.wired.co.uk/article/revolut-trade-unions-labour-fintech-politics-storonsky

Wired website, 'In India, Smartphones and Cheap Data Are Giving Women a Voice About 200 Million Women in the Country Are Illiterate. But Voice Memo and Image-Sharing Apps Make It Easier to Connect, Communicate, and Run Businesses', (4 January 2021), https://www.wired.com/story/india-smartphones-cheap-data-giving-women-voice/

Wonderful Payments website, 'Payment Initiation Services: A Game Changer for UK Businesses', (26 January 2023), https://blog.wonderful.co.uk/payment-initiation-services-a-game-changer-for-uk-businesses/

World Bank Group website, 'Access to Financial Services in Brazil', A study led by Anjali Kumar, (2005), 3, https://documents1.worldbank.org/curated/pt/738461468743954483/pdf/30858.pdf

World Bank Group website, 'Mexico: More Than Half of the Households Don't Have a Bank Account', (12 December 2012), https://www.worldbank.org/en/news/feature/2012/12/12/mexico-more-than-half-of-households-do-not-have-bank-account

World Bank Group website, 'Financial Inclusion and Inclusive Growth. A Review of Recent Empirical Evidence', (April 2017), https://openknowledge.worldbank.org/entities/publication/b90d407a-b789-5cbd-9f43-6e6f5438b8da

World Bank Group website, 'Expanding Financial Access for Mexico's Poor and Supporting Economic Sustainability', (9 April 2021a), https://www.worldbank.org/en/results/2021/04/09/expanding-financial-access-for-mexico-s-poor-and-supporting-economic-sustainability

World Bank Group website, 'The Role of Consumer Consent in Open Banking. Financial Inclusion Support Framework', (1 December 2021b), https://elibrary.worldbank.org/doi/abs/10.1596/37073

World Bank Group website, 'Chile - Financial Sector Assessment Program: Digital Financial Inclusion', (April 2022a), https://openknowledge.worldbank.org/entities/publication/3a19c0c0-ea9e-5031-915d-070db0580eec

World Bank Group website, 'Technical Note on Open Banking. Comparative Studies on Regulatory Approaches', (2022b), https://documents1.worldbank.org/curated/en/099345005252239519/pdf/P16477008e2c670fe0835a0e8692b499c2a.pdf

World Economic Forum website, 'The Next Generation of Data-Sharing in Financial Services: Using Privacy Enhancing Techniques to Unlock New Value', (September 2019), https://www3.weforum.org/docs/WEF_Next_Gen_Data_Sharing_Financial_Services.pdf

World Economic Forum website, 'At a Crossroads: The Next Chapter for FinTech in China' (March 2021), www3.weforum.org/docs/WEF_The_Next_Chapter_for_FinTech_in_China_2021.pdf

Worldline website, 'The Nordic Way - A PSD2 Whitepaper from Worldline Nordic', (2017), https://financial-services.worldline.com/content/dam/equensworldline/documents/whitepaper/Worldline_whitepaper_The_Nordic_Way.pdf

Yapily website, 'Why Nordic Countries are Perfectly Positioned to Lead the Way to Open Finance', (25 August 2022), www.yapily.com/blog/why-nordic-countries-could-unlock-open-finance

Yapily website, '20 Open Banking Use Cases to Help you Unlock Business Potential', (2023), https://i.yapily.com/OB-Use-Cases

Yolt website, 'Data Security and Open Banking, Dispelling Myths and Misconceptions', (2021), https://yts.yolt.com/images/logos/YTS_Whitepaper_Data-Security-1.pdf

Yougov website, 'Three Quarters of Britons Haven't Heard of Open Banking', (1 August 2018), https://yougov.co.uk/topics/economy/articles-reports/2018/08/01/three-quarters-britons-havent-heard-open-banking

Newspapers

Daily Business, 'ClearScore Buys Budgeting Platform Money Dashboard', (20 May 2022).

Financial Times

FT, 'An Open Door for Open Banking', (21 April 2023), https://www-ft-com.ezp.lib.cam.ac.uk/content/2b227007-3468-4b15-8117-68a30e0023a0

Bibliography 221

FT, 'Atom Bank Valued at £435mn as It Targets Market Listing Next Year', (16 February 2022)

FT, 'Banking Veteran Departs Revolut after One Year', (27 July 2020)

FT, 'Banks Brace for Next Wave of Digital Shake-up. Open Banking Is Yet to Provide a Flood of Innovation but Its Architects Are Sticking At It', (14 January 2019), https://www.ft.com/content/8f106e36-15bb-11e9-a581-4ff78404524e

FT, 'Beware the Promise of Salary Advance Schemes', (17 May 2022)

FT, 'BoE Hit Monzo with Tougher Capital Demands during Fundraising', (6 August 2020), https://www.ft.com/content/ca53305d-e44f-4f1c-a74e-dd2583b7c26b

FT, 'Brazil's Biggest Banks Battle for Reinvention in Digital Era', (4 April 2021)

FT, '"Buy Now Pay Later" Boom Fuels Consumer Debt Concerns as Transactions Soar', (12 February 2022)

FT, 'City Watchdog to Probe Revolut's 'Spoof' Takeaway Ad Campaign

'Fintech Firm Attracts IRE of Regulators after It Admits Using Falsified Data', (8 February 2019)

FT, Claer Barrett, 'Driven Round the Bend by Cashless Parking', (10 June 2022), https://www.ft.com/content/0fd91ff5-a7b0-46ad-965c-a88d343cb3e5

FT, 'Co-op's Big Adventure May Turn Sour', (18 March 2012), https://www.ft.com/content/4879ad2c-6e90-11e1-a82d-00144feab49a

FT, 'Emerging Markets "Leapfrog" the West in Digital Payments Race', (30 November 2021)

FT, 'Fintech Users Just Can't Get Enough of Traditional Banks', (7 January 2020)

FT, 'Half a Trillion Dollars Wiped from Once High-Flying Fintechs', (18 July 2022)

FT, 'How Monzo Is Banking On Customer Apathy', (23 April 2019)

FT, 'Klarna's Valuation Crashes to under $7bn in Tough Funding Round [From over $46bn Just over a Year Ago]', (11 July 2022)

FT, 'Klarna's Widening Losses Driven by Rapid Expansion', (28 February 2022)

FT, 'Lessons from the UK's First Fintech Failures', (21 March 2021)

FT, 'Lloyds Reshuffles Bankers as Part of Chief's New Strategy', (29 June 2022)

FT, 'Masthaven Launches Digitally-Focused UK Bank', (28 November 2016)

FT, 'Monzo Chief Vows to Scale up Business despite Fintech Turmoil', (14 July 2022)

FT, 'Monzo Takes a Step into the US Digital Banking Fray', Quoting Ronit Ghose, Head of Banks Analysis for Citigroup, (13 June 2019)

FT, 'Monzo Tells Almost 500,000 Customers to Change Pin', (5 August 2019)

FT, 'Nordea and DNB to Combine Baltic Operations', (25 August 2016)

FT, 'Revolut: Bitcoin Hype-merchant Or Bank?', (27 January 2021)

FT, 'Revolut Offers Dog Tricks as Bank of England Licence Talks Drag On', (4 February 2022)

FT, 'Revolut Leads Fintechs in Complaints to Ombudsman', (26 May 2019)

FT Lex, 'Revolut: Loans for Paydays after Their Heyday May Prompt Naysay', (19 August 2021)

FT, 'Revolut Reports Suspected Money Laundering on Its System', (17 July 2018)

FT, 'Revolut's New Hire Pledges to Improve Governance', (15 July 2019)

FT, 'Revolut's Russian Founder Stirs up Lithuania's Fintech Debate', (20 February 2019)

FT, 'Sainsbury's Considers Sale of Banking Arm', (1 November 2020)

FT, 'SoftBank's LatAm Fund Co-head Commits to Further Investments despite Losses', (26 March 2023)

FT, 'Starling Bank Faces Questions over Reliance on State-Backed Funding', (1 August 2022)

222 Bibliography

FT 'Starling Bank Matures from Digital Upstart to Mainstream Lender', (8 November 2021
FT, 'The UK Led the World in Open Banking—and Then Got Left Behind', (26 January 2023)
FT, 'The Virus Has Crushed the Challenger Bank Dream', (2 November 2020)
FT, 'Trustly: Payment Fintech Bypasses the Card Issuers', (16 March 2021), https://www.ft.com/content/dd8e60bc-e466-4f44-9ca1-2384afdfcc71
FT, 'Trustly Postpones $9bn Flotation after Regulator Flags Concerns', (3 May 2021)
FT, 'UK Banking: Mixing Mediocrity', (20 November 2020)
FT, 'Unity at Midnight Beckons with India's Tax Reform', (28 June 2017)
FT, 'Worldpay to Provide Loans to Small Businesses', (4 December 2015)
Fintech and Finance News, 'Belvo Receives Authorization to Develop Payment Initiation Solutions in Mexico', (30 June 2022), https://ffnews.com/newsarticle/belvo-receives-authorization-to-develop-payment-initiation-solutions-in-mexico/

The Guardian

The Guardian, 'Chair of UK Open Banking Body Resigns over Bullying Report', (1 October 2021a)
The Guardian, '"I Suffered Anxiety": Monzo Founder on the Pressures of Running a Digital Bank', (30 January 2021b)
The Guardian, 'Scammers Took £20,000 of My Wedding Savings but Revolut Won't Pay Me Back', (10 August 2022)

The Telegraph

The Telegraph, 'Monzo Boss Warns Open Banking Reforms Have "Zero Benefit"', (7 March 2020)

The Times

The Times, 'Fintech Bosses Accuse Starling Bank's Anne Boden of Stifling Innovation', (29 December 2021), https://www.thetimes.co.uk/article/fintech-bosses-accuse-starling-banks-anne-boden-of-stifling-innovation-rgd6jhhdj
Times of India, Yogesh Kabirdoss, 'Indian Bank Activates Account Aggregator System', (18 July 2022), https://timesofindia.indiatimes.com/business/india-business/indian-bank-activates-account-aggregator-system/articleshow/92955639.cm

Verdict

Verdict, 'TrueLayer CEO Accuses Monzo Founder Blomfield of Trashing Open Banking', (14 April 2021)

Legislation

Australia

Competition and Consumer (Consumer Data Right) Rules 2020
Treasury Laws Amendment (Consumer Data Right) Bill 2019

Bibliography

Bahrain

CBB Rulebook

Brazil

Law 12, 865 of 9 October 2013, SPB (Sistema de Pagamentos Brasileiro)
Provisional Measure No. 615 dated 17 May 2013 ('MP 615')

Canada

Canadian Payments Act 1985
Retail Payment Activities Act 2021

Chile

Law No. 21.314, 'Market Agents Law' (2021) Biblioteca del Congreso Nacional de Chile
Law No. 21.365 'Interchange Rate Law' (2021) Biblioteca del Congreso Nacional de Chile
Law No. 21.521 'To Promote Financial Competition and Inclusion through Innovation and Technology in the Provision of Financial Services' ('FinTech Ley') (2023) Diario Oficial de la Republica de Chile No. 43.442, CVE 2246446

European Union

Commission Delegated Regulation (EU) 2018/389 of 27 November 2017 supplementing Directive (EU) 2015/2366 of the European Parliament and of the Council with regard to regulatory technical standards for strong customer authentication and common and secure open standards of communication
Directive (EU) 2008/48/EC of the European Parliament and of the Council of 23 April 2008 on credit agreements for consumers and repealing Council Directive 87/102/EEC
Directive (EU) 2015/2366 of the European Parliament and of the Council of 25 November 2015 on payment services in the internal market, amending Directives 2002/65/EC 2009/110/EC and 2013/36/EU and Regulation (EU) No. 1093/2010, and repealing Directive 2007/64/EC
Payment Services Act (2010) 2010:751
Regulation (EU) 2016/679 of the European Parliament and of the Council of 27 April 2016 on the protection of natural persons with regard to the processing of personal data and on the free movement of such data, and repealing Directive 95/46/EC

Japan

Japan's Banking Act (Act No. 59 of 1981) was amended in 2018

Jordan

'Regulating Open Finance Services Procedures Instructions No. (12/2022)

South Korea

Electronic Financial Transaction Act

Iceland

Act No. 114/2021, on Payment Services' (2021)

India

Payment and Settlement Systems Act 2007

Indonesia

Board of Governors Regulation Number 23/15/PADG/2021 on the Implementation of the National Open API Payment Standard (SNAP Regulation)
Regulation Number 23/11/PBI/2021 on National Payment System Standard by the Blessing of Almighty God (2021)
Regulation Number 23/6/PBI/2021 on Payment Services Providers by the Blessings of the Almighty God (2021)
Regulation Number 23/7/PBI/2020 on Payment System by the Blessing of the Almighty God (2020)
Regulation Number 23/7/PBI/2021 on Payment System Infrastructure Providers by the Blessings of the Almighty God (2021)

Norway

'Act of 18 December 2022 No. 146 on Financial Contract' (the revised Financial Contracts Act)
Act No. 40 of 10 June 1988 on Financing Activity and Financial Institutions (Financial Institutions Act)' (1988)
Act No. 46 on Financial Contracts and Financial Assignments (Financial Contracts Act)

Liechtenstein

Zahlungsdienstegesetz' (ZDG) (2019)

Singapore

Personal Data Protection Act 2012 (2021 revised edition)

United Kingdom

Consumer Credit Act 1974
Financial Services and Markets Act 2000
The Electronic Money Regulations 2011

The Financial Services and Markets Act 2000 (Appointed Representatives) Regulations 2001
The Payment Services Regulations 2017

United States

DoddFrank Wall Street Reform and Consumer Protection Act (2010) (DoodFrank Act) 124 Stat 1376 Public Law 111-203

Cases

Case C-191/17 *Bundeskammer für Arbeiter und Angestellte (Austria) v ING-DiBa Direktbank Austria Niederlassung der ING-DiBa AG* (2018) ECJ 2018:809

Index

A2A (account-to-account) payment 20
Aadhaar number 155
account: aggregators 156–157; data holders 65; holder 20; verification applications 21
accountability mechanisms 65
account information service providers (AISPs) 19–20, 46, 106
account information services (AISs) 107
AccountScore 124
Account Servicing Payment Service Providers (ASPSPs) 19–20
Advanced Notice on Proposed Rule Making (ANPR) 66
Agricultural Bank of China 85
Allied Irish Bank 16
Adyen 122
'Ancillary Service Providers' 17–18
anti-money laundering 130; controls and procedures, FCA review 130–134; failures 136
Anti-Money Laundering/Combating the Financing of Terrorism (AML-CFT) 93
API Economy 14
application programming interfaces (APIs) 3, 11, 13–15, 46; architecture 17; bank customer data exposure 14–15; Chilean open banking/finance system 72; computer-to-computer relationship 14; data-sharing ecosystem 15; 'reverse engineering' practices 15; 'screen scraping' 15
Arab States of the Gulf 103
Association of Banks in Singapore (ABS) 84
Atom Bank 125–128

Australia and New Zealand Bank (ANZ) 78
Australia/Australian 78–80; open banking regime 17, 19; payments system 79–80
Australian Competition and Consumer Commission (ACCC) 8, 79
Australian Consumer Data Rights (CDRs) 105
Australian Securities Exchange (ASX) 123
Australian Treasury 78
'authorised push payment ('APP') frauds 136
automated clearing house payment initiation 21

'BaaS business' 131–132
Bahrain 104–106
'Bahrain Open Banking Framework' (BOBF) 104–105
Banco Bilbao Vizcaya Argentaria (BBVA) 125
Banco Central do Brasil (BCB) 151–152
Bank of China 85
Bank of Ireland 16
Bank of Korea 83
Barclays 16
Basel capital requirements 129
Basel Committee on Banking Supervision (BCBS) 21
behavioural economics 41
Belvo 68–69
Biden, Joe 66
Blomfield, Tom 126–127, 166
BNPL 123–124; regulation of 134
Boden, Anne 166
'Boost' 124
BPAY 80

Index 227

Brazilian Federation of Banks 149
Britton, Caroline 137
Burt, Peter 132
buy-to-let (BTL) specialist mortgage originator 126
Byungdoo, Sohn 83

Cambridge Centre of Alternative Finance 103
Canada 63–64
Canadian-based Wealthsimple 125
Canadian Department of Finance 7, 63
Canadian Payments Act 1985 7, 63–64
Card Domestic Scheme 108
Cathay United Bank 82
CBB Reporting Requirement Module 105
CBB Rulebook 105–106
Central Bank Digital Currency (CBDC) 108
Central Bank of Bahrain (CBB) 104–105
Central Bank of Indonesia (BI) 92
Central Bank of Jordan (CBJ) 109
Central Bank of Kuwait (CBK) 110–111
Central Bank of the UAE (CBUAE) 108
Chakrabarty, K. C. 156
Chartered Institute of Personnel and Development (CIPD) 123
Chesbrough, Henry 33
Chile/Chilean 69–73; card payment system 70–71; FinTech trends in 69–70; open banking/finance framework 71–73; reforms and 'FinTech Ley' 70–71
China: embracing open banking 86–87; opening-up reforms, internet finance and FinTech 85–86; path to follow 87–89
China Construction Bank 85, 87
Chinese National Internet Finance Association 88
Citibank Korea 83
CITIC Bank 86
City of London Corporation 34–35
ClearScore 120
Clydesdale Bank 42
Cobro Digital (CoDi) 8, 68
'Coleman Report' 78
Common Baseline document 91
Commonwealth Bank of Australia (CBA) 78
Competition and Markets Authority (CMA) 33

consumer: consent 21–24; education 171; education on open banking 170–173; financial data 12; financial transaction data 66; ownership 23, 41
'Consumer Access to Financial Records' (2020 Symposium) 65
Consumer Credit Act 1974 40
Consumer Credit Directive 134
Consumer Data Right (CDR) 8, 19, 79
Consumer Financial Protection Bureau (CFPB) 64–65
Contingent Reimbursement Model Code (CRM Code) 136
cooperative competition concept 83
Co-op Groups venture 121
Court of Justice of the European Union (CJEU) 19
COVID-19 pandemic 79
crypto assets 125
cryptocurrencies 127
crypto payments 21
CTBC Bank 82
Current Account Switch Service (CASS) 42
custom-made APIs 17
cyber-attacks 170
cyber risk 92

Danish Financial Supervisory Authority (DFSA) 55
Dubai Financial Services Authority (DFSA) 108
Danske Bank 16
data: access 13; account users 17, 65; aggregation and presentation of 6; APIs 14; breaches 170; -driven economy 23; -driven ecosystem 23; -driven financial environment 175; -mining 124; protection and financial services regulation 34; reciprocity 93; scope and usability 65; sharing and digital collaboration 84; -sharing ecosystems 4–5, 65, 171; -sharing processes 12, 15, 18, 22; transmission 13; user rights 66
'Data Recipients' 17–18
Davies, Richard 137
Deliberative Council 152
digital identities 21, 47
digitalisation 21, 92
Digital Moneybox 125
Dodd–Frank Act 15, 64–68

Dubai International Financial Centre (DIFC) 104
Dublin-based credit referencing business 124
Dutch central bank 42

Eftpos 80
Electronic Financial Transaction Act 83
Electronic Fund Transfer Act (EFTA) 58–59, 66
Electronic Know Your Customer (eKYC) 108
Electronic Money Association (EMA) 117
electronic payment funds institutions (IFPE) 68
embedded finance 120–122
Emma Technologies Ltd ('Emma') 119–120
e-money: accounts 19; operations 118; regulations 135
Espinosa, Juan Carlos 69
EU Payment Service Directive 2 (EU PSD2) 18, 105 (?)
European Banking Authority (EBA) 47, 168
European Central Bank (ECB) 46
European Data Protection Board (EDPB) 22–23
European Free Trade Association 6–7

Fair Credit Reporting Act (FCRA) 66
Far Eastern International Bank 82
Far EasTone Telecommunications Company 82
Farrell, Scott 8, 79–80
Farrell Inquiry 8
Federação Brasileira de Bancos (FEBRABAN) 149–150
Federal Deposit Insurance Corporation (FDIC) 135
'Finance-as-a-Service: API Playbook' 84
Financial Conduct Authority (FCA) 19 [there are more references than this]
financial inclusion 92, 156; and financial literacy 147; initiative 154–155; open banking and 173–175
Financial Information Providers (FIPs) 156
Financial Information Service Company (FISC) 82
financial information users (FIUs) 156

'Financial Infrastructure Transformation Programme' (FIT Programme) 108
financial institution user (FIU) 157
'Financial Market Commission' 71
Financial Ombudsman Service (FOS) 128, 134
Financial Portability Law 70
'Financial Sector Development Program' (FSDP) 107
Financial Services and Markets Act 2000 ('FSMA 2000') 119
Financial Services Authority (JFSA) 81–82
Financial Services Regulatory Authority (FSRA) 108
Financial Supervisory Commission (FSC) 82
FinTech 104; ecosystem 103; legislation 25; market 107; start-ups 11, 18; trends in Chile 69–70
FinTech Galaxy 106
FinTech Hive 104
FinTech Ley 8, 17, 73
'FinTech Strategic Implementation Plan' (FinTech Plan) 107
First Commercial Bank 82
Fleet Mortgage business 131

General Data Protection Regulation (GDPR) 22
General Requirements Module 105
Gilbert, Martin 137
Gill, Stanley 14
Glen, John 34
Goods and Services Tax Network (GSTN) 157
Goods and Service Tax (GST) 158
Government E-Marketplace (GeM) 158
Gramm–Leach–Bliley Act (GLBA) 66
Gulf Cooperation Council (GCC) countries 9
Gulf Council Countries (GCCs) 104

Hana Bank 83
Harper, Ian 78
Hashemite Kingdom of Jordan 109–110
Holmes, Richard 137
Hong Kong Association of Banks (HKABs) 90–91
Hong Kong Monetary Authority (HKMA) 89–90, 92
'Hong Kong Personal Data Privacy Ordinance' 22

Hong Kong SAR: four-phased approach 90; four-phased Open API approach 89–92; Hong Kong Monetary Authority (HKMA) 89–90; looking ahead 91–92
House of Representatives Standing Committee on Economics 79
HSBC 16, 127–128
HSBC Mexico 69
Hua Xia Bank 86
Hume, Jane 79

'Implementation Trustee Functions' 36
India: cheap mobile internet-enabled handsets 158–159; context 154–156; financial inclusion 156–157; NPCI role 157–158; PMJDY (Prime Minister's people wealth project) 158; sandboxes 157
Indian Banks' Association (IBA) 157
Indian Stack 155
Indonesia/Indonesian: Blueprint initiative 95; economy 92; financial reforms and open banking significance 92–93; open banking progress 93–95; regulators 93
'Indonesia Payment System (IPS) Blueprint' 92
Industrial and Commercial Bank of China 85, 87
Industrial Bank of Korea 83
Information Based Service Providers (IBSPs) 17, 72
information providers (IPs) 72
'Instant Bank Transfer' 20
Instant Payments Platform 108
Institución de Fondos de Pago Electrónico (IFPE) 69
InsurTech companies 69–70, 104
Integritetsskyddsmyndigheten (IMY) 134
'Interchange Rate Law' 70–71
International Monetary Fund (IMF) 68, 103–104, 150
International Monetary Fund Financial Access Survey for 2022 155–156
Internet Finance Guidelines 2015 86
Islamic bank licensees 105
Islamic FinTech firms 104
'isolated' open banking 167

Japan 81–82
Japan's Banking Act 81

Joint Regulatory Oversight Committee 38
Jordanian open finance services regulation 109–110

KidStart Ltd. 119
Klarna Bank AB 132–134
Klarna's business model 120–122
Kookmin Bank 83
Korea Development Bank 83
Korea Financial Telecommunications & Clearings Institute (KFTC) 83
Korean Financial Security Institute (KFSI) 83
Korean Financial Services Commission 82–83

Licensing Requirement Module 105
Lloyds Bank 16, 122, 127–128
London Stock Exchange 35

MacLean, David 137
'Market Agents Law' 70–71
Mazzucato, Marina 39
Mega International Commercial Bank 82
Menon, Ravi 84
Metropolitan Commercial Bank 135
Mexico 68–69
Microfinance Institutions and Ancillary Service Providers 106
Middle East and North Africa (MENA) region: Bahrain 104–106; financial system 103; Hashemite Kingdom of Jordan 109–110; Qatar and rest of the region 110–111; Kingdom of Saudi Arabia (KSA) 106–108; small and medium-sized enterprises (SMEs) 103; United Arab Emirates (UAE) 108
Minsheng Bank 86
Mizuho Bank 81
Monetary Authority of Singapore (MAS) 84
Money Changers Licensees 106
Money Dashboard 120
Monzo 126; and customer complaints 127–128; fraud 128; and US plans 128
Monzo card 127
Morrison, Scott 79–80
M&S Bank 124
MUFG Bank 81

multi-factor authentication (MFA) 170
'MyBank' 87
'MyMoneySense' 85

National Australia Bank (NAB) 78
National Automated Clearing House
    Association (NACHA) 15
National Banking and Securities
    Commission (CNBV) 69
National Digital Economy Strategy 108
National Financial Inclusion Strategy
    (PNIF) 68
National Financial System 151
National Open API Payment Standard
    (SNAP) 94
National Payments Corporation of India
    (NPCI) 155
'National Working Group' 94
Nationwide Building Society 16
'New Area of Smart Banking in
    Hong Kong' 91–92
New Payments Platform Australia
    (NPPA) 80
New Zealand 80–81
Nonghyup Bank 83
Nordic Capital 124
Nordic region 55–57
Norinchukin Bank 81
Northern Rock Bank 42
NuBank 153
Nutmeg 125

OakNorth 127
Office of Fair Trading (OFT) 45
Office of the Comptroller of the
    Currency (OCC) 128
'Open Banking Development Research
    Report' 87–88
Open Banking Implementation Entity
    (OBIE) 36–37, 168
Open Banking Module 106
open finance 12, 176; open banking to
    175–177
Open Finance Platform 108
Oxera and Nuffield Centre research 41

'Pay by Bank' 20
Payment and Settlement Systems Act
    2007 157
Payments Canada 7, 63–64
Payment Services Regulations 2017
    (PSRs) 167–168
Payments NZ Application Programming
    Interface (API) Council 80

People's Bank of China (PBOC) 85
'Pillar 2' 129
PMJDY (Prime Minister's people wealth
    project) 158
Pradhan Mantri Jan-Dhan Yojana
    (PMJDY) 155
Prime Minister's People Wealth Project
    155
'Privacy Commissioner for Personal
    Data' 22
Product APIs 84
Prometeo 68–69
Prudential Regulatory Authority (PRA)
    117, 133
PSD II see Payment Services Directive II
    (PSD II)

Qatar and rest of the region 110–111
Qatar Central Bank (QCB) 110
Qatar National Bank (QNB) 110
Quick Response Code Indonesia
    Standard (QRIS) 94

RBS 16
RegTech 104
Representative Office Licensees 106
Required Rulemaking on Personal
    Financial Data Rights 67
Reserve Bank of Australia (RBA) 80
Reserve Bank of India (RBI) 148, 157
Retail Banking Market Investigation
    Order 2017 36–37
Retail Payment Activities Act 2021 7, 64
Revolut 135–138

salary advance schemes 123
Sales & Marketing APIs 84
Santander UK 16
Saudi Arabia 106–108
Saudi Arabia Monetary Agency (SAMA)
    107
'Saudi Vision 2030' 106–107
Shanghai Pudong Development Bank 87
Shenzhen WeBank 86
Sherwood, Michael 137
Shinhan Bank 83
Singapore 84–85
Singapore Financial Data Exchange
    (SGFinDex) 84
Singapore Personal Access (SingPass) 84
Single Euro Payments Area (SEPA) 45
single invoice financing (SIF) 122
small and medium enterprises (SMEs)
    40, 103, 174; customers 91

Small Business Regulatory Enforcement Fairness Act of 1996 (SBREFA) 66
'SNAP Technical Standards' 94–95
South China Commercial Bank 82
South Korea 82–83
Standard Chartered Bank Korea 83
Starling Banks 128, 130–132
State Bank of India (SBI) 157–158
stress tests 129
strong customer authentication (SCA) 169–170
Sumitomo Mitsui Banking 81
Sunak, Rishi 36
supply-chain provider 35–36
suspicious activity reports (SARs) 130
Sutton Bank 135
Swedish Authority for Privacy Protection 134

Taiwan 82
TARGET Instant Payment Settlement (TIPS) 47
Tencent Cloud–WeBank Fintech Innovation Lab 87
Thai QR Payment interconnectivity 94
'Third Party Providers' (TPPs) 19–20
third-party service providers (TSPs) 82; in Hong Kong 17
Toscafund and Infinity Investment Partners 125
Transaction Accounts Identifier Directory—database 154
transaction APIs 84
Treasury Select Committee 36
Trustly Group AB 132
Trust Service Providers 106

UK Financial Intelligence Unit (UKFIU) 130
UK government: consumer behaviour 41–42; consumer demand 39–41; consumer lack of trust 42; OBIE surveys 43; open banking 36–37, 41–42, 184–185; Ron Kalifa report 34–36; success 34; surveys 43–44; treasury role 37–39
UK House of Commons Treasury Select Committee 166
UK Open Banking Limited 171
UK's National Crime Agency (NCA) 130
Unified Payment Interface (UPI) 155; application 156
Uniform Resource Locator (URL) of banks 168
United Arab Emirates (UAE) 108
United States of America 64–68; CFPB in October 2022 66–67; CFPB's initiatives 65–66; 'Open Banking Rule' 68; rulemaking developments 66
unrestricted investment accounts 19
US banking licence 128
US-based credit card companies 46
US Open Banking Rule 15

value: -added banking services 156; chain 33; propositions 33
Virgin Money 42

Wealthify 125
'WeBank' 87
Westpac 78
Wheeler, David 14
Wilkes, Maurice 14
Woori Bank 83

Yorkshire Bank 42
YouGov survey 43–44
Yuanta Commercial Bank 82

Zhejiang E-Commerce Bank 86

Printed in the United States
by Baker & Taylor Publisher Services